MAN AND SOCIETY

A NEW EDITION

VOLUME THREE

John Plamenatz

MAN AND SOCIETY

POLITICAL AND SOCIAL THEORIES FROM MACHIAVELLI TO MARX

VOLUME THREE

Hegel, Marx and Engels,
and the Idea of Progress

A New Edition
Revised by M. E. Plamenatz and Robert Wokler

Longman
London and New York

Longman Group UK Limited,
Longman House, Burnt Mill, Harlow,
Essex CM20 2JE, England
and Associated Companies throughout the world.

Published in the United States of America
by Longman Publishing Group, New York

First published 1963
Second edition 1992

British Library Cataloguing in Publication Data
Plamenatz, John
  Man and society: political and social theories
  from Machiavelli to Marx: Vol 3. Hegel, Marx and
  Engels, and the idea of progress. — New ed.
  I. Title II. Plamenatz, M.E. III. Wokler, Robert
  320.509

  ISBN 0–582–05541–5

Library of Congress Cataloging in Publication Data
Plamenatz, John Petrov.
  Man and society: political and social theories from Machiavelli
  to Marx/John Plamenatz. — A new ed./revised by M. E. Plamenatz
  and Robert Wokler.
    p. cm.
  Includes indexes.
  Contents: v. 1. From the Middle Ages to Locke — v. 2. From
  Montesquieu to the early socialists — v. 3. Hegel, Marx and Engels,
  and the idea of progress.
    ISBN 0–582–05540–7(v. 1): — ISBN 0–582–05546–6 (v. 2):
  — ISBN 0–582–05541–5 (v. 3):
    1. Political science—History. 2. Social sciences—History.
  I. Plamenatz, M. E. II. Wokler, Robert, 1942– III. Title.
  JA83.P53 1991
  3066.2′09—dc20   91–19404
                                                                         CIP

Set by 5 in 10/12pt Bembo Roman.
Printed in Malaysia by VP

To My Father

To My Father

Contents

Contents

Editors' Preface

John Plamenatz first conceived this work in the 1950s, as a set of twenty-eight lectures which he gave at Oxford and then at other universities. Substantially revised and extended over a number of years, these lectures were then recast once again, for publication in two volumes, in 1963. Subject only to occasional minor alteration, *Man and Society* has remained in print, in that form, ever since.

In his original preface Plamenatz observed that his text was 'not a history of political thought', but rather, as his subtitle made clear, a critical examination of some important social and political theories from Machiavelli to Marx. His interpretation of the ideas and assumptions of past thinkers was mainly designed to elucidate significant treatments of central problems in political and social thought which are still pertinent today. It was intended not only as a commentary on the doctrines of important thinkers but equally as a contribution to political theory by way of commentary – that is, through an assessment of the profound insights and fundamental errors of influential thinkers of the past whose ideas have continued to inform the beliefs of persons who reflect upon the nature of society and government. That critical approach was and remains the chief focus of *Man and Society*. In examining the views of others, Plamenatz sought to show why they still matter to us, why propositions put forward at times very different from our own may be judged in the light of their universal application, as their authors themselves so frequently imagined, and often postulated, was the case. Plamenatz believed that while the idiom of discourse of political and social thinkers is always particular and unique, the substance of their arguments, and the truth or falsity of their contentions, do not depend on the local and specific circumstances which give rise to them. Great political thinkers are themselves characteristically critical and innovative. In flouting the political assumptions or linguistic conventions of their age, they aspire to free themselves and their readers from dead dogma. They develop or cross-examine the ideas of pre-eminent thinkers of previous ages and thereby add to or break from traditions of discourse not circumscribed by the lifetime of any single figure. That wider context – indeed the whole of the discipline of political and social theory – is the main subject of Plamenatz's work, to which his critical interpretation of other doctrines itself forms a major contribution.

It would, however, be misleading to read his commentary only in that light. Plamenatz wished to show, to historians, that the meaning of theories was not determined solely by the circumstances that occasioned their production, and, to political scientists, that old theories are often deeper, richer and more lucid than new theories which ignore them. But crucial to both endeavours was the need for accuracy in the interpretation of past thinkers, for familiarity with the varieties of language they employed, for a proper grasp of the meaning they intended to convey through their writings, in so far as it remains accessible. In distinguishing a critical examination of past doctrines from an historical investigation of their origins, Plamenatz was anxious to ensure that he conveyed their sense, as well as their significance, correctly. He was convinced that anachronistic interpretations of ideas were no less discreditable to the political theorist than to the historian, and he went to great lengths to ensure the contextual reliability of his readings. His views on Marx came to be progressively refined by the historical research of other scholars, particularly that which was devoted to Marx's earlier writings, in the years prior to the publication of *Man and Society;* his interpretation of Hobbes, by contrast, was strengthened and reaffirmed in reply to recent scholarship which he regarded as more ingenious than plausible; the best-informed contextual readings of Locke prompted significant revisions of his lecture notes on the subject, especially with regard to the dating of the *Two Treatises of Government* and Locke's connection with the Glorious Revolution.

Over the past twenty-six years or so, readers of *Man and Society* may not have been sufficiently aware of the importance Plamenatz attached to the contextual interpretation of political doctrines, particularly with regard to relatively minor writers who helped more to shape than to transform the conventions and discourse of their age. In his lectures Plamenatz recognized, and indeed emphasized, the historical significance of thinkers who were not so much innovatory as re-presentative, who articulated the widely shared assumptions of their contemporaries but did not seek to undermine them, or whose contributions to political disputations were more polemical than philosophical, more apposite and influential within a particular context, because less abstract. For no other reason than that of sheer lack of space in a work already too long for a two-volume format, Plamenatz was obliged to compress his material, truncating certain chapters and deleting others. Because doctrines most circumscribed by local and contingent interests have less bearing on the aspirations of other thinkers in different cultures, he elected, when required to be more brief, to remove sections which were of more restricted, more exclusively historical, concern. This foreshortening of particular topics, including even the excision of whole periods of debate and controversy, somewhat reduced the breadth and scope of the original lectures. In restoring mainly that material – devoted above all to doctrinal disputes and to the cut and thrust of battles fought in pursuit of power as well as the truth – we have, now in three volumes, sought to rectify this abridgement. More than was possible in the two-volume edition of *Man and Society*, we have followed Plamenatz's initial scheme in joining the peaks of political argument, as he perceived them, not only to each other, but also to the foothills from which they separately rise.

To the original introduction of 1963 we have added a number of lines drawn from his preface to the lectures, which address what Plamenatz took to be the contribution to political theory of minor authors and their polemical writings. We have assembled two lectures on ancient and mediaeval thought, together with fragments of some earlier drafts, to form the new opening chapter in volume I of this edition, including some of the most historically discursive additional material, under the title, 'The Political Thought of the Middle Ages'. Chapter three of volume I, here entitled 'The Reformation and Liberty of Conscience', has been expanded in length by about one-third, embracing fuller discussions of the mediaeval church, the doctrines of Luther and Calvin, and the ideas of their disciples and critics, especially Knox and Castellion. Chapter six of volume I, now bearing the title 'Divine Right, Absolute Monarchy and Early Theories of the Social Contract', has been enlarged by a similar amount, incorporating material from one lecture which Plamenatz offered on contract theory before Hobbes and Locke. In this chapter will be found extended commentaries on Hotman, Mornay, Mariana and Suárez, previously eliminated; the sections on Hotman and Mornay, in particular, initially presented in the form of two much compressed footnotes uncharacteristic of Plamenatz's style, are hereby restored to their originally intended place in this work, more conspicuously, perhaps, than any of our other revisions; we have, moreover, followed the practice of most recent scholarship in attributing the *Vindiciae contra tyrannos* to Mornay rather than Languet. Volume I, chapter seven, entitled 'English Political Theory from the Breach with Rome to the Restoration', comprises material entirely unpublished before, distilled from two lectures in different formats devoted to Elizabethan and Jacobean political thought and to the English Civil War, to which we have appended another lecture on Harrington. In volume II, chapter five, we have incorporated sections from two lectures on Bentham and Philosophical Radicalism and a third on John Stuart Mill, clearly a centrally important figure in modern political thought, whose ideas had already engaged the attention of Plamenatz in his study of *The English Utilitarians,* but who, again on account of lack of space, received only passing mention before in *Man and Society*. In volume II, moreover, we have divided what was originally the longest chapter, on 'The Early Socialists, French and English', into two, now chapters six and seven, adding to each a few pages, where appropriate, drawn from a lecture devoted to the ideas of Saint-Simon. Volume III, embracing the last five chapters of what was volume II, remains largely unaltered, although we have made a number of slight changes to accord with our corrections to the other volumes and have amended the titles of three chapters.

In each case we have tried to shape the new material in a style and order closely approximating the initial format of the published work. Although the lecture variants of several other chapters contain substantial additional and striking differences as well, we have decided not to include any extracts which would have required major alteration to the text of the already printed volumes. In many instances, however, we have changed a term or phrase of the original version, sometimes to accommodate the intercalations, occasionally for the sake of fluency or coherence. We have corrected several passages in the light of evidence of which Plamenatz himself could not have been aware. We have also corrected or identified quotations – in a few cases thanks to the assistance of Dr Terrell Carver, Mr Alistair Edwards or Mr Michael Evans – whose previous citation was inaccurate or incomplete. Since particular themes are raised in the more historically contextual chapters that have great bearing upon the argument of the work as a whole, we have not attempted to reassemble those chapters so that they might incorporate the findings of recent scholarship or the most up-to-date interpretations of old issues and debates. In revising a text originally prepared several decades ago, we felt no duty to speculate on what

Plamenatz might choose to say if he were able to embark upon it now. It is therefore unavoidable that at least some of the material which is published here for the first time must reveal its age. For each chapter, we have, accordingly, appended a list of the most salient contemporary writings on the subject.

We have thus tried to remain faithful both to the published tomes and to the work originally projected, which was of markedly broader conception and more historical in focus. No opportunity arose before his death in 1975 for Plamenatz to make these revisions himself. In attempting to enhance and lend fresh impetus to the most durable and popular of all his writings, our aim has been, not so much to append additional material to an established text, as to impart new breath into old bones and therefore restore the full vigour and vision of *Man and Society*'s original design. We are grateful to Dr Chris Harrison and Mrs Joy Cash of Longmans for all their encouragement and patience; to the British Academy for enabling us, intermittently over a number of years, to meet and sort out the papers we required from a substantial corpus of other unpublished texts; to Dr Janet Coleman and Dr Mark Goldie for their invaluable comments on the new and revised chapters, for which, however, they bear no responsibility and with whose conclusions they do not always concur; and to Mrs Jean Ashton and to Miss Karen Hall for typing them and for their forbearance, in deciphering densely written passages, on demand.

April 1990

Preface

This book is not a history of political thought; it is, as its title implies, a critical examination of a number of important theories. It is not concerned to argue for some interpretations of these theories against others but to examine assumptions, ideas and attitudes.

The book is an expansion of lectures given at various times at three universities, Columbia, Harvard and Oxford. It is hoped that it will prove useful to students of social and political theory whose interest in the subject is more philosophical than historical; and the author has had in mind students in the United States as much as in Britain. He has aimed at lucidity but is aware that some parts of the book make difficult reading.

The most difficult part of all, which treats of Hegel, has been read by Professor H. L. A. Hart and Sir Isaiah Berlin, by Professor Herbert Deane of Columbia University, and by Mr William Weinstein and Mr John Torrance of Nuffield College, and the author is grateful to them for valuable comments and criticisms. He thanks Mr Alan Ryan of Balliol College for making the index. He also thanks his wife for reading the book in manuscript and suggesting improvements of grammar and style.

July 1961   J. P.

Introduction

The artist ploughs his own furrow; the scholar, even in the privacy
of his study, cultivates a common field. He is responsible to others
for what he does; he feels the need to explain his purpose, to justify
his efforts.

There are many things well worth doing not attempted in this book.
It is not, for the most part, a history of social and political thought; it
does not enquire how one thinker influenced another, and compares
them only to make clearer what they said. It scarcely looks at the
circumstances in which this or that theory was produced. And it quite
neglects several important thinkers. Althusius will get into the index
only because he is mentioned on this page, and so too will Vico, who
has been greatly and rightly admired. Grotius and Kant are mentioned
only in passing. If my purpose had been to produce a history, however
brief, of political thought from Machiavelli to Marx, this neglect or
scanty treatment would have been without excuse.

Every thinker, even the most abstract, is deeply influenced by
the circumstances of his day. To understand why Machiavelli or
Hobbes or Rousseau wrote as he did, we must know something of
social and political conditions in their day and country and of the
controversies then to the fore. But this does not, I hope, mean that
whoever discusses their theories must also discuss these conditions and
controversies. Is there to be no division of labour? Those conditions
and controversies have often been described, and the writer who
is primarily concerned with arguments and ideas need not discuss
them except to make something clear which might otherwise be
misunderstood. He must use his judgement: at times he may need to
make a considerable digression, and at other times a passing reference
or mere hint will be enough.

Those who say that to understand a theory we must understand the conditions in which it was produced sometimes put their case too strongly. They speak as if, to understand what a man is saying, we must know why he is saying it. But this is not true. We need understand only the sense in which he is using words. To understand Hobbes, we need not know what his purpose was in writing *Leviathan* or how he felt about the rival claims of Royalists and Parliamentarians; but we do need to know what he understood by such words as *law, right, liberty, covenant* and *obligation*. And though it is true that even Hobbes, so 'rare' at definitions, does not always use a word in the sense which he defines, we are more likely to get the sense in which he does use it by a close study of his argument than by looking at the condition of England or at political controversies in his day. These are, of course, well worth looking at on their own account. Nevertheless, we can go a long way in understanding Hobbes's argument and yet know very little about them.

No doubt, Hobbes is a special case. We can get more of his meaning by merely reading what he wrote than we can, say, of Machiavelli's or Montesquieu's or Burke's. It is a matter of degree. But, even in their case, we learn more about their arguments by weighing them over and over again than by extending our knowledge of the circumstances in which they wrote. Hobbes was not less a child of his times than they were. If we want to know why he wrote as he did, or why an argument such as his was produced and found exciting, we have to look at what was happening when he wrote; he was no more independent of his age than was Machiavelli or Burke. Of every really great thinker we can say that, compared with lesser men, he is idiosyncratic; he is, for a time, more liable than they are to be misunderstood because he has more to say that is unfamiliar. He uses the common language but uses it differently. But this is not more true of Hobbes than of Machiavelli. Hobbes belongs as completely to his period as Machiavelli does to his; and if, in order to understand him, we need take less notice of the circumstances in which he wrote, this is because his style and method are different. To understand the argument of *Leviathan* is one thing; to understand the age in which alone it could have been written is another. I do not deny that the second understanding may contribute to the first; I merely doubt whether the contribution is anything like as great as it is sometimes made out to be. Of course, it is of absorbing interest to see a great thinker in the setting of his age. How society and politics are related to political and social theory is as well worth studying as theory itself. Who would deny it? But that is another matter.

Students of society and government make use of ideas and assumptions inherited from the past. In this book I have not been concerned to trace the origins and evolution of these ideas, but rather to examine them critically by considering some of the most familiar and most famous theories which contain them. I have chosen these theories, rather than others, precisely because they are familiar, and because, between them, they contain most of the important ideas and assumptions still used or made, whether by students of society and politics or by persons engaged in political controversies. All these theories, in one way or another, are inadequate; they fail to explain satisfactorily what they set out to explain. They are also – though this is less important – 'out-of-fashion': by which, I am sorry to say, I mean no more than this, that sociologists and political scientists in many places (though not in all) now believe that they have less to learn from them than from one another.

These ideas and assumptions ought to be examined critically; and where can they be so examined to better advantage than in the context of well-known, long discussed and, in some cases, still influential theories? It is sometimes objected that the questions raised by, say, Hobbes or Locke are no longer relevant. But if we discuss social and political matters, we must still speak, as they did, of *law,* of *rights,* of *obligation* and of *consent.* By seeing how they used these words and what arguments they constructed, we learn to use them ourselves. By seeing where their explanations are inadequate, we learn something about what they sought to explain. To treat *right* as absence of obligation (which is what Hobbes did) may do for some purposes, but not for others. By examining critically the argument of *Leviathan* and *De cive,* we learn why this is so. It may be true, as Locke said, that the authority of governments rests in some sense on the consent of the governed; but perhaps it cannot do so unless consent is understood in a sense different from his. By seeing where his argument goes wrong, we are better able to construct another to take its place. If we do not get from Hobbes or Locke answers to the questions we now put, we do, by examining their theories, learn to put our own questions more clearly. And I take Hobbes and Locke for examples deliberately because they are among the most abstract of political theorists. Machiavelli, Bodin, Montesquieu, Hume, Burke, Hegel and Marx all take larger account than they do of history and of the machinery of government.

It is, of course, not only the great thinkers who produce the thought of their age; indeed, they are not even the largest contributors to it. No doubt, they are often the most original, but they are not so always, for they are sometimes only more lively and more vigorous than the rest. The others, the lesser thinkers, enormously outnumber them; and though, as individuals, they may give much less, what they give collectively is much more. What any thinker, however remarkable, has to give is incomparably less than what he takes from others; and the greater part of what he takes does not come from other great thinkers, but from many relatively minor figures, of which most are soon forgotten by posterity. Even in the period of their predominance, the great works do not cover all that is worth noticing. There are important shifts of opinion and outlook not mediated by genius; there are new ideas that find currency and endure, though no Hobbes or Hume has given them a memorable place in his theory.

Much of the political thought of the sixteenth century is to be found in treatises and pamphlets of real interest only to specialists; and yet that thought, taken as a whole, is historically of immense importance. The religious minorities, by pressing their claims against their governments, were not fighting for liberty of conscience but to secure privileges for themselves. Yet, as a result of their struggle, liberty of conscience – perhaps the most precious of all liberties – was eventually established. These minorities made it impossible for the governments of Europe to achieve domestic peace except by conceding religious liberty; and when this concession was eventually made, the greatest moral revolution in modern history was completed. In attempting to follow that revolution in thought and feeling, we must consider such writers not individually but in schools, examining the types of arguments they use and the general conclusions they reach. Our approach in addressing their doctrines must therefore be more historical than may be the case with regard to the pre-eminent thinkers.

The great advantage of these old theories is that they are both rich in content and familiar. If our purpose is to examine ideas used to explain society and government, these theories provide them abundantly, vigorously and attractively. They are a fertile field for the exercise we have in mind. Everyone agrees that students of society and government need to look carefully at the assumptions they make and the ideas they use; that – owing to the nature of their subject – they are especially liable to be the dupes of words. Yet there are now many who question the use of a close study of theories produced long ago in circumstances widely different from our own. It is therefore a point worth making, that such ideas are nowhere better or more economically studied than in these old theories. Nowhere *better* because of the richness and variety they present, and nowhere *more economically* because they have been sifted again and again, so that we can get down quickly to essentials.

The predominant figures in the history of political thought are not great for nothing, or just by chance. They are more original, more profound, than the forgotten or almost forgotten men, who are remembered only by scholars. Their theories are often better constructed; there is usually a greater weight of thought and feeling in their works, and they make a deeper and more lasting impression. Though most of what they offer their readers is taken from others, their powers of selection are unusually fine; they have perception and imagination and an eye for the important, and so their ideas, original to a much smaller extent than appears to the reader who knows little or nothing of their contemporaries, do none the less contain a large part of what is best worth preserving in their age. Most of their contributions to political thought, moreover, are far from dead; they are either still with us – though sometimes in forms we do not immediately recognize – or they are revived among us from time to time when occasion serves. The world is full, not only of Marxists and democrats, but of people who, though they mostly do not know it, are still using the ideas and arguments of Hobbes, or Machiavelli, or Montesquieu, or Hegel or Burke. These thinkers may have originated only a small part of our stock of ideas about human nature and politics, but they gave it the appearance still familiar to us. They mixed only a fraction of the ore, but they refined much of it, put their stamp on it, made it profitable and good currency for our use.

In some circles where the study of these theories is depreciated, there is nevertheless a keen interest taken in the ideas and assumptions used or made by the sociologist or the political scientist. There are sociologists and political scientists who put themselves to great trouble to define the terms they employ and to state their assumptions. They do not always do it well. They wish to be lucid, precise and realistic; they aim at explaining the facts and are in search of a vocabulary adequate to their purpose. It is impossible not to sympathize with them. Yet, for all their efforts, they are often more obscure, or looser in their arguments, or more incoherent, than the makers of the old theories which they neglect on the ground that they are irrelevant. A close study of these theories might be a good discipline for them. Or the social scientist, though he does not know it, repeats what has been said as well, or better, long ago. Ideas very like his own have been used long before his time, and yet he thinks them new because he has coined new words to express them. It is sad to read a book for which it is claimed that it breaks new ground, and to find it thin and stale.

Not for a moment do I suggest that these old theories provide the social scientist with all that he is looking for. They are not a stock of ideas sufficient for his purposes. They are inadequate for all kinds of reasons, some of which are discussed in this book. I suggest only that the study of them is still amply rewarding, and to no one more so than to the student of society who feels that he lacks the ideas needed to explain what he studies. Of course, he will not find the ideas he wants ready-made in these theories, but he will become more adept in the handling of ideas and a better judge of their uses. He will be more discriminating, more scrupulous, and perhaps also more severe with himself and his contemporaries. Bentham said that his purpose in writing *A Fragment on Government* was to teach the student 'to place more confidence in his own strength, and less in the infallibility of great names: – to help him to emancipate his judgement from the shackles of authority'. An admirable purpose. But today, in some intellectual circles, the authority of great names is less oppressive than is fashion, which is an even worse guide. If we neither neglect great names nor defer to them, but seek, to the best of our ability, to take their measure, we are then better placed to take our own.

It is said that, in the past, it was difficult, if not impossible, to study the facts, social and political, whereas now it is much less difficult. There are vastly greater records than there were, more easily accessible; there are methods now used to get at the facts which could not have been used in earlier periods; it is easier than it was to test hypotheses, and we are more sophisticated in making and testing them. The social sciences may have no spectacular achievements to their credit, but then it is not to be expected that they should. It is admitted that they differ greatly from the natural sciences, that there are difficulties peculiar to them, that their conclusions are less precise and more open to question. Such is their nature that – though they call for no less imagination, no less intelligence, no smaller talents from their devotees than other sciences – they afford lesser opportunities; and we are not to expect from them hypotheses as precise, as impressive, as revolutionary and as widely acclaimed as those of, say, Copernicus or Newton or Darwin or Pasteur. And yet it is claimed for them that they do now deserve to be called *sciences*, because those who practise them are seriously concerned to construct theories to explain the facts, and are self-critical and open-minded. As much as the natural scientists, they are imbued with the scientific spirit, even though their methods are more uncertain and their results looser and less well-established. The social scientist is much more apt than the natural scientist to talk nonsense and to make a fool of himself. This is one of the hazards of his occupation. Yet his occupation is science.

But the occupation of the great social and political theorists of the past was not science. They did not study the facts or did so only at random; they did not construct hypotheses and test them. They deduced their conclusions from axioms *a priori* and from definitions, or they relied on what they chose to consider the common sense of mankind. They were not scientific but speculative. What is more, their aim was often less to explain than to justify or to condemn. That they seldom distinguished between their aims is only one further proof that they were not scientists. And so it is sometimes held that their theories are much more impediments than helps to the social scientist, who need not rate his own achievements high to feel that, as compared with them, he is moving in the right direction, given that the object of the journey is to extend knowledge. Hence the need often felt by the social scientist to turn his back on these old and famous theories.

There is nothing arrogant about this attitude, with which it is easy to sympathize.[1] But there can be no real turning of the back on these old theories, whose ideas and assumptions still permeate our thinking about society and government, whether we know it or not. We are not free of them as the natural scientists are of the essences and entelechies of mediaeval and Aristotelian philosophy. We have still to come to terms with these thinkers of the past, to make up our minds about them, if we are to learn to think more clearly than they did.

These theories, moreover, were by no means entirely speculative, nor was their function always primarily to justify or to condemn. They were also, to a greater or a lesser extent, attempts to explain the facts – to explain what the social scientist aims at explaining. To examine them, as is still sometimes done, merely in order to establish how far they are internally consistent, is not an exercise of much use to the social scientist. Nor does it matter to him just which, among several different interpretations of a well-known doctrine, is the nearest to being correct. The enquiry perhaps most useful to him is an enquiry into the adequacy and relevance of these theories. How far do they provide a satisfactory explanation of what they seek to explain? How far are their assumptions and ideas useful for purposes

---

[1] There is more that is arrogant about the disparagement of the social sciences still common in England than about the claims made for them in the United States.

of explanation? Granted that the theories are in many ways inadequate or irrelevant, just why are they so? This book attempts, among other things, to answer these questions – and never more so than when it treats, sometimes at considerable length, of three among the more recent and still widely influential theories, those of Rousseau, Hegel and Marx.

The expositor and critic is bound to give what he honestly believes to be a fair interpretation of the doctrines he discusses. But, if his purpose is not to offer an interpretation which he believes to be an improvement on others, or to pronounce in favour of one among several current versions, he is not bound to argue the case for his interpretation. Since I have been concerned much more to examine the adequacy and relevance of assumptions, ideas and arguments than to establish that Machiavelli or Hume or Marx meant this rather than that, I have refrained from defending my interpretations, except where it has seemed to me that they might strike the reader as unusual or implausible.

Again, I have not considered every aspect of the most important theories; I have considered only those aspects which raised most sharply the issues I wanted to discuss. I have not considered, for example, what Montesquieu has to say about religion and its social functions, though in fact he has a great deal to say about it and says it in the most interesting way. The points I wished to make about religion, and its place in society, I have tried to make in discussing certain beliefs of Machiavelli and of Marx. It may well be that to someone whose field of study is the sociology of religion, Montesquieu has more to offer than either Machiavelli or Marx. Certainly, he treats of religion more elaborately and with greater subtlety than they do. But it seemed to me that their simpler and perhaps cruder treatment served my purposes better.

These theories are more than attempts to explain society and government, and more also than apologies for or attacks upon the established order. They are philosophies of life; and philosophies of this kind are often dismissed as useless or pernicious on the ground that they claim to be more than they really are.

They flourished, it is said, before the scientific study of man, of society and of government had properly begun; they pretended to a knowledge they did not possess. But now that men are beginning to see how to get this knowledge – how to study themselves and society to good purpose – they can do without these pretentious theories. When these theories are not, in the Marxian sense, *ideologies* (when their function is not to defend or challenge the interests of some class or group), they are merely personal statements. They express what somebody feels about man and man's condition in the world. Taken for what they are they may be interesting, but they must not be taken for more.

Certainly, the makers of these theories had illusions about them, and often claimed a knowledge they did not possess. I have already said in their defence that they took some account of the facts and made some attempt to explain them, and I do not suppose that the persons who call their theories 'ideologies' or 'fantasies' or 'mere personal statements' mean to deny this. I believe that these theorists took larger account of the facts and were more seriously concerned to explain them than their critics imply, but that is not what I now want to argue. Nor do I want to argue that the element of class or group *ideology* in these theories is smaller than Marxists have supposed. I want rather to insist that these theories – even when they are not attempts to explain the facts and do not serve to defend or challenge class or group interests – are more than mere personal statements, and that to call them so is grossly misleading. They do more than express personal preferences, even when those are preferences which many share.

Some of these theories are integral parts of a cosmology, of a sometimes elaborate theory about the universe and man's place in it; others are not. Hegel affirms that reality is an infinite Mind or Spirit seeking self-realization, an activity or process passing from level to level, and which is manifest, at its highest levels, in communities of finite selves – that is to say, in communities of men. His social and political theory is rooted in a philosophy which purports to explain everything; or alternatively (and this alternative is perhaps nearer the truth) his philosophy is an attempt to apply to all things ideas which make sense only when applied to human activities and social institutions. Others, as for example the Utilitarians, are more modest. The Utilitarians, for the most part, do not seek to improve upon or to add to the explanations of the physical and biological world offered by science; with rare exceptions they say nothing about divine or immanent purposes. They confine themselves to explaining man and his social behaviour. They take man as they think he is, as a creature of desires who seeks to satisfy them as abundantly as he can at the least cost to himself. They seek to explain his behaviour and all social institutions on this and a few other assumptions about man and his environment; and in support of their assumptions they appeal above all to what they take to be the common sense of mankind. Yet they, too, are concerned to do much more than explain the facts; they too seek to criticize and to persuade. They too have a philosophy of life which is something more than an explanation (however inadequate) of how men actually live.

All these theories, no matter how 'pretentious' or 'modest' they may be, are elaborate philosophies which contain a large element that is not science or conceptual analysis or ideology in the Marxian sense. They are what I venture to call, for want of a better word, practical philosophies or philosophies of man; they are forms of self-expression of which it is lamentably inadequate to say that they are mere personal statements. They are neither mere exercises in psychology – statements about how men feel and think and behave – nor mere excursions into morals. They involve much more than the laying down of ultimate rules (as, for example, the 'greatest happiness' principle or the principle of 'self-realization') or even the construction of elaborate hierarchies of rules.

There is always a close connection between a philosopher's conception of what man is – what is peculiar to him, how he is placed in the world – and his doctrines about how man should behave – what he should strive for, and how society should be constituted. The connection is there, multiple and close, whether the philosopher is a Rousseau or a Hegel, who does not agree with Hume that there is no deriving an *ought* from an *is*, or whether he is Hume himself. For Hume – though he believes that no rule of conduct follows logically from any description of man and his condition in the world – offers to show how man, being the sort of creature he is, comes to accept certain rules. Man and the human condition are, in some respects, everywhere the same, and therefore there are some rules which are everywhere accepted. They are not the only rules which men accept, and are not always in keeping with the other rules. Indeed, these other rules are sometimes preferred to them. Nevertheless, there are some rules which men everywhere accept, or would accept if they understood themselves and their condition; we have, therefore, only to understand what man is and how he is placed in the world to know what those rules are. This way of thinking is not confined to the natural law philosophers and Idealists; it is common to them and to the Utilitarians, and (as we shall see) there is a large dose of it even in Marxism.

In this book I am as much concerned to discuss these theories as *philosophies of life* as I am to examine critically the assumptions they make and the ideas they use in the attempt to explain the facts. And, here again, I confine myself almost entirely to what my authors have to say, attending hardly at all to the origins of their theories or the circumstances in which they were produced. I have already said enough, I hope, to show that this neglect does not come of a failure to appreciate the importance of what I have not tried to do. I have learnt much from many scholars, but the attempt to tread in all their footsteps would be absurd.

Man, as Machiavelli sees him, is self-assertive. He lives, not to seek God's favour or to serve some larger than human purpose, but to satisfy himself; he seeks security and something more; he seeks to make himself felt. He seeks reputation, to make his mark, to create some image of himself which is impressive to others. The stronger he is, the more he is willing to risk security for reputation. Man is both self-preserving and self-assertive; but Machiavelli sympathizes more with the second than the first of these needs. He values above all the two qualities which enable a man to assert himself: courage and intelligence. These are not just preferences which Machiavelli happens to have; they are rooted in his conception of what it is to be a man. Hobbes also sees man as self-assertive but sees him even more as in search of security in a world of self-seeking men; and he puts a high value on prudence and consistency of purpose. Organized society is a discipline which the prudent accept and to which the imprudent must be forced to submit. Rousseau sees man as the victim of society, as a creature who has lost his integrity. Society derives from his needs, develops his faculties, and yet is oppressive to him. As a rational and moral being, man is at once the creature and the victim of society, and can be cured of the ills it produces in him only in a reformed society. Bentham sees man as a subject of desires who, unlike other animals, can compare and foresee; he sees him as a competitor and collaborator with other men in the procuring of what satisfies desires. The proper function of rules and institutions is to ensure that competition and collaboration are as effective as possible – that they help and do not impede men in their efforts to satisfy their desires. Hegel sees man as a creature who becomes rational and moral in the process of coming to understand and master an environment; he sees him transformed and elevated by his own activities. He sees him as changing from age to age, and the course of this change as 'implicit' in his nature, in his capacity to reason and to will. Marx sees man as a creature whose image of himself and the world is a product of what he does to satisfy his basic needs; and yet he also sees him as a creature who comes in the end to know himself and the world, understanding his condition and accepting it, and who thereby attains freedom.

We have here six very different philosophies, even though there are elements common to several of them. And, though we can say of each of them that it was 'the product of its age' – though we can give reasons for its appearing when and where it did – we cannot say of any one of them that it is obsolete or irrelevant. They are ways of looking at man and society which are of perennial interest; we can find traces of them in philosophies much older than the ones which now seem to us to give fullest expression to them. Man and his social condition do change from age to age, but they also remain the same; and the different philosophies which men have produced reflect, not only how they and their condition have changed, but also the diversity of their reactions to what has not changed. Alfred North Whitehead once said that all later philosophies are footnotes to Plato. This may be extravagant but is not absurd, and is least extravagant when applied to Plato's views about man and society. Plato's theory of knowledge and Aristotle's logic have been superseded in a sense in which their political philosophies have not. That is not because epistemology and logic have made progress since their time as the study of man and society has not; it is because political philosophy has always aimed at something more than explanation. One explanation of what is involved in having knowledge or in reasoning may be an improvement on another. But with philosophy, in the sense in which I am now using the word, it is a different matter.

Today, in the social as in other studies, two kinds of enquiry find favour: the aim of one is to explain the facts, and when its methods are (or are held to be) adequate to its aim, it is called science; the aim of the other is to examine the ideas and methods used in explanation and in other forms of discourse, and when those ideas and methods are of wide application, it is sometimes called analytical philosophy. The theories expounded and criticized in this book, though by no means unscientific and unphilosophical in these two senses, are also more than science and analytical philosophy. Moreover (as I have said already, though in different words), as science and analytical philosophy they are often grossly inadequate. Therefore, since science and this kind of philosophy are in favour, these theories, which are often indifferent specimens of both, are in disfavour. And even when it is conceded that there is a large element in them which is neither the one nor the other, this element is written off as an aberration, due to a failure to understand what is the proper business of science or philosophy.

The suggestion is that these theories aim at extending knowledge but do not know how it is to be extended, or that they confuse other things with the extension of knowledge. They have several purposes but fail to distinguish between them, or have purposes so vague that they are not really purposes at all. They aim at explaining the facts or at elucidating ideas or at defining rights and obligations or at persuasion, and move from one aim to the next without knowing that they have done so. They are uncertain of purpose. The present-day critic, coming upon this confusion and trained to make the distinctions these theories too often fail to make, easily concludes that, if they have some purpose beyond explanation, elucidation, definition or persuasion – beyond the purposes familiar to him (and which he does not quarrel with, provided the man who has them knows what he is doing) – that purpose is illusory, rooted in misunderstanding. By all means let a political writer explain or analyse or persuade, but let him know what he is doing. For, if he does not know what he is doing, he will aim at the impossible, or will delude himself into believing he is contributing to knowledge when he is not, or will unconsciously seek to pass off his peculiar preferences as eternal truths.

I have already conceded that most of the great political and social thinkers of the past failed to make certain distinctions now commonly made, and that they were under illusions about their theories. Yet it is a mistake to conclude that, to the extent that they aimed at more than explanation, analysis or persuasion, their efforts were pointless or useless. Their theories have another function besides these, and a function which is not less important than they are.

Sophisticated man has a need to 'place' himself in the world, to come to terms intellectually and emotionally with himself and his environment, to take his own and the world's measure. This need is not met by science. It is not enough for him to have only the knowledge which the sciences and ordinary experience provide. Or perhaps I should say – to avoid misunderstanding – it is not enough for him to have only knowledge; for I do not wish to suggest that what he needs, and science and ordinary experience cannot provide, is knowledge in the same sense as they supply, merely coming to him from another source. Nor is it enough for him to have this knowledge together with a moral code and a set of preferences. He needs a conception of the world and of man's place in it which is not merely scientific – a conception to which his moral code and preferences are closely related. I have here in mind something more than the assumptions on which science and everyday experience themselves rest, assumptions which cannot be verified because they must first be accepted before it makes sense to speak of verification. This need is not felt by all men; and it is felt by some much more strongly than by others; but it is a persistent need. It is a need which can be met for some only by religion, but which for others can be met in other ways (unless any system of beliefs which meets it is to be called a religion). The theories examined in this book are systems of belief of this kind; or, rather, that is one aspect of them, and a very important aspect of some of them.

It would be profoundly misleading to speak of this aspect as if it were no more than a statement of preferences or a laying down of rules or a defining of goals. If it were only that, it would be possible to reduce it to a list, which is not in fact the case. A hostile or perverse critic may say that, as far as he can see, there is nothing more to it than that and a whole lot of verbiage besides, which to him means nothing. If he says this, there may be no arguing with him, beyond pointing out that it is perhaps a kind of verbiage in which he himself indulges when, momentarily, he forgets his opinions about it. When Rousseau or Hegel or Marx tells us what is involved in being a man, he is not – when what he says cannot be verified – either expressing preferences or laying down rules; he is not putting 'imperatives' in the indicative mood; he is not prescribing or persuading under the illusion that he is describing. He is not doing that or else talking nonsense. It might be said that he is telling his reader how he feels about man and the human predicament – or, more adequately and more fairly, that he is expressing some of the feelings that man has about himself and his condition. But he is not describing those feelings or just giving vent to them; he is *expressing* them, and the point to notice is that this expression takes the form of a theory about man and his condition. It could not take any other form. Thus, if it is an expression of feeling, the feeling requires systematic and conceptual expression. Only a self-conscious and rational creature could have such feelings about itself and its condition; and the theories which express these feelings, far from being statements of preference or rules of conduct passed off as if they were something different from what they really are, serve only to give 'meaning' to these statements and rules. Not that they are needed to make the statements and rules intelligible, to make it clear what the preferences are or what is involved in conforming to the rules; nor yet to justify the preferences or rules by pointing to their consequences. They give 'meaning' to them, not by explaining or justifying them, but by expressing an attitude to man and the human condition to which they are 'appropriate'; so that, even when we do not share the attitude, we understand how it is that those who do share it have those preferences and accept those rules. We do not infer the rules from the attitude, nor do we establish, in the manner of the scientist, a constant connection between the attitude and the rules and preferences; our understanding is different in kind from that of the scientist or the logician. It is neither an understanding of how things happen nor that some things follow from others; and yet it is an intellectual enterprise, a rational experience.

Man, being self-conscious and rational, has theories about himself and his social condition which profoundly affect his behaviour: theories which have not been, are not and never will be merely scientific. They will always be more than explanations of how he behaves and how institutions (which are conventional modes of behaviour) function. And they will always be more than statements of preference or assertions of principle and attempts to justify them; they will be more than 'personal statements' and more than exercises in persuasion. I do not say that there cannot be theories about man and society which are merely scientific, nor yet that any social theory which is more than merely scientific must have this particular more to it; I say only that the need for this more is enduring, and is in no way weakened by the spread of the scientific spirit.

But, it may be asked, granted that this is so, is not the study of these old theories, in so far as they do not attempt to explain the facts or do not examine the ideas used in explanation, of merely historical interest? They may once have been persuasive but are not so today, when the issues which inspired them are dead; and, to the extent that they do not seek to persuade but express what you have called attitudes to man and the human condition, our attitudes are no longer what they were. These theories, in this aspect of them, speak for their contemporaries and not for us; they belong to the past, and the study of them is mere history.

To this there are two answers. Issues and attitudes change less than they seem to, for the language used to express them changes more than they do. These theories are products of their age but are also ageless; their diversity shows not only how epochs and countries differ from one another but also the variety of man's attitudes to himself and his condition. It has been said that all men (or is it all thinking men?) are either Platonists or Aristotelians – which, though not literally true, makes a point worth making. So too, in similar style, we can say that in all ages there are Machiavellians and Marxists and Utilitarians, and even men who, like poor Rousseau, despair of the future of mankind while protesting that man is naturally good.

Secondly, man is an object of thought to himself and would not have the capacities peculiar to his kind unless he were such an object. His being a person, his sense of his own identity, his feeling that he has a place in the world, depend on memory – his own and other men's – for he has rational intercourse with them and belongs to enduring communities. Man is more than just the product of his past; he is the product of memory. The past 'lives on' in him, and he would not be what he is unless it did so. Thus, for him, as for no other creature, to lose his past, to lose his memory, is to lose himself, to lose his identity. History is more than the record of how man became what he is; it is involved in man's present conception of what he is; it is the largest element in his self-knowledge.

Man, being rational and capable of self-knowledge, puts to himself two sorts of questions, and science answers only one of them. The sort of question which science answers he puts both of himself and of what is external to him; but the sort which science does not answer he puts only of himself or of creatures whom he believes to be in his own condition. And these questions which science does not answer are also not answered by analytical philosophy. They are questions which have no final answers; for the answers to them differ from age to age and, perhaps even more, from person to person. These questions which science cannot answer are often put in the same form as the questions which science can answer. We may ask, 'What is man?', meaning 'What sort of creature is man?', and look for answers to the biologist, the psychologist and the social scientist. Or we can put the question which Pascal tried to answer in his *Pensées,* which is a different question altogether, though put in the same words. Pascal believed in God; but the need to put that question does not arise from this belief. An atheist may put it and find an answer which satisfies him, and yet remain an atheist. But the answer, whatever it is, is not a mere set of rules. The question, 'What is man?', as Pascal put it – a question which science cannot answer – is not to be reduced to the question, 'How ought man to behave?'.

Political and social theories of the kind discussed in this book are not the only theories, nor even the most important, which attempt answers to that sort of question; and of course they also put questions of other sorts. But this is an important element in them, and still as much worth studying as any other. The putting and answering of questions of this sort is an activity not less rational and not less difficult than scientific enquiry, and neither more nor less useful. These theories have helped to form sophisticated man's image of himself. No doubt, in primitive and illiterate communities men make do without them; but then they also make do without science. To ask, as some have done, 'What is the use of these theories?', is as pointless as to put the same question of science.

CHAPTER ONE
The Social and Political Philosophy of Hegel   I

As everyone interested in Hegel knows, his social and political theory
forms part of a general philosophy that is elaborate and difficult – a
philosophy that is metaphysical in the sense that it offers to explain
not so much how things happen in the world as why the world is
necessarily as it is. I am not, as a student of theories about society
and government, interested in the Hegelian metaphysic for its own
sake. It may be that its essence is beyond me, and I do not think I
should greatly mind if that were so. But I have to take notice of it
– though only in broad outline and in the most superficial way – for
two reasons: Firstly, because persons interested in Hegel's political
theory have taken a brief look at his metaphysical system and have
misinterpreted it. This, in itself, would not matter to us, except that
their misinterpretations have caused them to misunderstand what
Hegel says about society and the State. For instance, Hegel calls the
State *divine*, and also says that it is a *substance* and that citizens are its
accidents. It is easy, if the sense of these words is misunderstood, to
draw false inferences from them about his conception of the State.
Secondly, because we must do more than avoid certain common
errors about Hegelian metaphysics if we are to do justice to his
social and political theory. In expounding that theory, Hegel uses
concepts which belong to his metaphysical system. For example, he
calls the State *Objective Spirit*, and he calls Spirit a *concrete universal*.
To understand what he is saying about the State when he calls it a
spirit, we have to understand what he means by a *concrete universal*.
But this notion is the central notion of his metaphysics.

It may seem that I have brought myself to an *impasse*; for I have
admitted that the essence of Hegelian metaphysics may be beyond
me, and I have said that, if we are to understand his theory of the

State, we have to know how he uses the notion which is central to his metaphysics. My purpose is to expound and criticize the social and political theory of Hegel. Have I not as good as confessed that that purpose is beyond my power? Am I not stopped short at the very beginning of my enterprise?

I do not think so. The impasse, I hope, is more apparent than real. I suspect that the notion of the concrete universal, if we try to take it literally, is unintelligible – that it is a conflation of ideas which, taken together, do not really make sense. At the same time, I believe that the notion, if we take it metaphorically, does make sense; or, rather, I believe that it contains several notions which, if they are so taken, make sense. Hegel, if I may so put it, says to us, 'I mean by the concrete universal *this* and *that* and *the other*, and I mean it all literally'. Let us suppose that he defines it as A, B, C, D and E, all to be taken literally. My contention is that, though this combination, taken literally, makes no sense, several of its constituents, taken together and metaphorically, do make sense. Sometimes it may be A and B together that make sense, sometimes C and E, and sometimes B and E. I see the fundamental concept of the Hegelian philosophy as a family of concepts which are not quite what they are made out to be, but which are (most of them) highly effective in various combinations, each combination always going under the family name.

It is not the business of a political theorist to attempt a complete exposition or to offer a satisfactory criticism of a metaphysical system, even when that system is closely connected with a political theory which interests him. He need go no further, in his exposition and criticism, than what seems to him far enough to make the best sense he is able to make of the political theory. His exposition, therefore, is unlikely to seem adequate to anyone interested in the metaphysical system for its own sake. And his criticism is intended to be only superficial. Indeed, it is not so much criticism as a putting of his own cards on the table. He does not say, 'This and that part of the system are unacceptable for these reasons, which ought, in my opinion, to convince anyone who considers the matter closely'; he says, rather, 'I can make nothing of this or that part of the system, but I think that the author's political theory makes sense even without it'. The political theorist, criticizing a metaphysical system, does not attempt to argue an elaborate and careful case, meeting all objections to it which he can think of and which seem important to him. He merely takes up a stand, and has done as much as can be reasonably expected of him if he makes it plain just what that stand is.

This exposition and criticism, therefore, despite their superficiality, are necessary because they give notice how we intend to deal with the social and political theory of Hegel. As we have seen already, he calls the State Objective Spirit, and says that Spirit is a concrete universal. I shall reject as false or unintelligible much that Hegel says about the concrete universal. The rejection will not be criticism meant to satisfy the logician or metaphysician, for I neither regard myself as competent to make such a criticism, nor do I think it the duty of a social and political theorist to attempt it; but it will, I hope, help me to explain what I think is true or important or suggestive in what Hegel has to say about society and the State.

He was, I believe, a profound social and political theorist, and also a profound psychologist. Since I find his metaphysics unacceptable, I have to show what it is that is profound in his social and political theory, even when divorced from his metaphysics. Unfortunately, Hegel did not first produce a metaphysical system, using concepts appropriate to it, and then a social and political theory, using other concepts which his readers could understand without reference to his metaphysics. He used, as I have said, metaphysical concepts to expound his views about man in society and about the State. Therefore, anyone interested in those views, but who cannot accept the metaphysics, must learn to translate what Hegel says in his peculiar and metaphysical language about man, society and the State into more ordinary speech. If he refers to the metaphysical system, either to expound or criticize it, he does so primarily to make it plain how he proposes to render the translation.

If we treat Hegel's metaphysical language as largely metaphorical, we can, I believe, see that he uses it to say many important and true things not said by others before him, or not said nearly so well. No doubt, the convinced Hegelian will protest that this method is wretchedly inadequate. He might perhaps be moved to put his protest in such words as these: 'What you say makes no sense unless taken metaphorically actually makes excellent sense when taken literally, and that is how Hegel invites us to take it. Your exposition of Hegel's political and social theory necessarily misses a great part of the truth – indeed the essential part.'

That is a criticism to which the political theorist who adopts the line that I propose to take with Hegel is necessarily exposed, and which, as a mere political theorist, he cannot meet – at least not to the satisfaction of the critic. For to meet it he would have to do more than say that he could not accept the Hegelian metaphysical system for such and such reasons; he would have to prove that it is untenable. And I have already said that I cannot do this, and that it is not even my business,

3

as a social and political theorist, to attempt it. I must therefore admit that my account of Hegel's social and political theory may be seriously inadequate for the reason put forward by the hypothetical critic. I do not believe that it is; I believe that its inadequacies, whatever they are, are due to other causes, but this I cannot prove. A notion like that of the concrete universal may be unintelligible to someone either because, though it has a sense, he cannot get it, or because it has no sense. But he cannot be sure that it has no sense unless he can prove that it has none. I wish I could say that whatever in Hegel's philosophy is unintelligible to me is so for the second reason. Unfortunately, I cannot. I can say only that the arguments of the critics of Hegel's metaphysics seem to me more convincing than the arguments of his defenders, to the extent that I have understood them. Even if it were true that an account of Hegel's social and political theory must be inadequate if it assumes that the central concept (taken literally) of his philosophy is unintelligible, it would not follow that it must also distort his meaning. It might still be a fair account of part of his theory, and that part might be important. It is my hope that even Hegelians may say that my account of it, though it falls far short of the whole doctrine, is a fair enough interpretation, as far as it goes.

In reading the works of contemporary sociologists and political scientists, especially the more theoretical among them, I have often been struck by how much they have in common with Hegel. They have, I believe, as much in common with him as with Marx, and yet they are much less aware of their community with Hegel. His metaphysics and his vocabulary trouble them; they make little or nothing of him, and are easily tempted to dismiss him as a purveyor of nonsense. Nothing could induce them to take his philosophy seriously. If they were disposed to try to make sense of his social and political theory, they would, in all probability, discount his metaphysical beliefs. They would seek an answer to this question: What does that theory amount to, divorced from these beliefs? But that is precisely the answer that I am seeking. Even if it were true that whoever rejects the Hegelian metaphysics misses the essence of his theory of the State and of man's progress in society, the fact remains that it is those parts of the theory which still make sense when the metaphysical system is rejected that are important in contemporary social and political thought.

Croce once put the question, What is living and what is dead in the philosophy of Hegel? I believe that what is living still amounts to a great deal, but that we cannot see clearly what it is until we have extricated it from the clutches of what is dead.

I. HEGELIAN METAPHYSICS

1. Puzzles and Solutions

Hegel arrives at his doctrine about what reality essentially is by examining critically the attempts made before him to explain it – that is, by examining critically the philosophies prior to his own. As he sees it, these philosophies were all, in one way or another, faced by two kinds of puzzles – epistemological and logical – that they failed to solve, or to solve completely, and that he thinks are solved only by his philosophy, which asserts that reality is essentially spiritual, or the activity of Mind or Spirit, whereby it produces a coherent world and comes to full knowledge of itself and full satisfaction in the process of coming to know that world as its own product. I shall say more later about his conception of the world as essentially spiritual, but first I want to consider the puzzles which he believes that philosophies prior to his own had not completely solved.

a. Epistemological Puzzles

Philosophers have reflected about the nature of knowledge, distinguishing the knowing self or the act of knowing from the object known. In the course of this reflection, they have been caught up in all kinds of puzzles about what is independent of the mind and what is not. The same object appears different to different observers, and yet it is only one object and not as many as there are observers of it. We distinguish between changes in how an object appears to us and changes that happen to it. We distinguish between our dreams and our waking experience, calling only the first illusory. Ordinarily, we are not puzzled by such things, but when we reflect on the nature of our experience, we are puzzled. How do we distinguish between knowledge and illusion, between reality and appearance? None of the answers to this question given in the past is entirely satisfactory, though each, according to Hegel, has an element of truth about it, some of the answers being much nearer the truth than others. If we take philosophers who come only a little time before Hegel, we find Hume reducing all experience to mere clusters and sequences of impressions and their faint copies in memory; or we find Kant saying that space and time are forms of intuition (or ways in which what is given in sensation appears to the mind) and that concepts such as substance and cause are imposed by the mind on what it senses. Hume's theory allows nothing for the mind's activity. It treats mind as passive; or, rather, it neglects it altogether. For mind, Hegel tells us, is essentially active, and anyone who fails to notice this really leaves mind out of account. Kant makes a false distinction between things as they appear to us and things as they are in themselves, making the absurd assertion that we can know that there are things-in-themselves, quite independent of our minds, but that we can know nothing more about them than that they exist. Yet there is an element of truth in both their theories. Hume is right in holding that there is nothing outside the range of our experience, and Kant is right in holding that the mind creates the world which it knows. If we are to get over these difficulties, we must, Hegel tells us, realize that knowing or thinking and the object of knowledge or thought are but two sides of a single experience, separable in our minds but not in fact; and we must realize as well that knowledge is active and not passive.

b. Logical Puzzles

Philosophers, in explaining the world, have used certain basic concepts or categories, such as *being, substance, quality, change, cause* and *effect, finite* and *infinite*. These concepts were not, of course, invented by philosophers in order to explain the world; they were already present in ordinary speech, sometimes implicitly and sometimes explicitly. Philosophers have merely examined them, refined upon them and explained them. Hegel does not question the utility of these concepts or suggest that, as ordinarily used, they involve the user in obscurity or contradiction. He says only that, if they are examined critically, it is seen that they are contradictory in themselves.

Let me take an example to illustrate his meaning. Hegel thinks that the notion of being, critically examined, proves to be self-contradictory. For if we say of anything that it has only being, we attribute nothing to it, as mere being, without any other properties, is nothing. Thus the concept of being is seen to contain within itself the concept of nothing, which is its opposite, and it is therefore a self-contradictory concept. Hegel is even prepared to say that the two concepts, being and nothing, are identical, and also that they pass into one another. But the passing of these two concepts into one another gives us a third concept, which is that of *becoming*. We have here three concepts *dialectically* related to one another: the concept of being, the *thesis*; which passes into its opposite or *antithesis*, the concept of nothing; and the concept of becoming, which contains them both and is their *synthesis*. It is equally true, says Hegel, that the concepts of being and nothing are different and that they are identical; we cannot help but distinguish between them, and yet we also cannot help observing, if we take either in pure abstraction, that it is the same as the other. We have two concepts which we cannot deny are both identical and different, and we cannot see how they can be both until we pass to the concept of becoming, or of coming to be and ceasing to be. What is coming to be both is not and is; what is ceasing to be both is and is not; and so, in the concept of becoming, being and nothing are reconciled – that is to say, they are both necessarily contained in it, because it is unthinkable without them.

If we take the concept of *becoming* in pure abstraction, we see that it too contains its opposite, and is therefore self-contradictory, and then again that both it and its contradictory opposite are necessarily contained in some other concept; and so the process goes on until we eventually reach a concept which is not self-contradictory and which Hegel calls the Absolute Idea. Thus, for Hegel, the concepts in terms of which we describe and explain our experience form a hierarchy whose highest member contains all the others within itself. Therefore, the peculiarity, if I may so put it, of this hierarchy is that its highest member *is* the hierarchy, for it contains all the members below it. It alone is fully self-consistent, whereas the concepts contained in it, if they are considered in abstraction from it, are not self-consistent.

So far, we have been considering only concepts and not the reality to which they apply. Now, what is real cannot be self-contradictory; it must therefore realize the Absolute Idea, which alone is completely self-consistent. But only Mind or Spirit realizes the Absolute Idea, and from this it follows that reality must be spiritual. The puzzles and contradictions, from which we cannot escape when we consider what is involved in our having knowledge and when we analyse the concepts which we necessarily use to describe the world, can be resolved only if we think of the world in a certain way – if we think of it as Mind or Spirit rising progressively to a full knowledge of itself.

The philosophies prior to his own are of interest to Hegel for two reasons. They interest him because, by reflecting on their inadequacies, he can make his way to the true philosophy, and they also interest him as stages in the process whereby Spirit comes to full knowledge of itself. He thinks of them as necessary stages; and so, in his opinion, the study of the history of thought is an important part of the study of what reality essentially is and must be.

Spirit, says Hegel, is of its essence active; it is what it does. It is revealed only in its actions, and exists only as so revealed; it is by action and by reflecting on its actions that it constructs for itself coherent knowledge of a world and in the same process acquires self-knowledge. But we have seen that, for Hegel, knowledge and its object are but two sides of a single experience, so that Spirit, as it creates for itself coherent knowledge of a world, creates the object of that knowledge, which is the world. Since Spirit is active and is revealed only in action, Hegel speaks of it as self-creating; and since it comes to know itself in the process of knowing a world (that is, in the process of acquiring a coherent experience), he speaks of it as discovering itself in the world, or as positing a world in which it comes to full knowledge of itself as it comes to know that it has posited the world.

The process whereby Spirit comes to full self-knowledge is dialectical. Spirit is active in producing for itself coherent knowledge of a world, but it does not at first know that it has produced it; it therefore takes the world as something outside itself, contrasting itself, as Spirit, to nature as the opposite of Spirit. Then, as it reflects on its experience, it comes to know that nature, which it took to be external to itself, is its own product. As Hegel often puts it, Spirit negates itself in a world which it takes to be external to itself, and then negates that negation when it comes to know the world as a projection of Spirit. In other words, it comes to know itself as that which necessarily produces a world and cannot attain self-knowledge except by so doing.

Spirit necessarily acquires self-knowledge in a plurality of finite minds – of minds like yours and mine, of minds in the ordinary sense as understood by anyone ignorant of the Hegelian philosophy. Spirit is revealed to itself, necessarily, in a plurality of selves, because Spirit involves self-consciousness, and a self becomes self-conscious by distinguishing itself from other selves. Of course, it cannot distinguish itself from other selves unless it distinguishes itself from a world external to itself. Spirit is not conceived of by Hegel, as God is by most theologians, as a mind separate from ordinary minds and differing from them chiefly in being omniscient and omnipotent.

In the ordinary sense of mind (in the sense in which Smith and Robinson each have one), there are only finite minds. Spirit is revealed to itself only through finite minds; it is self-conscious only through their consciousness of it. Yet it is greater than any of the finite minds in which it comes to know itself. For, though each finite mind also acquires self-consciousness in the process of acquiring coherent knowledge of a world, this knowledge is not its sole product. Knowledge involves the use of concepts logically related to one another; in other words, it involves the use of a language, and a language is not the product of this or that finite mind but of many such minds related to one another. And these relations are not external, like the spatial relations between material objects; they involve communication. The knowledge through which any finite mind acquires self-consciousness and consciousness of an external world is the product of a community of minds.

Therefore, when Hegel says that Spirit reveals itself by producing a world and comes to full knowledge of itself as it comes to recognize the world as its own product, we must not suppose that he is talking about a process which happens separately in each finite mind. He is not saying that each of us reveals himself in producing a world, and exists only as so revealed; he is saying that Spirit which reveals itself in producing a world comes to know itself only in our knowledge of it. He is not a solipsist or a subjectivist; though Spirit is the whole of reality and is manifest, at higher levels, in a plurality of finite minds through which it obtains self-knowledge, each of these finite minds is only an infinitesimally small part of reality. Spirit, as Hegel puts it, is a concrete universal; it is a process whose nature is revealed through everything which is a part of it, and the end or goal of the process is self-knowledge achieved in a plurality of finite minds. If I have understood Hegel aright, only a part of the process which is Spirit is thus revealed in finite minds and in the forms of their communal life. But this part is the highest, for the end or goal of the process is self-knowledge, which is attained only in the knowledge of finite minds. The process which is reality is said by Hegel to be timeless, and so we have the paradox of a timeless process whose goal is self-knowledge, achieved only in the knowledge of finite minds whose experience is necessarily temporal.

Hegel – though he conceives of the whole process which is reality as spiritual – also uses the word Spirit more narrowly to refer to the higher stages of the process, the stages revealed in finite minds. So we find him treating all reality as spiritual, and also contrasting nature with Spirit, saying that Spirit arises out of nature and is a higher stage of the process in which they are both involved. If we think of Spirit as all reality, then nature is its product; if we think of it as the higher stages of the process which reality is, then Spirit emerges out of nature. And here we come upon another paradox, which, for the moment, I will only mention without comment. The process is dialectical; it involves contradiction and the resolution of contradiction, repeated over and over again, until a final stage is reached which involves no further contradiction. The process is spoken of as if it were both logical and teleological – as if the lower stages implied the higher ones, and also as if they produced them in order that the process should achieve its goal. This goal is the full self-knowledge of Spirit; and all the stages that lead up to it, since they imply it, are said to be explicit in it, and it

9

is said to be implicit in them. So, just as the Absolute Idea – the only fully consistent concept – contains all the other concepts in it, so the highest stage in the process of Spirit, the Absolute Spirit, contains all the lower stages. That a complex idea should be made up of simpler ones is readily intelligible, but it does seem odd to speak of a process whose ultimate stage contains all the stages leading up to it.

The concepts contained in the Absolute Idea are, we have seen, abstract and self-contradictory when considered apart from the whole which contains them. As it is with the Absolute Idea, so it is with Absolute Spirit; whatever is contained in it, whatever is its culmination, is said to be abstract and self-contradictory when considered apart from it. To understand anything which is involved in the process, we must understand that process as a whole. Even to understand its end, its culmination, we must understand the whole process, for the end of Spirit is that it should know itself. To understand what it is to be a finite self, we must understand what it is to be a member of a community, for a finite self is what it is only in a community of selves. And to understand what a community is, we must see it in relation to the whole process whereby Spirit attains self-knowledge. As revealed in the thoughts, purposes and feelings of finite selves, Spirit is, in the Hegelian parlance, subjective; as revealed in the forms of communal life, especially the State, it is objective.

2. *Why Hegel's Solutions are Unacceptable*

a. *Spirit and Nature*

The mere student of social and political theory, in attempting to take stock of Hegel's account of what reality essentially is and why it must be so, finds himself torn between two emotions – admiration and suspicion. There is a boldness and a magnificence about what he says, which cannot but impress. His is a high-sounding account; it is philosophy in the grand manner. But does it really solve the difficulties it claims to solve? Does it provide us with ideas which really help to make the world, and especially the social world, more intelligible?

Hegel – by his doctrine that knowledge and its object are essentially one (meaning, apparently, not that they cannot be distinguished, but that they are inseparable aspects of a single experience) – seems to create as many problems as he solves. Unless we can legitimately speak of things being as we know them to be, quite independently of our knowing them, how can we distinguish between truth and error? We can, of course, resort to a coherence theory of truth, saying that an opinion is true if it is compatible with those of our opinions which form a consistent or coherent body of opinions – a systematic whole which we treat as knowledge. But, in that case, it follows that an opinion which is compatible with the coherent system of our opinions at one time but not at another can first be true and then become false. It remains true while it fits in with the system, but, if the system changes (which it must do as the experience of mankind is enlarged), it may become false. I find it impossible to accept this; I would rather say, as most men do, that what was believed to be true on the best evidence then available has since been shown to be false. It seems to me that the Hegelian philosophy requires us to hold that this is merely another way of saying that what was true has become false, which it clearly is not.

If knowledge and its object are one, in the Hegelian sense, moreover, it surely follows that where there is no knowledge there is nothing. For, though we are told that Spirit is not be be confused with the finite minds in and through which it attains self-knowledge, we are also told that it reaches the level of self-consciousness only in them, and that only where there is self-consciousness can there be knowledge and thought. It would therefore seem that, where there are no finite minds, there is nothing.

But Hegel, though he seems committed to this conclusion, in fact avoids it. We have seen that he sometimes speaks as if nature were a projection of Spirit, and at other times says that Spirit emerges out of nature. As we have also seen, when he speaks in the second way, which he does the more frequently, he uses the word Spirit in a narrower sense. But it is in this narrower sense that Spirit involves self-consciousness and knowledge. Therefore, in the ordinary sense of mind, there could be a mindless world – a world without knowledge or thought or even feeling in it. It is true that Hegel says that Spirit, in this narrower and more usual sense, arises *necessarily* out of nature, and is higher than nature. Nature exists for the sake of Spirit; nature implies Spirit; Spirit is the *truth* of nature. Hegel says all these things, and I do not pretend to know what he means by the last of them, which is the oddest. Presumably, to say that Spirit is the *truth* of nature does not imply that, unless there is a mind to know it, there can be no nature; it must surely be only another way of saying that nature exists for the sake of Spirit, or else it must mean that nature is not fully intelligible except as giving rise to Spirit. But all this does not allow us to escape the conclusion that there could be a mindless universe. No doubt, if nature necessarily gives rise to Spirit, the universe could not remain mindless for ever, but it would have to be mindless before

Spirit and self-consciousness and knowledge arose in it. But how can this be, if, as Hegel says, thought and its object are *essentially* one? For Hegel, when he asserts the identity of thought and its object, does not mean merely that whatever is real is thinkable or knowable; he means that whatever is real is actually an object of thought. Or, rather, he means that whatever is real is both thought and its object.

If we want, as Hegel and his disciples do, to hold on to both these assertions – that thought and its object are essentially one, and that Spirit (in the narrower sense which involves the existence of finite minds that think and have knowledge) emerges out of nature – we are driven to speak as if there could be thought even with no minds to do the thinking. But this is surely nonsense. It is, I believe, the sort of paradox to which philosophers are driven when they have got themselves into a difficulty they cannot get out of.

I must also confess that I can attach no meaning to the assertion that Spirit arises *necessarily* out of nature. Hegel intends to convey by it something more than that the universe was once mindless, and that minds later emerged in it, not by chance, but from causes which would appear sufficient to us if we knew them; he intends to convey something deeper and altogether more difficult to grasp. Nature, he says, *implies* Spirit. When he says this, Hegel is perfectly well aware that the causes to which science points to account for an event do not imply it. He is not saying that nature is the cause of Spirit; he is saying that it is inconceivable that there could be a universe in which Spirit (which is essentially reason and will) does not arise. The process which is reality, and which includes the emergence of Spirit out of nature, is a *necessary* process; it is inconceivable that it should be otherwise than it is. For this process is the realization of the Absolute Idea, the only self-consistent concept. Reality, which is self-consistent, must therefore be an instance of this concept, and it must be the only instance, for the concept is of a Whole that is all-inclusive, a process which culminates in Spirit knowing itself.

b. The Deduction of the Categories

Hegel's deduction of the categories would appear to attribute to concepts contradictions which arise only when the concepts are misused or when mistaken theories are put forward about their use. Let us consider the example we took before – the assertion that something has only being. This is a meaningless assertion; it purports to say something and in fact says nothing. But that does not make *being* and *nothing* identical concepts. If we say that X has only being, we speak improperly; we speak as if there were something to which we were attributing being, whereas in fact there is nothing. If I were to say that X is only red (that is, has no property other than redness), I should be speaking nonsense, for nothing can have only this one property; but it would not follow from my nonsense that red and not-red are identical concepts. That being is not a property, while redness is, makes no difference to the argument; for Hegel speaks of being as if it were a property.[1] Thus – or so it seems to me – we have, at the very start of his *Logic*, a piece of false reasoning: that to predicate only being of something is to predicate nothing of it. The truth is, rather, that to predicate only being of something is to predicate being of nothing; but from this it clearly does not follow that to predicate being is to predicate nothing.

That is not the only kind of false reasoning to be found in Hegel's *Logic*, in his attempt to show that all our basic concepts involve one another and are free of contradiction only if we see them as a hierarchy whose highest member contains all the rest. His reasoning varies with the nature of the concepts he wants to prove, which are both different and identical. He does not, for example, use the same type of argument to prove that the finite and the infinite are identical as to show that being and nothing are so. Most people would suppose that finite and infinite are mutually exclusive terms. But, says Hegel, those who think this fail 'to note the simple circumstance that the infinite is thereby only one of two, and is reduced to a particular, to which the finite forms the other particular'.[2] W. T. Stace, who quotes this passage from William Wallace's translation of Hegel's *Logic*, comments on it thus: 'The infinite, according to this view, is limited by the finite, and is therefore itself finite.'[3] If I have understood this strange argument, it amounts, in effect, to the claim that *Whatever is finite is not infinite, and so the concept of infinity is confined only to what is not finite. But to be confined is to be finite, and so the infinite is finite*. In other words, because the term *unlimited* is limited in its application, *limited* and *unlimited* are equivalent terms. Hegel then goes on to deduce, from these two concepts, which are different and identical, a third

---

[1] The Idealists think it important to distinguish between *being and existence*. Universals, they say, do not exist except in particulars; but they can be thought of apart from particulars. When we speak of whiteness, without speaking of any white thing, we are speaking of something which does not exist; yet we are not speaking of nothing. Thus whiteness has being.

[2] *The Logic of Hegel*, trans. William Wallace (first published in 1873, 3rd ed. (Oxford 1975), § 95, p. 139.

[3] Stace, *The Philosophy of Hegel* (London 1924), § 200, p. 147. Looking at Hegel's argument as Wallace translates it, I did not trust myself to select the passage that gives the gist of it, and so I thought it best to allow a professed Hegelian to select it for me. This, as Stace sees it, is the clue to Hegel's meaning.

concept in which this contradiction is reconciled. The finite and the infinite limit one another, and yet are identical. But if A is identical with B and is also limited by it, we can say that it is *self-limited*. Only the self-limited is the truly infinite.

I offer these two examples to illustrate why I think that the attempt to show that our basic concepts form a hierarchy, whose highest member is alone free of contradiction, fails. I take the first example because it is the most frequently given by exponents of Hegel's philosophy, and the second because the concept of the self-limited or truly infinite is one that Hegel applies to Spirit. Reason and Will, which are aspects of Spirit, are self-limiting. Reason determines the limits of its own competence, and the will is self-determined whenever a deliberate choice is made. But this is mere playing with words; for the concept of self-determination, as applied to reason and will, is not a combination of the concepts of finite and infinite, as Hegel interprets them when he offers to show that they are both different and identical. Finite and infinite are concepts which apply to things that can be measured or quantified, and it does not make sense to say of such things that they are self-limiting. No finite space is self-limited; it is only limited by what is external to it. In the sense in which a quantity or series can be finite or infinite, it means nothing to say that it is self-limited, and it also means nothing to say that it is self-determined.

No doubt it does make sense to speak of the self-determined or the self-limited, when the self we have in mind is a self-conscious and rational being. But, in that case, the word *limited* is used in a different sense from that in which a space or a series is limited. If we take this second sense to be the literal one, then the other is metaphorical. We have here a line of reasoning which is by no means rare in Hegel; we are first invited to believe that two concepts which are mutually exclusive are also identical, and then we are offered a third concept which is said to contain them both and to 'reconcile' them. They are 'reconciled' in the third concept, presumably, because – though it contains them both and they contradict one another – it is nevertheless intelligible. If, however, we look more closely at what Hegel says, we see that the argument showing that the two concepts are identical is fallacious, and that the third concept does not really contain them, and can only be passed off as doing so because there is a verbal similarity between them. The connection between self-limitation, in the sense in which the term can be applied to the activities of a self-conscious and rational being, and the limited and unlimited, as applied to what can be measured, is not logical but etymological.

The concept of the truly infinite or self-limited is of great importance in the philosophy of Hegel, for with it we pass from the concepts applying only to nature to those which apply to Spirit as well. According to Hegel, it is the concepts which apply only to nature – to the material world – which are the more 'abstract' and the more obviously 'self-contradictory'. As we pass from them to the concepts which apply to Spirit and not to nature, we pass – so Hegel tells us – from the more to the less abstract, from the more to the less self-contradictory, till we reach the Absolute Idea, the only fully consistent concept. And so we get, unless I am mistaken, this strange result, that the less abstract concepts which apply to the higher levels of existence – the levels of rational endeavour – being nearer to self-consistency, apply to what is in itself more real than that which the more abstract concepts alone apply to. Thus Spirit, in the narrower sense, as consciousness, reason and will emerging from nature, is more real than nature. It is in the concepts which apply to it, but which do not apply to nature considered apart from it, that the contradictions involved in the concepts which do apply to nature are resolved. These concepts imply those which apply to *Spirit*. Therefore nature implies Spirit, and exists for the sake of Spirit. Hegel sometimes speaks as if nature existed in order to be known and used by Spirit, as if the material world were unintelligible except as being destined to be so known and used.

I must confess that none of this makes sense to me. I should have thought that concepts which are self-contradictory apply to nothing. But the Hegelian philosophy appears to rest on the contrary assumption, that self-contradictory concepts do apply to certain aspects of reality, which are therefore, taken in themselves, less rational and less real than other aspects, not being fully intelligible apart from them and existing for their sake.

Spirit, says Hegel, is a concrete universal. He calls it *concrete* to distinguish it from the *abstract* universal – from the concept which applies to any one of many instances. The abstract concept of circularity is fully realized in every instance of it, and there need be only one instance for it to be fully realized. But Spirit is not realized in each of its actions as an abstract concept is realized in every instance of it. Spirit is realized in the totality of its actions. It is revealed in its actions and exists only as so revealed. But it is not a mere collection of actions; for the actions that reveal it exhibit a character which it can know. Thus, if we consider Spirit in relation to the actions which reveal it, we see that it stands to them differently from the way in which an abstract universal stands to its particulars or a material whole to its parts. Hegel speaks of it as a universal which particularizes itself, or as a concept involved in a process of revealing or making explicit what it is potentially. Thus, he says in the *Philosophy of Right*, which is the most elaborate exposition of his theory of the State, that it is his purpose to reveal the development of will from concept to Idea.[1] He offers to show how from the bare concept of will it follows that will can only be realized or made actual in the State, in a community of rational beings who conscientiously accept the rules they are required to obey. This, clearly, is to use the words 'realized' or 'made actual' in a special Hegelian sense.

There are three ordinary uses of the word *realized* which are relevant here. We speak of a concept being realized whenever anything exists to which it can be applied. Realization, in this sense, does not involve growth or development or endeavour. We also speak of realizing an ideal. Whenever a person imagines a state of affairs which he thinks desirable and then succeeds in bringing it about, we may say that he realizes an ideal. This second sense involves the notion of endeavour. We also sometimes speak of growth or development as a process whereby something realizes its potentialities, as when we say that a seed comes to be, or is realized in, the mature plant. Hegel's concrete universal would appear to be a running together of these three quite different senses of realization. It is also more than that. Realization in the third sense, which is growth or development, is treated by Hegel as if it were a necessary process. There is here a running together of the notions of development and implication. The seed does not merely grow into the mature plant; it implies it.

Again, the concrete universal is not merely the sum of its particulars; it is not just the whole of which they are the parts; it is a whole contained in each of them. The finite self is one example of a concrete universal; it is not, we are told, the mere subject of its actions, the 'I' to which they all refer, for it is present in each of them in some deeper sense than that. A man's character is revealed both in the totality of his actions and in each of them; for it is not a bare subject that acts, but a man with a definite character. A community of selves is another example of a concrete universal; and again its character is revealed both in the pattern of life of the whole community and in each of its members; for each of them is what he is as a member of the community. The community is *reflected* in each of them.

Hegelians say that the concrete universal is a rich notion. No doubt it is; there is a great deal put into it. But if we take it literally, it does

[1] See Hegel's *Philosophy of Right*, trans. T. M. Knox (Oxford 1942), introduction, §§ 29–33, pp. 33–36.

not make sense. A concept does not develop; it has no potentialities to be realized. It can either be applied or it cannot, and its application adds nothing to it. It makes no sense to speak of it as particularizing itself, as if it were the cause of its own instances and revealed its essential nature the more fully, the more varied the instances it produced. A concept does not stand to its instances as a seed does to the mature organism that grows out of it. Nor can we say that the earlier stages in a process, whether it be a natural growth or a psychological or social development, imply the stages that follow it. If we describe the earlier stages, as they are in themselves, without regard to what comes after them, we cannot infer the later stages; we can infer them only if we know the process as a whole; and that is knowledge which we get from experience. From the fullest possible account of the actual properties of an acorn, we cannot infer that it will grow into an oak. Hegel seems both to admit and to deny this. He admits that if we knew only the earlier stages of a process, we would not be able to predict the later ones; but he also insists that, when we do know the whole process, we can see that it is necessary. This I find unacceptable. No doubt, if we do know the whole process, we can define its early stages by reference to the later ones; we can put into our definitions potential as well as actual properties. Having done that, we can speak as if the early stages implied the later ones; but the implication is in our definitions and not in the facts.

It does, I concede, make sense to speak of the self as revealed in the whole course of its actions, and it also makes sense to say that the self is present in each of those actions. And Hegel is right in contending that when we speak of the self in this way or use the pronoun 'I', we are doing something different from, or at least something in addition to, referring to a bare subject of conscious feelings, thoughts and actions. This is clear enough in the first case. Nobody supposes that the self revealed in the course of a man's life is the bare subject of all his experiences; for he would need to have only one self-conscious experience for that self to be revealed; he would need to be able to say 'I' only once in his life. The self revealed in the course of a man's life is his character, which is something complex and yet peculiar to himself; whereas the bare subject, considered apart from its experiences, is, like any other bare subject, a mere abstraction.

But the self revealed in the course of a man's life is not the self present in each of his actions. When we say that a man's self is present in each of his actions, we are not, I think, speaking of his character. True, his actions are influenced by his character, though even then they are influenced, not by his character as revealed during

17

the whole course of his life, but by his character as it was when he acted. Nevertheless, when we say that the self is present in each of its actions, we do not mean that a man's every action reveals his character, even though only in part. Nor do we mean that all his actions have a common subject. And yet, when we speak in this way, we do refer to something peculiar to creatures who are self-conscious. As Hegel saw, the experiences and actions of such a creature differ in kind from all other events known to us. Since man is, in fact, the only self-conscious creature, the only creature capable of saying 'I' known to us, we can say that human experience is unique. Man, being a self-conscious creature, is alone capable of passing false and true judgements on the situations he contemplates and in which he acts; he alone is capable of deliberation and choice. When he says to himself 'I see this' or 'I desire this' or 'I choose this', he is doing more than just stating a fact – which is, for instance, all that he is doing when he says 'the door is open'. He is, when he so speaks or thinks, being himself. According to Hegel, it is the peculiarity of the self that it does not exist unless it is self-conscious; and in being self-conscious it is necessarily active. Mere sensation may be passive, but any experience which involves self-consciousness is always active; it involves thinking. In one sense of the word action, only a self can be active; and when it is active – in the peculiar sense in which it alone can be – it is present to itself in the action (in mere thinking, or in consciously desiring, or in making a choice), and it exists only in being so present. This is, I think, what Hegel means when he says that the self 'posits itself'. All its actions involve self-consciousness, and it is not self-conscious except in action, and is a self in being self-conscious. Therefore, when I use the word 'I', I am not merely speaking or thinking about myself; I am not becoming aware of a self which existed, or could exist, apart from my awareness of it; I am being myself. I am exhibiting what it is to be a self.

Hegel was right in believing that a self-conscious creature has a character in a sense peculiar to creatures of its kind, and right also in believing that the statements whereby it expresses its self-consciousness are more than merely descriptive. A self-conscious creature develops in ways in which it could not develop if it were not self-conscious. Hegel used his notion of the concrete universal to express these beliefs. Unfortunately, that notion is more misleading than helpful; it suggests so much which is unacceptable that what is both true and important is apt to be lost from view. So also, in considering the relation of a community to its members, Hegel has important things to say which are easily overlooked if we allow ourselves to be too much put off by the words he uses to say them. Though it makes no sense to speak of a whole which is contained in each of its parts, or to speak of it as implicit in them, or of them as explicit in it, it does make sense, if we speak metaphorically, to say that a community is *reflected* in each of its members. This is so not only because men become rational and moral persons in the process of using a language and adopting norms of behaviour which are communal rather than merely personal, but also because a human community differs in important respects from other communities, its members being aware that they belong to it.

Hegel's notion of the concrete universal enables him to speak as if *mind*, a class-concept, were itself *a mind* as if it were present in finite selves as the finite self is present in its experiences. It enables him to speak of it as if it were itself active and conscious and self-conscious, and yet to insist that it is so only in and through finite selves. To anyone to whom the notion of the concrete universal is unintelligible (as it is to me), this looks like an attempt by Hegel to have his cake and eat it. He can deny that there is any self-conscious and rational mind apart from finite minds, and he can also speak of a mind or spirit which is infinite. He can say that Mind or Spirit is essentially infinite, and also that it is its nature to be revealed in a plurality of finite minds and to exist only as so revealed. The notion of an infinite mind, active and conscious only in finite minds, is one that makes no sense to me; and yet, as I hope to show, Hegel uses this notion to say a great deal that makes excellent sense about man and society. In my opinion, we can get at that sense only if we treat the notion as a bundle of metaphors, which Hegel employs now one and now another, as serves his purpose.

If I pass on directly to other topics, it is not because I feel I have done justice to Hegelian metaphysics, either in exposition or criticism; it is because I hope that I have said enough to make it clear what method I shall use in interpreting his social and political theory. I shall begin by discussing Hegel's account of the development of Spirit as revealed in the intellectual and social evolution of mankind, and then I shall go on to consider his theory of the State.

II. THE PROGRESS OF SPIRIT

By the progress of Spirit I mean the process whereby, as Hegel puts it, Spirit comes to know itself fully and to be satisfied, or, as we might prefer to say, the process whereby men come to understand themselves and the world they live in and attain the contentment of full maturity in so doing. This process is described in the *Phenomenology of Spirit* and in the *Lectures on the Philosophy of History*. Certain aspects of it are also described in the *Lectures on the History of Philosophy*, but we, as social and political theorists, are interested in the account in broad outline, and that we can find sufficiently in the *Phenomenology* and in the *Philosophy of History*.

In the *Phenomenology*, Hegel explains how Spirit appears to itself at each stage in its evolution towards complete self-knowledge and satisfaction, or, as we should put it, how men see themselves and the world at every stage. He also claims to show how these stages are necessary parts of a single process. He claims to see the process as a whole, to understand the significance of each stage as the men involved in it could not understand it; or, to use his language, he sees Spirit as it actually is at each stage and also as it appears to itself; he sees it as it is *in* itself and as it is *for* itself. Only at the end of the process, when Spirit attains complete self-knowledge and satisfaction, is it *for* itself what it is *in* itself – or, in other words, does it appear to itself as it really is.

Hegel begins by describing what knowledge is, how it consists of sensation, perception and understanding. He is not, at this point, explaining a process of intellectual and social evolution; he is merely explaining what goes to make up knowledge, properly so called. Knowledge is always, as he sees it, architectonic; it involves having a more or less coherent picture of a world. Even the child, as soon as it learns to think and to use a systematic language, is conscious of itself as living in a world in which it distinguishes itself from what is external to it.

Hegel then goes on to describe a temporal process: how one way of thinking about man and the world gives way to another. He links up, often in the most ingenious way, these pictures of the world – these *Weltanschauungen* – with moral attitudes and forms of art and religion. Much of his argument is specious; he wants to make everything fit into his scheme, and sometimes resorts to the oddest devices to achieve his object. The poverty of his argument, when it is poor, is often hidden by the obscurity of his style. Hegel has sometimes been accused of being a charlatan: he is so confident, so omniscient, and at times so tricky and so thin, that he annoys or disgusts the reader. It is difficult to believe that so acute and ingenious a mind could have been taken in by some of his arguments. More perhaps than any other philosopher of his calibre, he gives the impression of being intellectually dishonest. His are not the lapses of a slow or tired mind; he makes great claims for his philosophy, and claims that are unprecedented. For it is in his philosophy that Spirit attains full self-knowledge. We may expect, but we do not excuse, shoddiness in those who give us to understand that they have solved the riddle of the universe.

Yet Hegel's enterprise is not, taken as a whole, shoddy and trivial; it is exciting and bold, and even magnificent. He sees a process whereby man, by getting to know the world and to master it, also gains self-knowledge and self-mastery; he sees man, before he has achieved this knowledge and mastery, as a stranger in a social world which, though he does not know it, is the product of his own actions; he sees him transforming himself as he transforms his environment; he sees him learning gradually to be at home in the world.

This process, on its intellectual side, takes two forms: it is revealed in the attitudes of mind of the individual, in personal philosophies of life, and it is also revealed in the myths and dogmas of religion. A personal philosophy can be shared by many people, and indeed usually is so; it is not personal as being exclusive to the person who holds it but only as being how he sees the world and himself in it. It is the conscious stand he takes, though he may have motives for taking it (as Hegel clearly saw) of which he is unconscious. It is his faith, in the broad sense of that word. No doubt, it is connected with the myths and dogmas of his community, but it is different from them. Faith is personal, whereas religion, in this conception of it, is communal; religion consists of dogmas which the individual may not understand, or to which he may pay only lip-service. Religion, Hegel tells us, expresses a community's attitude to itself, though not explicitly; it is a manifestation of Spirit different in kind from a personal philosophy. In the *Phenomenology*, Hegel discusses both these forms in which Spirit reveals itself.

He believes that the progress of Spirit towards self-knowledge is necessary, every stage in it following logically from the one before it. Being necessary, it can be explained abstractly without reference to actual societies and historical events. That is what Hegel undertakes to do in this work. When he happens to refer to historical events, he does so only to illustrate a point. The facts of history provide only footnotes to the theme of the *Phenomenology*. Of course, since the process is necessary, it is in fact revealed in World History, but it can be explained, so Hegel believes, without reference to what has actually happened. Spirit first takes one form and then another, and we can see, if we know what Spirit essentially is, that it must be so. No doubt, since the process to be explained is the progress of Spirit towards complete self-knowledge, that process cannot be explained until it has in fact reached its goal; it cannot be explained until the course of

World History is complete. The events recorded by the historian – the events in and through which Spirit attains complete self-knowledge – must have happened before there can be a philosopher capable of explaining what Spirit essentially is (or, which is for Hegel the same thing, how Spirit attains self-knowledge); but the philosopher can make his explanation without referring to those events. For instance, Spirit passes necessarily through the stages which we call Stoicism and Christianity, but the philosopher can explain these stages without mentioning Zeno or Christ or Greece or Palestine. He can even – and here philosophy and modesty join hands – explain how Spirit attains complete self-knowledge without mentioning Hegel. As we read the *Phenomenology*, the actual societies and events and philosophies which correspond to what Hegel is describing come readily to mind; and this, he would no doubt say, is as it ought to be. For though it is not implied in the nature of Spirit that Zeno or Socrates or Christ or Luther had to do what they did, it is implied that there had to be the attitudes of mind which they expressed. In the *Phenomenology of Spirit* we have the intellectual history of mankind given to us without proper names.

In the *Lectures on the Philosophy of History* the same history is offered to us with proper names. We are not told merely what Spirit had necessarily to accomplish through finite minds and communities of such minds; we are given the names of the finite minds and the communities actually involved. This, however, is not the only difference between the two works. The *Philosophy of History* takes much larger account of institutions than does the *Phenomenology*, which is almost exclusively devoted to attitudes of mind and doctrines. The *Philosophy of History* also has much more to say about doctrines and social forms peculiar to the Orient or seldom found in Europe. In that respect it is broader in scope. The *Phenomenology* was completed in 1807, when Napoleon, whom Hegel greatly admired, was at the height of his power, whereas the *Lectures on the Philosophy of History* were delivered several years after Napoleon's fall. Hegel, from being an admirer of the conqueror of his country, had by then become a German patriot. Though the central theme of both works – that is, the ascent of Spirit to full self-knowledge – is the same, there are many differences between them; the earlier work is a mixture of epistemology and of an abstract philosophy of progress, while the second tells us nothing about the nature of knowledge and is an account of how progress actually occurred. Again, in the *Philosophy of History* Hegel is much less concerned than in the *Phenomenology* to explain how each stage appeared to the finite minds involved in it;

he tells us rather what each stage was *in* itself and, not for itself but for *us*, who, viewing it through his eyes, see it for what it was – an inevitable phase of a necessary process.

We have the *Phenomenology* in the form that Hegel himself gave to it, whereas we have the *Philosophy of History* only in the form in which it was put together by an editor from notes taken by persons who attended his lectures. The *Phenomenology* is the more impressive work of the two, and I shall devote more attention to it than to the *Philosophy of History*. I shall try to explain its general argument, and then offer some criticisms of it. I shall not consider in the same way the general argument of the *Philosophy of History*, but shall confine myself only to drawing attention to how it differs from the argument of the *Phenomenology*.

1. The General Argument of the 'Phenomenology of Spirit'

The Process of Spirit as Revealed in Personal Attitudes and Philosophies

a. Experience and Knowledge

Hegel begins by explaining what is involved in experience and knowledge. At the lowest level of consciousness, that of bare sensation, the subject does not distinguish between itself and what it senses. It is not, at that level, properly a self, because it is not self-conscious. At a higher level, the subject distinguishes between its sensations, and also between them and itself. It is at this level that it is self-conscious – that it is a self – for, in order to be a self, a subject must be self-conscious. As a self-conscious being, it can organize its sensations into a coherent experience, into a vision of a coherent world. As Hegel puts it, in his peculiar way, the self finds itself, as reason, reflected in a rational world. A rational world means, here, a coherent and intelligible world.

I find the details of Hegel's account of what constitutes knowledge difficult to follow. He appears to begin by saying that the self must be self-conscious before it can organize its sensations into a coherent world, and then later to speak as if it became self-conscious in the process of becoming rational – that is, in the process of organizing its sensations. No doubt, he believed that there are different levels of self-consciousness. But the details of his account, though modern psychology and epistemology might question many of them, need not detain us. We are concerned only with the broad outline. Hegel sees the self as constructing, out of its sensations, the world in which it lives. At the lowest level, where no distinction is made between the subject and object of consciousness – between sensor and sensed

– there is as yet no coherent experience; it is the self which constructs out of its sensations a coherent world within which it distinguishes between itself and what is external to it. The concepts which it uses to make sense of its sensations are not themselves given in sensation; they are applied to its sensations by the self. But these concepts are not the products of any one self; they form a system of concepts used *by a community of selves.* They are the products of many finite minds in communication with one another; and they are produced, not by one generation, but by many. They form a public language which every finite mind must learn if it is to become fully self-conscious and rational. The world as it appears to men, as they understand it and form purposes inside it which they strive to realize, corresponds to the language they use to build up a coherent picture of it.

Merely to see himself as existing in a world, man does not need to be a philosopher. He must use a system of concepts to construct a world (or, as those of us who are not Hegelians prefer to say, to construct a picture of the world); but he need not reflect upon the concepts he uses. He need not know what concepts are or how he uses them. He makes use of them without analysing what they are, and without thinking of himself as constructing a coherent picture of the world by means of them. He takes the world for granted.

So, too, man can change his concepts without reflecting upon how he has come to do so, and often even without knowing that he has done so. Hegel shows how, for example, at one stage of their development, men use (among others) the concept of substance to construct their picture of the world, and how, at a later stage, as in Newtonian science, they come to use the concept of force. They think of force as something independent of themselves which causes things to behave as they do; and they do not know it for what it in fact is – a concept invented by themselves to help them explain that behaviour in a way more satisfying to them. The Newtonian physicist thinks of himself as discovering force and not as inventing it, but he is mistaken.

There is much said about the nature of scientific knowledge and scientific progress in the *Phenomenology*, especially in the earlier parts of it. I dare say that Hegel was in some respects in advance of his time, and in other respects superficial or even perverse. I deal with this part of his theory only cursorily, for it is not of special interest to the student of his social and political theory; and I deal with it at all only because it explains what Hegel means when he asserts that Spirit, active in a plurality of finite minds, constructs a coherent world and becomes self-conscious and rational in the process of doing so. It constructs the world without knowing *how* it has done so, or even *that* it has done so, and so treats the world as something independent of itself. But eventually – so Hegel tells us – it necessarily discovers that the world which it begins by taking as independent of itself is its own product. It recognizes that the world is rational (or intelligible) because it is the product of reason; it recognizes itself in the world, as Hegel puts it, and so is at home in the world and is satisfied.

b. The Need for Recognition

We have seen that, for Hegel, only a self-conscious being can have knowledge, properly so called, for knowledge has for its object, not sensations, but facts, and facts are referred to in judgements which involve the use of a variety of concepts forming a system or a language. Self-consciousness and consciousness of a coherent world go necessarily together. Yet the self is not most sharply present to itself in mere knowledge, in contemplation of a world. It is most sharply present to itself as a subject of conscious desire. It can have desires without knowing that it has them, just as it can have sensations without knowing that it has them. But it cannot know that it has desires and express this knowledge without using the word 'I'. Though it cannot have knowledge unless it is in fact self-conscious, it can express its knowledge (when that knowledge is not self-knowledge), without referring to itself, without being sharply present to itself, without using the word 'I'. It is above all as a conscious subject of desire that the self is intensely self-conscious.

Hegel does not, of course, think of the self as *first* becoming self-conscious as a subject of knowledge and then afterwards becoming more intensely self-conscious as a conscious subject of desire. Desire, as much as sensation, is prior to self-consciousness and knowledge; the lower animals have desires as well as sensations and yet are not self-conscious and do not have knowledge. The self that rises to self-consciousness and knowledge is essentially active, and it would not be active unless it had desires. As it strives, at first blindly, to satisfy its desires, it becomes gradually aware of its environment; it comes gradually to acquire knowledge and self-knowledge. Thus the self becomes conscious of itself as a subject of desire in the same process as it becomes a self-conscious subject of knowledge. Nevertheless, it is, thinks Hegel, as a conscious subject of desire that the self is most sharply present to itself, and from this circumstance he draws some important conclusions.

The self, as it comes to see itself having an external environment, distinguishes itself from more than merely natural objects; it also distinguishes itself from other selves. It becomes self-conscious in the process of learning to distinguish itself from an external world which contains both natural objects and other beings like itself.

It is the peculiarity of a self-conscious being that all its desires are not natural appetites; for it has, apart from such appetites, a desire to be *recognized* by other beings like itself. The lower animals are without this desire; they have no sense of their own dignity or worth. They have no need to assert themselves, no need for acceptance or recognition, because they have no self-consciousness. This desire for recognition Hegel calls *spiritual*, because he thinks of it as a desire which goes along with self-consciousness, which he takes to be the essence of Spirit. It is the first among man's desires which is specifically human; it marks him off from the other animals.

At first, man wants to be recognized by others without according to them the recognition which he demands from them. He wants recognition for himself alone. This necessarily brings him into conflict with other men, for they too make the same demand on him. It almost seems that we have here a Hegelian version of Hobbes's war of all against all. But there is a difference. The conflict arises, neither from competition to satisfy natural appetites, nor from a desire for power as a means to their better satisfaction; it arises from a desire different in kind from the natural appetites and unconnected with them.

If all were equally resolute in demanding recognition from others and in refusing it to them, the conflict would end with the death of all, or with the death of all but one; and that one would have failed in his purpose, for there would be no one left to recognize him. But not all men are equally resolute; they all risk death for the sake of recognition, an action possible only to self-conscious creatures. Some, however, are less steadfast than others, and from fear of death recognize the others without being recognized by them. Some become slaves, and some masters.

Hegel speaks of this conflict as if it were both an effect of man's self-consciousness and a means to it, both as if men engage in the conflict because they are self-conscious and as if the conflict made them so. There is here an apparent contradiction, but it is only apparent. There are, for Hegel – as indeed there are in fact – different levels of self-consciousness. Or perhaps it would be better to say that the word *self-conscious* is used in different senses. As Hegel does not distinguish carefully between these senses, it is sometimes difficult to get his meaning; but in this case it is not too difficult. I take it that to demand recognition from others involves insisting on deference from them. It may involve more than this, but it involves at least this. It also involves, to use Kantian language, insisting on being treated by them as an end-in-oneself. To refuse recognition involves refusing deference; it also involves, again in Kantian language, refusing to treat others as ends-in-themselves. No doubt, the man who demands recognition is not able to use Kantian language and perhaps has no words to express his desire. He may merely demand services from others, but if he does, he demands them, not because he needs them, but because he needs to be important to others and to show that he is so by imposing his will on them. He is then like a child who insists on being the centre of attention. If the child is asked whether it wants to be the centre of attention, it may not even understand the question; and yet that is what it wants. And it wants it because it is a self-conscious creature.

Man has a sense of his own dignity or worth; he has it even though he is not able to express it in words. But his sense of this dignity or worth is insecure unless he is recognized by others as being what he takes himself to be. His self-importance depends on his being important to others, or on his being treated by them as if he were important to them. He would not insist that his dignity be recognized unless he had some sense of it. Hegel speaks of men's need to 'raise their certainty of being *for themselves* to truth', and to do that 'they must engage in. . .struggle'.[1] This, if we take it literally, means that man has a need to validate or verify his belief that he exists through conflict with other men. And this, certainly, is part of what Hegel means. But, presumably, he also means more than that. By the 'certainty of being for oneself', he cannot, I think, mean mere self-consciousness; he must mean by it what philosophers of the Kantian School are getting at when they speak of man's being an end-in-himself. He means what I have deliberately put in more familiar (but not therefore more precise) language by calling it man's sense of his own worth. A self-conscious being needs assurance both that it exists and that it has value, and it is through a conflict of wills with other self-conscious beings that it gains this assurance. This, I take it, is what Hegel means, because it is what makes the best sense of that part of his argument. For he says, in the sentence which follows the one from which I have just quoted, that 'it is only through staking one's life that freedom is won; only thus is it proved that for self-consciousness, its essential being is not . . . the *immediate* form in which it appears'. As we shall see, man is free because he is – in a sense not yet explained but to be explained later – 'his own end'.

[1] *Phenomenology of Spirit*, trans. A. V. Miller and ed. J. N. Findlay (Oxford 1977), p. 114.

Hegel, for all his insistence that Spirit makes its own world, and makes itself in doing so, lays heavy stress on the distinction between the subjective and the objective, or, as we might put it, between the private and the public. We have seen that it is not each separate self that builds up its own private world; it is a community of selves that builds up a public world by using a common system of concepts, a common language. So, too, though it is supremely important to the individual self how he thinks and feels about himself, he cannot hold firmly to what he thinks and feels unless he is recognized by others as being what he appears to himself to be.

c. Master and Slave

With Hegel's doctrine of the master and the slave, we come to the part of his *Phenomenology* which is of peculiar interest to the social and political theorist; and that part is in fact the major part. My interpretation of it owes a great deal to Alexandre Kojève's *Introduction à la Lecture de Hegel* (Paris 1947); it also owes something, though less, to Jean Hyppolite's *Genèse et Structure de la Phénoménologie de l'Esprit de Hegel* (Paris 1946). I have sometimes found Hyppolite's commentary more difficult to follow than the text it seeks to explain, though at other times I have found it illuminating.[1] My criticisms of the *Phenomenology* are mostly my own.

The slave, in working for the master, works on nature. He transforms it; or, to use Hegel's own expression, he *negates* it. In the process of transforming what he works on, he transforms himself. He is a worker, and therefore feels the need to make the most efficient use of his labour and his materials. As a worker, he gradually increases his understanding of nature and of himself; he acquires self-discipline. Though he has put himself in the power of his master, he inevitably, through his work, extends his own power. He gets power over nature and over himself. But the master does not acquire the same understanding of nature or the same power over it, nor does he learn discipline. He does not even get, from his recognition by the slave, the satisfaction that he seeks, because it is not the recognition of an inferior but of an equal which is truly satisfying. If I despise the man who recognizes my worth, his recognition of it does not give me the assurance I seek.

The master is in an *impasse*. He cannot give to the slave the

---

[1] But, since my German is too poor to enable me to follow so difficult a text, I have relied mostly on Hyppolite's translation of the *Phenomenology*, which I prefer to the English translation by J. B. Baillie, first published in 1910. (For this edition of the text, the editors cite the more recent and more accurate translation by Miller.)

recognition which he has demanded and obtained from him, for he has subjugated the slave and is served by him. The slave is the living proof of his worth, of his superiority, and is therefore indispensable to him; and yet he cannot find the satisfaction he needs, the full assurance of his own dignity, in his recognition by the slave. His condition, morally and intellectually, moreover, remains unchanged; he is the master of the slave. He is so from the moment that the slave recognizes him without insisting on being recognized in return, and his aim is merely to continue his mastery. He does not acquire knowledge and self-discipline in a struggle to master nature. He does not contrive and work to satisfy his appetites; he merely forces another man to work for him.

The slave, however, is not in an *impasse*; he is transformed by his work and by what that work involves; his condition, morally and intellectually, changes as a result of what he does. He acquires knowledge, power over nature, and self-discipline. Only fear keeps him docile; if he can overcome this fear, he can cease to be a slave. He does not need his master as his master needs him. He will come eventually to demand for himself the recognition which he gives to the master. His servile condition, though it does not satisfy him, is not such as to prevent his doing anything to improve it. He is not both attached to his servility and dissatisfied with it, as the master is to his mastery. When he comes, at last, to demand recognition for himself, he does not refuse it to others. The recognition of his demand does not involve putting others in a position which cannot satisfy them and which they must in time strive to change. The future, therefore, is with the slave. It is his destiny to create the community in which everyone accords recognition to everyone else, the community in which Spirit attains its end and achieves satisfaction.

This 'dialectic' of the master and the slave has been greatly admired. It has much in common with the Marxian account of the class struggle. Of course, the essence of the domination of man by man is explained differently by Hegel. The life and death conflict for mere recognition, for the satisfaction of a spiritual need, would no doubt seem to Marx sheer fantasy. But the assertion that the future belongs to the oppressed is altogether in the spirit of Marxian philosophy, and so too are the reasons given for the assertion. The slave is a producer, and in the course of production acquires the qualities – intellectual and moral, the knowledge, the skill and the self-discipline – which he needs to enable him to put an end to his servile condition. The slave evolves while the master remains unchanged. It is the slave, not the master, who comes to understand the limitations of his condition, who decides to put an end to it and who carries out his decision. The community in which everyone recognizes everyone – the community of equals – is his creation. All this that Hegel says of the slave, Marx says of the proletarian, though Hegel, as we shall see, has a very different conception of equality.[1]

d. Stoicism and Scepticism

The slave is dissatisfied with his servitude. For he, too, like his master, once strove for recognition, and abandoned his claim only from fear of death. But the desire for recognition does not disappear in the condition of slavery. It is a desire natural to every self-conscious creature, and the slave is such a creature. His work is educative; it forms his character. This education – although (as we have seen) it changes him – does not cause him to find satisfaction in his servitude; it does not weaken his desire for recognition. He comes eventually to differ from the master in being willing to recognize others; and this willingness proceeds from his seeing the justice of according to them what he seeks for himself, and not from fear.

Thus the self-conscious self is not satisfied either in servitude or in mastery. It is essentially free; it strives for independence, or (to use a Hegelian expression) it seeks assurance that it exists *for* itself. That the slave is dependent is obvious, while the master is dependent on the services of the slave and gets from him a recognition which does not satisfy.

It is at this point that there arises a form of self-consciousness, or (as I should prefer to say) an attitude of mind, of which Hegel says that it 'has . . . been called Stoicism', 'when it appeared as a conscious manifestation in the history of Spirit'.[2] It is an attitude which he says is *negative* towards the relation of master and slave. As Hegel puts it, the master does not 'find his truth' through the slave, and the slave does not 'find his truth' in the will of the master.[3] We can put this another way by saying that both master and slave have a conception of what man – as a self-conscious rational being – essentially is, a conception realized neither in mastery nor in servitude. Man is essentially free. I take this to mean that man, being self-conscious and rational, necessarily aspires to freedom, and is not satisfied until he gets it. But the Stoic does not stop at the belief that man is

---

[1] Sir Isaiah Berlin suggests that, in interpreting this part of the *Phenomenology*, I have read too much of Marx and of Kojève into Hegel. Certainly here, as in several other places, I owe much to Kojève.

[2] *Phenomenology of Spirit*, § 198, p. 121.

[3] See the *Phenomenology*, § § 192–4, pp. 116–7.

essentially free in the sense of necessarily aspiring to freedom; he also believes that man, if he only but knew it, always is (or always can be) free, no matter what his social condition. Merely by virtue of being self-conscious and rational, man is free, or can obtain freedom, whether he is master or slave.

This belief arises out of the master's and the slave's dissatisfaction with mastery and servitude. They are both dissatisfied, and yet they yearn for satisfaction and delude themselves into believing that they already have it, or that they can obtain it without ceasing to be master and slave. The belief involves a pretence, a withdrawal from the realities of life; it is a form of escapism. The Stoic conception of freedom Hegel calls 'abstract', whereas true freedom, he says, is concrete. We achieve freedom, not by withdrawing from life, but in life – not by affecting to despise the world but by getting satisfaction in it. The wisdom and virtue of the Stoic soon wear thin; they do not stand the test of experience; they prove in the end to be wearisome.

Scepticism is a more extreme form of what is, at bottom, the same attitude of mind; it is even more sharply negative. The scepticism here in question is not, of course, the scepticism of the English empiricists. English empiricism is essentially a theory of knowledge. As we find it in Hume, it involves no rejection of the world, no withdrawal from life, no pretending that nothing really matters. The scepticism that Hegel has in mind is that of the Greeks – the kind which asserts that nothing is good or evil, that nothing is certain and nothing worth striving for. It takes the world for mere show and illusion. It is a state of mind, an attitude to life, which, like Stoicism, is rooted in dissatisfaction; it is an even more extreme attempt to find freedom by rejecting the world. And, again like Stoicism, it does not satisfy. For the man who says that everything is illusion and that nothing matters must, in practice, behave as if it were not so. He says that life is worthless and meaningless. If he does not destroy himself (and he seldom does that), he must continue to live, which involves his acting as if life were not worthless and meaningless. He gives the lie to his creed merely by continuing to live, by having desires and seeking to satisfy them.

Though Hegel speaks of Stoicism as an attitude of mind common to master and slave, and of Scepticism as an extreme form of Stoicism, Kojève, in his book (which is much more a commentary on the *Phenomenology* than an account of Hegel's philosophy taken as a whole), treats them both as forms of servile consciousness. Kojève is apt to be too free in his interpretations, but I feel a considerable sympathy with him. Hegel's philosophy is like a ploughed field, water-logged, through which it is safer and quicker to walk on stilts, taking long strides, for fear of getting stuck in the mud. Or, to change the metaphor, it is more palatable taken in large doses than small. Hegel takes a broad and free view of the facts, and the interpreter is tempted to do the same with Hegelian theory. Kojève seems at times to ignore the details of Hegel's argument or to adjust them to suit his own lucid and masterly, indeed masterful, interpretation of it.

According to Kojève, the master, though not fully satisfied, is free; or he is, at least, freer than the slave. There is, in his case, no disparity that he is aware of between what he aspires to be and what he is; he fought for recognition and has achieved it. The slave also fought for it, and did not achieve it. It is therefore the slave rather than the master who makes an ideal of liberty. But the slave cannot be free unless he fights and risks his life for freedom, and this he is not yet ready to do. The doctrine that man, being essentially free, possesses the dignity proper to his kind, no matter what his social condition, is the doctrine of the slave who aspires to freedom without yet daring to fight for it. He persuades himself that he already has it; he retreats from the world into himself. But this attitude cannot satisfy; it comes to birth in order to justify not fighting for recognition, for freedom. It discourages action; it seeks refuge in speech and conjecture. But Spirit, to be satisfied, must find itself in this world; or, as we might put it, man achieves satisfaction, and freedom also, by creating a social world acceptable to himself, and not by seeking escape from it.

It was certainly Hegel's belief that all doctrines which preach withdrawal from the world or indifference to it are due to man's seeking to attain an ideal which is not yet clear to him and which he fails to attain. Man's progress is a search for freedom, but in the early stages of that search he does not know exactly what he wants. He gropes his way towards it, and comes to have a clearer idea of it as he comes closer to getting it. He does not fully understand what he aspires to until he has achieved it. In the course of his progress towards freedom, not finding what he seeks and having only a dim understanding of what it is, he is again and again afflicted by despair and by hope; he takes up attitudes of mind and produces doctrines which either keep alive his aspirations or reconcile him to his lot, or which do both the one and the other. Stoicism is an aspiration to freedom and also an attempt to reconcile man to his condition, which is not yet free; and so too is Scepticism. Freedom, as imagined by the Stoic and Sceptic, is inadequate, and the reconciliation is illusory. Stoicism and Scepticism are both creeds of man who has not yet achieved freedom. To that extent Kojève is right in his interpretation of Hegel. But Hegel does not, I believe, think of them as creeds of the slave rather than the master. They are creeds of the unfree who are confusedly aware of their condition and wish to shut their eyes to it. The master is, in some ways, freer than the slave, but in other ways he is not; he too is dissatisfied and unfree, and needs to delude himself.

e. The Unhappy Consciousness

Stoicism and Scepticism are, as we have seen, creeds of unsatisfied man – of man not yet at home in the world. But there is a human condition more poignant even than the ones expressed by these creeds. Hegel calls it the *Unhappy Consciousness*. The Stoic and the Sceptic both delude themselves that they are free in this world. The Stoic believes that, provided he is rational and self-disciplined – provided he has learnt to rise above his social condition – he has achieved all that man can achieve. The Sceptic says that the world is meaningless and illusory and yet continues to live in it, behaving as if what he said were not true; but he is not aware of his inconsistency. Both the Stoic and the Sceptic imagine that they have come to terms with life; they do not admit that, in this world, they are unfree. But the Unhappy Consciousness does admit this; it recognizes that it is not free. It is consciously wretched in this world. Hegel also calls it 'an alien Being',[1] and speaks of it as if it were a stranger to itself. It is a stranger to itself, presumably, because it is the essence of Spirit to produce a world and to come eventually to recognize that world as its product. Consciousness and its object are, Hegel tells us, inseparable; consciousness, by the use of concepts, constructs out of its immediate content (that which is merely sensed) a coherent world. It is a rational consciousness only in so far as it does so. It reveals itself as reason in constructing a rational (that is to say, coherent or intelligible) world. If, then, it sees itself as a stranger in this world, which it does when it is an Unhappy Consciousness, it is estranged from that in which it is revealed as a rational consciousness; it is estranged from itself.

The self-estranged Spirit seeks in another world the satisfaction which it cannot get in this one; it imagines an after-life. It projects itself into another, imaginary, world, in which are satisfied the aspirations which are not satisfied on earth. We have seen that man necessarily seeks recognition, that every self-conscious being needs to have its worth admitted by other such beings. And so in the next world, the imaginary world, the worth of every man is recognized by God. Man

---

[1] Ibid., § 208, p. 127.

asserts his sense of his own dignity, a sense which is frustrated on earth, by supposing himself infinitely precious to a Being infinitely greater than himself. In his image of another world, he expresses both a deep sense of his own unworthiness and a sense of his worth. He feels unworthy because of his condition in this world, where he is diminished in his own eyes. But he does not therefore puff himself up into something much greater than he feels himself to be; he sees himself, rather, as the beloved of a Being infinitely more worthy than himself. That Being he conceives of as essentially like himself. Into his notion of God man puts his sense of what Spirit is. And we have seen that, for Hegel, Spirit (though in itself infinite) is revealed in and through finite minds. Therefore, in worshipping God, man expresses his sense of the worth of the Spirit which is in him. This does not mean that man, without knowing it, worships himself. For man is finite, while Spirit is infinite. It means that man, without knowing it, worships what is revealed in creatures like himself and gives them their worth; he worships what still has to be fully revealed, what has not yet become fully actual.

The Unhappy Consciousness is clearly the Christian consciousness, though Hegel, in the *Phenomenology*, does not call it so. Christianity, for Hegel, is the religion of individualism; it is the religion which, above all others, asserts the intrinsic worth of the individual person. In the Hegelian sense of recognition, the Christian recognizes everyone. The master demanded recognition from the slave and refused it to him, and became a master because he was given what he asked for; the slave began by behaving as the master did, and became a slave only because fear drove him to give what he was asked for without insisting on it in return; whereas the Christian voluntarily gives to all men what he asks for himself. But in Christianity the equal worth of all men is recognized only in another world. It is therefore recognized inadequately. To be recognized adequately, it must be recognized for everyone by everyone in this world, which is the real world.

The Unhappy Consciousness is a necessary phase in the evolution of Spirit. The self must be thrown back upon itself; it must feel isolated in its environment, detached from it and oppressed by it, if it is to become deeply self-conscious. An intense self-awareness, which necessarily takes the form of self-estrangement, must precede the full attainment of freedom. In order to be free, man must consciously 'find himself' in the world; his acceptance of it must not be merely habitual. He is not free unless his acceptance of it is rational; he is not free until he knows what it is to act conscientiously and finds it possible to do so in the world. What Hegel calls 'the inward movement of the pure heart'[1] must be developed in him to the full; he must have an intense self-awareness. He must first feel himself to be a stranger in the world before he can become fully at home in it; he must have a profound sense of his own unworthiness before he can come fully to appreciate the dignity of man. The Christian alone with God is alone with what he obscurely feels to be the Spirit within him, though he does not yet know it as such. Intent on his relations with God, man is also intent upon knowing himself, for he has no privacy from a God who reads his innermost thoughts. The Christian feels himself close to God and yet remote from Him, supremely important to God and yet liable to be rejected by Him. This ambivalent attitude to God expresses man's intense self-awareness and anxiety about himself, and his sense of both his own worth and his unworthiness.

f. Spirit in its Immediacy

The three attitudes of mind which we have considered – Stoicism, Scepticism and the Unhappy Consciousness – are all symptoms of man's dissatisfaction with the world and with himself. If we look at history, we see that they all three come with the decay of the ancient city-state. Hegel, of course, using his abstract method, does not speak directly of the city-state or of its best-known example, the Greek *polis*. He speaks of Spirit existing 'in its immediacy'. But clearly he has in mind a community of the type of the *polis*, and I shall therefore refer to it, for the sake of convenience, by that name. In this type of community, the social order, or – as Hegel would put it – the ethical order or objective Spirit, is accepted by man, not critically, not after reflection, but as a matter of course. Morality is custom. There are two spheres of custom; there are the customs of the city and the customs of the family, or human and divine law. These two spheres are complementary, the customs of the city having their roots in the customs of the family. They may, to some extent or in some circumstances, clash, but men do not admit this or take it consciously into account.

The *polis* is a compact community; the citizens are the city. In the *polis* there is no contrasting the State with the individual, and no asserting of individual liberty against the State. In so far as the value of the individual is recognized, it is so within the family, in the honours paid to the dead. I do not quite follow Hegel's argument at this point, but he means, perhaps, that when we honour the dead we do not benefit either ourselves or them, and we need not express

[1] Ibid., § 217, p. 131.

gratitude or love. Grief and gratitude and love we may or may not feel or express, and yet we bury the dead with ceremony, and thus bear witness to our sense of the dignity of man.

Hegel uses Greek tragedy to illustrate how the two spheres of custom – the two laws, human and divine – clash. Antigone defies Creon; divine law requires that she should bury her brother, though Creon has forbidden his burial. She is certain that she is right, just as Creon is certain that he is. There is no conflict, either within her mind or within his, between two laws, and no conflict between passion and duty. The conflict is between Antigone and Creon. Neither of them is faced with a moral problem; neither of them has to make a morally difficult choice. The situation is tragic because Antigone, by her narrowness, brings her fate upon herself. By the only law which she recognizes, she does no wrong. Neither she nor Creon acts conscientiously, as we today understand conscientious action; she does what family custom, or divine law, requires of her, and he acts by another law. Her fate is terrible and yet necessary; it serves to bring out the narrowness, the inadequacy, of the law which she accepts. Though Antigone sees herself as the victim of fate, and learns nothing, and is not shaken in her convictions, whoever contemplates her predicament and Creon's – whoever understands them both – has already passed beyond her and him. Sophocles may not see her predicament as we now see it, but he already sees it as Antigone could not see it. In looking at her predicament through the eyes of Sophocles, we can see how her morality differs from ours, and also how reflection on her fate prepares the way for our own morality.

g. The Soulless Community

The compact community, where morality is custom and where there is no contrasting the individual with the State – the community in which Spirit is revealed 'in its immediacy' – gives way to what Hegel calls *the soulless community*, where the free man (i.e. the man who is not a slave) ceases to be a citizen and becomes a subject. He is not reduced to servitude; his status is embodied in his personal rights, and above all in his rights of property. In this type of community, law becomes elaborate and precise, and there develops a science of jurisprudence. It matters greatly that personal rights should be carefully defined and adequately secured. But, politically, the free man is no longer a master; he takes no effective part in government, and has no share in a general will. He is a private person, who looks upon the State as set in authority over him, necessary to his well-being but out of the reach of his influence. He is neither citizen nor slave; he is something between the two. He even ceases to fight for the State, which is defended by mercenaries. The example of the soulless community which Hegel has in mind is clearly the Roman Empire, for he speaks of it as dominated by a 'master of the world'.[1]

The private person – the possessor of personal rights – is not, in the same sense as the slave, a worker. He is personally free and therefore does not work for a master. Nor does he work for the community. His work is not service; he exerts himself for himself and his family, and his business is above all to maintain and to enlarge his property. It is in the 'soulless community' that Stoicism and Scepticism flourish.

h. *The World of Culture*
The soulless community – the world of universal monarchy, of elaborate private rights, of Stoicism and Scepticism – is succeeded by what Hegel calls the *world of culture*. It is the world of *Spirit in self-estrangement*, or, in other words – though Hegel avoids referring to actual societies and events – it is the Christian world or Western Europe from the establishment of Christianity and the fall of the Roman Empire until the French Revolution. Together, the 'soulless community' and 'the world of culture' cover all the phases in the evolution of Spirit from the phase in which it exists in its immediacy to the phases in which it finds itself *in* the world and attains self-knowledge and satisfaction. In the world of Spirit in its immediacy, Spirit is not yet self-estranged; it is not, of course, fully satisfied, for that it can be only when it has attained a self-knowledge which is still far off. But it is not consciously dissatisfied, and has no need to seek to reconcile itself to its lot in such attitudes and beliefs as Stoicism, Scepticism and Christianity. In the compact community of citizens, the ethos of the master predominates, and yet the worth of the individual, merely in virtue of his humanity, is not recognized. It is not recognized, not only because there are slaves as well as masters, but also because the masters are concerned with status and privilege and with the affairs of the community, and have no conception of freedom of conscience. The Greek idea of freedom is, in Hegel's opinion, inferior to the idea that gradually emerges in the world of culture and is eventually realized in the community where everyone is recognized by everyone.

i. *Forms of Individualism*
Spirit, estranged from the world and from itself, does not merely

[1] Ibid., § 481, p. 292.

seek the satisfaction denied to it in this world by imagining another; it also seeks satisfaction in this world. Hegel describes how it does so, and equally how, in the process, it comes gradually nearer to what it seeks and at last finds. It does not find it merely by chance; it does not make one unsuccessful attempt after another until at last it succeeds. It is transformed and educated by its efforts; it seeks satisfaction and does not find it, and reflects on its experience and grows wiser. In *In Memoriam* (section 1), Tennyson speaks of our rising 'on stepping stones of [our] dead selves to higher things' – a remark which comes close to how Hegel conceives of the progress of Spirit. Not that he thinks of man as being always, in each later phase, better than in the phase before it; he thinks of him, rather, as gaining in depth and understanding, so that, though he may sometimes be more wretched and evil, he is always more mature and more completely a man. To illustrate my point from drama, as Hegel loved to do, Hamlet is not a better man than the Oedipus of Sophocles, but he is a moral agent in a deeper sense.

Hegel discusses three attempts of Spirit to find satisfaction in the world, and explains why each of them fails of its object. They might be called three types of individualism. The first is the pursuit of pleasure. The individual seeks pleasure and judges the community and its laws as they help or impede the pursuit of it. But the pursuit of one pleasure after another cannot satisfy him, because each separate pleasure is momentary and a self-conscious being can find satisfaction only in what endures. I am not sure that I have taken the point of Hegel's argument, and so I shall not go into the details of it. Part of his meaning, perhaps, is this: A self-conscious and rational being can be satisfied only by a way or pattern of life which seems to it worthwhile. It needs, if it is to win happiness, not repeated success in achieving one disconnected end after another, but the sense of a life well lived or the feeling that it is making progress towards some goal which it makes persistent and rational efforts to attain. This is a common criticism of the pursuit of pleasure, and though Hegel uses uncommon language, he does not, any more than Burke did, avoid or despise common or received opinions. They often contain, he thinks, much wisdom. So I continue to hope that this criticism, which I find intelligible, is, if not the whole, then a part, of what Hegel means. He says that the pursuit of pleasure involves contradiction, meaning thereby, no doubt, that the man who makes pleasure his end in life seeks satisfaction where it is not to be had. He means perhaps more than this, but at least this as well.

The second form of individualism might be called romantic; Hegel calls it *the law of the heart*. It is the doctrine that man is naturally good. Let him follow the dictates of his heart, and all will be well with him. Man is natural and society is artificial. This second form is also self-contradictory, though it is so (as Hegel does not trouble to notice) in a different and more literal sense than the first. The man who takes up the doctrine is presumably not speaking only about himself. If his heart-felt sentiments are right, so presumably are other people's. But the sentiments of one man are not always shared by other men. So each man condemns the sentiments of other men when they conflict with those he feels himself, irrationally refusing to their sentiments the validity he claims for his own. The believer in this doctrine is inevitably driven to self-contradiction or absurdity. He begins by saying, 'Let every man act upon his heart-felt sentiments, for they are good', and he ends either by denying that the heart-felt sentiments of others which do not square with his own are good, or by insisting that they are not really what those who express them say the are – that they do not really come from the heart.

The third form of individualism Hegel calls *the virtuous consciousness*. It condemns conventional standards. The virtuous man claims knowledge of a moral truth superior to 'the way of the world'. But this truth is an abstract ideal; it is expressed in the form of general principles whose practical implications are not yet known by the persons who assert the principles. The ideal they cherish may be impossible; it can be tested only when people try to live up to it. Or it may be that the ideal is already to a great extent realized, though the persons who uphold it, owing to their ignorance of what is involved in the practical application of it, do not see that it is. Hegel's point, if I have understood it, might be put briefly in this way: An ideal which is used to condemn current practice is necessarily understood very imperfectly by those who proclaim it. It purports to put forward rules of conduct which differ greatly from accepted rules. But to understand rules of conduct we must know how they apply to concrete situations. If, for example, we proclaim the equality of all men, how is our proclamation to be understood? Presumably we are not saying that no man must have any right which every other man does not also have, for in every society there is a wide diversity of functions, and men doing different work must have different rights. Our proclamation acquires a precise content only when an attempt is made to put it into practice. We see then what it amounts to. We elaborate and qualify it in ways we could not foresee when first we made it. While we use it merely to condemn established ways, having only the vaguest notions of what implications it has in practice, our condemnation is blind; we use a criterion which we scarcely understand. Here, too, as Hegel sees it, we are involved in contradiction. We put forward an ideal for all men to live up to, but we do not know how far or in what way it can be realized, nor even to what extent it has already been realized. When we come to understand it more fully, we are apt to find either that it is unrealizable or that it is much nearer being realized than we thought.

j. The Ignoble and the Noble Consciousness

In the world of Spirit self-estranged – in the world of culture, as in the soulless community – man looks upon the State as alien to himself. He is expected to obey the State, but as a mere subject and not a citizen. He does not take thought on behalf of the State; he merely takes into account what the State requires of him when he thinks of himself. He is, as a member of the State, passive; he is active in his private life. In this type of community the pursuit of wealth is important.

There are some who willingly acknowledge the State power and seek satisfaction by accumulating wealth, while others are suspicious of the State and indifferent to riches, and are even inwardly in revolt against them. In persons of this latter kind is manifest what Hegel calls *ignoble consciousness*, in contrast with the *noble consciousness* of those who accept the State and who seek and respect wealth. Noble and ignoble do not, in this connection, express approval or disapproval; when Hegel uses the terms, he has in mind what he takes to be the typical attitudes of the privileged and the unprivileged orders in the West before the French Revolution.

In the world of culture, the State emerges and gathers strength as the nobles gradually abandon some of their rights. Presumably the rights here in question are rights of private jurisdiction and private war. Hegel calls them the 'essential nature' of the noble consciousness, which suggests that it was by virtue of them that the nobles were noble before they began to decline from their nobility. But their nobility is a social status; it consists of their rights; and the rights they must surrender before there can be an effective State power are rights of private jurisdiction and war. Eventually the nobles abandon more than these rights to the bearer of the State power, the monarch; they do more even than avow themselves ready to die for him. They become courtiers, and by their flattery raise the monarch high above themselves. They behave outwardly as if the great purpose of their lives was to serve and honour him. But this surrender of themselves to the monarch is more apparent than real. The class of persons who flatter and serve the monarch, who abase themselves before him as the embodiment of the State, really own the State; the public service is their property; the State is a form of their wealth.

Here, too, the keen eye of Hegel discerns a contradiction. The established social order rests on the distinction between the noble and the base. But when the nobles give up honour for riches, and the service of the State becomes for them principally a means to wealth, this distinction loses its point. Those whose position allows them to do so pursue wealth and power, but they get no real satisfaction from doing so. They become arrogant and superficial, while the unprivileged or the base grow angry and cynical.

It is not the noble and the wealthy who see the situation for what it is: it is rather those among the ignoble who stand closest to them, who are on the periphery of their closed circle, the poor clients and the attendants. Hegel finds in Diderot's *Neveu de Rameau* the model of the cynical rogue who has taken the full measure of the world and of himself, and who yet, in a sense, rises above the corruption in which he is involved because he understands it and is frank about it. Hyppolite, in his commentary on the *Phenomenology*, sees in Hegel's interpretation of Rameau's nephew an account of what is perhaps 'a pre-revolutionary state of the soul'.[1] The social and psychological condition of man which is treated cynically by Rameau's nephew is the source of anguish in Rousseau and of indignation in Robespierre.

Some take refuge from that condition in faith; but others seek to find a remedy for man in this world. Man's condition, they say, is due to his failure to see himself and the world as they really are. Man must be delivered from the irrational; he must learn that there is nothing mysterious, nothing miraculous, nothing unintelligible. He is a rational being, and everything is in principle capable of being rationally explained.

k. Rationalist Philosophy

There is therefore necessarily a conflict between those who put their trust in faith and those who put it in the intellect – between those who accept a revealed truth and those who are persuaded by rationalist philosophy. Hegel approves of rationalist philosophy for insisting that everything is intelligible, that the world is coherent and unmysterious, and that man can find complete satisfaction in it. The philosophers reduce God to a mere first cause, so that the conception of the divine no longer contains man's obscure sense of the Spirit in himself – what he is capable of, what must eventually be manifest in him. Perhaps

---

[1] *Genèse et Structure de la Phénoménologie de l'Esprit de Hegel*, p. 401.

without knowing it, they make God irrelevant to man; they deprive Him of humanity, making Him indifferent to man and man indifferent to Him.

Yet their contempt for revealed religion is rooted in ignorance. They do not understand its significance for man; they dismiss it as superstitious nonsense because they take it literally. They do not know that religion (and especially Christianity, which Hegel takes to be the highest form of religion) expresses – not explicitly but in *Vorstellung* – man's sense of what Spirit essentially is. *Vorstellung*, in this context, is usually translated as *representation*; so that Hegel presumably means that religious doctrines stand for truths which they do not express literally. If we are to make explicit the truths they stand for, we must take them metaphorically; we must translate them. The faithful, of course, do not take them metaphorically; they take them for literally true. And yet, since they do not (as the philosophers do) reject them as absurd, they must in some sense apprehend the truths contained in them. They must understand more than they are capable of putting literally. Both the faithful and the philosophers say that they take religious doctrines literally, the first to accept them and the second to reject them. But the faithful – since they do not reject them, since they find them significant – must read more into them than they literally say, and yet this more is more than they are capable of explaining. Those who have faith, therefore, know, in a sense, more than they are aware of knowing, and the philosophers, in rejecting the dogmas which they accept, do not apprehend this knowledge.

The world of culture is the world of Spirit 'in self-estrangement'. But with rationalist philosophy, we are on the threshold of the world in which Spirit finds itself, in which self-estrangement ends. Rationalist philosophy – the philosophy of the Enlightenment – is utilitarian; it asserts that the world must be adapted to man's needs. In itself, it is no more than a theory, but it is a theory which encourages action. It stimulates man's first deliberate and comprehensive effort to refashion society to suit himself.

1. Revolution

We are now at the phase in the evolution of Spirit which Hegel calls *absolute freedom and terror*. For Spirit, in the form of absolute freedom, 'the world is . . . simply its own will, and this is a general will'; it is 'a real general will, the will of all *individuals* as such', so that 'what appears as done by the whole is the direct and conscious deed of each'.[1]

---

[1] *Phenomenology of Spirit*, § 584, pp. 356–7.

Hegel describes this phase, as he does every other, in the most abstract terms, but clearly his description is inspired by the French Revolution. Therefore I shall speak of this phase, as I have done of several of the others, more concretely than Hegel does, but without, I hope, being false to his meaning. I shall call it the revolutionary phase.

In this phase of his development, man, as never before, claims that the world shall be as he wants it; he puts himself forward as the maker or re-maker of society. As Hyppolite puts it, 'Man is thus like a God and creator, who finds himself entire in the work of his hands, and that work is the terrestrial city'.[1] The revolutionary possesses adequately the notion of freedom, which is not, for him, mere absence of constraint; freedom must be realized in a community which gives effect to a general or universal will. This will is not what *I* want for myself or what *you* want for yourself or what *he* wants for himself; it is what *we* want for ourselves. It is not merely what is common to our wills; for, even if we were entirely self-regarding creatures, we should have some ends in common, because our interests would still sometimes coincide. It is what each of us consciously wills because we have a sense of belonging to a community which is precious to us as being the context that gives meaning and purpose to our lives. It is much the same as Rousseau's general will, which is not a harmony of selfish wills, nor yet a will in which the individual sacrifices his interests to the public good.

But Spirit, in the form of absolute freedom, is still not the realization of freedom. Hegel speaks of the 'undivided Substance of . . . freedom' ascending 'the throne of the world without any power being able to resist it'; and he says that 'in this absolute freedom, therefore, all social group or classes which are the spiritual spheres into which the whole is articulated are abolished'.[2] Translating his argument into more concrete terms, we might say that the revolutionary – the man who insists that the social order shall give effect to the universal will – though he has an adequate conception of freedom, fails to realize it because he seeks to do so by abolishing all hierarchy. Freedom is in fact realized in an elaborate social structure which allows of a great diversity of functions; but the revolutionary, though he rightly believes that freedom consists in the realization of a universal will, does not see that it cannot be realized except in a society whose structure necessarily involves hierarchy. Hyppolite, commenting on this argument, says that, for Hegel, 'the French Revolution failed . . . not because its principle was false, but because

[1] *Genèse et Structure de la Phénoménologie de l'Esprit*, p. 440.
[2] *Phenomenology of Spirit*, § 585, p. 357.

it sought to realize it immediately. . . . It is this immediacy which is here. . .an error'.[1] Now, the immediate, in the sense in which the term is used here, is the simple and undifferentiated, or what appears to be so to the unphilosophical mind.

Hegel's highly abstract argument suggests that the revolutionary sees in a stable, hierarchical social structure an obstacle to the universal will. He speaks as if the revolutionary believed that there is no freedom except where men can do, at any time, what they please with that structure, or even as if he believed that freedom were incompatible with any such structure. The claim that the universal will may do what it pleases with the social order is destructive of that order, and yet the universal will is made effective, and liberty achieved, only within a stable order. There is here, according to Hegel, a contradiction. He sees in the Terror an effort of the universal will to destroy all obstacles in its way. The nation, as the embodiment of the universal will, claims to suppress every particular will opposed to it. Thus it is that the assertion of absolute liberty leads to death.

We must remember that Hegel, in this part of the *Phenomenology*, does not refer by name to the French Revolution, though he very clearly has it in mind. He discusses what he takes to be a necessary stage in the evolution of Spirit. He does not say that, when certain things happen, they spring from such and such causes; he says that they must happen. Spirit cannot attain its end, mankind cannot achieve freedom, except by this process, whose every phase is implied by all the others.

m. The Moral Will

The contradiction involved in Spirit in the form of absolute freedom seeking immediate realization (or, as we might put it, in the revolutionary spirit) is that the universal will negates particular wills, although it is itself manifest only in them. There cannot be freedom except where there is harmony between the universal will and the particular wills required to conform to it. Spirit, reflecting on its experience in the revolutionary phase, rises to a higher level in which the negation of the particular by the universal will is no longer a process whereby some people, in the name of the universal will, coerce and even destroy others. At this level, the universal will is *internalized* as a moral will. The claim that the universal will shall govern the particular wills of individuals becomes the claim that, inside the individual, the moral will shall govern particular inclinations. The

[1] *Genèse et Structure de la Phénoménologie de l'Esprit* pp. 440–1.

claim of the individual to take part in realizing the universal will of his community gives way to the claim of the individual to live according to moral standards which he freely accepts. This is the passage from the revolutionary ethic to the realm of true morality, as men like Kant conceived it.

This morality is far indeed from the morality of Antigone. As Kant understood it, Antigone had no moral will – no conception of duties incumbent on her as a rational being. She felt no need to justify the principles of her conduct, either to others or to herself. She was merely *fated* to do her duty; she did what she had to do, what she was impelled to do by a force which seemed to her external to herself; she did what the gods required of her. In Kant's moral theory (and we are here concerned with an attitude which Kant elaborated and made explicit rather than with opinions peculiar to him), the moral will – the will to do one's duty – is contrasted with natural impulses, which have to be surmounted for duty's sake. Freedom and nature are opposed, and man achieves freedom by mastering his nature.

This attitude of mind, which Kant elaborated into a systematic philosophy, Hegel finds self-contradictory and sterile. It is, he admits, necessarily involved in the progress of Spirit, and it emerges at a late (and therefore high) stage of that progress. But though Hegel claims to do full justice to it, he is also strongly critical of it. His debt to Kant is great, and yet clearly he thinks that he has gone beyond Kant. Hegel stands to Kant rather as Aristotle stands to Plato; he does not deny his greatness, but is perhaps less fully aware of what he owes to him than where he differs from him. He puts him in a high place, but puts him there severely.[1]

Hegel's criticism of this attitude of mind can be put briefly thus: If morality consists in our doing our duty in spite of our inclinations – if it is a struggle against our nature – then, if the struggle were successful, nature would be suppressed in us, and we should cease to be moral; and yet the object of the struggle is just that suppression. I mention this argument because both Hegel and his commentators seem to think it important. But, having mentioned it, I hasten to add that I do not see the force of it. If we could suppress nature in us, we should have what Kant calls a holy will to distinguish it from a moral will. We should no longer have inclinations standing in the way of our doing our duty, and we should therefore cease to be moral. But Kant, so far as I know, does not think this outcome undesirable; he

---

[1] Though Hegel, in this part of the *Phenomenology*, is not concerned with Kant but with an attitude of mind which others have shared with Kant, he gives the impression that he is arguing against Kant without mentioning him by name.

merely thinks it impossible. To say, as he does, that we must do our duty for duty's sake is not to say that we should struggle against our inclinations merely for the sake of struggling against them.

Hegel puts forward another and better argument against the Kantian type of ethic. Duty for duty's sake is, he says, a empty notion. We cannot deduce from the notion of duty what we ought to do; nor can we consult our inclinations to discover our duties, for our duty is to resist them. If we ought to obey rules for their own sake, then it does not matter what the rules are, provided they are compatible with one another – provided they form a coherent system. But if that is so, then any set of mutually compatible rules is as good as any other. We have no criterion for choosing one set rather than another, unless we depart from our principle that we must do our duty for duty's sake. To avoid this absurdity, those who adhere to such a principle are driven to postulate an external legislator, a God who lays duties upon mankind. Though they say that the moral law is rational, their criterion for deciding what that law commands is purely formal, so that any set of mutually consistent principles would conform to it. To give content to the law, they must either tacitly abandon their criterion or must appeal to the will of God. But appealing to God contradicts the very notion of the moral will, because the essence of that will is that it is free. According to this notion, in doing our duty we conform to principles which we accept because we are convinced that they are rational; we do not bow to a will external to our own.

Hegel would agree with Hume that before an action can become a duty there must be a reason for doing it other than a sense of its being a duty. This, I take it, does not mean that a man can never perform a duty for duty's sake; it means only that there must be something about the type of action which he does for duty's sake that explains how it came to be considered a duty – something about it other than the sense that it is a duty.

n. Spirit Satisfied

It is not in the ideal of duty for duty's sake that man finds satisfaction. He finds it only where the principles which he is convinced are right are recognized to be so by others. A man who acts conscientiously expects that the principle which guides his action will be recognized by others. But he may find that it is not. He cannot insist on this recognition, and yet he feels that his convictions must, in the last resort, guide his own actions. He cannot hang back from action, waiting for other people to agree with him. He must act, and it is in the light of experience that his conviction is tested. A morality which is both generally recognized and conscientiously accepted emerges as a result of action. We test our moral convictions not so much by discussing them as by acting upon them; in no other way can we bring our convictions into harmony with one another and with the convictions of others. Hegel condemns what he calls the *beautiful soul*, so anxious that its actions shall be from the highest motives that it dare not act.[1]

As moral beings we are both active and self-critical, and we cannot be fully moral unless we are both. When we act, our action often falls short of our profession; we are mistaken about the motives of our action, which are not what we make them out to be. We discover our mistake by seeing how our action appears to others, and also to ourselves when we look back upon it.

There must be both action and judgement. The man who is merely judicial is apt to be hard-hearted. The mere judge cuts himself off from his fellows; he claims to express the shared values which hold men together, and yet, by his purely condemnatory attitude to wrong-doers, he makes outcasts of them and weakens the bonds of society. We must have judgement between men but also forgiveness. The judge who forgives identifies himself with the wrong-doer, just as the wrong-doer who accepts punishment as his due identifies himself with the judge.

Man is free when he is at home in the world, when what society requires of him is what he conscientiously wants to do. It is by action and by reflecting on his actions that man learns to adjust his convictions to his situation in the world, and so to be at home there. He cannot learn except by being active. By his strivings man creates a social order, and in the process transforms himself. Striving conscientiously for a variety of ends which differ at different stages of his spiritual and social evolution, he is involved in a necessary process which he comes to understand only when he has reached the end of it, although it has consisted, all along, of his own activities. When he comes to understand this process, he sees that the social order and the attitudes of mind making for freedom are products of his own activity; he sees this and is satisfied.

In the Hegelian idiom, this is to say that Spirit is satisfied when it is manifest in a community of selves who conscientiously desire what the community requires of them, which they can come to do only after the process of social, moral and intellectual evolution described in the *Phenomenology*. Spirit is satisfied when it knows the process which it is, which it can do only through the knowledge of finite minds.

[1] See the *Phenomenology of Spirit*, § 668, pp. 406–7.

At this point of Hegel's explanation, we are impelled to put several questions. Is it enough, if Spirit is to have complete self-knowledge, that that knowledge should be revealed in only a few, or even in only one, finite mind? Is it enough, if Spirit is to be satisfied – to the extent that its satisfaction depends on self-knowledge – that Hegel should have written the *Phenomenology*? Or must all finite minds know what Hegel knows? He gives no clue to the answer to this question. Kojève speaks as if it followed from Hegel's philosophy that Spirit must have the knowledge contained in that philosophy in order to have self-knowledge. But even if we grant this conclusion, as I think we must, my questions are still unanswered. Though we grant that the knowledge, in all essentials, is contained in Hegel's philosophy, we can still pertinently ask, Must all finite minds understand and accept this philosophy, if Spirit is to have complete self-knowledge? Kojève takes it for granted that, in Hegel's opinion, Spirit attained complete self-knowledge as soon as he had produced his *Phenomenology*. I am inclined to agree with Kojève, though less because the conclusion seems to follow from the general argument of that book than because of the impression of Hegel produced by a study of his philosophy.

We may also ask, Can Spirit attain self-knowledge, even though only in one finite mind, before it is manifest in a community of selves who conscientiously desire what the community requires of them? Kojève takes it for granted that it cannot; and it seems to me, this time, that his conclusion does follow from Hegel's philosophy. For how can Spirit attain self-knowledge before the completion of the process which constitutes Spirit itself? And, clearly, the process is not complete until Spirit is manifest in a community. Must we then conclude that the Europe dominated by Napoleon was such a community? For it was in that Europe that Hegel wrote the *Phenomenology*. According to Kojève, the highest manifestation of Spirit is Napoleon-revealed-by-Hegel.[1] Perhaps it would be better to say that it is the community dominated by Napoleon and explained by Hegel. Kojève puts and answers questions that Hegel failed to put. Indeed, writing the *Phenomenology* in such abstract terms, he did not need to put them. I shall return to them again later.

The Process of Spirit as Revealed in Religion

a. Hegel's Idea of Religion

So far we have been considering Spirit as it is revealed in the attitudes of mind and activities of individuals. For example, we have not

[1] See Kojève, *Introduction à la Lecture de Hegel*, p. 153.

considered Christianity as a body of doctrines and practices; we have considered only the predicament of the typical Christian – his needs, anxieties and aspirations. So, too, we have not considered the institutions of the community in which the noble and the ignoble consciousness flourish, but only the ambitions and the moods which constitute those attitudes.

But Hegel also has a theory of religions, as bodies of doctrine, apart from the moods and aspirations of their adherents. Religion is, he thinks, a way in which Spirit expresses its awareness of what it essentially is. Spirit is revealed in communities of finite selves, and the religion of a community expresses its sense of what it is in itself, as a manifestation of Spirit. The doctrines which make up the religion are, of course, lodged in finite minds, but they form, none the less, a system of beliefs which may not be present, entire, in any one finite mind. The system can be considered apart from the needs and hopes of the faithful. Just as a symphony played by an orchestra – though it exists as music only when it is played – has a significance apart from the feelings about it of the members of the orchestra, so a body of doctrine – though it is nothing apart from the finite minds in which it is lodged – has a significance beyond what they feel about it.

Religion, as a system of beliefs, is a manifestation of Spirit to itself which anticipates the full self-knowledge it achieves in the Hegelian philosophy. Religious doctrines do not reveal Spirit literally as it is; they reveal it in *Vorstellung*. What they reveal, in other words, is Spirit as it appears to those who have not yet found terms adequate to express what they have in mind. Hegel distinguishes three main types of religion – natural, aesthetic and revealed – and discusses the sorts of community in which they flourish.

b. Natural Religion

Natural religion flourishes where men have not yet acquired a sense of belonging to a rationally organized community, where they are creatures of custom and have no conception of an ethical order or body of rules and practices which form a more or less coherent system. They are not citizens, nor have they attained the 'subjectivity' – the heightened self-consciousness – of men in the world of culture and self-estrangement. They are not political, as the Greeks were, nor do they reject the world in the manner of the Christians. They have, indeed, no conscious attitude to the social order; they merely have attitudes which make them part of that order. They have gone almost no way towards producing a science of nature. Yet they are not beasts, but men; they are rational beings capable of systematic speech and are therefore aware of themselves as living in a world. Being rational they are not altogether uncritical; but they are not consciously critical. They are not investigators and have no standards of criticism. Hegel speaks of them as lacking self-confidence. He does not mean that they are diffident in their dealings with one another; he means only that they have not yet acquired a strong faith in man's capacity to understand the natural world and to use it for his own purposes. He speaks of them as partly 'dissolved' or submerged in nature. That is why their religion is pantheistic; they deify nature or those aspects of it which most impress them. They make gods of plants or animals, of the Sun and the stars, and even of light. Their religion is not to be confused with fetishism or magic. Men who practise magic merely guard themselves against – or else try to use – powers, noxious or salutary, attributed to natural objects; whereas men who have natural religion express, in their attitude to nature or to certain aspects of it, their sense of what Spirit essentially is. They express their sense that Spirit is what gives life or meaning to all things, or what governs all things. They attribute to what they worship in nature qualities which, though they may not know it (not yet having learned to distinguish Spirit from nature), are spiritual.

c. Aesthetic Religion

Aesthetic religion is the religion of peoples who are political and not yet estranged from the world. They have confidence in man's capacity to understand and dominate his natural environment; they are not half submerged in nature. They therefore deify man. Their gods are men rather more than life-size; they are immortal heroes just as their heroes are mortal gods. They are on familiar terms with their gods; they respect but do not stand in awe of them.

Later, in his *Encyclopaedia of the Philosophical Sciences*, Hegel distinguished between art and religion as ways in which Spirit is aware of itself, or, as he put it, 'closes in unity with itself'.[1] Art, according to this later view, is intuitive, and expresses what it intuits in the form of symbols. The artist sees in some aspect of nature or man the Spirit manifest in it, and he puts what he sees into his work. He thinks in symbols, which he need not be able to interpret. If it should happen that an artist can explain his work, it is not as an artist that he does so, but as a critic or philosopher. The artist can convey his message, and the spectator or auditor can take it in, without either of them being able

---

[1] *Hegel's Philosophy of Mind* (Part III of the *Encyclopaedia of the Philosophical Sciences*), trans. Wallace (first published in 1894, Oxford 1971), § 571, p. 301.

to put it into words. The art of an age or people expresses in symbols how Spirit appears to that age or people. Art, Hegel tells us, is Spirit revealed in its immediacy;[1] that is to say, it is understood, at that level of understanding which is artistic appreciation, without needing to be explained. This does not mean, of course, that appreciation cannot be cultivated, that there is no such thing as an educated taste, nor yet that appreciation is instantaneous and does not grow with time; it means only that a work of art can be fully appreciated without being explained.

How then does religion, as a form in which Spirit is aware of itself, differ from art? In art, Spirit is revealed sensuously and symbolically, whereas in religion it is manifest in the form of doctrines and myths. But art can be verbal and narrative as well as plastic and musical; it can also make statements. How then does art, when it is verbal and narrative, differ, as a way in which Spirit is manifest, from religion? For Hegel has told us that religion, like art, does not reveal Spirit literally as it is.

Religion differs from narrative art in making assertions which purport to be true and of the utmost importance. Religion is authoritative and didactic, as art is not. Though, as Hegel tells us, religion reveals the essence of reality only in *Vorstellung* – only figuratively – its priests, the guardians of its doctrines and myths, believe that what they teach is literally true, and that it is a truth necessary to men. Without it, men cannot fulfil their destiny, or cannot live as men should live. Religion purports to reveal the 'meaning of life'; it purports to teach men why they are in the world. The teachers of religion aim deliberately at deepening our understanding of the world and at improving the quality of our lives. They are apt to speak of men who reject the truth they offer as 'lost' or 'spiritually dead'. But art, though it is in fact a manifestation of Spirit, has no such conscious aim; even when it is verbal, it is not primarily didactic. If it deepens our understanding of the world, it does so unconsciously. Art is a form of self-expression, and Spirit is manifest in it because it is manifest in the finite selves who, through their art, express themselves. Religion, as distinct from faith – religion as a body of doctrines and myths, authoritative and didactic – is not a form of self-expression.

In the *Phenomenology*, Hegel is much less concerned to distinguish religion and art, as manifestations of Spirit, than he was to be later; yet the distinction is there already, implicitly. Why, then, does he call one of his three types of religion *aesthetic*, or religion in the form of art?

---

[1] Ibid., § § 557 and 560, pp. 293 and 294.

Presumably not because, where religion is natural or revealed, there is no religious art. When he calls a religion *aesthetic*, he is, I suppose, contrasting it with revealed and not with natural religion. Revealed religion is much more doctrinal than aesthetic religion, which puts what it teaches more in the form of myths than of doctrines. And myth is much closer to art than is doctrine.

Where there is a revealed religion, myth expresses nothing essential about Spirit which is not also expressed doctrinally; whereas, where religion is aesthetic, this does not hold. When he spoke of aesthetic religion, Hegel had in mind mostly the religion of the Greeks, which was less doctrinal than mythological. Where religion takes the form of art, there is little systematic theology, and the community's conception of Spirit is revealed in myths about the gods rather than in the form of doctrine. Though the beliefs embodied in these myths make up a more or less coherent system, they are not abstracted from the myths and put forward as doctrines. Or, if some of them are, others are not, so that there is more in the myths than in the doctrines; and piety consists more in accepting the myths than in adhering to the doctrines. No doubt, where there is revealed religion, there are myths as well, but there are no essential truths contained in the myths which are not contained in the doctrines.

If that is what makes religion aesthetic, then what Hegel calls natural religion is no less aesthetic than the religion of the Greeks. If he had been as much concerned to make a sharp distinction between Greek and Oriental, as between Greek and revealed religion, he might have preferred to call religions of the Greek type anthropomorphic rather than aesthetic. The term *aesthetic*, used in this connection, does not, I think, point to the distinction that really matters. Hegel would have done better to call his three types of religion natural, anthropomorphic and dogmatic, rather than natural, aesthetic and revealed.

d. *Revealed Religion*
Revealed or dogmatic religion is the religion of communities in which Spirit is self-estranged. Judaism and Christianity are examples of this type of religion. The Jews imagined a God from whom man is almost entirely separate, a God who is a master rather than a father, an angry and exacting God rather than a God of love. Since man's idea of God is his conception of what Spirit essentially is, and since Spirit exists in finite selves, men, when they imagine a masterful and angry God, express their sense of not being what they aspire to be, or (to speak metaphorically) of not being themselves. In Christianity, too, man imagines himself separate from God, from the Spirit which is in

him; but he also imagines himself reconciled with God. God the Father represents the Spirit which is in man, though man does not know it – the Spirit to which man aspires and which he feels is out of reach; God the Son represents man's sense that what he aspires to is nevertheless within his reach and must be realized in him; God the Holy Ghost represents man's sense that Spirit is revealed in a plurality of finite selves. In the doctrine that the Holy Ghost is present in the community of the faithful lies the implicit truth that the Spirit which is the essence of man is fully realized in a community whose members are perfectly at home inside it and are satisfied. In Hegel's opinion, the Christian conception of the Holy Ghost and of the Church are theological versions of his own concept of the concrete universal; they contain implicitly a truth which the Hegelian philosophy makes explicit. Though the coming of Christ, which is the reconciliation of man with God, represents the sense of the finite self that it is united with the Spirit, Christ must die in the flesh, if men are to see this truth more clearly – if they are to move from the less adequate idea that God has taken human form to the more adequate idea that God is present in a community of finite selves who attain what they aspire to as members of it. Christianity is, in Hegel's opinion, the highest religion; it expresses, at a certain level, the whole truth about the essential nature of Spirit. It reveals that truth as fully as it can be revealed short of being made explicit in philosophy.

e. Hegel's Religion

It has been both asserted and denied that Hegel was an atheist. His detractors seldom go far enough into his philosophy to raise the question, which seems to have interested only his admirers. My impression is that the atheists among them have wanted to claim him for one of themselves, but that most of the believers, more cautiously, have been concerned to show that it cannot be proved that he was an atheist. Many years ago I was rebuked by a bishop for venturing to say that, strictly speaking, Unitarians are not Christians, and I am now much more careful than I used to be about expressing opinions on such matters. I am uncertain whether or not Hegel was an atheist, and shall confine myself to making the statements that follow.

Hegel did not admit that he was an atheist, nor yet that he was not a Christian. He thought of himself, not as denying Christianity, but as making explicit the truths contained in it, as saying literally what it says figuratively. He thought it inevitable that, as soon as men began to speculate about themselves and their world, religion and philosophy should both arise, being intimately connected and yet different in kind. Religion expresses what a community senses about reality, but does not put into words which are true when taken literally; whereas philosophy consists of theories put forward by individuals whose purpose is to explain the world as it is and who deliberately challenge criticism. There is progress in both philosophy and religion. But philosophy, unlike religion, is scientific, in the broad sense that it seeks to prove what it asserts, inviting doubt in the hope of overcoming it; philosophy puts questions and argues for some answers rather than others. It offers what it takes to be a literal explanation. As one philosophy succeeds another, the explanation becomes gradually more adequate. Religion, too, makes progress; for though it does not give a literal, but a figurative, account of reality, and asserts rather than explains, it does increase in adequacy until it says in its own way all that there is to say. In Christianity, it is fully adequate; it says all that there is to say about the essential nature of Spirit, leaving nothing unsaid, though it says it only figuratively. It is not until philosophy becomes, with Hegel, a comprehensive and fully explicit account of reality, that it puts into words to be taken literally the entire truth implicit in Christianity.

This might seem to imply that the Hegelian philosophy supersedes Christianity. But Hegel never says that it does; he claims no more for it than that it supersedes the incomplete philosophies of the past. Yet he believes that Spirit attains complete self-knowledge only in philosophy, which implies that philosophy is superior to religion. It implies it because the end of the whole process – that is, Spirit itself – is this complete self-knowledge.

2. The Argument of the 'Phenomenology' Examined

The Defects of the Argument

a. A Process Unique and Necessary

I have already rejected as unacceptable two Hegelian conceptions: that of a Mind or Spirit which is revealed in a plurality of finite selves and exists only as so revealed, and that of a process of development whose every phase implies all its other phases. To speak of Spirit as self-conscious only in the consciousness of it possessed by finite selves is to use words to which it is impossible to attach a meaning; the concrete universal is unthinkable, and is merely a putting together of notions which do not make sense when thus combined. I shall add no more to what I have said already to explain why I reject it.

I should, however, like at this stage, to elaborate on what I said earlier about a logically necessary process of development. I have argued that such a process comes to appear logically necessary only if we include among the properties of each phase its relations with later and earlier phases. If we take into account only its inherent properties, we cannot infer from what it is, either what came before it or what will come after it. We must know the process before we can know what phases belong to it, and we learn what the process is only from experience. If we define the process as A succeeded by B succeeded by C succeeded by D, then the process implies each of its phases only because it is defined as consisting of them. A, B, C and D do not imply one another unless they are defined as phases of the process, which only experience teaches us that they are. Only experience teaches us that As develop into Ds. But Hegel's theory is not about As that develop into Ds; it is not about a process of which there are many examples. It is about something unique; it is about Spirit, which he says is such that it must develop in a certain way.

No doubt, some of the properties which Hegel attributes to Spirit are included in others. The ability, for instance, to discriminate is included in the ability to make a deliberate choice. It is possible to have the first property without the second, but not the second without the first. Thus, even when we are considering a unique course of development, we can say that some properties are logically prior to others. But this does not mean that, if the properties which are prior are acquired, the others must be so too; it means only that, unless they are acquired, the others cannot be. Otherwise, only experience can be our guide. It may teach us that one property is in fact always acquired before another, that α always comes before β. But experience is no help to us when we are dealing with a process which is unique; or it can help us only to the extent to which the process, or some part of it, is like some other process – that is to say, only in those respects in which the process is not unique.

Hegel has built up his account of a unique and necessary process by a variety of devices which ought not to be used as he uses them. He has seen that some properties are logically prior to others, in the sense already explained, and he has seen as well that, very often, where we find the first properties, we also find, sooner or later, the second. He has then simply concluded that where we find the first properties we must find the second – that the first properties logically require the second, just as the second logically require the first. Nothing can have β without having α, for α is included in β; and whatever has α usually acquires β. This moves Hegel to conclude that what has α *must* acquire β, in the same sense of *must* as that in which what has β *must* have α.

Hegel sees that man has acquired a certain conception of freedom, and he sees also that certain other conceptions are logically prior to it. Man has in fact acquired this conception, and must have acquired certain others, before he could acquire it. Hegel therefore feels entitled to speak as if there were here a necessary course of intellectual and moral development, as if it followed that because there could not be freedom (as he defines it) unless there were conscientious defiance of established conventions, there had to be freedom if there was this defiance. Indeed, he goes even further; he sees that man has acquired particular conceptions under given social conditions. He sees a connection between the social and the intellectual, and also a logical priority of some conceptions to others, as well as a temporal one; and so he includes social changes along with intellectual developments in the same necessary process.

Though he is quite well aware that temporal and logical priority are different, he does not distinguish between them when it serves his purpose to ignore that difference. He sees that some properties are included in others which come after them; they are logically as well as temporally prior to their successors. He also sees that, as a matter of fact, some properties usually come before others, and whenever his argument requires it and he can plausibly do so, he speaks as if, being temporally prior, they were also prior logically. Our modern conception of freedom, for instance, may plausibly be held to include the Greek idea of the citizen who has a say in the affairs of his community; the Roman idea of the legal person as a subject of precisely defined rights; and the Christian idea of the individual. If this is true, as Hegel says it is, then we have here at least three ideas included in our notion of freedom – three ideas logically and temporally prior to it. But Hegel has noticed that the Greek idea of the citizen came in time before the Roman idea of the legal person, and so he speaks as if the first idea were logically prior to the second, though it clearly is not.

If we know that A has developed into X (say, that primitive man, self-conscious and potentially rational, has developed into the West European as Hegel conceived him to be), and if we know how X differs from A, we know what properties A must acquire in order to become X. But this knowledge does not tell us in what order these properties are to be acquired, or which (if any) are logically prior to others. Nor can we conclude from it that A, being what it is, must develop into X. Man has, in fact, developed into other things besides the West European. From the properties which make up the humanity of man – the properties included in our definition of him – we cannot infer that he will develop in one way rather than another. But Hegel thinks that we can, for he believes that wherever we have the type of change which is called growth or development, what is temporally prior is also logically prior. He is wrong on two counts: biological growth is not a 'logical' process, and the intellectual and social development of man differs in kind from biological growth.

Hegel says that the process cannot be seen to be necessary until it is completed. I find this assertion puzzling. No doubt, if the process is thought of as culminating in the emergence of a creature capable of understanding it, then the process must be complete before it can be understood. If, for the moment, we suppose that there is no intelligence superior to man's, we rightly conclude that man had to evolve out of a creature like the ape before we could have any understanding of how man could evolve out of the ape; but we cannot conclude that there had to be a process of evolution from ape to man. Hegel is, I think, saying more than that the process, which he calls necessary, must produce an intelligence capable of understanding it before it can be understood; he is also saying that it must be complete in order to be intelligible. From this it would follow that, even if there could exist – independently of the process – a being capable of understanding it, that being could not understand it unless it were complete. The process is necessary and yet is unintelligible until it is complete. This is, I believe, Hegel's position, and it seems to me untenable.

b. Hegel Begs the Question

Having made up his mind that the process is logically necessary, Hegel sometimes uses the oddest arguments to show how one phase of it leads necessarily to the next. Let me give an example. Why should the type of community which Hegel calls an embodiment of Spirit in its immediacy ever pass away and something different take its place? Hegel admits that in this type of community men are happy; he does not find in it the phenomenon which he calls self-estrangement. Why then should it ever be superseded? The only reason that Hegel gives is that Spirit, at that stage of its development, is deficient in what he calls *ethical substance*. If it is to become fully developed, it must be self-estranged and must afterwards 'find itself' in a coherent world order which it recognizes as its own product.

But this reason is not properly a reason at all. It amounts to saying that something must develop merely in order to acquire a property which it lacks. And what is meant by its lacking a property? No more than its not having it? If that is all that is meant, the argument is absurd. No doubt, if something is to acquire a property it does not have, it must change; but its not having it is not a reason for its changing. Is the lack here in question a felt want? Who, then, feels it? Not the members of the community, for they as yet have no inkling of what it is they lack. To explain why this type of community gives way to another, we must show what there is about it which causes it to do so. But this Hegel does not do. And even if he did, it would not serve his purpose; for it would be a causal explanation, and a cause does not imply its effect.

Hegel is caught in a dilemma which he does not see, and which, if he did see it, he could not resolve. He speaks of a process which he says is necessary, and then, to explain what it is and how it is necessary, he gives an account of it, phase by phase. But when he comes to show how one phase leads necessarily to the next, he is often incapable of doing more than show how it falls short of its successor and what must come after it to make up the deficiency. He does not see that it only makes sense to say that the next phase has to make up for what is deficient in the phase before if it is assumed that the process is necessary. Or, if he can point to something about the phase which causes it to give way to its successor, he feels himself obliged to speak of that something as if it explained how the phase is logically prior to its successor; but again he can do this, with a show of plausibility, only because he has already taken it for granted that the process is necessary. He offers to show that this is so by showing how each phase of it leads inevitably to the next, and then (although he does not know it) his explanation of how any phase leads inevitably to the next assumes that the process is necessary.

c. Hegel's Irrelevance

Again, because he has made up his mind that the process is logically necessary, Hegel feels the need to include in it whatever he cannot afford to ignore, whether or not it fits into the process. He is a European writing for Europeans, and so, although his account does not refer to actual events – European or otherwise – it finds a place for all the more important types of community, philosophy, attitude of mind and religion of which Europe provides examples. Nothing important is left out, because it is assumed that it *must* have made its contribution to the final result. But this final result is not the state of affairs in Europe in Hegel's time as might be described by the most learned and impartial historians. It is not that, but the actualization of freedom, understood in a certain way. It is no doubt true that all the important phenomena, social and intellectual, then recorded in European history had contributed to make Europe what it was when Hegel wrote the *Phenomenology*, but it is not true that they all contributed to the actualization of what Hegel understood by freedom.

Is it necessary, in order that freedom should be made actual, that the compact community of the type of the Greek *polis* should be superseded by what Hegel calls the 'soulless community' with 'a lord of the world' to govern it? Is it necessary that this 'soulless community' should give way to the feudal system, and that that system should in its turn give way to absolute monarchies of the type which arose in Europe in the seventeenth and eighteenth centuries? Even if we allow that what Hegel calls 'self-estrangement' and 'the unhappy consciousness' are necessary to the realization of freedom, does it follow that so too are Stoicism and Scepticism?

If we took the Hegelian conception of freedom, which is admittedly complex, and broke it down into the simpler ideas contained in it, we should no doubt find that some of them are logically prior to others. They are all logically prior to the conception of freedom, and there are also no doubt some logical priorities among them. We could then put these ideas into a logical order, and argue that, unless they appeared simultaneously (which we might think most improbable), they must have appeared in a temporal order corresponding to the logical one. But the logical order would not be quite what Hegel had in mind, for though we might, for example, be able to say that A and B, unless they came at the same time as C, must have come before it, there might be no reason why A should have come before B rather than after it. We could also, no doubt, by studying history, discover a good deal about the social conditions that favour the appearance of these ideas. We could build up an account of a course of social and intellectual development culminating in the emergence of freedom. We could then say that such and such conceptions had to appear in roughly a certain order, and under certain conditions. But our account, to be plausible, would differ considerably from Hegel's. It would leave out, on the ground that it is irrelevant, much that he put in.

We might perhaps claim for our imaginary account that it described a *necessary* course of development, but that course would be necessary in a different sense from Hegel's. It would include what experience had taught us about how the ideas that make up our conception of freedom, and also the practices that realize that conception, emerged. We should then not say that freedom thus conceived had to be realized;

we should say only that, if it was to be realized, certain things had to happen. And we should not speak of logical necessity, otherwise than to insist that, where one conception includes another, it could not have emerged before it. We should make a very modest claim compared with the one that Hegel made.

d. Self-Consciousness and Contradiction

In his attempt to show how the evolution of Spirit is necessary, Hegel constantly reminds us that Spirit is self-conscious. Indeed, that of which the development is traced in the *Phenomenology* is called self-consciousness more often than Spirit, the word Spirit being applied more to the later phases of the process. Self-consciousness, at any point in its development except the last, is involved in contradiction; but, precisely because it is self-conscious, it becomes aware that it is so involved, and then surmounts the contradiction. Or, as we might put it, men take up an attitude which involves contradiction, but – precisely because they are self-conscious and self-critical – they eventually come to see the contradiction and so abandon the attitude, taking up another. The development, which is a progress or movement from the lower to the higher, is necessary because the beings involved in it are self-conscious. Though they are not aware of the process as a whole until it is near completion, every phase of it is reflected in their minds. The reflection may be mistaken; they may not see themselves and their situation as they really are, but they are, being self-conscious, inevitably also self-critical. Their mistakes and defects are eventually brought home to them, and once this has happened, they are no longer quite the same creatures they were before. Because man is a self-conscious being, he is transformed by his own activities.

It is true that a self-conscious creature is affected by its own activities in ways in which an unself-conscious creature is not. It is also true that its attitudes often change because it has come to believe that they are, in some sense, inadequate or defective. They often change for this reason, but not necessarily. Because man is self-conscious, it does not follow that he must discover the contradictions involved in any attitude he takes up; it follows only that he may do so.

What Hegel calls contradictions, moreover, are not, for the most part, literally contradictions; they do not involve logical inconsistency. Hegel, in the *Phenomenology*, is not so much concerned with systematic theories as with what might be called, in the popular sense, philosophies of life. He is not so much concerned to point out false reasonings as to show that certain attitudes of mind are produced by needs of which men are not conscious, or of which they are only half-conscious, and that the attitudes, for one reason or another, do not satisfy the needs that give rise to them. This is, indeed, what makes the *Phenomenology*, despite its pretentious metaphysics and obscure style, a fascinating and profound book. What Hegel calls contradictions are often no more than attempts to obtain satisfaction in ways that do not give it. But it does not follow that, because man is self-conscious, he must discover that these ways do not bring satisfaction, especially when he does not even understand the needs that he is groping to satisfy.

Let us consider, for a moment, what Hegel says about the Unhappy Consciousness. Men desire recognition in this world but they do not get it, and so they imagine another world in which they do get it from a God to whom they attribute the essential qualities of man. They need recognition in order to be satisfied, but while they seek that recognition in another world, being unable to get it in this, they are not satisfied. The contradiction consists in their seeking recognition where it is not to be found.

For my part, I do not see, even in this peculiar sense of contradiction, that there is one here; and, if there is one, I do not see why man, as a self-conscious being, must eventually resolve it. I do not see why the situation should be unsatisfying, or why, if it were unsatisfying, it should not last indefinitely. Even if we allow that men imagine another world to compensate for the recognition they do not get in this one, it does not follow that the compensation fails to satisfy, Hegel, at least, produces no good reason for thinking so; he merely takes it for granted that because man first wants recognition in this world, which alone is real, he can be satisfied only if he gets it in this world; he cannot be satisfied by the mere belief that he has it, or will have it, in a world which he has imagined but which does not exist. But recognition is not like food, which must be real before it can satisfy; for a man to be satisfied by recognition, it may be enough that he believes he has it.[1] Provided he has no doubts, why should he not be satisfied? Hegel does not do what he might have done; he does not attempt to show that belief in an after-life is apt to be too weak to enable a man to find, in the hope of what it will bring him, adequate compensation for what he lacks in this life.

And why, even if hope of an after-life cannot satisfy man, should he come to know this and to seek satisfaction where alone he can

---

[1] If I believe that I am recognized by a Being who does not exist and whom I do not expect to meet in this life, and if my belief in an after-life is mistaken, then I need never be disillusioned.

get it? Hegel does not suppose that man, knowing what he wants in this world and not being able to get it, deliberately imagines another world and seeks compensation in it; he does not suppose that man is a deliberate escapist. He does not offer us so crude an explanation of how man comes to believe in an after-life. Though man is dissatisfied in this life, he does not understand what makes him so; his faith is a remedy for a condition of which he is only dimly aware. The very notion of an Unhappy Consciousness supposes that man does not yet understand his own nature – that there is more to him than he himself knows. He is not yet, as Hegel put it, *for* himself what he is *in* himself. Man is a self-conscious creature. Indeed, he is; but his being so does not of itself make it necessary that he should overcome a condition whose roots, though they lie in him, are not known to him. Freud would agree that repression and sublimation are processes which occur in man because he is self-conscious and rational, because he has a need for what Hegel calls 'recognition' and therefore seeks satisfaction in ways peculiar to his kind. Being self-conscious and rational, he needs to justify himself to himself. Man alone is capable of self-knowledge, and therefore man alone feels the need to hide from himself. The subconscious in man is not the part of him which he shares with the lower animals; it is what it is, not in spite of his being self-conscious and rational, but largely because he is so. His mental ills, even those of which he is not conscious, are the ills of a self-conscious creature; they are the ills of a creature who, in Hegel's sense of the word, is spiritual, acquiring self-consciousness in the process of building up for itself a coherent picture of a world in which it strives to satisfy desires peculiar to its kind. Only a self-conscious creature could suffer from such ills and could find a remedy for them; but it does not follow, merely because it is self-conscious, that it must find it.

e. Rationalism and Revolution

Hegel often confuses what is required by his theory with what is required by the facts. He says, for instance, that the rationalist philosophers explain the world and show that it is rational (or, as we should say, that it is completely intelligible), but that Spirit needs to do more than explain the world; it needs to transform it. Not for a moment does he suggest that it is the philosophers who feel the need to transform the world, and are not content merely to explain it. It is Spirit that is still unsatisfied, and not the rationalist philosophers; and thus, in order that Spirit should be satisfied, there must be revolutionary zeal as well as critical philosophy. Spirit is manifest in both philosophy and revolution; it is both theoretical and active. It follows, therefore, from the nature of Spirit that there must be both rationalist philosophy and revolution. The philosophers need not themselves be revolutionaries, but there must come to be revolutionaries after there have been philosophers, because it is in the nature of Spirit that there should be. Hegel's explanation is no explanation at all. He ought to show us how men, when they succeed in explaining the world, come inevitably to want to transform it; he ought to show us how rationalist philosophy and revolution are connected in human minds, for it is in such minds that Spirit is manifest. Instead of that, he merely tells us that there must be both rationalist philosophers and revolutionaries, because Spirit is active as well as theoretical. We might as well say: Love and jealousy go necessarily together, and therefore, since John is in love, James is jealous.

Hegel's theory requires him to hold that men come to have a new attitude to (or philosophy of) life, because they have failed to find satisfaction in an old one. As he might put it, for example, Spirit seeks satisfaction in Stoicism, discovers contradictions in it and hence passes on to something else. It does not occur to him that an old philosophy may come to seem unsatisfying because a new one has begun to take its place. As he sees it, there must be something wrong with the old philosophy which causes it to lose its hold on men and allows a new philosophy to supplant it. But this is by no means always so. There may be all kinds of reasons, other than anything inherently unsatisfying about it, which cause a philosophy of life to be supplanted. External conditions may change, and men may acquire ambitions which they did not have before; or they may have ideals imposed upon them which are unsuited to them and which they come to discard. A philosophy of life is not a scientific theory which is abandoned or modified because it is seen not to fit the facts. Nor does it lose its hold on men because it is logically inconsistent. The contradictions which Hegel claims to see in the philosophies he discusses are not – though he pretends otherwise – for the most part, logical inconsistencies; they are much more often failures to satisfy. Stoicism, he tells us, leads to boredom, and the systematic pursuit of pleasure defeats its own end. But is this so, always? And when it is so, what makes it so?

Stoicism is not boring to the man who is by temperament suited to it. Nor is the systematic pursuit of pleasure always self-defeating. We do not all come to terms with life in the same way. Hegel takes no account of the possibility that there may be several perennial philosophies, which take different forms in different ages, but which remain essentially the same from age to age, each of them attractive to only some people. There are Stoics now, as there were in the ancient world. Their explicit beliefs may be considerably different, but their attitude to life is at bottom the same. There are also sceptics and hedonists and believers in an after-life; their beliefs, too, have changed with the times, but the philosophies that come nearest to satisfying them have remained true to type. Hegel's theory requires him to hold that one type of philosophy gives way to another until at last there is left a single philosophy which is completely satisfying, and also that a philosophy is supplanted only because it has been found to be inherently unsatisfying. Both these opinions seem to me mistaken.

f. Master and Slave

One of the most admired parts of the *Phenomenology* is the dialectic of the master and slave. It has caught the imagination of several of Hegel's interpreters, and they have made much of it. Kojève, in particular, has expounded it with extraordinary force and lucidity.[1] Hegel, in this dialectic, points to certain quite fundamental aspects of human and social experience. I hope to make clear what they are, confessing that I would not have seen, as clearly as I do now, how Hegel conceived of them, if I had read only his *Phenomenology* and not also Kojève's commentary on it. Yet I believe that there are, in this part of Hegel's argument, important defects which Kojève has not seen, or at least has not seen to be important, for he has not troubled to mention them.

Man's desire for recognition – his longing to seem valuable in his own eyes and to have others admit his value – leads to a conflict which Kojève, interpreting Hegel, calls a conflict of pure prestige. Man cannot be certain of his value unless others admit it, and he requires of them what he will not – except from fear of death – accord to them. As a result of this conflict some become masters and others slaves.

I should not quarrel with Hegel for insisting that the desire for recognition is the pre-eminently human desire – that it is strong and persistent only in self-conscious and rational beings, that with them it takes forms unknown in other creatures, and that they become more fully self-conscious and develop their reasoning powers largely in the process of seeking to satisfy it. I should agree with him that conflicts of pure prestige are enormously important in human life, which owes its specifically human character much more to them than

[1] See his *Introduction à la Lecture de Hegel*, pp. 170–86.

to conflicts for what satisfies the appetites which man shares with the other animals.

But what Hegel forgets – and I am surprised that a family man should forget it – is that the human being first engages in conflicts of pure prestige in the nursery. It is there, and not on the battlefield, that man wins his first victories and sustains his first defeats. And by the nursery, I do not mean the room set aside for children in the homes of the well-to-do; I mean the relations in which children, in the process of becoming self-conscious and rational, stand to one another and to adults in the family circle. It is true that, to begin with, a child cannot distinguish between itself and its environment, and that when it comes to make this distinction, it comes also to distinguish between itself and other selves. It is true also that, as it becomes aware of other selves, it behaves towards them as if they existed only to satisfy its appetites. It does not at first require recognition; it merely has appetites, and gives vent to them until they are satisfied; it then gradually comes to be aware, as it acquires self-consciousness, that its appetites are satisfied by others. When it comes to this awareness, it tries to make others do what it wants; it does so, at first, in order that they should satisfy its appetites, and then, later, also to show its power over them. But the persons whom it seeks to make subservient to itself are much more powerful than the child; and they soon instil in it, usually without aiming to do so, a lively sense of its dependence on them. Even the most self-willed and spoilt child is often frustrated; it has it frequently brought home to it that its power is limited. Being aware of its dependence on others, it seeks to please them. It acquires self-esteem in the process of endeavouring to be the sort of person they approve of. Thus, though it may be true that – almost as soon as it can distinguish other people from itself – it seeks to make them subservient to its wishes, and also that it needs recognition in order to have self-respect, or a secure sense of its own worth, there can be no question of its enslaving others. It gains recognition by its own obedience.

I should have thought that the need to dominate and the need for recognition are distinct, and that the first precedes the second. The child wishes everything to happen the way it wants; when it becomes aware of other people besides itself, it wishes them to satisfy its desires as soon as it gives vent to them. No doubt, it soon acquires an appetite for power; it asks for what it does not really want, just for the sake of asking and getting. But an appetite for power, at this stage, consists merely of the need to express wishes for the pleasure of having them gratified. The child with this appetite may not be in the least concerned about what other people think and feel towards it; it may, as yet, have no need for recognition. I suspect that the need for recognition comes with frustration and a sense of dependence; the child needs to placate adults, and is therefore interested, not just in getting them to do what it wants, but in their feelings towards itself. It wants to be important to them, and this desire soon becomes the most persistent and absorbing of all. It is, as Hegel implied, the predominantly human and educative desire. It is abnormally strong in man because he is self-conscious and rational, and it also serves to deepen his self-consciousness and to develop his reasoning powers. But it is a desire born of a sense of dependence and a need to placate; and when it first appears in the human being, it makes him docile rather than aggressive. A child seeks recognition from grown-ups rather than from other children, and from children older than itself rather than from younger ones, and is apt to be docile towards them provided it can earn their recognition by docility. This docility, of course, is not slavishness; the child is not seeking to make itself a mere instrument of their wills, but is seeking their approval by conforming to what it believes are their standards.

Mastery and slavery are facts that have to be explained; they have their social and psychological causes. They may even mark a usual phase in the social and intellectual development of mankind. Slavery, in one form or another, has existed in many, and perhaps even in most, human societies. John Stuart Mill, who was – much more than Hegel – a thorough liberal, conceded that slavery, or at least a high degree of dependence of some men upon others, might be necessary to produce habits of regular and hard work, and might therefore have been beneficial to mankind. I would not deny this; it may be so. It may be true that slavery could hardly have been avoided and that the world is now a better place, even by standards acceptable to the liberal, than it would have been had there never been slavery. I am not concerned to challenge this claim. I deny only that Hegel, in his dialectic of the master and the slave, has shown that mastery and slavery are necessarily involved in the process whereby man becomes a deeply self-conscious creature with a lively and urgent sense of his own dignity – the sort of creature for whom freedom can be a supreme value.

g. Slavery and Progress

In an argument which has found admirers, Hegel contends that, whereas the slave is progressive, the master is not. This is so, he thinks, partly because the master is in an *impasse*, being unable to get real satisfaction from his recognition by the slave, whom he cannot recognize without forfeiting his mastery, which he will not do voluntarily; and partly because the slave is a worker, and through his work attains understanding of, and power over, both nature and himself, as the master does not.

The first of these reasons holds only if there is just one master, or if, where there is more than one, they do not form a community. But clearly there is more than one master, and there is also a community of masters, as Hegel tacitly admits. He speaks of a community which is concrete Spirit in its immediacy, whose members are citizens. This is the type of community of which the Greek *polis* is an example. In it there are both masters and slaves, and presumably the masters recognize one another, or otherwise the community would not subsist. Now, according to Hegel, the recognition extended to the master by the slave is not fully satisfying because the master does not recognize the slave. He is recognized by an inferior, by a person worthless in his eyes, and therefore is not satisfied. This implies that the recognition of an equal is satisfying; so that, if there are several masters and they recognize one another, they are all satisfied. Hegel's argument is merely that a man's sense of his own worth is secure if that worth is recognized by others, and that the recognition is fully satisfying only if it comes from persons whose worth he in turn recognizes. His argument is not that recognition cannot be fully satisfying to anyone who gets it unless everyone recognizes everyone else. Thus, provided there is a community of equals who recognize one another, that recognition is fully satisfying to them, no matter how many slaves there may be. This is what follows from Hegel's remarks about recognition and about the reasons which makes servile recognition unsatisfying. His argument that servile recognition cannot satisfy the master rests therefore on the tacit (and absurd) assumption that there is only one master or that, if there is more than one, they do not recognize one another. Unfortunately, Hegel's style encourages this kind of false reasoning. He is interested in the master and the slave as types, and so he speaks of the lordly and the servile consciousness, or of *the* master and *the* slave, as if there were only one of each.

Hegel's other reason for holding that the slave is progressive while the master is not is historically more important. It asserts a doctrine of which Marx was to make great use – that it is the oppressed rather than the oppressor who makes progress, because he is enlightened and disciplined by work. But it is not true that only the servile and the oppressed work; the free and the oppressors do so as well. Slavery and oppression are possible only in a community, and wherever there is a community, there is some form of government or management.

This too is work, and it is work as disciplined and as educative as any done by slaves or serfs or hired labourers. How are we to distinguish between work and activity which is not work? Work, presumably, is regular and obligatory. If these are the properties which distinguish work from other kinds of activity, then government and management are as much entitled as anything else to be called work. Even if we say that work is essentially service, we cannot deny that the ruler and the manager also serve. They are not free to do as they please; they carry out obligations; they do what is required or expected of them, and there are sanctions to ensure that they do it. Even in the economic sphere, they have as much interest as the servile and the oppressed in raising production; they study nature and themselves just as closely, and are just as inventive. If they are less progressive, it cannot be because they are not disciplined and enlightened by the work they do. On the contrary, they are – much more than the servile and the oppressed – the intellectual and reflective class.

I am not, in saying this, trying to suggest that there is really no such thing as oppression or exploitation; I am not saying that so-called oppressors or exploiters serve the oppressed and exploited just as much as they are served by them. Admittedly, when the oppressors serve, they serve only their own class, and the rewards of their labour are incomparably greater than the rewards of the oppressed, because they dominate the community. Nor am I denying that they have much more leisure than the oppressed. Though I suspect that the hardest workers are usually to be found among them, because their work is more absorbing and more rewarding than menial labour, I concede that many of them do little or no work. But to concede this is not to admit that their work is less disciplined and educative than the work of the servile and subordinate.

If the slave is progressive, at least potentially, in some respect in which the master is not, he is so not because he is a worker and is transformed morally and intellectually by his work; he is so, rather, because it is much more obviously his interest than the master's that all men, and not only some, should be free. Once you allow that freedom is good and that all men can have it, you must conclude that, if some men, owing to their position in society, are more disposed than others to demand universal freedom, they are, in at least one respect, the more progressive. But this has nothing to do with the effects upon them of their work.

h. An Odd Account of Revolution
Hegel's account of absolute freedom and terror – or revolution

(though he does not use that word) – is awkward and obscure; it is an unsuccessful attempt to make the course of events square with his theory. As we have seen, he says that for Spirit, in the phase of absolute freedom, 'the world is . . . simply its own will, and this is a general will'.[1] In other words, the revolutionary believes that the world ought to be as men wish it to be – that society exists for men, who have the right to mould it to their will. And the will here in question is the will common to them all, the universal will. The revolutionary sees freedom as the realization of this will, and to that extent is right; but he seeks to realize it by abolishing all social ranks and classes; he seeks to realize it *immediately*, as Hyppolite puts it in trying to explain Hegel's meaning. It is there that the revolutionary is mistaken, and his mistake leads to terror. And all this – so Hegel would have us believe – is necessary; it is a necessary phase in the evolution of Spirit.

We may ask, what is involved in trying to realize the universal will *immediately*? We have seen that, in Hegelian parlance, the *immediate* is the simple and undifferentiated, or what appears to be so to the unphilosophical mind. The revolutionary has an adequate conception of freedom and therefore understands that it is not mere absence of constraint; he understands that freedom is realized only when the universal will is made effective in a social order. This being so, it follows that the attempt to realize the universal will *immediately* is an attempt to realize it in a single and undifferentiated social order, a community without social ranks and classes. It is that attempt, apparently, which leads to terror.

The point of this argument escapes me. Hegel admits that the revolutionary has an adequate conception of freedom – that he sees it as the universal will realized in a social order. The universal will is, indeed, his object; his supreme desire is to see that will embodied in the laws and institutions of society. The revolutionary presumably does not deny that in society there is a considerable diversity of functions, that every society has a definable structure; he merely wants to ensure that that structure accords with the universal will – or, as we might put it, with principles of justice which he believes all men would accept if they considered them impartially and saw their practical implications. In believing this he may be simple-minded; there may be no such principles. But that is irrelevant here; and, in any case, his belief is not one that Hegel would reject. No matter how simple-minded the revolutionary, he does not want to do without a social structure, and therefore does not want to do without a hierarchy. He wants to

---

[1] *Phenomenology of Spirit*, § 584, pp. 356–7.

transform the social structure and the hierarchy to accord with his conception of justice. He does not want to abolish *all* social ranks. He may perhaps say that this is what he wants, but, if he says it, he is using the term *social ranks* in a narrow sense to refer to the kind of hierarchy he dislikes – as, for example, to hereditary classes. But that is not the sense of *social ranks* required to make sense of Hegel's argument. A society without hereditary classes is not simple and undifferentiated; it may be – and indeed, unless it is small and simple, it must be – elaborate in structure. It must be hierarchical, and must have social ranks. An attempt to abolish hereditary classes or unearned privileges is not an attempt to abolish *all* social ranks, *all* hierarchy; it is not an attempt to make society simple and undifferentiated. But Hegel says that, when Spirit takes the form of absolute freedom, there is an attempt to abolish *all* ranks, *all* hierarchy.

Now, an attempt to abolish all ranks and all hierarchy – if it is made in any but the smallest and simplest societies (and it is not them but countries like France that Hegel has in mind at this stage of his argument) – is tantamount to an attempt to abolish organized society. How then can Spirit, at this stage of its evolution, have an adequate conception of freedom? Or, as we should prefer to say, how can man have it? The adequacy of the conception consists in freedom's being acknowledged to be a universal will realized in a social order. The claim of the revolutionary is that society shall conform to the universal will. He can have no adequate conception of freedom unless he understands that there must be a structure of authority to hold society together – unless he understands that there must be hierarchy, even though neither wealth nor rank is inherited.

Hegel cannot condemn the revolutionary for wishing to change society; for, if he has an adequate conception of freedom which he sees is not yet realized, he must wish to change society in order to realize it. Hegel could condemn him, as Burke does, for acting in haste and ignorance; but that condemnation would have nothing to do with the necessary evolution of Spirit. He could also condemn him for attempting what is both impossible and undesirable: for trying to ensure that the momentary will of the people, no matter what it is, always prevails. He might have argued that this attempt is self-defeating; he might have said that trying to give immediate effect to the will of the majority must lead to chaos and then to oppression and terror, so that, eventually, it is not the will of the majority, but that of a ruthless minority, which prevails. If Hegel had put forward this argument, he would have been more convincing, for it may be that the institutions most likely to ensure that the people get what gives them enduring satisfaction will often prevent their getting what, at the moment, they happen to be clamouring for.

Indeed, I do not wish to deny that Hegel may have meant to say this as well. Reading his highly abstract argument, it is often difficult to see just what he does mean. He may also have meant to say that, where there is no democracy, every citizen can be free, accepting the social order as being in harmony with his enduring will, or even that democracy prevents the full realization of freedom.

It may have been Hegel's intention to use these two more plausible arguments as well. I do not exclude that possibility. But the argument he makes the most of is that the revolutionary wants to achieve freedom by abolishing all social ranks. That argument is either out of place or else does not square with Hegel's admission that, at this stage of the evolution of Spirit, men have an adequate conception of freedom.

Nor is it clear why the attempt to abolish all ranks should lead to terror. Hegel's argument amounts to no more than this: revolution, or the attempt to realize universal freedom *immediately* (in the Hegelian sense of immediate), is necessarily destructive, and therefore the sole achievement of universal freedom is death. And this death, he calls – coming down suddenly from the heights of abstraction to homely language – 'the coldest and meanest of all deaths, with no more significance than cutting off a head of cabbage or swallowing a mouthful of water'.[1] But in what does the destructiveness of revolution consist? Apparently, in the attempt to achieve universal freedom by abolishing all social ranks. Now, the abolition of social ranks is the destruction of institutions; it is not the killing of men. Hegel's argument seems therefore to be that the destruction of these particular institutions leads necessarily to killing. It may be so, but it is not self-evident. Yet Hegel has nothing more to say about it than this. He does not offer to show how the attempt to destroy these institutions leads to killing; he moves directly from this destructiveness to death, as if the first logically implied the second. It is only because he puts his argument in such abstract terms that its absurdity escapes notice.

The abolition of all ranks is clearly impossible. For the attempt to abolish them is made by an organized power, and organization involves hierarchy. It is also impossible to ensure that the momentary will of the people always prevails. Thus, we have here one aim, which Hegel clearly (though mistakenly) attributes to the revolutionary, and another which can be attributed to him and whose attribution is more

[1] Ibid., § 590, p. 360.

plausible; and both are aims at the impossible. Can we say, then, that Hegel believed that revolution leads inevitably to killing because it aims at the impossible? He may have believed it. Yet this belief, if it is merely asserted and not argued, carries no conviction; for it is by no means obvious that merely aiming at the impossible leads to killing. But there is here a possible line of argument that does make sense, and Hegel may have had it in mind without putting it into words. People who have power and who try to achieve the impossible, believing it to be possible and also important, are quickly frustrated, and made angry and suspicious; they suspect treachery and ill-will and take easily to extreme measures. They look upon themselves as spokesmen for the community, or as guardians of its enduring interests, and so, when they find things going seriously wrong, are apt to blame others rather than themselves and to feel justified in punishing them. When, after centuries of accepting society for what it is, men seek to transform it, they easily lose control of the course of events they have set in motion, and in their bewilderment and panic resort to violence. But this argument – even if Hegel had it in mind – has nothing to do with the development of Spirit as he imagined it.

i. Hegel and Napoleon

As we have seen, it seems to follow from Hegel's philosophy being possible that the process whereby Spirit achieves self-knowledge is complete, for that self-knowledge is knowledge of the process which is Spirit and is revealed in finite minds. Hegel is such a mind, and this knowledge is revealed in his philosophy; therefore (unless we assume that it must be revealed in all finite minds), the existence of that philosophy proves that the process which is Spirit is complete. But Spirit is both Reason and Will; it is fully actual and satisfied when it attains complete self-knowledge, and when it is manifest in a community of selves who conscientiously desire what the community requires of them. It would appear, too, that Spirit cannot attain full self-knowledge unless it is manifest in such a community, for the process must be complete before it can be fully known, and Spirit is as much Will as Reason.

It would seem, then, that the Europe in which Hegel wrote the *Phenomenology* – the Europe dominated by Napoleon – must be the community whose members conscientously desire what is required of them, the community which is completely free. But this is surely an odd conclusion to a philosophy which makes the realization of freedom its central theme. Hegel admired Napoleon as perhaps only a German is capable of admiring a conqueror of his own country, as Goethe admired him, and Beethoven too before the First Consul turned Emperor. Napoleon was never admired by intellectuals in France as he was in Germany. The Napoleon that Goethe and Hegel admired – without perhaps seeing him for what he was – was much more than a soldier; he was, they thought, the heir of the Revolution. In the place of terror he put order, and he knew how to make men secure in the possession of the rights granted to them by the Revolution. He extended to the territories he conquered the civil liberties which the Revolution brought to Frenchmen. It was still possible, in 1807, to think of Napoleon as a liberator rather than an oppressor. Hegel shared an admiration which was still respectable, and which it would be absurd to call abject or servile. It would be more than unjust; it would be stupid to speak of Hegel as if he were a crude worshipper of power or a quisling. Yet it is odd that a man who could speak of freedom as he did, making so much of the claim to be allowed to live conscientiously, should have implied that freedom was achieved in the Europe of his day.

According to Kojève, Hegel saw in Napoleon the fully satisfied man, the man who knew what he had to do and how to do it, the man completely at home in the world. He saw him as the instrument of the universal will, the legislator whose laws are entirely acceptable. Since Napoleon is not mentioned by name in the *Phenomenology* – not even as is Antigone to illustrate a point – we must suppose that the opinions about Napoleon attributed to Hegel by Kojève are opinions to which Kojève thinks that Hegel is committed by his philosophy. If the attribution is just – and perhaps it is – it serves to show that Hegel's ideas about how freedom is realized were as inadequate as those of the revolutionaries.

The Merits of the Argument

I shall speak more briefly of the merits than of the defects of Hegel's argument, not because the merits are slighter, but because they are more easily explained. The mere exposition of an argument as rich and varied as that of the *Phenomenology* brings its merits to light. But what Hegel says abstractly and obscurely can be put more concretely and lucidly, so that often little else is needed to establish the value of what he says than to translate it into plain English.

a. The Self and its Environment
If we take such Hegelian expressions as 'negation', 'self-development',

'self-estrangement' and 'the self finding itself in what is external to itself' metaphorically, it is often possible to make excellent sense of what Hegel says; and this sense, as I remarked before, is at least part of what he means, though it may still (if we are to believe his admirers) fall far short of his whole meaning. Hegel, for instance, speaks of the self as *negating* what is external to itself when it acts upon it or consumes it. When a man eats something he is said to negate it, and so also when he changes its character to make it useful. If we take 'negating' to mean 'transforming something for a purpose', we do not take it literally but metaphorically; and yet we take it to mean part of what Hegel meant by it. And this is also true, if, by 'self-development', we understand man's developing his potentialities by his actions; and, by 'self-estrangement', his feeling frustrated in society and having a sense of his own unworthiness; and, by 'the self finding itself in what is external to itself', his coming to understand himself in relation to his environment and thereby finding satisfaction. These are not the only meanings of such expressions, even when we take them metaphorically; and therefore, if we are to do justice to Hegel's argument, we must not always translate them the same way. I take these particular examples only as illustrations, though I think they give us the most important meanings of the expressions they translate – or, to speak more cautiously, the most important meanings which the non-Hegelian can accept.

If we interpret those expressions in these ways, we find in the *Phenomenology* an elaborate and suggestive account of how man acquires self-knowledge and self-discipline in the process of reacting to, acting upon and acquiring knowledge of, an environment which he distinguishes from himself and in which he seeks satisfaction. It is by acting in an environment and by acquiring a systematic understanding of it that man becomes a rational and purposeful creature, with a conception of a coherent world and of himself as a person distinct from other persons.

b. *The World and Language*

It is true that this systematic understanding – this capacity to create a coherent picture of a world – depends on the creation of a language, which is the work, not of each man separately, but of many men able to communicate with one another. Language is the product of a community, and every man uses it to acquire knowledge both of an external world and of himself in that world. Man becomes self-conscious, rational, purposeful and moral as a member of a community.

c. Recognition and Self-esteem

It is true also that man is much more than a creature of appetites which he seeks to satisfy. He desires to have value in his own eyes; he needs to have some conception of himself which he finds satisfying. To be assured of his value, he needs to have it recognized by others. He needs self-respect, which he cannot have unless he is respected by others. Admittedly, some men are much stronger than others, and are much less dependent on the good opinion of their neighbours, but this is a strength which they acquire by education, in the process of adapting themselves to a form of communal life. It is an independence which grows out of dependence. A man's self-esteem, no matter how invulnerable, rests on his acceptance of certain values, which he either gets from others by example or precept, or which he evolves for himself in reaction to how others treat him. No man's self-esteem, moreover, is anywhere near being invulnerable; even when he is indifferent to the opinions of most men, there are nearly always some whose opinions he values. There are always some circles in which he could not bear to be despised. Hegel was right in treating the need for recognition as the pre-eminently human need, and also as the pre-eminently educative need in the sense that a man's character is formed largely by what he does in his endeavour to satisfy it. That need for recognition is the need of a self-conscious and rational creature able to see himself as living in a coherent world with other creatures like himself.

d. Man, the Producer and Product of Society

Every social order is a product of human activities which differ in kind from the activities of other animals because men are self-conscious and are capable of speech and communication, and therefore of relations – practical and emotional – of which other animals are incapable. Society is, as Hegel saw, the unintended product of specifically human actions – of actions that are purposeful and involve reasoning. Yet, though man has, in this sense, produced society by his activities, he need not know *how* he has done it, nor even *that* he has done it. He may feel 'estranged' from society; he may be unable to acquire inside it the self-esteem and recognition which he seeks. This phenomenon of estrangement or *Entfremdung* is, psychologically and socially, of the greatest importance. Hegel was the first predominantly secular thinker to give it a name and to try to explain it. We can, I think, see the idea of estrangement already present in the social theory of Rousseau, but it is there, as it were, under the surface and is never brought into the full light of day. There is nothing like a systematic attempt at explaining it. It is not an idea lightly touched upon by Rousseau; he seems to be again and again on the point of making it explicit, and yet never quite succeeds in doing so. He is absorbed by it, and yet does not see it for what it is. Hegel, however, does makes it explicit and gives it a central place in his theory of man and society.

e. *The Rôle of the Unconscious*

In the *Phenomenology* he distinguishes, in many connections, between Spirit as it appears to itself at a certain stage of its evolution and as it really is at that stage; he distinguishes self-conscious mind as it is *for itself* from as it is *in itself*. It is *in itself* what it is *for us* – *we* being the author of the *Phenomenology*, together with those of his readers capable of understanding him. This distinction between the *for itself (für sich)* and the *in itself (an sich)*, if it is applied to the mind, sometimes comes very close to the distinction made by modern psychology between the conscious and the subconscious. Much more than any social theorist before him, Hegel is aware that what man knows about himself is, or may be, only a small part of what there is to know. Everything that goes on in our minds is discoverable, but not therefore discovered; and the process of discovery is long and painful. This is a conclusion to which the *Phenomenology* points as clearly as any contemporary work on psychology.

f. *The Concept of Freedom*

There is a great and important difference between the Greek and the modern conceptions of freedom, which Hegel – if he was not the first to notice it – was the first to emphasize and explain. That difference is, as he said it was, connected with the notion of conscience. In all communities law and custom are disobeyed, but there is a difference between disobedience and rejection. It is one thing to disobey the law when moved by passion or appetite, and quite another to condemn it as unjust. The man who disobeys conscientiously deliberately prefers a higher law to the law which he is required to obey. Condemnation of positive law and custom takes, to begin with, the form of an appeal to the commands of God against the commands of men, and then later becomes an appeal to a law of reason – a law supposedly discoverable by considering what sort of creature man is and what rules of conduct are incumbent upon a creature of his kind. Even if we believe (as Hegel did not) that no rules of conduct derive logically from man's being the sort of creature he is, we can still agree that man, until he has conceived of rules superior to positive law and custom, and has sought to justify them by an appeal to something more than the mere will of God, is incapable of the idea of freedom such as we now have it.

g. Freedom and Law

Where men have this conception of freedom, they cannot in fact be free except in a society in which what is required of them accords with what they think is right or good. Law and custom must not stand in the way of their living what they think is a worthwhile life. If men are to be free, there must be, as a sociologist might put it, harmony between subjective values and imposed norms. And the sociologist would agree with Hegel that subjective values, even where they do not square with imposed norms, are always deeply influenced by them – or, in other words, that a man's conception of what is desirable largely depends on the standards to which, at one time or another, he has been required to conform. Only social creatures can be socially maladjusted – by which I do not mean merely that they must be in society before they can be maladjusted (as a man must wear shoes before he can feel uncomfortable in them), but that they must have values, which can only be acquired in society, before they can have the needs and aspirations which society frustrates. To be consciously unfree and to aspire to freedom, a creature must be self-conscious and must be able to make value-judgements. Therefore only a social and moral creature can be consciously unfree and can desire freedom; and it can only have freedom when what it finds desirable is compatible with what it is required to do.

h. The Social Rôle

No doubt, it is a mistake to call a community a mind or Spirit. Yet those who make this mistake often do so, I suspect, because they have noticed a fact about communities which many fail to notice and which they think supremely important. A community's being a community depends on more than how its members behave; it depends also on how they feel and what they think about it. A human community is not adequately described as a number of persons related to one another in certain ways, or among whom a certain pattern of behaviour prevails. The members of a human community are aware of themselves as being members of it; they are aware also of the relations in which they stand to one another. A human mother does not merely bear children and nurse and protect them; she also knows that she is a mother, and in knowing this is aware of herself as a member of a family. The peculiarity of social relations is that they involve awareness of what they are. This awareness is not, of course, the kind of knowledge that the sociologist aims at; but it is conscious acceptance of a social rôle. A human mother behaves like a human mother because she knows that she is one. Thus, we can say that truly social relations, which exist only between human beings, are what they are because the beings involved in them acknowledge that they are so involved; and there is a sense, therefore, in which a human community is what it is only because it is, as Hegelians would put it, 'reflected' in the minds of its members.

i. The Concept of Ideology

Hegel's conception of systems of beliefs (or, as we should now say, ideologies) whose function is to reconcile men to their social condition or to compensate them for it – systems which would not exist if men were not dissatisfied with that condition – is admirable. It enables him to give a much more plausible explanation of religion than the eighteenth-century philosophers gave. They explained religion as a product of curiosity combined with ignorance, or as arising from the need to appease irrational fear. Hegel explains it as expressing, figuratively, the aspirations of frustrated men. Of course, this is not the whole of his explanation. He insists that religious beliefs are essentially, even though not literally, true – which is to claim more for them than that they express the aspirations of the dissatisfied. But it is, historically, the more important part of his explanation – the part which Feuerbach accepted and developed, and which Marx took over from Feuerbach.

When I say that this conception of ideology is admirable, I do not mean that it gives us the whole truth about religion; I am sure that it does not. But it is a conception which can be applied to much more than religious beliefs. It is a good idea, a fruitful hypothesis. As we find it in Hegel, this conception, moreover, is free of several of the defects which spoil the Marxian theory of ideology. There is no suggestion in Hegel that the function of ideology is primarily to support class interests, or that it is to be dismissed as fantasy because it serves to reconcile the dissatisfied to their condition. Yet Hegel agrees with Marx that it is only because men cannot find happiness in this world that they imagine another and aspire to it.

Those who have faith, in perhaps a deeper sense than Hegel had it, would not deny that faith helps to reconcile man to his worldly condition; they would not deny that unhappiness often inspires a man with faith, and that faith makes him less unhappy. And they mostly would not claim that the articles of their faith are to be taken quite literally. They would be inclined to admit that some of these articles mean more, to the literal-minded, than they appear to say. But they would deny that man has faith *only* because he is dissatisfied in this world; they would assert that man, even if he got in this world all the satisfaction he could get, would still need faith.

j. The Idea of Progress

Progress, as Hegel conceives of it, is an altogether richer idea than we find in any social theorist before him. The idea of progress, as we find it in Condorcet, is simpler, shallower and less suggestive. Hegel's account of it is more impressive, both in its central theme and in its details. I have no wish to praise mere size and complexity. It is astonishing how much Hegel knew or guessed at. In criticizing so vast and so pretentious a theory, and a theory vulnerable on so many different grounds, it is easy to lose sight of what makes it admirable: the grandeur of its conception and the originality and subtlety of many of its arguments. A vast theory is almost certain to have many faults, and sometimes has few virtues. But Hegel's theory abounds in virtues as in faults. Unfortunately, men are not builders with ideas as they are with bricks and stones; any vast and elaborate intellectual structure which they put up is almost bound to be shoddy. So it is with the *Phenomenology of Spirit*; many of its deductions are plays on words, and others are trivial or silly. In England, and more particularly in Oxford, we are not trained to make the best of such a thinker as Hegel. We are easily put off by his arrogance and his obscurity, and we are disgusted by the poverty or (as it sometimes seems to us) the dishonesty of his arguments. His faults strike us first and blind us to his virtues. Among philosophers interested in man as a moral and social creature, there have been not a few who are more lucid, more self-critical and more rigorous than Hegel. But has there been another as imaginative since Plato?

III. WORLD HISTORY

Hegel's *Philosophy of History* is much simpler and easier to read than his *Phenomenology of Spirit*. It is not an account, in the abstract, of how Spirit progresses to complete self-knowledge; it deals with historical events and actual societies. Thus it deals with what is already familiar to us. It purports to explain these events and societies as manifestations of Spirit, and often uses abstract language when speaking of Spirit; but we can always, if we are at a loss to understand that language, turn to what Hegel says about the Greeks or the Romans or the Germans in the hope of getting his meaning. His arguments in the abstract and his versions of actual events throw light upon one another. Moreover, the form of the *Lectures on the Philosophy of History*, as the title indicates, is more popular; Hegel was concerned to make himself understood by an audience which was not necessarily familiar with his philosophy. The version which we have of these lectures is not even directly from the pen of Hegel and was never revised by him. It was put together after his death mostly from notes taken down by those who listened to him. Hence a certain carelessness in the arguments, as well as many gaps. The *Philosophy of History*, though much more readable, is also, when closely studied, much less impressive than either *the Phenomenology of Spirit* or *The Philosophy of Right* – the other two works of special interest to the social and political theorist.

Though the *Phenomenology* is not, properly speaking, a philosophy of history – because it makes no open reference to historical events – it is, as we have seen, largely inspired by historical events, and by actual philosophies, religions and forms of communal life, as they appeared to Hegel. Therefore, if I were to expound the general argument of the *Lectures on the Philosophy of History*, I should inevitably be repeating much that I have already said in discussing the *Phenomenology*. I shall thus confine myself to matters not treated of in the *Phenomenology* or only lightly touched upon, and which seem to me to raise issues worth discussing. Hegel was a considerably older man when he gave the *Lectures on the Philosophy of History*, and the state of Europe was then very different from what it had been when, at the height of Napoleon's power, he wrote the *Phenomenology*.

The *Philosophy of History*, if we compare it with the *Phenomenology*, makes it clear how heavily, in his account of progress, Hegel relies on European experience. It also emphasizes the importance of great men, the special qualities and destiny of the Germanic peoples, the superiority of Protestantism over Catholicism and the defects of liberalism. It reveals, much more obviously than the *Phenomenology*, how selective Hegel's method is: how he takes notice only of what suits his purpose, or else how, where he cannot ignore what does not suit it, he twists it to make it suitable. There is no process of social transformation described in the *Philosophy of History*; we are told how a number of societies are manifestations of different phases of Spirit – how they form different stages in the evolution of mankind. But how one type of society gives way to another is not explained.

1. Hegel's European Bias

We have seen that the *Phenomenology* is an account of progress in the abstract, purporting to show how the self-conscious mind moves necessarily through certain phases until it attains complete self-knowledge and satisfaction. Though the account is abstract, we soon notice, if we consider these phases, that there are historical events and practices corresponding to them. But we perhaps do not notice that the events and practices are nearly all European. Only when he discusses the Unhappy Consciousness[1] and natural religion[2] does Hegel appear to have non-European examples in mind. We know from his earlier writings that he thought of Judaism as a form of self-estranged Spirit, so that the Unhappy Consciousness is Jewish as well as Christian; and it is clear that what Hegel calls natural religion (which is not to be confused with natural religion as philosophers and theologians conceived of it in the seventeenth and eighteenth centuries)[3] is more Asian and Egyptian than European. And yet, though it is almost entirely on European experience that the *Phenomenology* rests, this fact is not brought home to us because the whole argument is so abstract. We are told that natural religion is inferior to aesthetic religion, but we are not told that natural religion is Asiatic and Egyptian while aesthetic religion is Greek. We are told that a certain type of religion is the highest of all, but we are not told that that type is Christianity, and so it is not brought home to us that the highest type of religion flourishes in Europe.

The *Philosophy of History* takes much larger account of non-European experience than does the *Phenomenology*, but – precisely because it makes open reference to actual societies, forms of art, religions and philosophies – it drives home how entirely European are the institutions and attitudes of mind which Hegel believes are necessarily the highest. Spirit attains self-knowledge and satisfaction in Europe. The essence of reality is Mind or Spirit, moving necessarily towards self-knowledge, freedom and satisfaction, which it attains in the civilization to which Hegel belongs. Though he is often ingenious in his distinctions between one oriental culture or religion and another, he treats them all as inferior to Greek civilization. He discusses four worlds or civilizations – the Oriental, the Greek, the Roman and the

---

[1] *Phenomenology of Spirit*, §§ 206–30, pp. 126–38.
[2] Ibid., §§ 684–98, pp. 416–24.
[3] They meant by natural religion beliefs about God attested by reason alone and not by revelation, whereas Hegel meant by it the attribution of divine or spiritual qualities to animals or the sun or stars or other natural phenomena.

German; and though it may be open to question whether he considers the third superior to the second, it is abundantly clear that he regards the first as the lowest and the fourth as the highest. Oriental civilization is the lowest because it is the furthest removed from the realization of freedom, defined as the concordance of the conscientious and rational will of the individual with the laws and customs of his community. In other words, it is the lowest because the furthest from realizing a European ideal. But Hegel cannot admit that it is the lowest merely from the European point of view; he cannot allow that this European ideal is one of several, of which none is intrinscially superior to the others. For that would be to admit that the European ideal is parochial or provincial, whereas he thinks he has proved that it follows from the very nature of Mind that it is the highest ideal. But to anyone who cannot accept this proof, the *Philosophy of History* necessarily wears a provincial look; it sets up the standard of one part of mankind to judge all mankind.

It was no novelty, in Hegel's day, for Europeans to treat non-European ways and ideals as inferior to their own. Montesquieu, so much praised for his breadth of mind and freedom from prejudice, was not less convinced than Hegel of European superiority. But Montesquieu merely took that superiority for granted. He never sought to prove that European ideals were the best; he was content to find in climate and geography obstacles in the way of other peoples attaining those ideals or even coming to conceive of them. Indeed, he made excuses for them; he explained why through no fault of their own they could not be like the Europeans. His was the plain, unmetaphysical arrogance of the Frenchman or the Englishman.

2. World–Historical Individuals

In the *Philosophy of History*, Hegel speaks of *World–Historical Individuals*[1] who are, if I may so put it, chosen vessels of the Spirit. By their actions they help to change accepted institutions and ways of thought; they help to establish new forms which reveal Spirit at a higher level. Hegel sometimes speaks of these great men as if they had a deeper insight than their contemporaries into 'the needs of the age', while on other occasions he suggests that they need not have this insight but may act from selfish or wicked motives, or be shortsighted. They may fail to achieve what they set out to achieve, and yet, by their actions – though

---

[1] See the *Philosophy of History*, trans. J. Sibree (New York 1956 edition), especially the introduction, pp. 29–33.

neither they nor their contemporaries know it – they contribute to the progress of Spirit. Hegel speaks of Reason working through them; he speaks of *the cunning of Reason*,[1] using men for purposes of which they know nothing. Though the chosen vessels of the Spirit are not always worthy vessels, they serve their turn.

What are we to make of all this? What is involved in having a deeper insight into 'the needs of the age'? This is not, I think, an empty phrase; some men do have a deeper insight than others into the needs of their time. Some, like Socrates, see further than was seen before them into human nature or into the condition of man in society, and propose remedies for human ills. They are the wisest men of all; they have the deepest insight. Others, like Luther, without perhaps seeing much further than their neighbours into man's nature and his social predicament, make claims never made before, or never at so opportune a moment. They too are wise, though in a lesser degree; they too can plausibly be said to have a deeper insight into the needs of their times, for they have judgement enough to see that the claims they make will receive wide support. They have a sense of what is troubling men and what claims will find a response.

Men can have this wisdom or deeper insight, in the higher as much as in the lower degree, without in the least seeing how their wisdom contributes to the realization of freedom. If, then, we believe that freedom, as Hegel conceived of it, is desirable, and that men's wisdom has in fact contributed to its achievement, we call such men agents of progress. Yet, when we do so, we give them a title they never aspired to, and which perhaps would have been meaningless to them; for they did not understand, as we do, the historical significance of their wisdom. Indeed, if the Hegelian philosophy is true, it follows that men, until they come near to Hegel's time, cannot understand the historical significance of what they do; for freedom (and whatever comes with it) is fully intelligible only when it is on the point of being achieved. The further men are from its achievement, then (no matter how wise they may be) the less they can understand it. The course of history, which Hegel says is a progress towards freedom, cannot be seen to be so by those involved in it until the process is near to completion.

What of the men who are no wiser than their own generation, who see no further into human nature or the social condition than other men, but who are, nevertheless, called great men? Though they act from ambition and even from worse motives, they too can be

[1] Ibid., p. 33.

agents of progress. Without knowing that they do so, they may set in motion processes which in fact contribute to the achievement of freedom. Indeed, they may contribute more to it than the men of deeper insight. What is Hegel's attitude to them? They are, he admits, justly condemned by the standards of their time. But this much could also be said of the wise men. By the standards of their time they too are justly condemned, and not the less justly because they have seen a need to change those standards.

Hegel admits that the merely ambitious are justly condemned, and yet seeks also to justify them without troubling to distinguish between them and the truly wise. Now, it does, I think, make sense to say that Socrates, though justly condemned by the standards of his time, was nevertheless justified, because he acted by different standards which those who say he was justified believe to be higher. They do not blame the men who condemned him, but they say that Socrates was right to conform to standards which he believed to be higher, and they also say that they share his belief. But the merely ambitious do not conform to standards which both they and Hegel (who seeks to justify them) believe to be higher. Their actions are bad by the standards of their own day and by Hegel's standards, and they have no standards of their own which they sincerely believe to be higher than the standards that condemn them. It makes no sense to say of them that they are justified. Even in the community which is truly free – in Hegel's sense of freedom – such actions as theirs are condemned. Of Socrates it could be said that he asserted principles which a later age accepted – even though his own age rejected them; and this, to the believer in progress, is a justification of Socrates. But Socrates is justified, not because by his actions he helped (though he did not know it) bring about something good, but because his actions were right by standards which were already his and which those who justify him accept.

If great men who are ambitious or wicked can be justified merely because the unforeseen consequences of their actions are good, then so too can little men. If thousands of petty criminals by their crimes produce unintended good, they are as much justified as the great criminal. This is a conclusion we cannot avoid if we accept justification in Hegel's peculiar sense. Yet I feel sure that Hegel would never have accepted it. He aspired to greatness and sympathized with the great, even in their crimes. He took it for granted that all important change, especially change for the good, is due to the initiative of great men, or rather (and this for him comes to the same thing) of men who have made a great name for themselves; it did not occur to him that it may just as often be due to the actions of large numbers of little men with no great individual among them to move them to action.[1]

3. The German World

By the German world, Hegel means the civilization which emerged in the West after the spread of Christianity and the invasions of the Roman Empire by the barbarians. Thus the German world includes Italy, Spain and France. The peoples belonging to it are of mixed origin, as Hegel well knew, and it might therefore seem that there is no racial or national pride behind his use of the word German in this context. Perhaps he calls the fourth of his civilizations *German* merely because it resulted from the invasion of the Roman Empire by German tribes; perhaps he uses the word merely to refer to a type of society or culture. He could hardly call it Christian, for the Slavs are not less Christian than the West Europeans, and yet they have no place in this fourth civilization; and he may not have wanted to call it simply Western because the Roman Empire, his third civilization, was also in large part western.

I would not deny that this is one reason why Hegel speaks of a German world, But it is not the only reason. He also attributes to the Germans a special quality, which he calls *Gemüth*, and which he clearly thinks of as a native quality of the German people – the *Volk* – and not as a quality acquired by men who belong to a certain kind of civilization, no matter what their racial origin.[2] *Gemüth*, or heart, is – in his eyes – a racial characteristic. Again, he speaks of the 'time-honoured sincerity' of the Germans.[3] He says that they need Christianity to discipline them but also suggests that they are somehow destined by their inborn qualities to raise Christianity to its highest level. Protestantism is, he thinks, German, and is also a higher form of Christianity than Catholicism.

Within the German world, Hegel distinguishes the pure German peoples (the Germans, the Scandinavians, the Dutch and the English) from the Romanic peoples (the French, the Italians and the Spaniards), and claims for them that – having achieved in Protestantism a deeper sense of freedom than the Romanic peoples – they do not need to make a revolution of the kind made by the French in 1789.

[1] Sir Isaiah Berlin suggests that I have not allowed enough for Hegel's idea of great men as artists who 'understand the material they work in' – the situation they dominate and affect – though they may not be able to describe it. Having genius, they are better instruments of Reason than are masses of lesser men.
[2] *Philosophy of History*, IV.i.1, pp. 350–2.
[3] Ibid., IV.iii.1, p. 414.

Hegel has been criticized for his nationalism and racialism, in my opinion too harshly. Nationalism takes with him a comparatively harmless form, and if other writers later twisted his doctrines to suit their purposes, he is not to blame. But we ought to notice that the considerable traces of nationalism and racialism to be found in Hegel's writings are in no way logically connected with his philosophy. The notion of Spirit making itself actual in world history does not entail that pure peoples are any better adapted than mixed peoples to achieving higher forms of Spirit. For the purposes of Hegel's theory, the *Volk*, whether it constitutes one or several political communities, does not need to be pure. Hegel admits that the ancient Greeks, whom he greatly admires, were of mixed origins, and yet he treats them as one people. If the Greeks did not attain the highest levels of Spirit, this was due to their place in history, coming before the Germans, and not to their mixed origins. Not until he comes to consider the German world does Hegel feel the need to prefer pure peoples to mixed ones. It was a need still unexpressed (and perhaps unfelt) when Napoleon was at the height of his power and Hegel was writing the *Phenomenology*; it comes to the fore only with the German revolt against Napoleon and the defeat of the French. As a show of feeling it is neither unnatural nor contemptible; it is merely out of place in a philosophy of history of the Hegelian kind.

It seems never to have occurred to Hegel that the German-speaking peoples were as much Catholic as Protestant, and that the Catholics among them were not less German than the others. Indeed, it is in the most stoutly Protestant parts of Germany – in Saxony, Brandenburg, Pomerania and East Prussia – that the admixture of Slav blood is the greatest. It is also odd to call the English a pure German people, seeing how much they are Celtic as well as German by racial origins; and the Welsh and the Scots are even more so, and yet are more fiercely Protestant than the English.

4. Hegel's Protestant Bias

I would not quarrel with Hegel for preferring Protestantism to Catholicism. That is his own affair. But some of the grounds of this preference seem to me mistaken. It is the special merit of Luther, Hegel tells us, that he first clearly put forward the claim to freedom implicit in the notion of conscience – the claim that a man must be inwardly convinced of the rightness and truth of the rules and doctrines he accepts. The priesthood of all believers is, he thinks, a doctrine of freedom, and it is clearly Protestant rather than

Catholic. Since Spirit in its maturity is free, Protestantism is a higher form of Spirit than Catholicism; it puts the honest conviction of the believer in the place of external authority.

To this argument there are two objections. In the first place, Luther did not understand the full implications of his own doctrine, because in practice he denied anyone's right to read into Holy Scripture what he (Luther) said was not there. He allowed some room for honest differences of opinion, but took it upon himself to set the limits to that room. Secondly, the Catholic Church also expects its adherents to be honestly convinced of its authority; it puts a value on inward conviction and not on mere obedience and outward conformity from no matter what motive. It offers reasons for accepting its authority. If it is true that it matters what men believe, and not merely that their beliefs should be sincere – if it is the case (as Luther did not deny) that there is a truth necessary to salvation – then it is reasonable to suppose that God established an authority on earth to ensure that this truth was brought to men.

The first of these objections is less important than the second. Hegel was very willing to admit that the full implications of an epoch-making doctrine are not understood by the persons who initially put it forward. It is true that Luther would not in practice, in spite of his proclaiming the priesthood of all believers, agree that no one must be molested for the way in which he interprets Holy Scripture, and that he rejected, even more harshly, the plea that anyone has the right to deny the Scriptures as untrue or irrelevant. Yet the claim, that every Christian (that is, everyone who honestly believes that the Scriptures reveal the Will of God) is entitled to interpret the Scriptures, was of momentous significance and did, in the long run, make for freedom.

The second objection is more serious. In practice, Catholic priests may often be content with mere obedience and outward conformity among their flock; but as much could be said of Protestant pastors, Catholics do not hold that anyone who is received into their Church, no matter what his motive, will be saved provided he is obedient; they hold, as much as Protestants do, that only sincere belief is acceptable to God. If Hegel had been more anxious to be fair as between Protestantism and Catholicism, he might have noticed that – though the doctrine of the priesthood of all believers has the seeds of freedom in it – the Protestant doctrine of grace (whether Lutheran or Calvinist) is more illiberal than the Catholic. The doctrine that a man must deserve grace in order to obtain it is nearer being Catholic than Protestant. The orthodox Lutheran (not to speak of the Calvinist), if we compare him with the Catholic, is much nearer believing that whether a Christian has the faith necessary to salvation depends entirely on whether he receives the grace of God and not on how he exercises his freedom of choice.

Hegel considered both the separation of Church and State and the division, within the Church, of priests from laymen as necessary stages in the evolution of Spirit. If certain feelings and ideas which men have about themselves are to reach full maturity, there must be a Church separate from the State. The Christian idea of man is deeper and richer – more adequate to reality – than the Greek or Roman idea, and it needed a Church in order to reach full expression. The separation of the Church from the State serves to preserve and to deepen aspirations that, in the society in which there is that separation, cannot yet be realized. The division of the Church into priests and laymen is a mark that men – though they have acknowledged their duty to realize these aspirations (an acknowledgement expressed in the form of a desire to serve God) – are still too weak and ignorant to realize them. The aspirations are there, kept alive and enriched by the Church, but still lacking are the disciplined will and the mature understanding needed to make them come true. In the vision of Heaven, the Church preserves ideals which mankind are destined to achieve in this world. As Spirit progresses, or (and this for Hegel is the same thing) as its capacity to seek and find satisfaction in this world increases, both these divisions – that of the Church from the State and that of priests from laymen – become less marked. The State achieves the possible while the Church aspires towards the ideal, and as the ideal becomes possible the separation of Church and State loses its importance. In Protestant countries, that separation, and the division between priests and laymen, are of less account than in Catholic countries, and this, for Hegel, is a mark of Protestant superiority.

He says that in the Catholic Church the priest is a mediator between the layman and God, and he even speaks as if he believed that the lay Catholic does not venture to communicate directly with God but only indirectly through the priest. Did he really believe that Catholic priests discourage prayer? Or that lay Catholics pray only to the saints and not to God? Hegel knew that the Lutheran pastor, when he administers the sacraments or gives spiritual guidance, endeavours to bring the faithful closer to God and not to stand as a screen between them. Why then should he suppose that the Catholic priest acts with a different intention? In all this I see much prejudice and little reason.

Except for the doctrine of the priesthood of all believers, I see nothing about Protestantism – in either its Lutheran or Calvinist form – which accords better than Catholicism does with Hegel's conception of freedom.[1] The Protestant doctrine of grace, especially in its Calvinist form, accords with it less well; and what could be less Hegelian in spirit than Luther's doctrine of justification by faith? No one believed more than Hegel that a man is justified by his works – that it matters more what he does than what he claims, however sincerely, to believe. It is indeed a Hegelian principle that the real quality of a man's faith is revealed only in his works.

5. His Dislike of Democracy

Hegel regarded himself as the philosopher of freedom. The world, he said, is essentially Spirit, and Spirit is essentially free. Yet he was not attracted to liberalism or to democracy. Why was this so?

Freedom, as he conceived it, is realized in a community wherein what law and custom prescribe accords with the dictates of the individual conscience – or, in other words, where the individual can live as he sincerely believes that he ought to live. Now, this conception of freedom is very much the same as Rousseau's; it is implicit in the doctrine of the general will. Rousseau believed that freedom can be realized only in a community all of whose members take part in making the law. Hegel disagreed with him, but the grounds of his disagreement are not made altogether clear.

That a democratic society *may not* realize freedom, in Hegel's sense of it, is obvious; and yet it may be that freedom in his sense can be realized fully only in a democracy. Hegel considers the first possibility and not the second; he sees the dangers of democracy but not its opportunities. In the *Philosophy of History* he does not so much argue against democracy as exhibit his distaste for it. He says that the 'abstract' French doctrine of the rights of man is too individualistic, treating men too much as atoms. He objects to what he calls 'the atomistic principle, which insists on the sway of individual wills, maintaining that all government should emanate from their express power, and have their express sanction'.[2] Liberalism (by which he means partiality for the abstract doctrine of the rights of man) has, he thinks, a special appeal in Catholic countries, where it is a weapon against the Church, but elsewhere it is going 'bankrupt'.[3]

This line of criticism, which is common to Hegel and Burke,

[1] No doubt, some of the sects preached doctrines more liberal than either Lutheranism or Calvinism, but Hegel says nothing of them.
[2] *Philosophy of History*, IV.iii. 3, p. 452.
[3] Ibid.

seems to me irrelevant. What is the point of calling the doctrine of the rights of man 'abstract' and 'atomistic'? Any doctrine which attributes rights to individuals is, in a quite obvious sense, 'atomistic'; it is a doctrine about individuals, about the 'atoms' which compose the social whole, and not about groups or communities or institutions. To call it atomistic or individualistic, in this sense, is merely to define it; it is not to make a criticism of it. The doctrine that all sane adults should have the vote is no more 'atomistic' than the doctrine that nobody with less than £1000 a year should have it. It is also no more and no less abstract, for it makes a claim for individuals considered apart from the actual situations in which they are placed.

Hegel's criticism of the doctrine of the rights of man ceases to be pointless only if it is interpreted as meaning that those who assert this doctrine are unaware of the difficulties in the way of putting it into effect, or else do not see that the rights they claim for all men would – if all men had them – prevent their getting the freedom they strive for or ought to strive for or will come eventually to desire. But, as a matter of fact, many liberals were well aware of these difficulties, and differed from Hegel only in believing that they could be surmounted. There is nothing atomistic or abstract about this belief. It may be mistaken or it may not, and Hegel produces no arguments to show that it is so. A liberal or a democrat might accept the Hegelian conception of freedom (and even the metaphysics associated with it) and might then insist that freedom, thus conceived, cannot be achieved unless the rights of man are made good.

He might insist on this with a good show of reason. Freedom, as Hegel conceives of it, is not habitual obedience to law and custom; it is a conscientious and critical acceptance of them. It could plausibly be argued, as Rousseau tried to argue, that such acceptance is possible only in a democracy. Hegel produces no arguments that could be used to prove Rousseau wrong; at least, he produces none in the *Philosophy of History*. Hegel's condemnation of democracy rests on the same line of false reasoning as Burke's. The democrats assert that democracy is a condition of freedom. Burke and Hegel reply that where there is democracy, freedom is faced with peculiar and great dangers. Their reply, as a warning to democrats is timely; but as a condemnation of democracy it is pointless unless it is shown that the dangers are insurmountable.

6. Stagnation and Progress

We have seen that, in Hegel's opinion, progress is necessary: Spirit is essentially active, and moves necessarily from phase to phase until it reaches full self-knowledge and satisfaction. Why, then, we may ask, should some peoples (e.g. the Oriental peoples) be unprogressive? Why should they be confined to expressing Spirit only in its less developed forms? They are not late-comers on the stage of history. On the contrary, they are the first peoples to have been civilized. The march of progress, as Hegel imagines it, is a kind of relay race, with some peoples taking up where others have left off. The idea that it is just such a race may perhaps be true, or partly true, but it certainly does not accord with Hegel's belief that progress is a necessary and dialectical process.

The various forms – psychological, social and ideological – in which Spirit is manifest, develop (so Hegel would have us believe) contradictions of which Spirit eventually becomes conscious and which it therefore surmounts, thus moving inevitably from phase to phase. These forms and contradictions, and the consciousness of them, exist only in and through finite rational minds – or, in other words, in and through men. We should therefore expect every people to move necessarily from one phase of Spirit to another. We should expect a people to progress as long as it continues in existence; for while it exists it is involved in the life of the Spirit, which is necessarily progressive. We should not expect it to go so far and no further. We should not expect it to stagnate.

And why, if it does stagnate, should some other people carry on from the point where it left off? Each phase, we are told, develops out of the phase before it, and we are also told that each phase is manifest in the life of a community of rational beings. How, then, if one phase is manifest in one community can the next phase be manifest in another, which has not even passed through the earlier phase? Or, if we concede that this is possible, how can we say that one phase develops necessarily out of another? Let us suppose that men, if they reach a certain pitch of anger, necessarily resort to violence. That being so, if James reaches that pitch of anger, it is he who is necessarily violent, and not John.

It might be said, in defence of Hegel, that one people or community can assimilate the experience of another. It might be said that the Romans assimilated the experience of the Greeks and even (though less plausibly) that the 'Germans' assimilated the experience of the Greeks and the Romans. But it can hardly be said that the Greeks assimilated the experience of the Oriental peoples, all of whom – so Hegel tells us – manifest phases of Spirit prior to the Greek phase. No doubt, the Greeks were stimulated by their contacts with the Egyptians and with the peoples of Asia Minor; but it is a far cry from this kind of stimulation to the assimilation needed to save Hegel's theory. The Greeks never absorbed the cultures of the East, and Hegel does not even pretend that they did. The Oriental peoples lived through certain phases of Spirit, and the ancient Greeks lived through certain other and higher phases. It was necessary that the lower Oriental phases should come first, and that the higher Greek phases should emerge out of them, but it was apparently not necessary that the Greeks should absorb the cultures of the Orient; it was enough that they should be stimulated by them. This I find unacceptable. I do not doubt for a moment that there are unexplained mysteries in the real world. But there ought to be none in the world as Hegel explains it; for it is his belief that the world, which is the progress of Spirit, is not only intelligible in principle but is also in fact understood – that is, by Hegel and by those who understand him.

Whatever our idea of progress, we can always find some peoples who cease to make progress, who stagnate. We may also, if we study the available facts carefully, be able to discover the causes of the stagnation. We may do this even if we accept Hegel's idea of freedom, and therefore believe that anything makes for progress which helps to achieve that idea. There must be reasons why the Oriental peoples ceased to make what Hegel called progress. But these reasons, if we could discover them, would be evidence against the truth of his philosophy of history, for they would show how a certain phase of Spirit failed to give rise to the phase which, according to him, necessarily comes after it. There must also be reasons why the Greeks reached what in the Hegelian scale is a higher phase of Spirit than the Orientals, without needing to assimilate Oriental culture, and these reasons, too – if we could find them – would be evidence against Hegel's theory.

His philosophy of history differs in one important respect from Marx's. There is, Hegel tells us, a necessary course of development of Spirit, which he describes, abstractly and without open reference to particular events, in the *Phenomenology of Spirit*. In the *Philosophy of History*, he gives concrete examples of Spirit in various phases of its progress; he discusses these phases in what he believes to be their logical and necessary order. But, even in the *Philosophy of History*, he makes not the least attempt to show how a society in one of these phases passes into the next; he never describes a process of *social transformation*. All that he does is give us a series of tableaux; and this is as true when he is speaking of European as of Oriental civilizations. He presents the Greek world to us as a manifestation of

Spirit at one level, and he shows what, at that level, Spirit was still lacking. He then presents the Roman world to us, showing how it differed from the Greek. Finally, he presents to us the German world, explaining it as the fullest and deepest manifestation of Spirit. It is true that he shows us (or at least attempts to show us) that the German world has absorbed and transcended the Greek and Roman worlds. But he never attempts to show how the Greek world was transformed into the Roman world, or how the ancient world was transformed into the modern. Spirit necessarily attains full self-knowledge and satisfaction, and in order to attain them must pass through certain phases. First there is one phase, and then the next, and then the next, and so on to Spirit's full flowering. We are told that it must be so, because such is Spirit's nature; the world is not intelligible unless it is Spirit, and since the world is intelligible it therefore is Spirit. Yet there is nothing about any phase, as Hegel describes it, which explains why the next *must* come after it; we only know that it must because the full maturity of Spirit, which is inevitable, requires that it should. But this explanation is absurd, for unless each phase leads necessarily to the next, the full maturity of Spirit is not inevitable.

Whatever the shortcomings of Marx's philosophy of history, he at least does not confine himself to presenting us with a series of tableaux, each an image of something higher than the one before it. He describes a process of social transformation, and tries to explain how it happens – how one phase of it gives way to the next.

CHAPTER TWO

The Social and Political Philosophy of Hegel   II

I. HEGEL'S THEORY OF THE STATE

1. General Observations

a. Why Man Needs Freedom

Spirit, Hegel tells us, is made actual in communities of finite rational minds. As we have seen already, it does not follow from this that Spirit is a mind in the same sense as Socrates or Luther was one. Yet what does follow from it is – for reasons which I tried to give earlier – unacceptable; it entails taking literally what only makes sense metaphorically. The State, says Hegel, is the highest type of community in which Spirit is made actual, and Spirit is made actual necessarily. Spirit, he tells us, is essentially free.

If we take all this metaphorically, forgoing resolutely (or with reluctance) the deeper wisdom which it may contain for those who find it possible to take it literally, what can we make of it? We must, I think, interpret Hegel's meaning thus: Since man is a rational and self-conscious creature capable of deliberate choice, he puts a supreme value on freedom, which he can attain only in the State. This is not the whole Hegelian doctrine of the State, even when that doctrine is taken metaphorically, but it is fundamental to it. Put thus succinctly, it is not self-explanatory; it calls for elucidation and elaboration.

b. Society an Unintended Product of Human Action

Hegel also says that the State is *objective will*, and he calls freedom, which is realized in the State, *the will that wills itself*.[1] These expressions

---

[1] See his *Philosophy of Right*, op. cit., especially § § 258 and 270, pp. 155–7 and 164–5.

could mislead us into believing that Hegel thought that man has created the State in order to get or to preserve freedom. But, as we have seen in studying the *Phenomenology*, this is not so. Hegel believes that man does not even fully understand freedom until the process which brings it about is almost complete. According to his philosophy it is only as members of a community, as creatures belonging to a moral and political order, that men come to conceive of freedom and to desire it. Though he speaks of Spirit creating the world in which it is made actual, and also speaks of it as existing only in and through finite minds, he does not think of these finite minds as deliberately creating the world. On the contrary, the world, in so far as it is produced by finite minds, is the *unintended* product of their activities.

We are not, for the moment, interested in the whole world but in society, which is only a part of the world. We may then say that, in Hegel's opinion, society is the unintended product of men's activities. If men did not have the potentialities they do have, there could be no society; but equally, if it were not for society, men would not realize their potentialities. By their activities they produce their social environment, and, in the process of doing so, they transform themselves, becoming rational and purposeful creatures capable of deliberately pursuing, within a social order, what they have come to believe is desirable. That Hegel calls this process logical makes no difference here; for by calling it so he does not mean to imply that men have deliberately produced society in order to get what they want.

The contemporary sociologist, while rejecting or ignoring Hegelian metaphysics and the claim that social evolution is a logically necessary process, might accept Hegel's account of how man produces society and what society does for him. He might agree that primitive society is the undeliberate, unforeseen and uncomprehended product of human activities, and that men acquire, in the process of being formed by society, the purposes and the knowledge – theoretical and practical – which make rational and moral creatures of them. It is only then that men, educated in society, can conceive of projects to change it.

The sociologist's main objection to Hegel might be that he speaks too often of the State where he ought to speak of society. It is not the same thing to say that man becomes rational, moral and freedom-loving in the State, as to say that he becomes so in society. Hegel's doctrine of the State is open to serious criticism. But it is not open to the criticism that he looks upon the State as a product of human will, or that he thinks of it as existing to provide for needs or appetites which men could have outside society.

c. *Morality and Freedom*

Hegel, as we have seen, makes much of man's self-consciousness and of his rationality. These two qualities are, he thinks, closely connected; only a creature capable of abstraction and comparison – capable of using concepts – can distinguish between itself and what is external to itself, including other selves. It can also distinguish between itself as a subject of thoughts and desires and the thoughts and desires of which it is a subject. Because it is conscious of itself as a subject of desires, it is led inevitably to seek an end which is more than the satisfaction of one desire after another. For it soon discovers that all its desires cannot be satisfied, and that some must be sacrificed to others. It learns to think ahead, to compare its desires, to consider the chances of satisfying them and the consequences of attempting to satisfy them. Nor can the self stop at establishing a system of preferences among its desires; for it is aware that there are other beings besides itself whose needs and actions it must take into account. It must adapt itself to other selves; it must adapt itself to a community of selves. If this adaptation took the form of mere prudence, with each person trying to get for himself whatever he could safely or conveniently get, every man would think of other men as standing in the way of his getting more. Man can be fully satisfied, completely free, in a community only when what he wants is compatible with what other people want. But this, in practice, involves more than just learning to do without what he cannot get; it involves more than just putting up with rules which restrict his actions for the sake of others and their actions for his sake; it involves more than the sense of getting as good terms from others as he can in the circumstances reasonably expect to get. It involves accepting the rules inwardly; it involves desiring the public good and the moral order for their own sakes. The man who respects the rules with nothing in view other than his own advantage acts, as Hobbes said, reasonably. But reasonable though he may be, he is not truly satisfied; for he gets, not *all* that he wants, but as much as he can safely and conveniently have. If he could get everything that he wanted, he would be better satisfied, or he imagines that he would be; he reconciles himself to what he can get only because he cannot reasonably expect to get more.

But if he accepts the rules inwardly – if he desires justice, if he wants to be a good neighbour and a good citizen – then he may be fully satisfied. For then he is not reasonable and just merely for the sake of satisfying as many as possible of his desires; he actually desires to be reasonable and just. He seeks satisfaction in a way of life which is capable of giving complete satisfaction. In practice it may be difficult to get this satisfaction, but in principle it is possible. A community of completely selfish persons, no matter how reasonable they were, could not be fully satisfied; but a community of moral persons, provided they were reasonable, could be. Now, for Hegel, to be fully satisfied is the mark of freedom. Man is fully satisfied when he knows what he wants, endeavours rationally to obtain it, and succeeds. But man cannot be free in society unless he desires to be just and his conception of justice accords with the established order; and again, he cannot be free unless he desires justice as much as ends private to himself, and unless those ends accord with his notion of justice. Yet again, man cannot be free outside society, for it is in society that he acquires purposes which he can rationally pursue; and it is also in society that he comes to conceive of freedom and to desire it.

Hegel remarks, in the *Philosophy of Right*, 'If we hear it said that the definition of freedom is the ability to do what we please, such an idea can only be taken to reveal an utter immaturity of thought, for it contains not even an inkling of the absolutely free will, of right, ethical life, and so forth';[1] and he also says that 'it is only as thinking intelligence that the will is genuinely a will and free'.[2] Freedom is the ability to do what we deliberately choose to do, and is conceivable only to creatures who live in a moral order. They cannot attain freedom, moreover, until that order is one that seems good to them, desirable for its own sake and not only as a means to their private ends.

d. Morality and Rationality

Actually, Hegel is not content to say that man, if he is to get full satisfaction, cannot stop at establishing an order of preferences among his desires; he also says that it is only as a moral person that man can establish such an order rationally. To the extent that man is moved only by impulses and appetites, he has what Hegel calls an arbitrary will. We are told that 'the contradiction which the arbitrary will is . . . comes into appearance as a dialectic of impulses and inclinations; each of them is in the way of every other – the satisfaction of one is unavoidably . . . sacrificed to the satisfaction of another. An impulse . . . has no measuring-rod in itself, and so this determination of its . . . sacrifice is the contingent decision of the arbitrary will'.[3] In other words, it is not a rational decision. Only after a man has become a moral being, after he has acquired some values, can he rationally prefer some of his impulses to others.

[1] Ibid., § 15, p. 27.
[2] Iid., § 21, p. 30.
[3] Ibid., § 17, p. 28.

Hegel therefore thinks himself entitled to conclude that only a rational (which is for him also a moral) will is free. The arbitrary will, wanting incompatible things, is necessarily frustrated time and again. The rational will, which does not aim at the satisfaction of one impulse after another but seeks rather to live up to a self-consistent set of standards, need not be frustrated. It will be free if its standards accord with the laws and conventions of society. But a rational will does not emerge in the privacy of an individual mind unconnected with other minds; it is the product of a life lived in society. There is therefore for Hegel (as there was for Plato and Rousseau) always a close connection between the rationality of the individual will and the rationality of the social and political order. The individual can have a coherent and viable system of ambitions and principles only where social and political conditions are favourable.

Bentham would not have been much impressed by Hegel's criticism of the arbitrary will. We can imagine him putting this question to Hegel: 'What is the point of your assertion that an impulse has no measuring rod in itself? Do you mean that a man cannot know that one of his impulses is stronger than another or that he cannot weigh the consequences of indulging them and then decide to indulge one rather than the other on the ground that, in the long run, he will get greater satisfaction by doing so? But we know from experience that a man can do this. If, then, he does it, he acts rationally.'

No doubt, Bentham would be right. It is often possible to prefer one impulse to another on this ground, and such a preference would be rational, as that word is ordinarily understood. Hegel does not deny that this kind of preference is possible. He admits that the arbitrary will 'may proceed either by using intelligence to calculate which impulse will give most satisfaction, or else in accordance with any other optional consideration'.[1] He does not make it clear how far he thinks it possible to choose between impulses by making calculations of this kind, and he also speaks of these choices, where they can be made, as acts of 'the arbitrary will'. Whether he really means to deny that they are rational choices, even though he admits that they are intelligent, I do not know. This part of his argument is by no means clear. But, despite its obscurity, it looks very much as if Hegel were denying that we can establish a hierarchy among our impulses merely by calculating how much satisfaction they are likely to bring – that he is denying one of the assumptions on which the Utilitarian philosophy rests, the assumption that we can, by considering the pleasures and

[1] Ibid., § 17, p. 28.

pains likely to result from indulging our impulses, formulate rules enabling us always to choose rationally between them.

If this is part of what Hegel means when he contrasts the arbitrary with the rational will (and I do not see how it can be denied that it is), it would seem that he is right and Bentham wrong. More often than not, if to maximize pleasure and to minimize pain are our sole objects, we have no rational ground for preferring one impulse or appetite to another because we cannot make the calculations needed to achieve our object, even if we were omniscient. Hegel, though he puts his point obscurely, is (if I have not misunderstood him) nearer being right than Bentham; it is as a creature who accepts certain norms which cannot be derived from a comparison of the satisfactions to be obtained from indulging his desires that man acquires a rational order of preferences among those desires. It is nearer the truth to say, with Hegel and the other Idealists, that man has a rational order of preferences because he has moral principles than to say, with Bentham and the Utilitarians, that it is because he has such a rational order that he acquires moral principles. The Utilitarians might agree with Hegel that it is in society that man comes to have moral principles, and perhaps also that it is as a creature having a rational order of preferences that man comes to desire freedom; but they necessarily part company with him when he says that the will which is not moral is arbitrary, and that the arbitrary will is not free; for if he is right in saying so, Utilitarianism cannot stand.

I have said that Hegel is nearer being right than Bentham. Yet he is not entirely right. When he says that only the rational and moral will is free, he means to assert more than is acceptable. If by a moral creature we mean one capable of making deliberate choices and value-judgements, we can say that only a creature who is moral in this sense conceives of freedom and desires it. That, very probably, was part of what Hegel was saying; but he was also saying more, and more than is true. He was also saying that man is free only when he desires and is able to do what he ought to do. He was implying that a wicked man is not free – which is to imply more than that only a creature who is moral in the sense defined above conceives of freedom and desires it.

No doubt, if man is to have freedom, as Hegel understands it – if he is to be able to live up to his own principles – those principles must be consistent with one another and also viable or practicable. It is irrational to adhere to principles which are not consistent with one another, and irrational also to seek to apply them where, though they are mutually consistent, they cannot in fact be applied. Therefore, we may say that, if man is fully to achieve freedom, he must have a rational will. Unless he has it, he will be frustrated both by his own actions and by those of other people. But it does not follow, when a man does act in a way which is inconsistent with his own principles, that his action is not free. It may be free though it has consequences frustrating to the person who performs it. In so far as we do not live merely from hand to mouth – in so far as we have principles and wish to be true to them – we cannot live as we want to live unless we have what Hegel calls a rational will; and if we cannot live as we want to, we are not free. This makes good enough sense, but we must not make false inferences from it; we must not speak as if, because man by his own action can diminish his freedom, the action whereby he diminishes it is not free.

We must make distinctions which Hegel and the Idealists fail to make; we must distinguish what constitutes a free action from what makes freedom desirable or attainable. Unless men had values by reference to which they could prefer some of their appetites or impulses to others, they could have no enduring ambitions and aspirations; and unless they had them, they would not care for freedom as they do. These values emerge in social intercourse and are not utilitarian; they are not accepted because men have estimated (however roughly) the satisfactions to be derived from indulging their various impulses. And a man who has come to value freedom cannot fully attain it unless his ambitions are compatible with one another, which they will not be unless he has what Hegel calls a rational will and that will accords with what he terms the universal will. We may accept all this, and yet deny that a man does not act freely when he acts wickedly or when the motive from which he acts does not form part of a coherent set of principles.

We may also insist that, though it is as a creature engaged in social intercourse that man becomes moral, his principles may be perfectly consistent with one another and yet be inconsistent with established laws and conventions – that is, with the universal will. He will then not be free, for he will be required to conform to rules which he does not accept. Yet he may be entirely rational. No doubt, it would be irrational of him to seek to apply his own principles regardless of the consequences – to behave as if the social order were already what he thinks it ought to be. But it would not be irrational of him to seek to reform that order.

Hegel, presumably, does not believe that the laws and conventions of a community always form a consistent and viable system, for he admits that some communities are higher (and therefore more rational) than others. He even admits that a man who challenges authority (such as Socrates) may be more rational than the authority he challenges. But he does seem to take it for granted that the individual's will cannot be fully rational except where there is a fully rational universal will. That is to say, though he does not hold that the individual – to be fully rational – must conform to law and convention, no matter what they are, he does assume that there must be a self-consistent and viable legal and moral system if the individual is to be fully rational. I can see no reason why this should be so.

Hegel also takes it for granted that there is constant progress towards full rationality and towards harmony between the rational will of the individual and the universal will. He does not allow that there could be several legal and moral systems, several universal wills, very different from one another, and yet each as self-consistent and viable as any of the others; nor does he allow that there could be widely different types of individual will, all of them equally rational. He does not, for instance, allow that the universal will manifest in the Greek city-state or the moral will of the citizen in such a state could be as fully rational as the universal will manifest in the modern State or the moral will of the modern citizen. He cannot allow it without undermining his conception of World History as the necessary progress of Spirit towards complete self-knowledge and rationality. But what he cannot allow may well be true.

e. Rationality and Law

According to Hegel, there is always a close connection between the individual's rational will (his principles and aspirations in so far as they form a coherent and viable system) and the universal will, the laws and conventions of his community. These laws and conventions are the fruits of the experience of many generations of men who have sought to achieve their purposes and who have had to adjust those purposes to one another, to the purposes of other men, and to the means at their disposal. The individual acquires a rational will in the process of learning to take his place in a social order; or, in other words, he acquires it by partaking in the life of a community having a universal will or system of laws and conventions which give it its distinctive character. Since Hegel conceives of a very close connection between the individual's rational will and the social order within which he acquires that will, he finds it easy to say of a man's rational will that it is the universal will manifest in him. And his metaphysical system – his conception of reality as universal Spirit or Mind manifest, at its higher levels, in the rational activities of communities of finite selves – seems to him to justify this manner of speaking.

Now, if we reject the Hegelian metaphysic, we have to say that this way of speaking, taken literally, does not make sense. We have to deny that the universal will, embodied in law and convention, is identical with the rational will of the individual. But we can take what Hegel says metaphorically, and it then becomes a theory about the conditions, psychological, social and moral, of desiring freedom and attaining it. That theory may not be wholly true; but whatever its measure of truth, it is intelligible and ingenious. It is a theory worthy of study and deserving respect. Moreover, it is not a theory read into Hegel's words, which it was never his intention to assert. It was his intention to assert it. That it was also his intention to assert more than this does not make it any the less his intention to assert this as well. When we take Hegel metaphorically and refuse to take him literally, we do not part company with him, while pretending not to do so. We are still dealing with Hegelian theory, though with only a part of it; and if we concentrate on this part to the neglect of the other, it is because the other part means nothing to us.

Hegel says that the will is *essentially* free, and that his purpose, in the *Philosophy of Right*, is to show how the concept of will is necessarily realized in a community of free persons. His purpose is to explain what he calls 'the proper immanent development' of the will from concept to Idea – the Idea of a concept being that in which it is most fully realized. He believes that it follows logically from the concept of will that it must be realized in communities of free persons. If we take this quite literally, we can hardly make sense of it. The concept of will is presumably the concept of deliberate choice, which involves the use of reason. It would seem that wherever there are creatures making deliberate choices, the concept of will is *realized*. What is the realization of a concept except its application to actual things or events? It is realized whenever there is anything real to which it applies. The concept of will is as much, as completely, realized in a prison as in a community of free persons. We must therefore suppose that Hegel is using the term *realized* in some different sense. The concept of will is not realized, in his sense of realization, wherever there is a genuine instance of deliberate choice; it is realized only when creatures capable of deliberate choice constitute a community of free persons. But realization, understood in this way, is clearly not *necessary*; it does not in the least follow from there being creatures capable of deliberate choice that there must eventually be a community of free persons. Admittedly, only creatures capable of deliberate choice could form such a community or could want to form it; but that does not allow us to say that they must eventually form it or even that they must come to desire it.

This doctrine, that the concept of will is eventually realized in the State, or the community of free persons, is another example of something we have come across before: the deliberate running together of different ideas or sets of ideas. In this case the ideas run together are that of a concept and what it applies to, on the one hand, and that of the less and more developed, on the other. It would be misleading to call this a confusion of thought; it is quite deliberate. Knox, explaining Hegel's purpose, says, 'We are tracing the development of the will from concept to Idea. The start of a process of development is abstract in comparison with its end . . . "immediate", not yet mediated and made explicit in and through the later stages; e.g. a man's character is built up in the course of his life, but it was implicit and undeveloped in his childhood'.[1]

We owe it to Hegel and to his disciples to say that this running together of ideas that most people think are best kept apart is not due to a failure to notice that they are different; it is deliberate and is held to be justified by the Hegelian philosophy taken as a whole. Indeed, it is held to be the key to a deeper insight. We may protest that concepts do not develop into anything but either have or do not have instances; we may boggle at calling childhood the concept of manhood, or a child's will more abstract than a man's. We may protest at applying to concepts categories which apply to things. But we must not suppose that the Hegelians do not know what they are doing. To them our protests seem misplaced, if not philistine, due to a failure to understand the essence of their philosophy, which alone gets to the heart of reality. They are the protests of the superficial who cannot help being what they are.

But if nature has condemned us to superficiality, what are we to make of Hegel's theory of the State, of his 'tracing the development of will from concept to Idea'? We can find in that theory a number of assertions about the social and psychological conditions of the capacity for deliberate choice; we can also find the doctrine that creatures having this capacity come eventually to conceive of freedom and to attach a supreme value to it, though they can attain it only when certain further conditions – social and moral – hold. No doubt, Hegel speaks as if the conditions of deliberate choice – the coming to conceive of freedom and to desire it, the conditions of attaining it

---

[1] *Philosophy of Right*, translator's note 1 to § 34, p. 319.

– were all implicit in (that is, logically deducible from) the capacity for deliberate choice or the will. This we can firmly reject, and yet hold that his beliefs about the conditions of deliberate choice and the conditions of freedom make excellent sense and may be largely true. They are certainly worth close study.

f. The Duty of Obedience

In justice to Hegel we must notice that his theory of the State is not a doctrine of political obligation. As we shall see later, there is a doctrine of political obligation implicit in that theory, and there is also another doctrine, which is not implicit in it but which Hegel puts forward tentatively and almost furtively – as if he wanted, without seeming to do so, to persuade people to accept it. There is, as I shall try to show later, an ambiguous and somewhat repulsive doctrine of political obligation contained in the *Philosophy of Right*, a doctrine more hinted at than openly propounded, a doctrine not even in keeping with the Hegelian conception of the State. Nevertheless, the *Philosophy of Right* is not, and is not meant to be, a doctrine of political obligation. We have Hegel's own word for it when he says that his book, 'containing as it does the science of the state, is to be nothing other than the endeavour to apprehend and portray the state as something inherently rational. . . . The instruction which it may contain cannot consist in teaching the state what it ought to be; it can only show how the state, the ethical universe, is to be understood'.[1] His work aims neither at teaching the State what it ought to be, nor the citizen how he ought to behave. It purports to explain what the State is, which of course involves explaining what it is to be a member of the State. That this explanation, as he conceives of it, also involves explaining what it is to be a rational and moral being does not in itself make it a doctrine of political obligation.

Hegel tells us that man is free only as a member of a community whose laws and conventions he can conscientiously accept. This purports to be a statement of fact; it may or may not be true. Whether or not it is true, it does not imply that a man ought always to accept the laws and conventions of his community; it states only that he cannot be free unless he is able to accept them conscientiously. As we have seen already in discussing the *Phenomenology* and the *Philosophy of History*, and as we shall see once more when we consider the *Philosophy of Right*, Hegel does not believe that freedom is realized in a community whose members accept its laws and conventions

[1] Ibid., preface, p. 11.

merely from habit. To be able to attain freedom they must accept the established legal and moral order conscientiously, which they can do only when they have reached a certain level of intellectual and moral maturity. Conscientious acceptance of law and convention is possible only in what we might call – using words which Hegel did not use but which seem to convey his meaning – a self-critical and sophisticated community. Hegel admired men like Socrates and Luther who defy authority and thereby help to raise mankind to what, in his opinion, is a higher level. It is clear, then, that he did not believe that the individual ought always to accommodate his principles to the laws and conventions of his community. I think we may say that he believed that the individual, more often than not, is perverse or irrational when he defies authority, that he is blinded by prejudice or self-interest, that he is confused or self-contradictory or does not see clearly the consequences of his principles. He probably believed that men in authority are more often right than the rebels who defy them. This is the impression that most of his readers derive from his books, and from none more than the *Philosophy of Right*. Yet he clearly does not believe that rebels are always wrong. Indeed he cannot believe it and reconcile that belief with his philosophy of history. Hegel is a believer in progress; he holds that some states and civilizations are better than others, and that the better ones supersede the less good. He therefore cannot condemn the men who, by their defiance of authority, help to give currency to better principles. His approval of Socrates and Luther is not fortuitous; it fits in admirably with his doctrine of progress and does not conflict with his conception of the State. Logically, he can condemn all disobedience and non–conformity only in the highest type of State, the State which is in the fullest sense a community of free persons.

Even this condemnation does not follow logically merely from what Hegel says about the nature of freedom and the conditions of attaining it. It follows only if it is assumed that freedom, and therefore also the type of community in which freedom is realized, are good. Hegel, of course, makes this assumption. That is why we can say that the *Philosophy of Right*, though its purpose is not to put forward a doctrine of political obligation, does contain such a doctrine implicitly. Once we accept Hegel's philosophy, it follows that, if freedom is the essence of will – if creatures capable of deliberate choice come necessarily to desire freedom and cannot find complete satisfaction until they attain it – freedom is desirable. Therefore the State, as the ethical universe (or, in other words, as a community of rational beings involved in a system of moral relations with one another) in which freedom is realized, is also desirable. But it is desirable only to the extent that freedom is realized in it or its realization is brought nearer by it.

This is the doctrine of political obligation implicit in Hegel's account of freedom and of the State. But, as I remarked earlier, there is also put forward equivocally in the *Philosophy of Right* another doctrine of political obligation, which is repulsive to the liberal as this one is not, and which is not in keeping with what Hegel says about freedom and the State. I shall discuss that doctrine later. For the moment, my purpose is only to remove a source of misunderstanding which sometimes leads people to suppose that Hegel's conception of the State commits him logically to assert a duty of complete submission to established authority.

2. Aspects and Forms of Social Life, Considered Generally

a. The Presentation of the Doctrine

Since Hegel's political philosophy is part of a general philosophy which explains reality as essentially Spiritual, and treats Spirit as a process of development which is necessarily dialectical (every phase in the process generating within itself a tension or contradiction which comes eventually to be resolved and whose resolution constitutes a passage to the next phase), it is presented to us in the form of an explanation of two dialectical triads. The first consists of abstract right, morality and ethical life, and the second of the family, civil society and the State. Abstract right and morality constitute the thesis and antithesis of the first triad; they necessarily go together and yet there is a tension or contradiction between them which is resolved only in ethical life. The family and civil society constitute the thesis and antithesis of the second triad, and Hegel also says of them that they are necessary and yet *contradictory* of one another, the contradiction being resolved in the State. His dialectical scheme implies that the three moments of the first triad are related to one another in much the same way as the three moments of the second. But this, as we shall see, is far from true. Hegel's dialectical scheme, applied to society and the State, is quite artificial. The sense in which there is a contradiction between abstract right and morality is quite different from the sense in which there is one between the family and civil society.

b. Abstract Right and Morality

By abstract right, Hegel means the claims which a man makes to assert his individuality – for man, as a rational and purposeful creature, is essentially a bearer of rights. Though it is part of Hegel's philosophy that man becomes rational and purposeful only as a member of a social order – as a partaker in what he calls ethical life – he does not, in the section of the *Philosophy of Right* in which he discusses abstract right, speak about the social order. That is because his purpose is to explain, not how man comes to make claims, or to assert rights, but rather the significance of his doing so. Therefore, it is only at a later stage of the argument that we see how man, as a bearer of rights, is also necessarily a social being; at this stage, what Hegel seeks to bring home to us is that man expresses his awareness of himself as a rational and purposeful creature by the assertion of rights.

By morality, Hegel means the feelings and intentions of man, not as a mere creature of appetite, but as a bearer of rights and obligations. He includes in morality what he calls conscience, or the claim of the individual to be allowed to act on principles which he is inwardly convinced are right. But conscience is not all that he means by morality, for morality exists in every society, just as abstract right does, whereas the claim which Hegel has in mind when he speaks of conscience is not (as he admits) made in all societies.

Clearly, abstract right and morality are aspects and not forms of social life; they are involved in social life and cannot exist apart from it. This Hegel never for a moment denies, even though, in the *Philosophy of Right*, he explains the aspects (or, as an Hegelian might put it, *deduces* them from the concept of will) before he explains the whole of which they are aspects. Yet, this manner of proceeding, though it is required by the type of explanation at which Hegel aims (which moves from the more abstract to the more concrete, from the partial to the complete), can be seriously misleading, as I hope to show.

Abstract right and morality are complementary, and there cannot be the one without the other. Men who have rational purposes and moral sentiments are creatures who make and recognize claims; they are social creatures forming communities, and where there is a community there are more than just uniformities or patterns of behaviour. There are rules which those who conform to them or reject them are aware of and which they choose to obey or to disobey. The making of claims, the assertion of rights and the expression of moral sentiments are of the essence of social or ethical life.

So far, so good. But Hegel goes further. He is not content, after he has explained abstract right and morality, to show how they are complementary – how they are but two aspects of social life and are inconceivable outside it. He also treats them as contradictory opposites in a dialectical triad. They not only go necessarily together but are also necessarily *contradictory*. But *contradictory* in just what sense?

The Hegelian concept of *contradiction* is extraordinarily loose. In Hegel's political philosophy, as in his philosophy generally, it is applied to concepts, to states of mind, to distinct but inseparable aspects of a whole and to different forms of life. He always speaks as if he were using the word *contradiction* in what is, at bottom, the same sense – and indeed his doctrine that reality is a logically necessary dialectical process requires that he should so use it. But, though Hegel strives to create the illusion that he uses the word consistently in the same sense, and no doubt deceives himself into believing that he does so, the truth is that he uses it in several different senses. When he says that two concepts contradict one another, he often means that, considered in a certain way (which he thinks is an inadequate way), they exclude one another logically, in the sense that, if one of them applies to something, the other cannot do so; and the contradiction is resolved when, considering the two concepts in another way, we see that both can apply to the same thing. But when, in his philosophy of man in society and his philosophy of the State, he says that two states of mind or two aspects or two forms of social life contradict one another, he sometimes seems to mean no more than that they can be effectively contrasted with one another – positive statements about the one alternating with negative statements about the other – while at other times he seems to mean that some sort of tension or incompatibility necessarily arises between them.[1] When two things, psychological or social, are contradictory in the first of these senses, the contradiction is resolved when they are included in or superseded by something which combines their contrasted characteristics; and when they are contradictory in the second sense, the contradiction is resolved when they are included in or superseded by something in which the tension is relieved or the incompatibility removed. The two things said to be contradictory are also said to imply or entail one another – which sometimes seems to mean that they are inseparable aspects of a whole apart from which they could not exist, and at other times that they are stages in a process which Hegel regards as being, for some reason or other, necessary.

It is easy to see the sense in which abstract right and morality are supposed to imply one another. But in what sense is there a *contradiction* between them? No doubt, abstract right and morality, as Hegel describes them, can be effectively contrasted with one another. Yet this is not all that he has in mind when he calls them contradictory.

---

[1] These two are not the only senses of *contradiction* when it is applied to states of mind or to aspects or forms of social life, but they are, I believe, the most important.

He also means to assert that a serious tension or incompatibility necessarily arises between them.

Abstract right and morality can, of course, be incompatible, and they often are so. It often happens that our moral sentiments are out of keeping with our society's system of rights. But are they incompatible necessarily? In primitive and static societies, rights and obligations are usually very much in keeping with moral sentiments. No doubt, even in primitive societies, rights are infringed; men's passions move them to steal or in some other way to violate right. But there is – as Hegel knew – a great difference between violating right and challenging it in principle. In all societies rights are violated, but they are not in all societies called in question. Men do not, in all societies, acquire *moral* sentiments which move them to challenge recognized rights. Only in sophisticated, self-critical and dynamic societies are rights widely challenged on moral grounds; only in them is there a conflict between abstract right and morality of which men become conscious.[1]

It may be that there is never complete harmony between recognized rights and moral sentiments; it may be that even the most seemingly static society is never quite as static as it seems, and that there is always some adjustment of right to morality or of morality to right, though it goes unnoticed. But Hegel, when he treats them as necessarily contradictory, has more in mind than this; he is suggesting that they must grow to be so seriously incompatible that men become aware that they are so and challenge established right on moral grounds. He is suggesting much more than is true.

And yet he is also saying something which is both true and important, though he does not say it clearly. He is saying that, unless established right and morality come into so sharp a conflict that men notice it and are disturbed by it, a certain idea of freedom (which in his eyes is the most precious) does not emerge. This is the idea of freedom as moral autonomy. Only where men have come to challenge on principle – and not merely to violate – established right, does the claim arise that what a man is required to do shall not be contrary to what he is convinced is right. This is the claim which Hegel calls the claim of conscience. Since he also says that freedom is realized where what men are required to do is in keeping with what

---

[1] Even in such societies, many more rights are accepted than challenged; even in a quickly changing social environment, men ordinarily approve of much more than they disapprove. The illusion to the contrary arises because disapproval is so much more self-conscious and vocal than approval, so much more noticeable. If right and morality were more incompatible than compatible, society could hardly hold together.

conscience dictates, it follows that, before there can be freedom in the sense of moral autonomy, established right and moral sentiments must first come into a conflict sharp enough to disturb men so deeply that they challenge established right, and that afterwards harmony must be restored. This we may accept. But then we accept only a part of what Hegel says. We accept only that, *if* there is to be a certain kind of freedom, right and morality must first come into conflict and then be 'reconciled'; we do not accept that there must be this conflict and that reconciliation.

What Hegel understands by conscience is only a part of what he calls morality, though it is the part he attends to most. Believing, as he does, that the realization of freedom is necessary, he is committed to the assertion that the conflict which is a condition of its being realized is also necessary. And yet he makes admissions which undermine this assertion, though he does not see that they do so. For example, he admits that men can respect right even though they do not make the claim which he thinks is of the essence of conscience. They must, of course, have sufficient motives for respecting established right, and some of these motives will be, in the broad sense of the word, moral sentiments. In all societies men are moved by shame or a desire to be approved by their neighbours or a sense of honour, and all these can be called moral sentiments. But a man moved by any or all of them is not moved by conscience as Hegel understands it. That Hegel is aware of this is proved by his account, in the *Philosophy of History*, of non-European societies. In these societies (as he describes them) the claim of conscience – the claim that a man not be required to do what he is convinced is wrong or to leave undone what he is convinced is right – is absent, and the idea of freedom as moral autonomy does not arise. Hegel does not say that in these societies established right and moral sentiments are always in perfect harmony; he does not deny that they may be in conflict. Perhaps he would admit that they sometimes are; but, if they are, the conflict apparently does not give rise to the peculiar claim of conscience and to the highest conception of freedom.

Abstract right and morality, when they do conflict, can only be reconciled in ethical or communal life. Thus ethical life is their *synthesis*, not only in the sense that they are inseparable aspects of it, but also in the sense that it is the sphere in which the tension between them is resolved. It is also, presumably, the sphere in which the tension arises, though Hegel does not trouble to say so, because his attempt to explain man in society dialectically does not require that he should say it. The synthesis is neither logically nor temporally posterior to the elements whose contradiction is resolved in it, for they are merely parts of the whole which it is and have no being outside it.

c. Family and Civil Society

The three 'moments' of the dialectical triad we have been examining are inseparable – two of them, abstract right and morality, being aspects of the third, ethical life. Abstract right and morality can be in conflict, and must be so if men are to rise to the idea of freedom as moral autonomy, and the conflict must be resolved if this freedom is to be achieved, for it can be achieved only in a community where what men require of one another (the claims they make) accord with their deepest conviction about what is right.

The three moments of the second triad (the family, civil society and the State) are not related to one another in the same way as are the three moments of the first. Where there is right of any kind, there is also some kind of morality, and the two are mere aspects of social life. But it is not true that, wherever there is any community of the family type, there is always some form of civil society, and that neither family nor civil society is ever found outside the State. The type of family which is found together with civil society is by no means the only type, and if it is *negated* by civil society it is so in a different way from the way in which morality, in the form of conscience, *negates* abstract right. Civil society does not challenge the family; there is no conflict or tension between them which needs to be resolved in the State; or, if there is, Hegel does not explain what it is. He says merely that civil society arises from the 'break-up' of the family, which is, presumably, the sense in which it *negates* the family. And this sense, as we shall see in a moment, really makes no sense.

I do not deny that what Hegel understands by *civil society* has arisen from the break-up of a certain type of family; but I do deny that it was necessary that it should arise, and also that the type of family out of which it in fact arose is the type that Hegel has in mind in the *Philosophy of Right*. The type of family, whose dissolution in fact brings civil society into existence, has often endured for centuries without showing any sign of dissolving into civil society. No doubt, there are causes for that dissolution wherever it occurs, but there is nothing about that type of family requiring that it should dissolve into civil society. The dissolution, when it happens, is only contingent in the Hegelian sense of that word; it has its sufficient causes but those causes are not inherent in the structure which dissolves. The family whose dissolution gives rise to civil society is the extended family or clan, the kinship group; and it can endure, as I have said, for centuries without dissolving into civil society. There is nothing about it which requires that it should dissolve and give way to civil society. When it does disintegrate, it is not because it is so constructed that there naturally emerges from it a form of life which supersedes it, as the butterfly emerges from the chrysalis; it disintegrates as a result of foreign invasion or penetration or from some other cause which is no part of the form of life of which it consists.

Civil society, as Hegel conceives of it, may be roughly defined as a community of producers of the kind described by the classical economists, together with the public services needed to maintain order inside it. Clearly, there have been many societies which were not civil in this particular sense – tribal societies with the family, in one shape or another, as the only important type of community. Where communal life is tribal, there is neither civil society nor the State, as Hegel describes them. Civil society and the State emerge as the tribe and the clan disintegrate. We may therefore say that civil society *negates* one type of family. But it stands to that type of family in a quite different relation from that in which morality stands to abstract right. Far from being complementary, far from being inseparable in fact, this type of family and civil society are mutually exclusive. As civil society emerges, the tribe and the clan disappear. Where morality is in conflict with abstract right, harmony may be restored between them, for they both survive the conflict. In their case, the *negation* can be *negated*. But it cannot be so in the case of the family and civil society, if the family we have in mind is the type whose disintegration coincides with the emergence of civil society.

When civil society does emerge – and it need not do so – one type of family gives way to another; the extended family gives way to the small family familiar to us in many parts of the world. It is, of course, this small family that Hegel has in mind in the *Philosophy of Right*; it is the family typical of commercial and industrial societies, having inside them a structure of authority of the kind we refer to when we speak of the State. It is that family of which he says that civil society arises from its breaking up.

But it makes no sense to say this. The father of the small family, the breadwinner, is a member of civil society; and when his children become old enough to leave the home, when they are capable of playing an independent part in civil society, when they become members of it, they usually found families of their own. The small family comes into being when a man and a woman marry and have children, and it breaks up when the children leave home and the parents eventually die. Small families are continually dissolving and other small families are taking their place. From the break-up of these small families, other such families arise. This is the truth of the matter. What is not true is that civil society arises from their breaking up. It is there all the time; it is the social environment in which families of this type are born and have their being and cease to be. Where we find civil society, we must also expect to find the type of family which alone Hegel is concerned to explain *philosophically*. Though the two are not complementary aspects of a whole – as abstract right and morality are – though it is conceivable that they could exist apart from one another, the fact is that in practice they are found together. But in just what sense is civil society the *negation* of the family which Hegel describes?

No doubt, civil society and the family can be contrasted with one another. They can be shown to be in some respects opposite. In civil society rights and obligations are precisely laid down, formal contracts are made and disputes settled by supposedly impartial persons bound by fixed rules, whereas in the family they are not. In civil society most services are paid for, and in the family they are not. In the family there is great forbearance and little respect for privacy; in civil society there is little forbearance and great respect for privacy. And so we might go on for a long time, contrasting the one form of communal life with the other. In many ways civil society is the antithesis of family life; we can make many true statements about it which would be false if we made them about the family. Indeed, it may be that civil society differs more from the small family which thrives along with it than from the extended family which disintegrates with its appearance; for husbands and wives and parents and children in the small family are perhaps more intimately and less formally bound to one another than are the members of the extended family, so that the ties between them are in even greater contrast with the ties between members of civil society. Nevertheless, civil society does not arise from the break-up of the small family, and there is no tension or conflict between them which is eased or settled in the State.[1]

If we use the word *family* in a wider sense than Hegel uses it in the *Philosophy of Right*, we can say that the family, in the shape of the clan and the tribe, comes temporally before civil society, and even that civil society comes before the State. Thus we have here a time sequence which we do not have with abstract right, morality and ethical life,

[1] A man's family obligations can (and often do) conflict with his obligations as a member of civil society, and when they do, the State can sometimes intervene to resolve the conflict. But this is not what Hegel has in mind when he speaks of the State as the synthesis of the family and civil society.

since the first two cannot exist apart from one another and are merely aspects of the third. But with the appearance of civil society, the type of family out of which it emerges gives way to another type, and it would be nearer the truth to say of this other type that it arises out of civil society than that civil society arises out of it. Civil society comes in time before the small family. As Marx and Engels (and others before them) have insisted, the small family, as we know it in the West, is in part at least a product of capitalism. It might even be argued that it is also in part a product of the State, for it could hardly exist except where there are forms of inheritance and contract not to be found in tribal societies and which require for their enforcement a type of authority that is not tribal but political.

Order in civil society cannot be maintained by the same methods as in the tribe; there is a need felt for a quite different structure of authority, and when this need is met we have what is called the State. A community of producers and consumers of the kind described by the classical economists cannot long subsist where there is no State. Thus, though civil society precedes the State historically, it does so by only a small interval. Civil society and the State, as forms of ethical or communal life, are closely connected to one another and also to the only type of family with which Hegel is concerned. But these connections, close though they are, differ greatly from the connections between abstract right, morality and ethical life generally.

Hegel's method not only conceals these differences; it also inclines him to say what is false or to suggest it. It inclines him to say that civil society arises from the dissolution of the kind of family which he has in mind, whereas in fact it arises from the dissolution of quite another kind; it also inclines him to suggest that the sort of conflict between morality and abstract right required to produce the idea of freedom as moral autonomy must take place, whereas in fact it need not do so.

d. Hegel's Sophistry and Perceptiveness

But we must be just to Hegel. Let us admit that his attempt to explain the State *dialectically* as a synthesis of two *contradictory* forms of ethical or communal life is a failure; let us admit that he does not prove what he sets out to prove, which is that freedom is necessary because it is implicit in the very concept of will, and therefore cannot but be realized in communities of rational and purposeful creatures; let us admit, too, that he forces the facts, psychological and social, into a mould in which they do not fit. Yet is is astonishing how much, despite his Procrustean method, he takes into account, how perceptive and ingenious he is. Though he sometimes (and indeed often) selects for notice the trivial or the irrelevant because it helps him to make a show of explaining matters *dialectically*, he seldom neglects what is truly important. This Bismarck of philosophy is adept at papering over the cracks, but he is also a social and political theorist of genius, and not all his word-play and tricks of argument can hide his genius. I venture to compare him with a musical (or other) critic using a ponderous vocabulary and style not suited to his subject. Unfortunately, being as insensitive to language as he is sensitive to music, he revels in his vocabulary, and his readers, if they are to learn anything from him, must suffer at his hands. He punishes as he enlightens, but there is no denying his deep understanding of music; he cannot help saying much that is admirable about it though he speaks pretentiously.

I propose to discuss in turn the two triads into which Hegel forces the social facts which interest him. I shall discuss the first very briefly, and the second at greater length; and when I discuss the second, I shall attend much more to the State than to the family or civil society.

3. Abstract Right, Morality, Ethical Life

a. Property and Contract

To discover how Hegel conceives of abstract right, we cannot do better than look at what he says about property. 'The rationale of property is to be found', he says, 'not in the satisfaction of needs, but in the supersession of the pure subjectivity of personality. In his property a person exists for the first time as reason'.[1] Hegel does not mean to deny that property helps to satisfy needs, and he is not concerned to explain its origins. He is not trying to answer such questions as 'How does property arise?' or 'Why do men desire property?'. He is trying to explain how property enables men to live in the way in which rational beings need to live if they are to be satisfied. As a rational being seeking to order his life systematically, man needs property. But man does not first choose how he shall live and then set about acquiring property in order to be able to live as he has chosen. It is in the process of acquiring rights, in the process of coming to think of himself and to be recognized by others as being a subject of rights, that man comes to conceive of a way of life as possible and desirable for himself. Both the desire and the ability to lead a purposeful and rational life arise from man's being a possessor of rights, from his having a status, a definite

---

[1] *Philosophy of Right*, addition 24 to § 41, pp. 235–6.

place, in a stable community. We have already seen how, for Hegel, man acquires self-knowledge and self-mastery, and a sense that he is a distinct person in a community of persons, in the process of learning to understand and to control an environment. Part of this process is the acquisition of property, of things set aside for his own use in an ordered life and acknowledged by others to be his. Even inside the family, the child insists on his rights of property; he does so, not merely to satisfy his animal needs, but to assert himself as a person among other persons in a community.

We can respect someone's property simply by not interfering with his use of it and by not using it ourselves. This is a tacit recognition of his rights. The recognition becomes more explicit when property is exchanged and contracts are made. It is chiefly in the process of dealing in property with others that men come to have explicit and precise titles to what they have acquired for their use.

b. Crime and Punishment

Where there are rights, they may be infringed. The infringement of a right is a wrong. When the wrong is unintentional – when the doer of an action does not know that his action violates a right – he commits a civil offence; when he knowingly makes a false pretence of right, he commits a fraud; when he deliberately violates a right, he commits a crime. Hegel tells us that wrong *negates* right, and is in turn *negated* when the offender makes compensation or the swindler or criminal is punished. Punishment, he says, is 'a negation of the negation',[1] for it negates a fraud or a crime which itself has negated a right. His dialectical philosophy moves him to speak in this way, which seems odd to us; but we need not cavil at it.

Hegel also speaks of the *will negating itself* when a man commits a fraud or a crime. This too is a way of speaking suggested by his need to fit everything into a dialectical pattern. But, this time, we must take exception to it because it contradicts what he himself says about the universal will. No doubt, Hegel's metaphysic enables him to treat Spirit (and therefore Will as an aspect of Spirit) as something greater than finite minds, even though it exists (at its higher levels) only as manifest in their activities. Will, in this larger sense – the universal will – is realized in the community to the extent that its members desire in conscience to behave as established laws and conventions require. Since Will, in this larger sense, exists only as manifest in particular wills, Hegel feels himself entitled to speak of crime and fraud as the

[1] Ibid., addition 61 to § 97, p. 246.

will negating itself. The universal will is manifest in particular wills, and it is also particular wills that commit crimes and frauds.

But, even if we do not question Hegel's account of how the universal will is related to particular wills, we can question his right to speak in this way. Will in the larger sense – the rational or universal will realized in the community of conscientious citizens – exists in the criminal only in so far as his actions are in conformity with it. Those of his actions that go against it are by definition not manifestations of the universal will. Thus, though they may *negate* it, in the sense of being in conflict with it, we cannot logically say that, when they occur, the will negates itself. The universal will cannot negate itself, because the acts of will that do negate it are not its own acts. This follows from Hegel's own account of the universal or rational will. If it could negate itself it would not be rational.

Yet even here Hegel has a point worth making. Nobody can do wrong deliberately without knowing what right is. A man can do something which violates right; he can know how his neighbours will describe his action and behave towards him if they are aware that he has done it; he can know what to expect from them and can know that it is unpleasant; he can do and know all this and yet be without a sense of right and wrong. In that case, punishment will be in his eyes merely something unpleasant to be avoided. But if, in spite of his deliberate violation of right, he is capable of feeling as his neighbours do about justice, he will see, not merely that he is liable to suffer for his action, but that he deserves to suffer. If that is his state of mind, then, if he comes to be punished, he will, in a sense, participate in his own condemnation; he will enter into the feelings of those who sit in judgement over him and inflict punishment on him. To do wrong deliberately is more than to do what you know will bring painful consequences upon you if your neighbours know you have done it; it is to act against your own principles. If, when you call an action wrong, you mean more than that it is ordinarily condemned, if you condemn it yourself, then, when you perform such an action, you act against your own principles. At the time that you act, your principles may not be present to your mind, but afterwards, as the saying is, the true nature of what you have done is 'brought home to you'. It is brought home to you by the reactions of others, by their punishment of you; but, if it is brought home, you are driven to apply your principles to your own case. The wrong you have done is not brought home to you unless you see your action as others see it. And it is less likely to be brought home to you if they act in anger or for the sake of vengeance than if they seem to you to be acting impartially for the sake of justice. By the manner of their condemnation, 'they bring you to yourself'; or, to speak more literally, they place you in a situation which inclines you to pass on yourself the judgement they pass on you.

c. *The Claims of Conscience*

This brings us to what Hegel calls morality, to our feelings and attitudes towards the standards to which we are required to conform and also towards other standards which we may prefer. By an attitude I mean something that includes both feelings and opinions. Some of these feelings and attitudes, such as shame, self-respect and concern for reputation, we may have without ever challenging established laws and conventions. Hegel is less interested in them than in what he calls 'the right of the subjective will that . . . whatever it is to recognize as valid shall be seen by it as good'.[1] He also, a few lines further on, says, 'The right of giving recognition only to what my insight sees as rational is the highest right of the subject'. Until we have asserted this right (and it is in practice asserted by challenging established standards), we are incapable of freedom as Hegel understands it. Merely to assert that right is not, of course, to have freedom; if there is to be freedom, the right must be both asserted and made good.

Oedipus killed his father and married his mother without knowing that he was the son of his victim or of his wife, and when he discovered how he was related to them, he was horrified and in his shame put out his own eyes. He was guilty, so he believed, of parricide and of incest, although he had acted in ignorance. He had in fact killed his father and slept with his mother, and his ignorance could not alter the facts; and so, as it seemed to him, he was guilty. We should now say that his sense of guilt was out of place, because he did not know what he was doing at the time that he did it; we should say that he was the victim of circumstances. But that was not how Sophocles felt about it, or the audiences that watched his play. We feel, as the ancient Greeks apparently did not, that a man is responsible for what he does only if he understands what he is doing. This notion of responsibility goes along with the claim we have just discussed; they are both, so Hegel tells us, involved in our notion of freedom.

'Children', says Hegel, 'have no moral will but leave their parents to decide things for them. The educated man, however, develops an inner life and wills that he himself shall be in everything he does'.[2] Children,

[1] Ibid., § 132, p. 87.
[2] Ibid., addition 68 to § 107, p. 248.

we know, are often wilful and decide many things for themselves. Hegel does not mean that children always do what their parents tell them and never act on their own initiative; he means that they ordinarily do not challenge their parents' decisions about what is right and wrong. They are wilful and disobedient, but they do not criticize the standards they are required to conform to. Yet the educated man (not the learned or the clever but the morally educated man) does criticize these standards, though not necessarily to reject them. He is morally educated because he has considered them critically, accepting some and rejecting others on what seem to him to be rational grounds. His acceptance is not a mere act of the intelligence, as when a man admits a statement is true after having weighed the evidence for and against it; it is also something more. There may be an act of will, a decision, involved even in mere intellectual acceptance; but here there is also something different in kind. Here the man makes the standards his own, or (to use an expression of the psychologists) he *internalizes* them. As Hegel puts it, in stranger and more elaborate language, *he wills that he himself shall be in them.*[1]

The internal standards of one man may not accord with those of another. If every man is allowed to do what he inwardly believes to be right, there may in fact be very little freedom; for one man's conscientious action may prevent another's. That every man should be a law unto himself is an ideal impossible of attainment. But conscience, says Hegel, is not a man's claim to do what he pleases; it is his claim to do what he sincerely believes to be right. Now, to say that an action is right is to say that any man, in a given situation, ought to do it. When we say that an action is right, we are not, in Hegel's opinion, expressing or giving vent to our feelings about it; we are putting forward a rule of action which we believe is valid for anyone who finds himself in the situation to which the rule applies. As Hegel puts it, 'Conscience is therefore subject to the judgement of its truth or falsity, and when it appeals only to itself for a decision, it is directly at variance with what it wishes to be, namely the rule for a mode of conduct which is rational, absolutely valid, and universal. For this reason, the state cannot give recognition to conscience in its private form as subjective knowing'.[2] We may not wish to put it quite as Hegel does; we may hesitate to speak of the literal truth or falseness of the pronouncements of conscience, which are moral judgements. Yet we ordinarily do believe that it is possible to argue

[1] Ibid.
[2] Ibid., § 137, p. 91.

rationally about the validity of moral judgements. This belief is not denied but asserted by the conscientious man. The man who merely says, 'I feel this way about it, and you feel differently, and there's no arguing between us', is not being conscientious. The conscientious man is not expressing a personal preference; he is asserting a principle which he claims is universally valid.

Let us remember that Hegel is, in his own opinion, primarily concerned to explain the facts. It is, he thinks, a condition of freedom that men should make the claim which he dignifies by the name of conscience – that they should claim to be allowed to act as they honestly believe is right. But, clearly, it is not enough that they should make this claim; they must also be able to realize it. They must *all* be able to realize it, or else some men will be free and others will not; and, in practice, they can realize it only in a community. It follows, therefore, that they can realize it only in a community whose laws and conventions are accepted in conscience by them all. Hegel is not saying that where a man's principles do not accord with established laws and conventions, he is necessarily wrong. He is not saying that such a man is right or wrong. He is saying merely that such and such are the conditions of freedom. If the claims of conscience are not even put forward, and laws and conventions are obeyed merely from habit or self-interest or some other motive, there is as yet no freedom. If the conscientious claims of some men conflict with those of others, then not all men can be free; and this is also true if these claims conflict with established laws and conventions. Only when such claims are compatible with one another and do not conflict with established laws and conventions can all men be free. Hegel is not denying that freedom is difficult to achieve, that it cannot be achieved unless men are willing to look critically at the claims which they put forward for conscience' sake, that a long process of adjustment is needed before the claims of conscience can be brought into harmony with one another and with established laws and conventions. Far from denying all this, he insists upon it; but he insists also that the process of adjustment which leads eventually to freedom is rational. Only the conscientious man can be free, but he can be free only if his conscience – to use an expression of Hegel's which this time is an expression in ordinary use – is *educated*.

In my desire to do justice to Hegel's account of freedom, I have perhaps created the impression that he was more liberal than he actually was. No doubt, he was inclined to believe that the man who defies authority for conscience' sake is much more often wrong than right. His sympathies were much more with authority than with the rebel. But that does not affect his account of freedom, which a man might accept even though his sympathies were different from Hegel's. He was quite willing to admit that the critic of authority may be right. He says that the 'existing world of freedom' (meaning the actual community or form of ethical life) may become 'faithless to the will of better men',[1] and also that, in the age of Socrates, what the world recognized as right and good could not satisfy the will of such better men.

4. The Family and Civil Society

a. Hegel's Conception of Communal Life

When he speaks of ethical life, Hegel calls it 'substantial' or 'substance', and says that individuals are its 'accidents'.[2] He is moved to speak in this way by his metaphysical beliefs, and therefore no doubt means to convey much that anyone who rejects those beliefs, or can make nothing of them, cannot accept; he is moved by his doctrine of the concrete universal. Yet Hegel, by this manner of speaking, also means to convey more than this; he also makes assertions which are intelligible even to persons to whom his metaphysical beliefs mean nothing.

Ethical life is communal life, and when Hegel calls it substantial and says that individuals are its accidents, part of what he means is that it is always as a member of a community that man becomes – both in his own eyes and other people's – a moral person. Whatever it is about himself that he values, as well as his capacity to value it, he acquires as partaker in ethical or communal life. Hegel also means, when he calls ethical life substantial, that it is desirable for its own sake. Men are so made that they cannot realize their capacities except as members of a community; and when they see themselves as members of it, the community is never, in their eyes, merely a means but also an end. Their aspirations are those of social beings, and are achieved when they play whatever part attracts them in society; their conceptions of themselves are the conceptions of social beings. Society is not the external means of their achieving their aspirations; it is the medium in which they are achieved. As Hegel sees it, it is a condition of men's realizing their capacities that the communities they belong to should seem to them desirable for their own sake. All ambitions, all aspirations, are doubly social; they are possible only to

[1] Ibid., § 138, p. 92.
[2] Ibid., § 145, p. 105.

121

creatures having faculties which are quickened in society, and can be achieved only through activities and enjoyments which have no meaning outside a social context.

All this, suitably qualified, makes admirable sense, I should wish to qualify it in two ways. Though few would take exception to the doctrine that man is destined by his nature for ethical or communal life – if all that were meant by it were that the capacities peculiar to man are developed in him in communal life – many would reject it, if it were taken to mean that man – in order to develop these capacities – must live in the kind of community which Hegel approved of or in any other particular kind. The capacities which interest Hegel, and which most people would agree are essentially human, are reason and deliberate choice. Presumably, even in a community like Auschwitz or Belsen, men reason and make choices. We must therefore suppose that what Hegel means is not that men can reason and make deliberate choices only in a certain type of community but rather that, being rational and capable of deliberate choice, they can lead fully satisfying lives only in that type of community. I see no reason why this should be so. It may be true that men, being rational and deliberate, are fully satisfied only where they have a coherent set of values and find it possible to live by them. But these conditions may hold just as much in an African tribe as in a liberal society of the Western type. There is no argument from the capacities peculiar to man to any one type of community in which alone a creature having these capacities can be fully satisfied. Thus man might be fully satisfied in a community where freedom, as Hegel understands it, is unknown.

Secondly, it is misleading to speak of the community, as Hegel so often does, as if it were an entity which is active in the same sort of way as a man is. While it makes sense to say that it is as a member of a community that man becomes rational, purposeful, moral and attached to freedom, it is seriously misleading to say that society or the State makes him so. Society or the community or the State – except where we use these words elliptically to mean those who govern or exert the greatest influence on others – is not active. It is merely a sphere of activity, a living together of men. It is true that Hegel often speaks of man as becoming moral in society, and insists that society (or ethical life) exists only in and through individuals; but he also, and not less often, speaks as if society *made* men moral, as if it had a mind and will of its own and moulded them to that will.

It may be objected that, in making this last criticism, I am being over-precise. To say that society makes man moral is surely only another way of saying that man becomes moral in society. The second way of speaking may be the more accurate, but most people understand the two ways in much the same sense. Do we not all often speak in the first way? Why, then, should we object to Hegel's doing so? I agree that we all often do speak in the first way, and that it would be pedantic to object to Hegel's doing so, if that were all that he did. But it is not all that he does; for he sometimes draws, from this first way of speaking, conclusions – theoretical and practical – which cannot properly be drawn if it is equivalent to the second. Though Hegel is not as illiberal as he is sometimes presented as being, he is illiberal; he does play down the individual. He does sometimes come very close to suggesting that, because society makes us rational and moral, we ought not to challenge established laws and conventions. He also sometimes speaks as if the State stood to the citizen as God the Creator stands to His creature, man. He insists so much that man owes everything to the communities he belongs to, and above all to the State, that he seems to be suggesting, without wishing to put it into crude words, that he also owes absolute obedience.

Franz Grégoire, in his *Études hégéliennes* (Louvain 1958), in the essay on the divinity of the State, reminds us that Hegel is apt to call anything divine which he regards as a manifestation at a high level of rational Spirit. Thus, he calls the family divine as well as the State. Except for art, religion, and philosophy, the State is, in his system, the highest manifestation of reason; it is a higher manifestation than the family and so is more often called divine. Grégoire believes that Hegel also calls the State divine to give force to his repudiation of the contract theory, which makes the State a human device. It is as if he were saying, 'The contract theorists claim that man made the State, but I say that man, as a rational and moral creature, is a product of the State'. Hegel also disliked the romantic individualism fashionable at the time that he wrote the *Philosophy of Right*. The romantics were proclaiming their right to free themselves from social conventions in order to be more fully themselves, and Hegel was eager to tell them that – without society and the State – they were nothing. He disliked, too, the traditional Christian rejection of this world. The aspirations which the Christian expresses through his belief in another world are to be realized only in this world, in the community of free men, the rational State. For all these reasons, Grégoire tells us, Hegel was impelled to call the State divine.[1] For these reasons, too, no doubt, he spoke with what seems to us an exaggerated respect of other forms of ethical life. This may be true; but not even a philosopher, when

[1] See Étude IV, pp. 221–356.

he uses such words as *God* and *divine*, can altogether deprive them of their customary associations, either for his readers or himself.

b. The Family

Hegel's views about family life are very much in keeping with the upper middle-class conventions of his day, and are less remarkable in themselves than for the vocabulary they are dressed up in and some of the arguments used to support them. Yet this part of the *Philosophy of Right* exhibits, as much perhaps as any other, one of his greatest and least noticed virtues: good sense. Hegel is thought of as the most abstract, the most metaphysical and the most grandiose of philosophers; he is also – when he comes down to details, as he quite often does – realistic and shrewd. No doubt, he sometimes deals, rather pretentiously, either in commonplaces – as when he tells us that marriage, though it involves a contract, is not essentially contractual; or in a mixture of the commonplace and the half-truth – as when he says that the family is 'specifically characterized by love'.[1] But when he says that 'the punishment of children does not aim at justice as such; the aim is more subjective and moral in character, i.e. to deter them from exercising a freedom still in the toils of nature and to lift the universal into their consciousness and will',[2] he is not uttering a commonplace but is saying, in a style which is fortunately unique, something well worth translating into plain English. Children are punished less because they deserve punishment than in order to be made moral; they are not only taught by precept and example; they are also taught by the infliction of pain. They are made to suffer not so much because they have done wrong as because they need to have what is right driven home to them. It is not only, nor even mostly, by listening to reason that young children learn to behave; it is much more by being made to suffer when they do not do what they are told.

Hegel would agree with Rousseau that we must not reason too much with children, for if we do, 'we leave it open to them to decide whether the reasons are weighty or not, and thus we make everything depend on their whim'.[3] This is so, presumably, because young children cannot reason properly, and it does them no good to treat them as if they could do already what they cannot yet do. Though they cannot yet reason, they must be made to act reasonably; they must be made to act as they would act if they were reasonable. They need firm guidance, and will be the more reasonable, when they

[1] *Philosophy of Right*, § 75 and 158, pp. 58–9 and 110.
[2] Ibid., § 174, p. 117.
[3] Ibid., addition 111 to § 174, p. 265.

attain the age of reason, for having had it. The feeling of inferiority and subordination is not bad for children because it is only temporary; it produces in them a longing to grow up and to be accepted by grown-ups as equals. If children are treated like adults when they are still children, this will only prolong their childishness. In spite of his difficult style, Hegel needs only a few sentences to say all this; there are psychologists and sociologists today who take many pages to say less.

c. Bentham and Hegel Compared

If Hegel had studied Hume's or Bentham's theories of the State, he would doubtless have said that they fall far short of the truth, taking no account of what the State essentially is. What Bentham or Hume called the State would have seemed to him merely an aspect of civil society. According to Hume or Bentham, government exists only to maintain order, so that citizens can pursue their private ends without getting too much in each other's way. All that matters is that the needs and desires of individuals should be satisfied. Men compete and also co-operate, but whichever they do they care only for their own personal advantage or for that of other individuals for whom they happen to be concerned. Bentham in fact believed in universal egoism; or it might be better to say that he often spoke as if that were what he believed, without troubling overmuch about the implications of what he said. But it was not merely this belief that shut his eyes to what Hegel understood by the State; for Hume, who did not believe in universal egoism, was in this respect as blind as Bentham. Hume and Bentham both differ from Hegel in assuming that all ultimate ends are individual or private, in the sense that what men desire for its own sake is always some personal good, their own or someone else's. They assume that the function of all institutions, political no less than economic, is either to satisfy the needs of individuals or else to serve ends which are individual or private in the sense just defined. We may desire the good of another person without hope of benefit to ourselves, but we always desire the good of individuals; nothing is desired for its own sake except the good of individuals. Therefore, strictly speaking, the public good is merely a sum of private goods or a means to private good; whatever is good in itself – be it pleasure or happiness or knowledge or virtue or anything else – is always private. John may desire the happiness of James, but James's happiness is his alone.

We can make this assumption, not only without assuming that men are always self-regarding, but also without assuming that all institutions have been deliberately contrived to satisfy personal needs and serve private ends; but if we do make it, then what we call the State is only a part of what Hegel calls civil society. No matter what our views about the selfishness of men or the origins of institutions, if we hold that the only function of society and government is to satisfy the needs of individuals and to serve private ends, we do not have what Hegel would allow to be an adequate conception of the State. We have only a conception of civil society, because civil society is the whole system of economic and political relations considered as satisfying individual needs and serving private ends.

d. Civil Society is Educative

Hegel, nevertheless, insists that in civil society we do more than acquire the skills we need in order to collaborate and compete successfully for the satisfaction of personal needs and the attainment of private ends. Life in civil society is educative; it inclines the mind to appreciate the values embodied in the State. In working together to promote private ends we acquire public ends; we begin to value the collaboration for its own sake and not just for what it brings to individuals. Moreover, life in society multiplies our needs, and this, says Hegel – arguing against Rousseau and the ideal of the simple life – is good. The needs we acquire in society bind us to one another and to the community even more firmly than the needs we are born with or acquire merely in the process of becoming physically mature. These needs are, he says, more universal and also – in another sense of the word – more natural. They are more universal, presumably, not in the sense of being more common (for what could be more common than the natural appetites?) but in the sense of being more intimately connected with our principles, with the rules of conduct and standards of excellence we accept, with what Hegel calls the universal will. They are more natural in the special Hegelian sense of being peculiar to creatures of our kind, having the capacities which distinguish us from other animals. They are the needs of rational beings; they are needs born of reason in us, and we become the more rational for having these needs. We would not have them if we were not rational, and we perfect our reason in the process of satisfying them. The simple life, to the extent that it leaves some of our faculties undeveloped, is not natural; for it is, according to Hegel, the nature of man to develop his faculties to the full.

It is best, perhaps, not to take sides in this dispute between Hegel and Rousseau, for they both play on words and indulge in paradoxes. Hegel's conclusion – that it is a mistake to aim consciously at the simple life – may be more generally pleasing than Rousseau's, though his arguments are not more impressive.

e. Social Classes

Collaboration and competition for the satisfaction of needs, or the division of labour, give rise to three social classes – the agricultural class, the business class and the universal class. Now, how a political theorist divides society into classes depends, when it is not determined merely by custom, on the kind of interest he takes in society, on what he wants to explain about it. Hegel made these particular distinctions because the first – between the agricultural and the business class – was traditional, and the second – between the universal class and the other two – suited his theory of the State. His agricultural class includes all who work on the land or get their incomes from it, no matter how rich or poor they may be; it includes landowners and peasants and farm labourers. His business class includes all who are engaged in commerce and industry, both employers and employed. The agricultural class is a country class, while the business class is urban. The universal class consists chiefly of magistrates and civil servants; its office is to maintain order and to do justice; it looks after the public or universal interest, and that is why it is called the universal class.

It is interesting to see how these class divisions differ from those made by the classical economists or by Marx. To the classical economists, it was also important to distinguish the landowners from the merchants and industrialists, but not more important than to distinguish owners of property from labourers with nothing to sell but their labour; while for Marx the second distinction was the most important of all. Hegel's Prussia was still a 'backward' country, commercially and industrially; the division that mattered most, socially, was between the landowners in the country and the merchants, shopkeepers and craftsmen in the towns. Wage-labourers, rural and urban, were mere dependants of their social superiors; politically they counted for nothing, and the same was true of the peasants. Moreover, Hegel was not an economist. Though he says that these classes arose out of the division of labour, he is not much interested in their economic functions. He is interested rather in their character and temperament, in their attitudes to life and to themselves; and he is interested in them less for what they are intrinsically than for what they contribute to the *ethos* of the society in which – so Hegel hopes to show – freedom is realized. It is a society of the Prussian type. The illiterate classes – the silent classes, with no spokesman of their own in the State – he scarcely notices; he treats them as mere appendages of the classes above them. Though he includes peasants and farm labourers in the agricultural class, the character of that class, as he draws it, is predominantly the character of a class of landowners. So, too, the character of the business class is predominantly the character of a class of independent and enterprising men. Interested, as Hegel is, primarily in the political and intellectual life of a country, it is not surprising that he should almost lose sight of classes which in his day and country were still unimportant, intellectually and politically. The classical economists took notice of these classes because they played distinct parts in the process of production which it was their business to explain, and Marx took notice of them both for that reason and also because he made it his mission in life to define and to fight for their interests.

Neither the classical economists nor Marx were admirers of the Prussian or any other State. The classical economists, like the Utilitarians – many of whose assumptions and prejudices they shared – believed that the only proper function of the State is to maintain order, so that it interfered as little as possible with what private citizens do in pursuit of their interests, while Marx defined the State as an instrument of class oppression. Marx was a Rhinelander who disliked Prussia and was deeply influenced by French and English political and economic theory; Hegel was an admirer of Prussia, the country which – perhaps more than any other in Europe – had been civilized and made strong by the government. Prussia owed much more to her public officials than did either France or England. The kings of Prussia and their officials had made the country strong and prosperous, sometimes even against the wishes of the agricultural and business classes. The Prussian monarchy and bureaucracy were enterprising; they were the great initiators of reforms. No wonder, then, that Hegel speaks well of what he calls the universal class, the officials who are not gentlemen engaged in public affairs but servants of the State with a tradition of devoted, intelligent and impartial service. In two other of the great monarchies of Europe, in Austria and Russia, the officials were also powerful but were less enterprising and perhaps also less public-spirited than in Prussia. Hegel was the first of the great political philosophers to find a large place for bureaucracy in his theory of the State. He saw the officials, not merely as subordinates, but also as makers of law and policy; he saw them as what they already were in Prussia and were soon to become in every powerful and well-governed State, even the most democratic. But he did not regard them as undisputed masters of the State; he did not, as we shall see in a moment, want them out of reach of criticism or out of touch with the people.

f. The Judicial System

With the emergence of civil society there arises a system of positive and precisely defined law with professional courts to interpret and enforce it; it is above all the business class which feels the need for this kind of law. The business class are involved in a wider range of transactions, and are more enterprising, more litigious, more concerned to assert the rights of the individual, and therefore more consciously freedom-loving than the agricultural class. When abstract right becomes positive law, interpreted and enforced by independent courts, it becomes the more conspicuously impartial and universal. The courts are no respecters of persons, for they are concerned only to do justice; and yet, in another sense, they do respect the person – the individual, the bearer of rights and duties – scrupulously.

Hegel, who ordinarily has so much respect for professionals, for the learned and the trained – for men with strong motives for living up to the high standards of their profession – has also a good word to say for the jury system. Juries, he says, judge the facts in a case and do not interpret the law, and any body of men who have some education and proper guidance are able to do that. When a man is condemned by his peers, the justice of the condemnation is more forcefully brought home to him; he is condemned by men who, in their feelings and opinions, probably stand much closer to him than do judges and lawyers. Where there are juries, moreover, trials must be carried on in a manner intelligible to laymen. Hegel's defence of the jury does not rest on the belief that jurymen are more likely than judges to reach correct decisions about the facts; it attributes no special wisdom or insight to untrained men. Juries do not improve the quality of justice; they merely make it more evident that justice has been done.

g. Corporations

Hegel was neither a socialist nor a champion of private enterprise. He approved of guilds and of other corporate bodies. They give, he thought, a common status and common standards to groups useful to society; they serve to maintain the dignity of their members and to remind them of their obligations. They help the needy among their members without humiliating them. The less the need for private charity, the better – presumably because private charity is good neither for giver nor taker. If we compare Hegel with the Utilitarians, we find him much less inclined to assume that the poor and the unsuccessful probably deserve their fate.

He believed that the rapid expansion of wealth could, and often did, lead to pauperism, and he thought it the duty of society to look after the poor. He laid that duty, not on the rich individually, but on the government or else on corporations which included both rich and poor. Whether the poor get assistance must not depend on the whim of the rich; they must get it as a matter of right, and yet must also prove that they need it. This is how I interpret Hegel's dislike of private charity, and his praise of corporate bodies because they can help the poor without humiliating them. Hegel also believed that the rapid expansion of wealth produces an 'inner dialectic' of civil society, leading to a search for overseas markets.

Some of Hegel's admirers have made much of these beliefs, and have suggested that, even as an economist, he is a precursor of Marx. Does he not say, as Marx does, that the rapid expansion of wealth produces poverty and also floods the domestic market with more goods than it can absorb?[1] Does he not here touch upon what Marx was to call the contradictions of capitalism? No doubt, he does. But he makes these suggestions merely in passing, and without attributing much importance to them. Were they suggested to him by what he had himself observed, or did he pick them up from someone else? I do not know. They are crumbs from his table, which become loaves in the social theory of Marx. They mean much less to him than his belief that government does not exhaust its duty when it protects rights and enforces contracts; it must also protect the weak against the strong, which involves more than giving them merely what they are legally entitled to. It is for society to see that poverty is relieved, and also that children are educated, even if necessary, against the wishes of their parents.

5. The State

a. What the State Is

I have said that the Utilitarian theory of the State would seem to Hegel to be merely a theory about civil society. How, then, does Hegel's State differ from civil society? How can we tell the two apart? Have they separate institutions?

Positive law, the courts of justice, the police and the administrative

[1] See the *Philosophy of Right*, § 195 and addition 124, pp. 128 and 269.

departments are as much organs of civil society as of the State. To the extent that their function is to reconcile and promote personal or private interests, they are organs of civil society; to the extent that they serve to hold together a community whose members value it for what it is, they are organs of the State. Society, conceived as a means to the realization of personal interests, is civil society; whereas, conceived as a legal and moral order in which men acquire these interests and others too, and to which they grow attached for its own sake, it is the State. To conceive of society only in the first way is to conceive of it inadequately. So Hegel tells us.

'The state is actual', he contends, 'only when its members have a feeling of their own self-hood and it is stable only when public and private ends are identical. It has often been said that the end of the state is the happiness of the citizens. That is perfectly true'.[1] Bentham, had he read these sentences, might have said, 'This is something with which I can perfectly agree, provided it is suitably interpreted'. But the interpretation which would suit Bentham would not suit Hegel. Not only because, in Hegel's opinion, the happiness in question is not a sum of pleasures, but also, and above all, because it is the happiness of a citizen, of a man whose private ends have no meaning apart from the social context in which they are to be realized. The ends of a citizen – of a member of society and of the State – no matter how private they may be, are the ends of a moral and rational being, and are not to be understood except in terms of situations and values which are essentially social. These values, which are part of what Hegel means by the *universal will*, are *involved* in private ends. If we explain them, after the manner of Bentham, as if their function were to make easier the attainment of private ends which are perfectly intelligible apart from them, we misunderstand them; we have a false conception of what society is. Public and private ends are not merely closely connected, in the sense that the first must be realized if the second are to be so too (because men will not ordinarily get what they want unless there is justice), nor in the sense that they arise together out of the same experience (because men acquire their values as they acquire their private ends in the mere process of living); they are also involved in one another in the sense that they are not intelligible separately. Men's interests and purposes as distinct from their mere appetites – their ends as moral and rational beings – have no meaning apart from the social relations they stand in and the values they accept. Nor can these relations and values be understood apart from those interests

[1] Ibid., addition 158 to § 265, p. 281.

and purposes. This, I believe, is part of what Hegel is saying when he says that private and public ends are identical.

I have already touched on this theme when I was discussing what Hegel understood by civil society, and I now want to go more fully into it in the hope of making clearer what I believe to be the strong and the weak points in Hegel's conception of the State. I think it a mistake to speak, as he does, of the identity of private and public ends, and I also think that he draws some false conclusions from their close connection. Nevertheless, by insisting that they are involved in one another, he points to important truths neglected by the contract theorists and the Utilitarians – truths whose importance he fully recognizes, though he never succeeds in putting them clearly.

By a private end Hegel means, presumably, some such thing as the happiness or dignity or wealth or virtue of an individual; a man's happiness may be desired by himself or by some other person, but in either case is merely a private end, in the sense that it is a state or condition of an individual. By a public end Hegel means, say, justice or some form or aspect of the social order or the victory of one's country. He believes, as Bentham does not, that public ends are desired for their own sake and not only as means to the achievement of private ends; and since he believes this, we can assume – in spite of his saying that public and private ends are identical – that he does not hold, with Bentham, that the public good is merely a sum or collection of private goods or something which is a means to private goods. And here, surely, Hegel is right and Bentham wrong; it simply is not true that men desire for their own sake only states or conditions of the individual and other things merely as means to such states or conditions.

It is also true (and it is implied by Hegel, if not clearly stated) that social values, which cannot be reduced to sums of private good or means thereto, are so intimately connected with men's private ends that these ends are unintelligible apart from them. The connection is there no matter how selfish a man may be. Let us suppose, for the sake of argument, that Hegel's hero, Napoleon, was entirely selfish – that he never cared for the good of anyone besides himself except as a means to his own good. Napoleon's ambition was to be a great general, an emperor, and to play a unique rôle in history. The playing of such a rôle involves living up to standards of excellence which are social; and we cannot say that Napoleon accepted the standards in order to fulfil his ambition, because his ambition was precisely to live up to those standards. Napoleon's selfishness did not consist in his accepting the standards as means to his private ends; it consisted in his caring for nobody's private ends but his own. Having private interests or ambitions, as distinct from mere natural appetites, involves accepting values which give to those interests and ambitions their distinctive character. We cannot therefore treat these values, as Bentham does, as if they were accepted because they make easier the attainment of private interests and ambitions.

And yet it is misleading to say, as Hegel does, that private and public ends are identical. Though to accept the values involved in a private ambition is not to accept them as a means to the attainment of that ambition, neither is it to desire them for their own sake. A man cannot have private ends without accepting some values, but he can have private ends without also having public ends; he can accept the values (and the institutions connected with them) without its being his purpose to preserve or enlarge them. They are not the objects of his endeavour; they are not his ends. He still has only private ends, true though it may be that he could not have them unless he accepted certain values and institutions.

Of course, men do have public ends; they strive for the preservation or reform of institutions and values because they find them desirable or undesirable in themselves, quite apart from their consequences for individuals. The contrary belief is not borne out by experience; and if that belief is widely received, it is so probably because such theories as those of the Utilitarians have supported it. One of the simplest ways of explaining the social order is to treat it as if its function were to make easier the attainment of their own purposes by the individuals involved in it. But, though men do have public as well as private ends, a man need not have the first in order to have the second, and the two are never identical. They are different in kind, however closely they are connected in fact.

Here, too, we must make a distinction which Idealist critics of Utilitarianism usually fail to make. A social order is maintained or altered, not only because men pursue private ends inside it, but also because men are attached to laws and institutions for what they are or might be apart from how they affect private ends. Therefore, in all societies, we must expect to find both public and private ends pursued for their own sake. We must not, when we seek to explain a social order, treat public ends as if their function were to serve private ones; we must remember that, closely connected though they always are, the first are no more means to the second than the second to the first. But it does not follow that, because we find both public and private ends in every society, we must also find them in every man formed by society – that whoever has the second must also have the first.

Though Hegel says that public and private ends are identical, he does not mean to deny that they can and do conflict. He means only that in the fully rational community they would not conflict. Clearly, private ends can conflict with one another and with public ends, and the same is equally true of public ends. So, too, both private and public ends can conflict with values not involved in them. All this Hegel readily admits; private and public ends, though always in any society intimately connected, are not always in harmony.

But, though he admits this, he also asserts that eventually, in the community of the rational and the free, in the fully evolved State, there will be complete harmony between them. Indeed, this is part of his meaning when he says that public and private ends are identical. He says that, when they are what they ought to be, they form part of a single fully consistent system of behaviour and belief, and also that they must become what they ought to be. The State is what it ought to be (or, to use Hegel's idiom, becomes *actually* what it is *essentially*) when there is this harmony, and there must eventually be this harmony. It can emerge only out of conflict, and it must emerge.

Here, too, we cannot agree with Hegel; but we must take care to define the limits of our disagreement. Because we refuse to admit that this harmony is necessary, we are not bound to deny that the attainment of freedom, as Hegel understood it and as it is widely understood and cherished today – freedom, as the ability to live in accordance with principles critically examined and deliberately accepted – involves both conflict and reconciliation. Freedom, thus understood, is likely to be greatest where, following upon conflicts which are at once social and psychological – conflicts which have both deepened men's understanding of their principles and their devotion to them – harmony has come nearest to being restored. As creatures having aspirations and seeking to realize them, we come to conceive of freedom and to desire it ardently. If we are to achieve freedom, we must neither abandon our efforts to realize what we aspire to nor refuse to alter our aspirations; we must continue to aspire and to endeavour but must also reflect on our efforts and our goals and correct them, changing both ourselves and our environment. We must come to terms with life, neither resigning ourselves to wanting only what we can easily get nor persisting in endeavours beyond our powers. Both the idea of freedom and its realization are fruits of our actions and reflections as rational creatures operating in a social order which powerfully affects us but on which we too impinge. Thus, in a community where freedom is understood as the ability to live in accordance with principles critically examined and deliberately accepted, there is likely to be the more freedom, the greater the harmony between public and private ends. This too is good Hegelian doctrine, and is not a commonplace and is acceptable.

b. The Three Powers of Government

Hegel distinguished three powers within the State: the power to determine the universal will, which is the legislative power; the power to settle particular cases in conformity with the universal will, which is the executive power and includes, presumably, the taking of both administrative and judicial decisions; and the power of subjectivity or the 'will with the power of ultimate decision', which he calls sovereignty.[1] It is the sovereign power which expresses the unity of the State.

Hegel is most obscure when he speaks of sovereignty; he does not make it clear what is included in that power, nor why he thinks it is best exercised by an hereditary monarch. Since the executive power is defined as the 'subsuming of cases' under laws, it seems reasonable to exclude from it the making of policy. Must we then include policy-making in the sovereign power? Hegel says that 'there is a distinction between the monarch's decisions and their execution and application, or in general between his decisions and the continued execution or maintenance of past decisions'.[2] This suggests that the making of policy is the business of the monarch, and is therefore part of the sovereign power. But the carrying out of policy often requires legislation. Does sovereignty include the power of initiating laws? Hegel does not say. He says merely that 'in a well-organized monarchy, the objective aspect belongs to the law alone, and the monarch's part is merely to set to the law the subjective "I will" '; and he also says, the monarch 'has only to say "yes" and to dot the "i" '.[3] If this is so, then the monarch has only to ratify the decisions of others and to symbolize the unity of the State. Are we, then, to conclude that the sovereign power is only formally vested in the monarch and is actually exercised by others in his name? Or should we say that the sovereign power is itself merely formal? The first alternative seems the more likely, except that the passage from which I have just quoted is the only one that reduces the monarch to merely saying 'yes' and dotting the 'i'. Elsewhere, it is suggested that

[1] Ibid., § 273, p. 176.
[2] Ibid., § 287, p. 188.
[3] Ibid., addition 171 to § 280, p. 289.

the monarch takes an effective, and sometimes even a decisive, part in government. Unfortunately, it is never made clear what that part is.

Hegel tries to fit the three powers of government into his dialectical scheme, but, since he fails to make a clear distinction between the sovereign and the executive powers, this part of his argument is unusually obscure and unconvincing. We are told that the sovereign power is the power in which the other two powers are reconciled. Sovereignty is vested in the monarch; he has the last word, he is the reconciler, the restorer of harmony. But, if the executive power is as Hegel describes it – if it is merely administrative and judicial and does not include the making of policy – there is little chance of a serious conflict between it and the legislative power, for it merely 'applies the law to particular cases', without challenging it or demanding that it be changed. It is not the administrator or the judge, it is the maker of policy, who is likely to get involved in disputes with the legislature, should it refuse to make laws needed to implement policy. Hegel, by not including the making of policy in the executive power, suggests that it is a function which pertains to the sovereign power vested in the monarch. If that is so, then we must conclude that the monarch – the sovereign, the reconciler of contradiction – reconciles his own power with the legislative power; we must conclude that he is, in this triad, both synthesis and antithesis. Or if, to avoid such an odd conclusion, we say that the sovereign power is merely conciliatory and excludes the making of policy, we contradict Hegel. The attempt to fit the three powers of government, as Hegel defines them, into a dialectical triad fails completely.

Nor is it clear why the sovereign power, no matter what its functions, must be vested in an hereditary monarch. Granted that the State needs a symbol of unity, somebody to 'bear its person' and to speak for it on solemn occasions, why is an hereditary monarch better suited to this purpose than, say, an elected monarch or a president? In the past, for a variety of reasons, hereditary monarchy was the most widespread form of government. The nations have become used to it, or else have come to expect attributes in the head of the State, even where he is not an hereditary monarch, which they never would have expected if hereditary monarchy had not once been the prevalent form. Thus, there are attached even to the American presidency certain attributes which might never have been attached to it had not the founding fathers, as men of British extraction, been familiar with British monarchy. The hereditary monarch, for historical reasons, has been the typical head of the State, and hereditary monarchy has seemed to many peoples over long periods of time the most 'natural' form of government. And even today, when it seems so no longer, the popular image of the head of the State owes a great deal to the traditional rôle of the hereditary monarch. But all this, though true, is nothing to Hegel's purpose; for it does not establish that, in a general way, an hereditary monarch is better suited to be a symbol of the State's unity than is a president.

If we look at the champions of hereditary monarchy in the sixteenth and seventeenth centuries, we find none of them using Hegel's argument in favour of it. They are either believers in the divine right of kings, or they use historical or utilitarian arguments. Bodin insists that in France sovereign power has always belonged to the king whose title to the throne is determined by the Salic Law. Hobbes admits that the sovereign need not be a monarch but thinks that there are advantages to his being so and to his succeeding by hereditary right. Pascal's brief arguments in the *Pensées* amount to little more than this: though proofs of competence are required in holders of lesser offices, they are not required in the holder of the supreme office; and though that may seem unreasonable, it is not so, given the insatiate ambition and vanity of men; for the greater the power attached to an office, the more bitter and dangerous the contests for it, so that a rule which avoids this contest for the supreme office, on which all other offices depend, is in the general interest. No doubt, the effective power of the kings of France in Bodin's time or in Pascal's was no greater than the power of the President of the United States today, but in the France of those days it would not have been possible to elect kings as peacefully as presidents are now elected in the United States. France needed powerful monarchs and also needed to avoid contests for the monarchy, and so there was a strong argument for hereditary succession. But where the head of the State is chiefly a symbol of unity, the argument for hereditary monarchy is much less strong.

c. Representative Assemblies

Though Hegel was no democrat, he believed that there ought to be a legislature representative of the better educated and politically more articulate classes whom he identified with the people. He thought it important that these classes should be represented because in that way the State, as he put it, enters 'the subjective consciousness of the people'.[1] The government and the people must be in close and continuous touch with one another; the people must know what the government intends, and the government must know the moods, grievances and aspirations of the people. The Estates

[1] Ibid., addition 179 to § 301, p. 292.

of the realm speak for the nation; they are the ears and the eyes of the people focused on the government. They have the right to be heard and the right to be informed, presumably because the government ought not to rule without consulting the people's wishes and cannot rule effectively without some measure of popular understanding. Moreover, it matters to the people that they should be heard; if they are silenced or disregarded, they are apt to become ungovernable.

The Estates, as Hegel puts it, are but one *moment* of the legislature; they are not the whole of it. It is not their business, he thinks, to initiate legislation; they are there not to make proposals so much as to discuss them and either accept them or make objections. Presumably, he thinks that proposals of law will mostly come from the king's ministers, who know the facts. Unlike many of his contemporaries, Hegel recognizes, at least implicitly, the importance of the executive,[1] the maker of policy, even in the legislative sphere. We can say this of him, because, though he does not make a clear distinction between the sovereign and the executive power, he leaves us in no doubt that, in his opinion, the Estates do not ordinarily put forward proposals of law. But would he give to the Estates the right to reject the legislative proposals of the government? Or would he confine their right to making objections and imposing delays, the executive getting its way in the end, if it is determined to do so? There is nothing in the *Philosophy of Right* to indicate how Hegel would have answered these questions, if they had been put to him.

There is nothing undemocratic or illiberal about the belief that the initiative in legislation belongs to the executive rather than to the representative assembly, even where, as in Prussia, the executive is appointed by an hereditary monarch. It is borne out by the experience of all modern states. The liberals and radicals of the early nineteenth century who assumed that it is for popular assemblies to make laws and for governments merely to carry them out were much less realistic than Hegel. But a political theorist cannot be called liberal – even as that term was understood in Hegel's time – if he does not allow that the executive, though appointed by the monarch, ought to be responsible to parliament or to the Estates. If the king's ministers can put their measures through, when the Estates have voted against them, then the government is not responsible to the Estates. It is not a responsible or parliamentary government; and the mark of the early nineteenth-century liberal was that he believed in that kind

[1] Using this word now as it is ordinaaarily used in England, and not as Hegel sometimes uses it in the *Philosophy of Right*.

of government. Though, if we study the text of the *Philosophy of Right*, we cannot say that Hegel unequivocally rejected responsible government, we also cannot say that he unequivocally accepted it.

His attitude to the Estates is not unlike his attitude to juries. They are the popular element in government, just as juries are the popular element in the administration of justice. He makes several claims in their favour, but they are all modest claims. The Estates are indispensable to really good government, but they must not be allowed to do more than they can do well, which is not very much. They are a link between the people and the professionals. Government explains its intentions to the people through the Estates, and so gains the people's confidence, without which it cannot govern efficiently. The need to make legal arguments intelligible to juries brings the law down to the level of the ordinary citizen, convincing him that justice is indeed being done. Government must remain close to the people, must react quickly to their needs, must take account of their feelings and prejudices; but it need not, in the sense of the radicals, carry out their will.

Hegel insists that the universal will, of which he speaks with so much respect, is not to be confused with the momentary will of the people. Though much that he says about the universal will reminds us of what Rousseau says about the general will,[1] there is this great difference between them: Rousseau's general will emerges in a popular assembly debating under certain ideal conditions, whereas Hegel's universal or rational will is not the product of an assembly. Hegel does not deny that the Estates help to formulate the universal will. That they do follows, indeed, from their being a part of the legislature. But their contribution to its formulation is modest, and there is no reason to suppose that when the Estates differ from the government they are the more likely to be right.

Hegel wanted the Estates to represent classes and corporations rather than masses of individual citizens. He was against territorial constituencies. There should be an hereditary upper chamber representing the agricultural class, and a chamber elected by corporations representing the business class. Clearly, he thought that the nobles – the great landlords – could be trusted to speak for all who worked and lived on the land. He was against an extended franchise, even among the business class; it would lead, he thought, to indifference and to the formation of caucuses. He wanted a small but independent

[1] Hegel's criticism of Rousseau's general will (*Philosophy of Right*, § 258, pp. 156–7) is quite unfair; actually his *universal will* is much closer to Rousseau's *general will* than he cares to admit, though Rousseau's conception, unlike his, is democratic.

electorate; he did not want the voters manipulated by party agents. Nor did he want the Estates reduced to silence or overawed by the government; he wanted their power limited but freely exercised within those limits.

In all this, except that he cared less for responsible government (and I admit that the exception is important), he was not more illiberal than Burke and the old Whigs. In some ways, indeed, he was more liberal than they were. He was much more concerned than they were that government should be clean, and he disliked incompetent amateurs not subject to control. He had a good word to say for juries, but none for justices of the peace ignorant of the law and intent on defending the privileges of their class. He condemned the purchase of commissions in the Army and the sale of offices in the State. He was a severe critic of practices long defended by both Tories and Whigs in England but nowadays condemned in all civilized states. He had, I am sorry to say, a keener eye for the abuses than the merits of the English system of government; he was a less generous and perhaps a less candid critic of the English than was Montesquieu. But the fact remains that what he denounced as abuses are now admitted to have been so by most English historians. I will not say that *History* has proved Hegel right, for that would be too Hegelian a sentiment for my taste; I will say only that, if we accept certain moral and political principles which most Englishmen now do accept, we have to conclude that he was right.

d. *Freedom of Speech*

Hegel was a believer in freedom of speech. Where there are Estates meeting regularly to speak for the nation, there is likely to be well-informed and responsible criticism. And where there is informed and responsible criticism, it is safe to allow great freedom of speech, for the responsible critics will show up the irresponsible. It is not possible to have responsible criticism without also having irresponsible criticism, and it is therefore wise to ensure that you do not get the second kind without the first. The longer the public are offered both kinds, the better they are able to discriminate between them and the more impressed they are by the first kind. Do not be too anxious to silence fools and adventurers or you will silence useful critics as well, but rather give what opportunities you can to the intelligent and the responsible.

Hegel laid three limits on freedom of speech; he said that there must be no libel, no incitement to rebellion and no 'contemptuous caricature' of the government.[1] The first two are today still regarded

[1] Ibid., § 319, pp. 206–7.

as offences in all countries acknowledged to be liberal, and the third could be prosecuted in Hegel's time even in Britain. He favoured religious freedom and the separation of Church and State, saying that it is not for the State to determine what the citizen shall believe. The State can rightfully forbid the propagation of a doctrine only if it is subversive. He advocated civil rights for Jews and the toleration of Quakers who refuse military service on conscientious grounds. I suspect that he cared for the freedom of the individual – though not for the privileges of parliaments, diets and Estates – rather more than did most English Tories, and perhaps even more than the Whigs in the era before the first Reform Bill.

e. Relations Between States

Though Hegel is often obscure and sometimes equivocal when he discusses the internal structure of the State, he says nothing to which his critics have taken strong exception on moral grounds. They have, of course, condemned him for calling the State divine and for saying that the members of the State are its 'accidents', having no value except as belonging to it. As I have tried to show, his critics have misunderstood the significance of these remarks, which are indeed open to criticism, though not on the grounds usually chosen. But this 'worship' of the State is not prominent in Hegel's discussion of its structure and the distribution of power inside it. The worst that can be said of this part of this theory is that it exhibits a strong distrust of democracy; and nobody, least of all an honest democrat, need be shocked by that.

Hegel's critics have been shocked more by what he says about relations between States than about the State's constitution. It is here, if anywhere, that he is more than equivocal – that he seems to be putting forward a doctrine which many people would condemn as immoral.

He admits that there are rules which ought to govern relations between States. He does not suggest that they are merely maxims of prudence; he speaks of them as if they were customary and also moral rules. These rules are in fact often, if not usually, disobeyed by States when they think it their interest to disobey and there is no impartial authority to enforce obedience. So far, there is nothing to object to in what Hegel says. He merely asserts that there are moral principles which States ought to conform to, although in fact they often disregard them because there is no power strong enough to ensure respect for them.

But he does not leave the matter there. 'The relation between states is', he says, 'a relation between autonomous entities which make mutual stipulations but which at the same time are superior to these stipulations'.[1] It is the word *superior* which is here equivocal and perhaps also objectionable. In what sense are States superior to the treaties they make? Are they superior to them merely because, if they choose to break them, they cannot be sued or legally punished? *Superior* is an odd word to choose if that is all you want to say. It suggests more than this; it suggests that it is right for a State to break a treaty if it finds it to its advantage to do so. If this is what Hegel means, he contradicts himself, for he has already said that there are rules which States ought to obey and has included respect for treaties among them. It is absurd to say both that there is a rule which ought to be obeyed and that those to whom it applies are superior to it. If there is a relevant moral rule, then those to whom it applies have a duty to obey it, and they therefore cannot be superior to it. Unless by *superior* Hegel means, in this context, *not suable* or *legally punishable*, he is plainly guilty of bad logic and is also putting forward an immoral doctrine. My own impression is that he means more than this and that the charge against him is just; for I find it hard to believe that, if he had wanted to convey no more than that States which break treaties are not legally answerable for what they do, he would have said that they are superior to the treaties they make. He was equivocating; he was saying obliquely what he was reluctant to say outright. He did not have the candour of Machiavelli. In this he was not exceptional; there were many people who thought as he did about the relations between States and who were as reluctant as he was to say precisely what they thought.

f. War

According to Hegel, the State is never more sharply present to its members than when it is at war with other States; it is then that their sense of community is strongest. War is good for the moral health of the people. Hegel did not look forward to perpetual peace; he neither expected nor desired it. He has been accused of glorifying war.

This accusation seems to me extravagant and misleading. Even if we grant that Hegel glorified war, the kind of war that he glorified is not the kind that we are nowadays desperately afraid of and wish to avoid at almost any cost. War was much less destructive in Hegel's time than it has since become, and also probably much less demoralizing. War does stimulate some virtues, social as well as military. The Prussians

---

[1] Ibid., addition 191 to § 330, p. 297.

had fought a hard war against Napoleon, a war which had led to domestic reforms and to a burst of patriotism which also had other good effects. It is not surprising that a German who had lived through the war of liberation should have believed that war is good for the moral health of a people. Because we now have so much more reason to fear war, it does not follow that the claims made for it a century and a half ago were altogether false; there was, at that time, a large measure of truth to them. Moreover, to point out, as Hegel does, that war has good effects is not to glorify it – at least not in the sense intended by those who make this accusation against him. Hegel does not advocate continuous or frequent wars, or suggest that war is the noblest activity of man.

6. Observations on Hegel's Theory of the State

a. False Charges Against Hegel

I am conscious that, in discussing his theory of the State, I have defended Hegel from criticism more than I have criticized him. I have not done so because I come closer to sharing his views than those of other political thinkers whom I have been less concerned to defend, but because he has been so much more, and so much more crudely, misrepresented. He has even been treated as an arrogant and pretentious sciolist, a sycophant, a man without originality or penetration, who purveyed the most vicious doctrines under cover of an elaborate but empty metaphysic. No one, not even his worst detractors, have denied him a certain cleverness; they cannot deny that, if he was a charlatan, he was a most successful one, whose victims were not men-in-the-street but men of letters and intellectuals.

That these charges are grossly unjust must, I think, be evident to anyone who has read the *Phenomenology of Spirit*, the *Lectures on the Philosophy of History* and the *Philosophy of Right* at all attentively. Whatever Hegel's faults as a social and political theorist, it ought not to be said of him that he lacked originality and penetration. To say that is almost like saying that Dante lacked passion, or Shakespeare lacked imagination, or Voltaire lacked wit, or Goethe lacked breadth of mind; it is to deny him the qualities which are most clearly and pre-eminently his own. To refute Hegel's grosser critics, even a summary account of his social and political theory is enough.

There are, however, other charges brought against him which are partly false and partly true. For example, it has been said that he was a believer in the *totalitarian* State. This is an ambiguous and misleading charge. The word *totalitarian* is not to be found in Hegel's writings; his varied and peculiar vocabulary does not include this particular epithet, which belongs to our century. Hegel said that it is only as a member of the State that the individual has value, that he realizes his essence by becoming rational, moral and free. If to believe this is to believe in the totalitarian State, then Hegel did believe in it. But then this belief, though perhaps mistaken, may be harmless. Harmless, I mean, from the point of view of the liberal; and it is the man who prides himself on his liberalism who is most apt to bring this charge against Hegel. For to say that the individual has value, in this sense, only as a member of the State is *not* to imply that he ought always to obey established laws, nor yet that, even when he ought to obey them, he ought not to criticize them. If we accept this belief, we are not committed to condemning Socrates and Luther, or even the American and French revolutionaries. Hegel's conception of the State commits him only to saying that the individual ought always to obey established laws and conventions when the State is at the highest level of its development; and we have seen that the State, at this level, allows considerable freedom of speech. It is only in the State where freedom is realized that the duty of obedience is absolute. This is all that follows logically from Hegel's account of how man realizes his potentialities and becomes what he is destined to be and ought to be only as a member of the State.

If Hegel had said (or implied) no more than that the duty of obedience is absolute where freedom is fully realized, the liberal would be hard put to it to find fault with him. But, unfortunately, he said more than this; he said enough to suggest that the Prussian State of his day came very close to being a State where freedom was fully realized. This has been denied by Eric Weil in his book, *Hegel et l'État*, where he quotes several passages from the *Philosophy of Right*, to show that the State there described by Hegel differs considerably from the Prussian State of the 1820s. My impression is that Weil makes too much of these passages and partly misinterprets them. I agree with him that the fully mature State, as Hegel describes it in the *Philosophy of Right*, is not the Prussia of his day, but I suspect that Hegel did not see nearly as great a difference between them as Weil supposes.[1]

But this does not seem to me the important point. Whatever the difference between the State described in the *Philosophy of Right* and the Prussian State, both are undemocratic. We can therefore say that,

---

[1] See Weil, *Hegel et l'État*, first published in 1950, 4th ed. (Paris 1970), chs. i, iv and v, pp. 22–3, 55–62 and 72.

in Hegel's opinion, the State in which freedom is fully realized is not democratic. He does not merely say that it *need* not be democratic; he says that it *must* not be. Now, this is not a conclusion which follows from his conception of the State or from his remarks on what the individual owes to the State; it is merely a conclusion he reaches in the account he gives, in the *Philosophy of Right*, of the structure of the State. No doubt, he believes that he has derived this structure logically from his conception of the State as a community of rational and free persons. But the belief is mistaken. Logically, democracy is just as compatible with Hegel's conception of a community of rational and free persons as is the constitutional monarchy described in the *Philosophy of Right*. Indeed, I should go further that that; I should say that Hegel's conception of the State as essentially a community of the rational and the free, though it does not entail that the fully mature State is a democracy, does powerfully suggest it. If Hegel's conception of freedom had been the same as Hobbes's or even Locke's, this might not be so; but in fact it comes much closer to Rousseau's conception and to Kant's. A man is free when he can conscientiously, and not merely from habit, accept the laws and conventions of his community. There are grounds, psychological and sociological, for believing that he is most likely to do this when he has a say in making the laws. There may well be democracy without freedom in that sense; it may even be that democracy generates forces that tend to destroy or diminish freedom. But this is only to say that democracy is not a sufficient condition of freedom; it is not to deny that it may be a necessary condition. There are grounds for believing that it is, though Hegel never considered them.

He was against democracy and was also in several ways illiberal. But that does not make him a champion of the totalitarian State in the sense in which liberals today condemn it. Far from believing that one party ought to control the State, he attacked democracy partly because he feared that it might lead to party government, which he took to be the domination of the State by one faction inside it. The universal will, expressed in the law, should emerge, according to Hegel, from the interplay of many forces independent of one another. He wanted the well-to-do and the educated to have much more influence, in proportion to their numbers, than the poor and the ignorant; he wanted professional servants of the State to make policy and not merely to carry it out. Like Burke and like Montesquieu, he wanted a balance of power within the State, with some groups and classes having much more power than others on the ground that, by tradition and education, they were more responsible, less narrow, and more competent. We might call him a Whig, except that he was more critical of parliaments and less mistrustful of public officials than the Whigs were, and also much less willing to have power fall into the hands of persons with nothing to recommend them except birth or riches. He believed much too strongly in what the French revolutionaries called *la carrière ouverte aux talents* to be a Whig. It is true that the cry of 'careers open to talent', as it was raised in Hegel's time, was not equivalent to the call of the socialists for equality of opportunity. The suggestion was not that the system of property should be changed in order to allow the poor and the ignorant to develop their talents, but rather that those who had developed them should not, by reason of their humble birth, be denied the opportunity of using them for the benefit of society and themselves. Yet Hegel did believe in equality of opportunity in a sense in which the Whigs did not.

b. His Excessive Claims for the State

Though Hegel is not a totalitarian, in the bad sense, it cannot be denied that he makes extravagant and false claims for the State. It may be true that man is rational, moral and free (in Hegel's sense of freedom) only as a member of society, but it is not true that he is so only as a citizen – as a member of the State. Hegel speaks of other forms of ethical (or communal) life besides the State; he speaks of the family and of civil society. Yet he calls the State the highest form.

But in what sense is the State *higher* than other communities? Can we say that it is higher because it includes them? Hegel speaks of the State as that in which the family and civil society – the only other forms of ethical (or communal) life he takes into account in the *Philosophy of Right* – are 'reconciled'; and it would therefore seem that this is at least part of what he means.

If that is what he means, he is clearly wrong. There are many communities which are not included in the State; there are many ways in which citizens of different States are socially related to one another. Even the relations proper to the family and to civil society can and do subsist between members of different States. There are also churches and many other kinds of associations which transcend the limits of States. Clearly there is no community (unless we treat all mankind as one community) of which it can be said that any association or body having a member in common with it has none outside it. No State includes all the communities and associations to which its citizens belong. Nor can we say that it is only in the communities and associations which fall entire within the limits of the State that man acquires the qualities which, in Hegel's eyes, make him a rational, moral and free being (i.e., a person who has become *actually* what he is *essentially*). It is not here a question of our being concerned with values which Hegel neglects, and our therefore rejecting his doctrine that it is in the State and in communities included in the State that man achieves whatever makes human life valuable. Even if we accept only the values that Hegel accepts, we must reject this doctrine.

The State possesses certain attributes (which I need not define for the purposes of my argument) that other communities and associations do not possess; some of these attributes go by the name of sovereignty. Because the State is sovereign, it can act upon other communities and associations in ways in which they cannot act upon it; and it is widely admitted that it alone should be sovereign. Thus we can say that the State is higher than other communities in a quite usual sense of the word higher; it can control them as they cannot control it. But this sense of higher is not the sense required to justify the claims which Hegel makes on behalf of the State. Because the State possesses these attributes, it does not follow that it does more than other communities and associations to make men rational, moral and free; nor does it follow, merely from these attributes, that a man ought always to put loyalty to the State above other loyalties.

I have argued already that it means nothing to say that the family and civil society are reconciled in the State, and that therefore the State is higher than they are in the way that one moment or aspect of a Hegelian triad is higher than the two others which are 'reconciled' in it. The family and civil society are not contradictory, except in the sense that some statements which are true of the first are false of the second; there is therefore no need for them to be reconciled. If we take the concepts of the family and civil society, as Hegel defines them, they are not self-contradictory or logically inconsistent with one another, and if we take the realities to which these concepts apply, they are not incompatible or antagonistic.

It is true that the State keeps the peace between both individuals and groups; it provides for the settlement of disputes without recourse to violence. In that sense, it is conciliatory; but when we think of the State in this way, we have no more exalted a view of it than Bentham had. The State as the conciliator of interests and the guardian of the peace – the State as the Utilitarians defined it – is in Hegel's opinion merely a part of civil society. In the sense in which the State is something more than civil society (a sense which expresses, I admit, important truths neglected by the Utilitarians), it is not a community in which other communities are reconciled; it is rather a community whose members have certain feelings towards it. It is, as far as its institutions go, much the same community as civil society; it differs from it mostly in the spirit that informs it. If, when Hegel distinguishes the State from civil society, we suppose him to be saying that there is something about a community, and especially about a political community, which is altogether missed by such explanations as the Utilitarians give, we may well agree with him; but this something has really nothing to do with the reconciling of a contradiction between the family and civil society. Moreover, this something is not peculiar to the State, nor always more marked in it than in other communities, nor confined to communities included in it.

c. Why No World-State?

In the *Philosophy of History* and in the *Philosophy of Right*, Hegel takes it for granted that for Mind or Spirit to be made fully actual, there is no need for a world-state; he takes it for granted that the nation-state or the system of such states is the highest manifestation of Objective Spirit. This does not, in my opinion, square with his conception of Spirit, which, he tells us, is essentially one. Spirit, in the form of rational self-knowledge, is fully and explicitly made actual in a single, coherent, all-embracing philosophy. This philosophy may develop out of many incomplete and partly inconsistent philosophies but must itself be fully consistent and complete. Why, then, should Spirit, in the form of rational will, not be made fully actual in a single community whose laws can be conscientiously obeyed by all its members? The universal will necessarily finds expression in the laws and conventions of a community of finite minds. If Spirit is essentially one, there can be only one universal will and therefore only one fully rational and free community. No doubt, that community will include other communities and associations inside it, just as the nation-state does. Hegel admits that the universal will, in so far as it is manifest in the nation-state, is not realized as fully as it might be while the individuals and associations inside the State are in conflict with one another, or rather, while the differences that arise between them cannot be resolved by methods which they all accept as rational and just. How, then, can the universal will, in so far as it is manifest in a system of states, be fully realized while those states resort to war with one another because there are no methods for settling disputes between them which they all accept as rational and just? But if there were such methods and they were effective, there would be a world-state. It seems to follow from Hegel's conception of Mind or Spirit that the fully rational and free community must be a world-state.

d. Success and Justification

Though Hegel is logically committed only to saying that the laws of the fully developed – or completely rational and free – State are always to be obeyed, he does sometimes create the impression that the laws of any state ought always to be obeyed, except by great men or, as he puts it, by World-Historical Individuals. I have already criticized this strange doctrine, and I must not now repeat what I said before. But there is another criticism often made against Hegel, and made justly.

For all his talk of conscience and freedom, he was impressed by power and even by the ruthless use of it. If he had not been, he would not have spoken as he did of History justifying those who succeed, even when they act from evil motives. It is one thing to say that good sometimes comes of evil, and quite another to say that the evil is justified even when the person who commits it never intended the good. And, as we have seen, it is only the great criminal whose crimes are justified.

Hegel's position here is by no means the same as Machiavelli's. Machiavelli neither condemned nor justified the great criminal; he merely argued that great crimes have sometimes to be committed if power is to be achieved, or the State to be saved or enlarged. He despised the man who refrains from crime only because he lacks the courage to commit it, because he lets 'I dare not' wait upon 'I would'. But he never said that the great criminal is justified; he never sought to elevate him morally. He spoke only of men; he did not speak of larger than human purposes working through men and justifying their wickedness when that wickedness contributes to those purposes. Nothing so logically absurd and morally perverse as the doctrine of justification by unintended good consequences is to be found in his writings. He admired courage, firmness of purpose and intelligence, but he did not revere power, as Hegel did. He was not ignoble; he was not vulgar in that particular way.

I have been concerned only with Hegel's doctrine, and have felt bound to insist that, taken as a whole, it does not have some of the implications which his detractors have read into passages taken out of context. But I would not deny that there is an unpleasant tone about the writings of a man who appears to have believed that the Universal Mind had attained full self-knowledge in his philosophy. His manner is against him; it suggests a colossal arrogance. And we do well to mistrust the arrogant, especially when they speak of freedom.

CHAPTER THREE
Marx and Engels   *I*

I shall discuss only the social theory of Marx and Engels, saying nothing about their philosophical materialism and their account of how we acquire knowledge. I shall limit myself in this way for a number of reasons, of which the most important (and perhaps the only one worth mentioning) is that it is doubtful whether we need to understand these aspects of their philosophy in order to understand their social theory. I do not deny that philosophical materialists may be disposed to hold some views about society and social change rather than others; I do not deny that there have been and still are certain connections between theories about matter and mind and the nature of knowledge and theories about society and the State. The intellectual history of mankind does not consist of streams which flow without ever touching one another; it is one broad river, and how men look at one part of life is deeply influenced by how they have learnt to look at others. Much the same fashions affect, from time to time, all or most branches of study. I would not deny anything so obvious, so well attested by history.

I deny only that certain theories, because they are often found together, or because they are intimately connected as parts of the intellectual life of one man or group of men, therefore stand or fall together or are unintelligible if they are studied apart from one another. Whatever the proper analysis of matter and mind, of physical and mental events, and of the relations between them, I do not see how it can affect the question of whether or not a particular theory about society is true. The social theorist, when he speaks of physical and mental events, speaks of them as all men do, and to understand him we do not need to know what his views are (if, indeed, he has any) about matter and mind. Marx and Engels have been called materialists and economic determinists, and economic determinism has also been called a form of materialism. But economic determinism is not a theory about physical and mental events or a theory of knowledge; it is a theory about how certain forms of social activity – all of them, even those which work on matter for the satisfying of basic needs, 'mental' as well as 'physical' – are related to one another. Economic determinism might still be true even if Marx's views about matter and mind were false or so obscure as to be unintelligible; and if economic determinism is itself obscure, it is so not because it rests on some other obscure theory but on its own account.

Marx's theory of knowledge, which I have never understood, has sometimes been called a form of pragmatism and sometimes a form of naïve realism. Perhaps it is one or the other; perhaps it is not. This is a question which neither interests the social theorist nor inhibits him as an interpreter and critic of Marxian social theory. Admittedly, Marx has something (though not much) to say about science, which he treats as genuine in contrast to spurious knowledge, and also about how science, as an activity of man in society, is related to man's other social activities. But we need not enquire into what he understood by knowledge to discover how he thought science was related to these other activities; because, when he spoke of these relations, he spoke of science as we all do. A pragmatist or a naïve realist (assuming, for the moment, that Marx was one or the other) might have views altogether different from Marx's about the relations between science and, say, economic production, and yet say nothing inconsistent with pragmatism or naïve realism.

Marx's philosophical materialism and his theory of knowledge have never, I believe, been taken seriously except by people who have been attracted to his social theory; they are meagre and enigmatic, and are less often masticated than swallowed whole as adjuncts to the main course. They are sometimes discussed by persons who are not Marxists, though scarcely ever for their own sake, but rather for the sake of completeness. There is, after all, a literal and obvious sense in which no account of Marxism is complete unless it discusses all aspects of the thought of Marx and Engels, and explains why they thought their materialism and their theory of knowledge were logically connected with their social theory. But, unless this logical connection is there, we do not need to look into their materialism and theory of knowledge in order to understand their social theory. I take it for granted that the connection is not there; it seems to me so obvious as not to be worth an argument. If I were enquiring how Marx and Engels came by the ideas which constitute their social theory, I should think it my duty to look into these other sides of their thought; for it may be that their materialism and their conception of what constitutes knowledge disposed them to hold certain views about society. But I am not enquiring into the genesis of their social theory; I am concerned only to explain what it is, and to consider how far the ideas it contains help us to understand social facts better than we otherwise would.

The social theory of Marx and Engels is incomparably more interesting than the other parts of their thought; it is studied for its own sake, and those who reject it also learn from it. Students of philosophy scarcely ever mention Marx except when they are actually studying his philosophy, whereas students of society often mention him, and even more often use his ideas, when they are studying society and not his theories about it. The study of Marxism as a social theory is therefore more than intellectual history; it is a study of ideas which – either in the form he gave them or else modified – are still widely used. In studying Marxist social theory, we add considerably to our understanding of how men think about society; in criticizing it, we help to make clear our own views about society.

To forestall criticism, there is one point I would like to make to justify my neglect of Marx's philosophical materialism. It does sometimes happen that a theorist employs, in order to explain man in society, conceptions taken over from his logic or metaphysics or theory of knowledge in such a way that we cannot be certain how he uses these conceptions in his social theory unless we study these other aspects of his thought. For instance, we need to know something of Hegel's logic and his metaphysics to understand how he uses certain very abstract concepts, in senses peculiar to himself, to construct his theory of the State. We cannot understand his social and political theory unless we do this, and it is well worth doing because that theory is one of the greatest of its kind. Yet I believe that everything that is important and really intelligible which Hegel says about society and government (and there is a great deal) can be said without using his peculiar concepts; I believe that it can all be translated into more ordinary language – language which can be understood by anyone who knows nothing of Hegel's logic and metaphysics, without anything valuable being lost. But, of course, the translation has to be made, and in order to make it, we have to understand, in some sense of understanding, both of the languages in question. It may be that Hegel's critics are right, that some of his concepts are empty or perverse;[1] but even if they are, they do

---

[1] I say *perverse*, rather than *self-contradictory*, because they involve the *deliberate* putting

form, together with his other concepts, a coherent system. There are rules which govern the use of Hegel's concepts, even though some of the concepts are empty; both his sense and nonsense are systematic, and we can learn to talk nonsense according to his rules. That is to say, faced by certain of Hegel's concepts – which he in fact goes to considerable trouble to explain – we can either accept or reject them; and if we reject them as empty or perverse, we must conclude that there is an element of nonsense in the doctrines which contain them. And yet – since Hegel is a systematic thinker who puts his cards on the table, telling us how he intends to use them – we can learn to discriminate between what to us appears the sense and the nonsense in his theories, and we can then put the sense into our own words. And, since it is not in his *Philosophy of Right* nor even in the *Phenomenology of Spirit* but elsewhere that Hegel puts his cards on the table and makes clear his intentions, we have to look at his logic (which is a form of metaphysics) in order to understand what he says about society and government – in order to extricate the sense from what we cannot help calling (though with all respect) the nonsense in the *Phenomenology* and the *Philosophy of Right*. Once we have done this, we have done all we can do to make Hegel's social theory as fully intelligible as it can be made, and we are then able to explain the theory to the man who knows nothing of his general philosophy as well as to the man who knows a great deal. To learn how Hegel uses his peculiar vocabulary, we must go to his logic and metaphysics; but I believe that, once this is done, we can say all that is valuable in his social and political theory without using that vocabulary.

We cannot say as much for Marx and Engels. They are not systematic thinkers as Hegel was; they nowhere clearly explain their ideas and intentions. And to the extent that they are systematic and lucid, they are much more so in their social theory than anywhere else. Their philosophy, as far as I can see, throws little light on their social theory; it gives us no insight into how they use ideas peculiar to themselves to explain society and government. If we are to get any such insight, we must get it from the social theory itself.

I shall also say almost nothing of Marxian economics, though my motives for this neglect are different from my motives for

---

together of what, to Hegel's critics, seem clearly incompatible ideas. Hegel is often as well aware as his critics of what he is doing. He admits that, taken in one way, they are incompatible, but insists that, taken in another – more profound or more adequate, way – they are not. As he sees it, those who – because they cannot follow him – accuse him of nonsense, are blind; while they in their turn say that they are not blind, because they know the meanings of the words used by Hegel and see that it makes nonsense to use them as he does.

neglecting Marxian philosophy. Marx was as much – as elaborately, as systematically and no doubt as lucidly – an economist as he was a social and political theorist. He was not a very coherent or clear or precise thinker in any field; but I dare say he possessed these qualities in as ample measure when he discussed the production and distribution of wealth as when he discussed the social order more generally or the functions of government within that order. Indeed, since economics (thanks to the work of the classical economists) was already, in Marx's day, as it still is now, a more developed field of study using more precise ideas than sociology, it is probable that Marx's account of how the capitalist economy functions is nearer being coherent and lucid than is historical materialism, which is his account of how society changes and how different forms of social activity are related to one another. It is probably more coherent and lucid, but also less original and suggestive. Marx is held in much greater esteem by sociologists than by economists – except, of course, when the economists happen to be Marxists. His reputation as an economist has fluctuated considerably among economists who were not Marxists; and some academic economists in the West have even tried, perhaps successfully, to enhance that reputation. Attempts have even been made to see in Marx anticipations of Keynes, and these attempts have also been contested.

If I were to discuss Marxian economics, I could at best hope to do no more than reproduce what other people have said; and I shall refrain from doing that. It is the Marxian account of society and of social change and the Marxian theory of the State that I shall discuss, for they are still of absorbing interest to the social and political theorist. I have already written a book about them,[1] but I hope that I shall not repeat in other words what I said there. Since writing it, I have read several books about Marxism, and two in particular, which have caused me to change my mind about some things, and to want to put my views about others differently. These two books are the second and much enlarged edition of M. M. Bober's *Karl Marx's Interpretation of History* (Cambridge, Mass. 1948), and H. B. Acton's *The Illusion of the Epoch* (London 1955). My book was published a year before Acton's, but I greatly regret I did not read Bober's book before I wrote mine. At the time, I wanted to make up my own mind about Marxian social theory undistracted by the opinions of others, and I thought it better to risk making my own mistakes rather than to repeat other people's. I now think that was unwise. These are two excellent books from which I have learnt a great deal.

[1] *German Marxism and Russian Communism* (London 1954).

I shall present my appraisal and criticism of Marxian social theory in the form of answers to four questions. What, according to Marx and Engels, is the *basic* determinant of social change, and in what sense is it *basic*? What did they understand by social classes and class struggles, and why did they say that class interests are irreconcilable? What did they understand by 'ideology', and how did they conceive of its function in society? What did they think is the function of the State in societies divided into classes, and what did they predict would disappear in the classless society? Each of these is not a single question so much as a group of questions so closely related to one another that they can hardly be treated apart. The questions are meant to draw attention to those aspects of Marxian theory which are still most in need of elucidation (or perhaps the better word is *disentanglement*) and most worth elucidating. Marxism has been so often and so severely handled by critics that most people are willing to admit that the theory, taken as a whole, is unacceptable. It is, they say, unacceptable, and they quickly go on to add that there is a great deal to be said for it. There is much wider agreement that the theory is both defective and valuable than about the respects in which it is so. There are still critics of Marxism who are misled by the theory they criticize. My aim is to be as precise as I can be, without, I hope, being tedious.

I. WHAT, ACCORDING TO MARX AND ENGELS IS THE BASIC DETERMINANT OF SOCIAL CHANGE, AND IN WHAT RESPECT IS IT BASIC?

1. Foundation and Superstructure

Let me begin by citing once again some often-quoted sentences from the Preface to Marx's *Contribution to the Critique of Political Economy*: 'In the social production of their existence, men inevitably enter into definite relations, which are independent of their will, namely relations of production appropriate to a given stage in the development of their material forces of production. The totality of these relations of production constitutes the economic structure of society, the real foundation, on which arises a legal and political superstructure and to which correspond definite forms of social consciousness'.[1] This short passage is part of what Marx called 'the general conclusion' which he reached in his study of economics, and which, once reached,

[1] Marx and Engels, *Collected Works* (London 1975–), vol. 29, p. 263.

'became the guiding principle' of his studies,[1] presumably not only of economics, but of society generally. In it he seems to be making several distinctions: between production and the relations into which men enter in production; between these relations and the laws and political institutions arising from them; and between these laws and institutions and what he calls the forms of social consciousness corresponding to them. We have, first, production, then relations of production, then laws and political institutions, and lastly forms of consciousness: these four things co-exist, and yet there is an order of dependence asserted among them. It is production which brings men into these indispensable and unwilled relations; it is out of these relations that law and government arise; and it is to law and government that forms of social consciousness correspond. As we shall soon see, there are all kinds of difficulties with this formulation: there are difficulties about what is to be understood by the four things distinguished from one another, and also about the nature of the relations asserted between them. I want, nevertheless, to draw attention to the actual words used by Marx, or, rather, by his English translators. Though some of these words, in this context, have an indefinite meaning, there is a limit to the plausible interpretations which can be put on them.[2]

There has been controversy between critics of Marxism as to whether the theory makes the technique of production or the economic structure in a broader sense the basic factor determining the general character of social life. Acton and Bober prefer the first alternative;[3] Sidney Hook, in *Towards the Understanding of Karl Marx*, prefers the second.[4] The passage I have quoted seems to settle the matter in favour of Hook, for Marx there distinguishes production from the relations of production, which he calls the 'economic structure' of society and the 'real foundation' on which law and government and forms of social consciousness all depend. But the matter cannot be settled that easily. For the passage, studied more closely, favours Bober and Acton rather than Hook. Though it is true that Marx calls the 'economic structure' the real foundation of social life, it is equally true that he says that

---

[1] Ibid., p. 262.

[2] The most compelling Marxist treatment of this subject is G. A. Cohen's *Karl Marx's Theory of History* (Princeton 1978) – see especially chs. 6 and 8. For an alternative view, partly inspired by Plamenatz, see Steven Lukes, 'Can the Base be distinguished from the Superstructure?', in *The Nature of Political Theory*, ed. David Miller and Larry Siedentop (Oxford 1983), pp. 103–19. For a reply to Lukes, and a critique of Plamenatz, see Cohen's *History, Labour, and Freedom* (Oxford 1988), chs. 2 and 3.

[3] See Bober, *Karl Marx's Interpretation of History*, 2nd ed., Part I, ch. i, pp. 6–11, and Acton, *The Illusion of the Epoch*, pp. 135–7.

[4] See Hook, *Towards the Understanding of Karl Marx* (London 1933), ch. 12, pp. 125–9.

that structure consists of relations into which men enter, whether they like it or not, because they are engaged in production. If the economic structure is basic in relation to law, government and forms of consciousness, is not production basic in relation to the economic structure? We have here four aspects of social life distinguished by Marx which we can, for brevity's sake, call A, B, C and D. Acton and Bober say that A is basic, while Hook insists that it is B. The passage I have quoted, read superficially, seems to favour Hook. But even if we could not, as in fact we can,[1] find other passages in Marx and Engels to support Acton and Bober, we may wonder whether the point at issue is worth an argument. Does it matter whether we call A or B *basic* in relation to C and D, given that B arises, as Marx says it does, out of A? Moreover, though Marx, in this particular passage, distinguishes what he calls the 'forces of production' (i.e. the materials, tools and methods involved in production) from 'the relations of production' arising out of them, and calls these relations the 'economic structure' of society, his usual practice is to include the forces of production in the 'economic structure'.

Nothing is gained by treating the economic structure or relations of production, rather than production itself, as basic, unless it is assumed that that structure is to a considerable extent independent of production – that there are other things besides production making it what it is. This Hook sees clearly, for he says, 'The social relations of production . . . cannot therefore be regarded as the automatic reflection of technology. On the contrary, the development of technology is itself often dependent upon the system of social relationships in which it is found'.[2] That is how we have to interpret Marx if we want to make his position stronger by insisting that it is the economic structure rather than the actual process or technique of production which is basic; and, as I have said already, we can

[1] For instance, there are these well-known passages: 'In acquiring new productive forces, men change their mode of production; and in changing their mode of production, in changing the way of earning their living, they change all their social relations. The hand-mill gives you society with the feudal lord; the steam-mill, society with the industrial capitalist.' Marx, *The Poverty of Philosophy, Collected Works*, vol. 6, p. 166. – 'The bourgeoisie cannot exist without constantly revolutionising the instruments of production, and thereby the relations of production, and with them the whole relations of society.' Marx and Engels, *Communist Manifesto*, sect. I, ibid., p. 487. – 'As individuals express their life, so they are. What they are, therefore, coincides with their production, both with *what* they produce and with *how* they produce. Hence what individuals are depends on the material conditions of their production.' Marx and Engels, *The German Ideology*, I, *Collected Works*, vol. 5, pp. 31–2.

[2] *Towards the Understanding of Karl Marx*, ch. 12, p. 126.

find evidence in the writings of Marx and Engels to support this interpretation.

As there is evidence to support both the one interpretation and the other, how are we to settle the matter? Should we say that, where there is a conflict of evidence, we ought to accept the interpretation which makes the better sense? Hook's interpretation makes the theory more plausible, and there is evidence in favour of it as well as in favour of the interpretation which makes the theory implausible. Is that not reason enough for preferring it? Ought we not, in justice and charity, to give Marx and Engels the benefit of the doubt?

I shall answer the last question by saying that there is no doubt here of which to give them the benefit. The evidence does not make it uncertain what position Marx and Engels took, for there is good evidence that they sometimes took one position and sometimes the other. We can be reasonably certain that they sometimes treated the economic structure of society as *basic* and at other times the process of production, and that they sometimes spoke as if the structure were entirely determined by the process and at other times as if it were not.

Hook's version of it may make the theory more plausible; it may seem to accord better with the facts than the version of Bober and Acton. I do not myself believe, for reasons which I hope to make clear later, that Hook's version does accord very well with the facts; but I do admit that, at a first glance, it seems to do so better than the other version. It is an apparently better version, not as being more in keeping with the text, but as being *apparently* more in keeping with the facts. If we ignore the facts and take account only of the text, we may say that, whereas the Bober-Acton version is more in keeping with what Marx and Engels tell us about the basic pattern of social change, Hook's version accords better with their explanations of actual social transformations – as, for example, the decay of feudalism and the rise of capitalism. In other words, their own accounts of major social revolutions do not accord with their formulations of the basic pattern of social change.

Yet it is because they have their own peculiar conception of social change that they use some of the expressions most characteristic of them. Why, for example, should they speak of 'relations of *production*' unless they believe that these relations, which they call the real foundation of the legal and political system and of the moral order, are determined by the character of production, by the natural resources at men's disposal and the tools and methods they use to produce what satisfies their needs?

If, then, I am right, the Marxian terminology suggests one version (which I have called the Bober-Acton version) of what Marx and Engels thought was the ultimate determinant of social change, while their explanations of the rise of capitalism and of other great social transformations suggest another version (which I have called the Hook version). This is one reason among others why their theory is so confused and confusing.

I have said that Hook's version, if we do not examine it too closely, is the more plausible of the two in the sense that it seems to be more realistic – to come nearer to fitting the facts. But if we accept it, there is no longer any point in calling the Marxian theory, as both Marx and Engels call it, *materialist*. Not, of course, because Hook's version takes the theory further away from *philosophical materialism*, which is irrelevant when we are discussing a social theory, but because it plays down the importance of actual production. If the Marxian social theory is *materialist*, it is so because it asserts that it is how men produce what satisfies their needs which determines the general character of the moral, political and legal order in which they live. Hook's version, if we accept it, deprives Marxian social theory of the right to be called *materialist* in the only sense of that word which makes sense when it is applied to a social theory. If the relations of production – the so-called foundations of the social order – are determined by other things as well as by the character of production, those other things can only be morality, law and government, or what Marx and Engels call the 'forms of social consciousness'; they must belong to what the two masters call the superstructure of society in contrast with the *material* basis. Thus, Hook's version, in spite of the evidence in its favour, does, if I may use the expression, knock the bottom out of Marxian social theory in a way that the Bober-Acton version does not; it makes it a theory radically different from what its authors intended it to be.

2. The Sense of the Distinction

What could be meant by calling one part of social life fundamental or basic in relation to the rest? If we choose to call production basic, what exactly is the point of doing so?

Clearly, if there is to be social life at all, the species engaged in that life – which in the case that interests us is the species *man* – must survive. Man survives by producing what satisfies his hunger, his thirst, his need for shelter. If men are to be able to engage in other activities besides the production of what they need to keep them alive, they must at least engage in that production. In this obvious sense, production is basic. No one would wish to deny it. But Marx and Engels were concerned to say more than this; they were concerned to do more than utter a truism. They wanted to say that the *character* of production determines in general the character of social life. It is true that they said other things not compatible with this – things which have moved Hook and others to offer what seemed to them more reasonable versions of Marxian theory; but it cannot be denied that they often did say this, and thought it important to say it. They also sometimes spoke as if this followed from production's being basic in the sense which nobody would wish to deny – as if it followed that, because men must engage in production if they are to be able to do other things, the character of production determines the character of their other activities. But the conclusion clearly does not follow.

Production is *basic* in relation to social life generally in the sense that it makes it possible. It is also *basic* in another sense, if not to all other aspects of social life, then to some of the most important; it is basic in relation to them in the sense that it creates the need for them. For instance, wherever there is production in society, there is a need for some rules of property. Or again, given a division of labour on a large enough scale, there is a need for organized government. And doubtless there are other things, which are not themselves parts or aspects of the productive process, for which a need arises because there is production, or because there is one type of it rather than another. But, though we admit that wherever there is production there is a need for some rules of property, we need not hold that the type of production determines what these rules are; nor need we, if we grant that a division of labour beyond a certain scale creates a need for government, go on to say that the form of government is determined by the form of that division of labour. To avoid confusion of thought, let us distinguish between *requiring* and *determining*. I shall say that one thing *requires* another, when, given any form of the one, there is a need for *some* form of the other, and that one thing *determines* another, when, given a particular form of the one, there arises a particular form of the other.

The degree of particularity does not much matter. Several governments differing considerably from one another can all be reckoned governments of the same form or type, and so too can systems of property and modes of production. If, for example, we want to say that the mode of production *determines* the system of property, we do not have to show that every change in productive technique, no matter how small, produces a change in the system of property; but we do have to do *more* than show that wherever there is *any* production in society there is a need for *some* rules of property. The least we must do is distinguish between several modes of production and several systems of property, and show how each of these modes creates a need for one of the systems. We must do at least this, and we must also take care not to include in what we call the determining factor anything which belongs properly to what we say is determined by it.

3. Relations of Production

Marx says that production (or, as he often puts it, the 'forces of production') determines the relations of production; and presumably he includes in what he understands by production (or the 'forces of production') the resources, tools and methods which men use to produce whatever they do produce. I have spoken elsewhere[1] of how difficult it is to establish what exactly Marx and Engels mean by 'relations of production'; they seem to have alternately in mind two different types of relations without ever making a clear distinction between them. Sometimes they seem to be referring to relations involved in actual production – to forms of co-operation in production – and sometimes to relations which arise because production creates a need for them. An example of the first kind would be the relation of a foreman to the men whose work he directs; an example of the second kind would be the relation of the owner of a piece of land to anyone required to respect his title to it.

Acton distinguishes three types of relations which might be called 'relations of production': those involved in the actual use of particular tools and techniques, those which are needed to make production go smoothly (which he calls paratechnological), and those which arise when commodities are produced for exchange.[2] As an example of the first kind, he gives the relations in which the crew of a ship stand to one another because they co-operate as they do to sail that particular kind of ship; as an example of the second kind, he gives the tacit agreement that land which has been dug shall not be trampled; and, though he gives no instance of the third kind, presumably because he thinks it superfluous to do so, I suppose that we can take for an example the relation of debtor to creditor. To this threefold distinction I prefer the simpler distinction which I said that Marx and Engels never make, though it is suggested by the way in which they use the expression 'relations of production': the distinction between relations involved in actual production and relations which arise because production creates

[1] In my *German Marxism and Russian Communism* ch. 2, pp. 21–8.
[2] Acton, *The Illusion of the Epoch*, pp. 159–68.

a need for them. The first kind of relations I had already clearly in mind before I read Acton's book, saying that they exist wherever there is a division of labour, and change more or less as methods of production change,[1] but my conception of the second kind is the clearer for my having reflected on Acton's threefold distinction. My second kind is merely his second and third kinds put together; and they are put together because there is, in my opinion, no need to distinguish them in order to explain and criticize this part of Marxian theory. The important distinction to bear in mind, if we are to see where that theory is defective, is between relations actually involved in production and relations for which the need arises because there is production; distinctions between kinds of relations not involved in production but arising out of it are, for this purpose, irrelevant.

Marx says of relations of production that, though they are determined in the first place by the character of production, they do not change to keep pace with changes in the character of production. He says that these relations, 'from forms of development' of the productive forces, turn into 'their fetters';[2] or, in other words, that from being relations for which the need arises because production has a particular character, they become obstacles to efficient production because the character of production has changed. He also says that property relations are the legal expression of relations of production.[3] It would seem, therefore, that relations of production, as Marx understands them, are relations for which the need arises because there is production and not relations actually involved in production; it would seem that it is relations of our second kind and not our first which best qualify to be 'forms of development' of and 'fetters' upon productive forces, and to have said of them that relations of property are their legal expression. The relations involved in production must change as production changes, and therefore can hardly become fetters upon it; nor are property relations their legal expression.

If, however, we treat our second kind of relations as being what

[1] *German Marxism and Russian Communism*, ch. 2, p. 24.

[2] See the Preface to *A Contribution to the Critique of Political Economy*. in Marx and Engels, *Collected Works*, vol. 29, p. 263.

[3] Ibid. In my *German Marxism and Russian Communism* (ch. 2, pp. 23–4), I said that, since relations of property are called the *legal expression* of relations of production, these two sets of relations cannot be identical, and I went on to say that, if they are not identical, it is impossible to discover what relations of production are. To serve Marx's purpose they must be more than relations involved in production, and yet, if they are not relations of property, what can they be? I now think that I was taking Marx too literally in refusing to treat relations of property and relations of production as being the same.

Marx calls relations of production, we are involved in other difficulties, not less serious. Why say of them that property relations are their legal expression, implying that they can be distinguished from them? Why not just call them property relations, and have done with it? Except when they are defining them, Marx and Engels nearly always speak of relations of production as if they were the same as relations of property. Why, then, do they sometimes feel the need to use expressions which suggest, if they do not actually say, that there is a difference between these two sets of relations, one set being the legal expression of the other? Presumably because they want to exclude law from what they call the economic structure of society, and therefore feel the need to suggest that relations of production can be defined without bringing the notion of law into the definition. 'The totality of these relations of production constitutes the economic structure of society, the real foundation, on which arises a legal and political superstructure.' Law belongs to the 'superstructure', while these relations belong to the 'foundation'.

Unfortunately, it is quite impossible to define these relations except in terms of the claims which men make upon one another and recognize – except in terms of admitted rights and obligations. Where there are such rights and obligations, there are accepted rules of conduct, rules which require and forbid and are supported by sanctions; there are, in the broad sense of the word, laws. But it may be that, by taking law in some other quite usual but narrower sense, we could so define relations of production that this narrower sense of law was not brought into the definition. Thus, making a distinction between law and mere custom, we could point to primitive societies and say of them that they have customs but no laws. In these societies without law there would of course be relations of production and relations of property, though it would not be permissible to call the second kind the 'legal expression' of the first.

I shall consider this expedient again later, when I discuss not only Marxism but any theory which seeks to explain morality, custom and law as determined by something in society more *basic* than they are. For the moment, it is enough to say that this expedient, even if permissible, would amount to a revision and not an interpretation of Marxian theory. There is no reason to believe that Marx and Engels would have admitted that in a primitive society without law as distinct from paternal or patriarchal rule, there would be no 'legal expression' of the relations of production.

If we identify relations of production with relations of property (as I think we must if they are to have any identity at all), it becomes

163

easy to see that they are not determined by what is produced and how it is produced. Given any one form of production, widely different systems of property are compatible with it. Some, no doubt, are excluded; the property relations of a tribal society are not compatible with industrial production as we know it today. But the variety of systems of property compatible with any one form of production is so great that it makes no sense to speak of forms of production *determining* systems of property. We can only make what we say look sensible by tacitly including the system of property in our notion of the form of production, and then saying that the form determines the system. We think we are making a statement of the type 'A determines B', which makes sense whether or not it is true, whereas what we are really saying (though we do not know it) is that 'A plus B determines B', which does not make sense. Thus we say that capitalist production determines capitalist relations of property, without stopping to consider whether we can explain what it is about that type of production which makes it specifically capitalist, except in terms of the relations of property which we say are determined by it.

Moroever, it is easy to see that the system of property often has a great influence on the form of production. Let us take a simple example. Where there is agriculture, there is property in land. Though the need for this kind of property arises from the cultivation of the land, the actual rules of property can vary considerably. Two communities using much the same methods when they first take to agriculture may have different rules about the inheritance of property in land; in the one, the custom may be primogeniture – all the father's land passing to his eldest son – and in the other, it may require the equal division of the father's land between all his sons. There will soon be many more large estates in the first community than in the second, enabling it to develop new methods which cannot be used in the other community. Marx, when he says that relations of production can act as fetters on productive forces, admits that the system of property can affect production. But the way he puts it does not do justice to the facts. The system of property is not merely a negative influence; it is also positive. It does more than put obstacles in the way of what is already there; it also creates opportunities – much larger opportunities, even, than are suggested by the example I have just given. One system of property as compared with another, by allowing a greater concentration of wealth in a few hands, may lead to quicker progress in the sciences and a more rapid improvement in productive techniques. The system of property determines the pattern of effective demand, which in turn has a great influence on what is produced and how it is produced.

These, it might be said, are obvious points. Are we to believe that Marx and Engels did not see them? I am not suggesting anything of the kind. If we look, for instance, at Marx's account of the rise of capitalism, we find him admitting readily enough that property relations have a powerful influence on productive methods. Part of the first volume of *Capital* is taken up with explaining how the decay of feudal relations of production made possible the development of new productive methods.[1] There is no question here of the methods of production peculiar to capitalism being born in the womb of feudal society and then gradually transforming it into capitalist society as feudal relations of property – now become fetters on these methods – give way to other relations more in harmony with them. As Marx describes the transformation, capitalist methods of production could emerge only because feudal relations of property were already giving way to others. There were no limbs to break the fetters until the fetters were broken.

Both Marx and Engels are often ready to admit the obvious. Their fault is much less that they turn a blind eye to it than that they do not see its implications for their basic theory. If the relations of production or property owe their character only in part to the form of production, if they in turn can profoundly affect production, and if they cannot be defined without using moral or normative concepts, what is the point of calling them relations of *production*? And what is the point of calling them the real foundation of law and government and of all forms of social consciousness? Since they owe their character only in part to the form of production, may they not owe it equally to the other sides of social life? In what sense, then, are they the real foundation of these other sides?

4. Fundamental and Derivative

So far, I have been discussing only the Marxian distinction between an economic foundation and a non-economic superstructure of society; and I should now like to broaden my argument to cover, not only Marxian theory, but every attempt to distinguish, among the larger aspects of social life, between a fundamental causal factor and what is derivative from it. No doubt, if we take a small enough part of

[1] See especially *Capital*, vol. I, trans. Ben Fowkes, intro. Ernest Mandel (London 1976), Part Eight, chs. 26–7, pp. 873–95.

social life, we can easily show that it is derivative, in the sense that it is much more affected by the rest of social life, or even by some other part of it, than it affects the rest or that part. If we take something like fashion in dress, we can show that it greatly depends on certain other things which it hardly influences. But if we take larger sides of social life, like religion or science or government, it is no longer plausible to treat any of them as fundamental or derivative in relation to the others.

To get our bearings in this matter, we need to keep firm hold of a distinction usually ignored by Marxists and by other writers who put forward theories like theirs; we need to distinguish between forms of social behaviour (or kinds of social activity) and characteristics or features of social life which are not forms of behaviour. Of these features the most important, for our purpose, are rules of conduct. Production, government, art and science are kinds of social activity or forms of behaviour. Law and morality are not; they are features of social life, involved in all kinds of *social* activity. Or, at least, if law, in some narrower sense, is not involved in all kinds of social activity, morality and custom most certainly are. All properly social relations are moral and customary; they cannot be adequately defined unless we bring normative concepts into the definitions, unless we refer to rules of conduct which the persons who stand in those relations recognize and are required to conform to.

Going along with these rights and obligations, there are mental attitudes which it would be misleading to call feelings because they involve thought as well as emotion. The relation of a mother to a child is properly a social relation, not because the mother gives birth to the child or feels affection for it or desires to protect it, but because she recognizes that she has obligations towards it. And the mother becomes a mother in the eyes of her child, not when the child learns that she gave birth to it, but when it comes to make certain claims upon her and to recognize (though not necessarily in so many words) certain obligations to her. It knows her for its mother when it comes to understand that she plays a certain unique part in its life, when it is aware of itself as a person standing in a special relation to her; though, of course, it need not be able to define that relation. Creatures having this kind of awareness feel differently towards one another because they have it; the love of human parents for their children, and of their children for them, differs profoundly from the natural affections of other animals.

Human beings feel about one another as they do because they become self-conscious and conscious of other selves (as other animals do not); and this they become in the process of learning to see themselves in moral and customary (and therefore social) relations to one another. Even the most private relation – the one which seems the exclusive concern of the persons involved in it – is, in this sense, a moral and a social relation. Even a clandestine love-affair in which there is no question of marriage usually imposes obligations on the man and the woman who have it, though it may matter to no one but themselves what they do. The lover and his mistress have more or less definite ideas about what each has the right to expect from the other; they are not creatures of mere desire or habit; they see themselves as standing in a certain relation to one another, as having parts to play because they are in that relation. How they think of the relation is not mere private fantasy; it derives from ideals accepted by others besides themselves – from ideals which they have taken over much more than they have made them. Even being in love consists of more than having certain feelings towards another person; it consists also in making, or hoping to be allowed to make, certain claims on that person, and in admitting, or hoping to be allowed to admit, certain obligations. The quality of the feeling involved is closely bound up with these claims and obligations.

Since claims and duties and mental attitudes are involved in all social relations – in every side of social life, no matter how primitive – since they are part of what we mean when we call a human activity social, we cannot take any side of social life and say that it determines, even *in the last resort* – whatever that may mean[1] – men's moral and customary relations and their attitudes towards one another. We can, of course, say that certain things are necessary conditions of social life. We can say that, if human beings were able (as some animals are) to look after themselves without help from the time they were born, they might never have come into customary and moral relations with one another. We can say that, if human children did not need to be protected and fed by their parents for many years, there might be no family life and therefore none of the social relations and affections involved in that life. We can say that, if men had not co-operated to produce and exchange goods and services, they might never have been drawn into such broad communities and into so many and such varied social relations. We may feel the need to insist more strongly on these points, converting *might* into *would*, when we come across someone saying that man is a social creature merely because he is a rational animal. True, we may say, unless he had natural capacities,

[1] It is usually a saving phrase to which the user attaches no definite meaning.

including reason, which other animals lack, he could never be a moral and social creature; but that is only part of the truth, because these capacities are developed in him by life in society. Unless he had had certain biological needs and had co-operated with other men in order to satisfy them, he would not have developed his powers of reasoning and have become a social and a moral creature.

But to say these things is to imply absolutely nothing about the relative importance of different forms of social activity as influences upon one another. The biological needs peculiar to man are satisfied by many forms of family life, which in their turn give birth to other needs, which are social and moral and not biological. Therefore the biological needs do not determine what form of family life there shall be; they merely create a need for some form of it. Co-operative production and exchange, in some form or other, are found in all societies, but the form they take in any society cannot be defined without reference to the social relations they involve. We cannot pass from such statements as 'unless men had biological needs peculiar to their kind, there would be no families', or 'unless men co-operated to produce and exchange goods and services, there would be no communities larger than families', to conclusions like 'how men satisfy their biological needs determines moral relations inside the family' or 'how men co-operate to produce and exchange goods and services determines social relations inside the community'. We cannot do it, because how men satisfy their needs and how they co-operate cannot be adequately defined without bringing these relations into the definition.

I have argued that any theory which postulates a fundamental causal factor to explain social change is mistaken. But that does not forbid our making any kind of distinction between the fundamental and the derivative; it forbids only the kind of distinction made by Marx, which commits the maker to holding that what is fundamental determines the character of what is derivative.

We can usefully make a quite different kind of distinction between the fundamental and the derivative. This distinction is worth discussing, not only for its own sake, but also because, though neither Marx nor Engels makes it explicit, it is implied by much that they say. I suspect that Marxism has been more effective than it would otherwise have been because its votaries have confused this implicit and useful distinction with the explicit and unrealistic one. They are apt to read the first into the second whenever it helps to make better sense of an argument advanced by Marx or Engels.

To elucidate the implicit and useful distinction, I must first make certain other distinctions between rules of conduct. Speaking broadly, we may say that rules of conduct are moral or customary or legal.[1] A rule may fall into all three of these broad categories, or into any two, or into one only. When we call a rule moral, without ourselves wanting to commend the behaviour it prescribes, we mean that people recognize (though they may not always carry out) the obligations it lays upon them whether or not there are sanctions attached to the rule. In calling the rule moral we have in mind the attitude towards it of the people who have to decide whether or not to obey it. Thus we, as students of society, may call it moral even though we ourselves disapprove of it. When we call a rule customary, we have in mind, not people's attitude towards it, but the fact that they usually conform to it, whether from habit or self-interest, or because there are sanctions attached to it, so that whoever is deemed to have broken it is liable to suffer from how other people behave towards him because they believe he has broken it. There are customary rules with no sanctions attached to them and towards which people do not have the attitude that would make moral rules of them. There are therefore some rules which are not obligatory in either sense – which people do not feel obliged to obey and which they are not required to obey. They too are involved in social relations, but not more than the others. Though many rules do not impose obligations, it is still true that every enduring relation between persons – every relation which we call social – does involve rules which do impose them.

In primitive societies, customary rules supported by sanctions, though quite often disobeyed, may never be challenged on the ground that they conflict with higher or better rules, so that the distinction which seems so important in more sophisticated societies – between what the community exacts and what morality requires – may never be made. Morality and obligatory custom may there exactly coincide. Also in such societies, there may be no law, unless we define law so widely as to include any rule which imposes obligations or confers rights. But if we define law as a rule of conduct declared or applied by legislatures and courts of law, then we can say that there are societies having only customary and moral rules and no laws. We can also show that custom and morality are prior to law in this narrower sense of law.

[1] This is only one possible classification among several. It is not meant to be exhaustive: it does not include rules which are invented for a specific purpose (e.g., a game) and with no sanction attached to them other than that refusal to obey them frustrates the purpose for which they are invented. But it does include nearly all rules in which the social scientist is interested.

I said that Marx and Engels did not use this distinction between custom and law to support their theory. They also quite explicitly put morality into what they called the 'superstructure' of society, resting on a 'real foundation' consisting of social relations. They spoke, moreover, as if they did not know that there are rights and obligations – moral or customary or both – involved in all social relations. They were not as explicit about custom as about morality; they did not put it resolutely into the superstructure.[1] But though, when we call a rule customary, we are not also saying that it is moral, we have seen that most rules held to be moral are also customary, and that the most important customary rules, those holding the family or some larger community together, are also moral. Therefore, if we put morality into the superstructure, it hardly makes sense not to put custom there as well; or, if we put custom into the foundation, we cannot reasonably keep morality out of it.

But may we now put law, as distinct from custom and morality, into the superstructure? Or, better still, perhaps, may we not put law there together with the customary and moral rules which arise in society when it comes to have law? Could we not, in this way, distinguish between custom and morality which are prior to law and custom and morality which are not? If we can show that law emerges to satisfy some need which custom and morality existing before there was law did not satisfy, we can then perhaps go on to show that the custom and morality which come along with law satisfy that same need. Though Marx and Engels never did this, it may still be worth doing; it may be a revision of their theory which helps to make better sense of it, and which is also in keeping with much that they said.

This, at first glance, is an attractive suggestion. Marx and Engels often speak as if the function of law were primarily to maintain what they call the 'class structure' of society, enabling some classes to exploit others. But, clearly, if we understand by law any rule supported by sanctions, we have to reject this account of law. For, unless there are already some rules supported by sanctions, and, in particular, rules of property, we cannot explain how society ever comes to be divided into classes. It is only if we distinguish between custom and law, in a narrower sense of law, that we can hope to show how, in a society without law, customary rules of property and inheritance operate to divide men into classes, and how, as a result of this division, there arises a need for rules of a different kind – rules connected with the emergence of specifically political

---

[1] Ordinarily, Marx and Engels did not distinguish between morality and custom any more than between custom and law.

institutions, and therefore declared and enforced in ways not known before. Though Marx and Engels did not in fact offer this explanation, they did say that society becomes political as a result of being divided into classes. We could even, I think, by appropriate selection, gather all the elements that go to make up this explanation from their writings. So that, although it is not their explanation, it is not altogether foreign to them.

Again, though Marx and Engels often speak as if all morality were class morality, they do not always do so. They admit, for example, that there have been and still are classless tribal societies, and they never dream of denying the obvious – that these societies too have their moral codes. They predict a classless society in the future, which they say is to have the highest morality of all. They also sometimes admit that all systems of morality, class and classless, have some features in common. Can we not say, then, that even in societies divided into classes there is a large part of morality which is not class morality and which therefore does not belong to the superstructure? Only in this way can we avoid the patent contradiction between these two positions: that all morality is class morality, and that men must stand in social (and therefore also moral) relations to one another before they can come to be divided into classes.

When society becomes political, what were once mere customs may become laws. Customs which were originally in the common interest, moreover, may come to be laws which are in the interest only of the rich. For example, customary rules of inheritance and other rules of property, which to begin with were generally acceptable, may have led in time to such great inequalities and exalted some people so much above the others, that the rules would eventually have ceased to be accepted by the great majority were it not that they had become laws – were it not there had emerged new methods of enforcing obedience to them and of persuading the majority that they ought to obey them. The minority could not for long have been secure in their privileges unless new sanctions had replaced the old, unless organized government had arisen to protect property, unless much that used to be mere custom had become law, unless an important part of morality had become class morality.

This does not mean that all law must be class law. Many old customs will continue to be in the general interest, even after society has divided into classes and government has emerged, and the new sanctions will also operate to uphold them. There will as well be new laws made in the common interest. It will come to be thought the business of government and the courts to declare and enforce the important rules, whether they are in the common interest or only in the interest of the privileged. For what is in the common interest is also in the interest of the privileged, who are part of the community. It will come naturally to them – being the rulers of the community – not to distinguish their own peculiar interest from the common interest, but to run the two together. Therefore, not even all law will be class law. Yet it may still be true that, historically, the emergence of law, as distinct from custom, is a mark that society is becoming divided into classes – that the methods of declaring and enforcing law (which make it law as distinct from mere custom) arise along with the division of society into classes.

It may be that, in some such way as this, we could make a cleaner distinction than Marx and Engels ever made between two sides of social life, one of which we might call – quite plausibly – *fundamental* in relation to the other. But, if we make the distinction along these lines, we abandon economic determinism, because we treat as fundamental all sides of social life which existed before the division of society into classes. Morality and custom we refuse to treat as derivative. Society is the matrix in which classes are born, and whatever was social before there were classes can be treated as prior to what develops in society when distinct classes appear inside it. As we shall see later, we cannot even treat what Marx understood by *ideology* as belonging entire to the derivative side. But we can made a distinction which is not altogether remote from Marx's purpose, seeing that he, too, often spoke of what he put into the 'superstructure' as if its essential function were to serve class interests.[1] To call what must exist before there can be classes fundamental or basic in relation to what emerges when they appear is, I think, an allowable use of these words. And this distinction is better than Marx's because it enables us, as his does not, to decide what to call basic and what derivative. It provides us with a criterion which we can use, even though, in practice, owing to our ignorance of the facts, it may often be difficult to decide whether some form of social behaviour or some feature of social life is or is not basic.

But basic in this sense is not basic in the orthodox and explicit Marxian sense. It does not imply that what is basic determines what is derivative from it – that the forms and features of social behaviour which must exist before classes can arise determine the forms and features which emerge with them or after they have arisen. It does

---

[1] Though, of course, he could not do so consistently. Some of the things he and Engels put in the superstructure are so obviously present in tribal societies – which they admitted are classless – that, when they had these societies in mind, they could not treat those things as if serving class interests were their essential function.

not deny that what is derivative, after it has arisen, can affect what is basic just as it is affected by it, nor yet that what is derivative can change drastically without being moved to do so by what is basic. It does not imply that we can in any society, class or classless, sort out men's social activities into two groups in such a way that, as the one changes, so does the other. Though it allows us to call co-operative production and exchange basic forms of social behaviour, and morality a basic feature of it, it does not allow us to say that government and law, which are derivative, do not change to any great extent except in response to basic changes, or do not affect them as deeply as they are affected by them. Basic or fundamental, in this sense, means only primary and universal. Morality and custom are, for example, fundamental in relation to law because they must exist before there can be law, and because they are common to all societies while law is not; they are not fundamental in the sense that, where there is law, they determine its character while it does not determine theirs.

5. Science as a Social Factor

In the Preface to his *Contribution to the Critique of Political Economy*, Marx distinguishes, among the things belonging to the superstructure, law and government from the forms of social consciousness corresponding to them. These forms of consciousness he calls ideological, and I shall consider later, and at some length, what he and Engels understand by ideology. At the moment I want to discuss only what they have to say about science. Though sometimes – no doubt incautiously – they come close to suggesting that science, too, is a form of ideology, they usually treat it as something quite different. Science is clearly not law or government, and so, if it is not a form of social consciousness corresponding to them, it must belong to the foundation and not the superstructure. As it is not, equally clearly, a relation of production or property, it must be part of the process of production, part of what Marx calls the 'forces of production'. In the Marxian scheme of things social, there is nothing else that it can be; and so we find Marx, in the first volume of *Capital*, speaking of the 'productive forces of labour' which 'come into being' through 'the conscious *use* of the sciences, of mechanics, chemistry, etc. for specific ends'.[1]

Some commentators friendly to Marx, arguing that it is unreasonable to include science among the forces of production, have denied that he did anything so unreasonable. No doubt, there are

[1] *Capital*, vol. I, Appendix (trans. Rodney Livingstone), II, p. 1024.

some passages in Marx, and in Engels too, which could be used to support this contention. But a bandying of quotations to and fro cannot settle the matter one way or the other. The important question is not, how many quotations are there in favour of this interpretation or the other? It is, rather, which interpretation is most in keeping with the theory? And there is no doubt about the answer to this question. In the Marxian scheme of things, there is no place for science except among the forces of production.

But it only makes sense to treat science as an inherent part of the process of production if men engage in science primarily to solve practical problems. Medicine is studied primarily to cure illness. The labours of a doctor are as much productive as those of a miner; and it is not absurd, though it may be unusual, to speak of the labours, say, of Sir Alexander Fleming as part of the productive process, since he undertook his researches in order to find a cure for disease. That he enjoyed his work and cared little for financial gain is nothing to the point; there are unskilled labourers of whom we can say as much.

But most science is not practical; it is undertaken to solve not practical but theoretical problems; it aims at nothing more than knowledge. It may later be put to practical use, but it need not be. Often centuries pass before any practical use is made of a scientific discovery, and the use was not intended or foreseen by the discoverer. Science can make great progress, as it did in the ancient world, and yet affect productive techniques very little. Pure science is, of course, in one sense, a productive activity; it aims at knowledge, and when it is successful – when its hypotheses pass the tests they are put to – it can be said to have produced what it aims at. But then, in this obvious sense, all human activities which have a purpose are productive if they achieve their purpose.

It might be argued that the findings of pure science, while they are not applied, have no important social consequences – that it is not until they are used to improve, or at least to change, productive techniques that they have such consequences. It may be said that society was very little affected by Greek science, because that science, for all the progress it made, was not applied to industry and agriculture, or was so only to a small extent. But this argument is unacceptable unless we reduce it to a tautology by defining an important social consequence as one which results from a change in productive technique. The progress of Greek science, affecting production very little, affected Greek philosophy – and through that philosophy, Greek ethics and Greek religion – very considerably. As people's understanding of the world changes, so too do their conceptions of themselves, of how they ought to live, of what they are destined for. These conceptions may not themselves be scientific; they may not follow logically from any conclusions the natural sciences reach, but they are, nevertheless, deeply influenced by science. Theology is not science, as we ordinarily use the word and as Marx used it; nor is metaphysics, nor is ethics (understood as a doctrine about how men should behave and not merely as an explanation of what they are doing when they pass moral judgements or how they come to make them). Science teaches men nothing about God; yet how they conceive of God does depend considerably upon what science teaches them about the world. The theology of a scientific age differs from the theology of an unscientific age; and so too do its ethics and metaphysics.

Not only does science affect these other forms of intellectual activity, which Marx would call ideological, but they also affect science. Scientific progress is sometimes slowed down, and at other times quickened, by theology and metaphysics. The mental discipline and curiosity stimulated in one field of study may be diverted to another. The universities of Europe, founded principally for the study of theology and law, contributed powerfully to creating the intellectual climate in which modern science was born.

Even if we leave aside pure science and its social consequences, science is not related to practice in the simple way needed to make plausible Marx's conception of it. Science creates practical problems just as fast as it solves them. Just as knowledge may be sought (or, if it is already available, used) to solve a practical problem, so a problem may arise out of an increase of knowledge. Because men have knowledge which they did not have before – because their conception of the world is different – they see opportunities where they used not to see them. They come to want things they used not to want because they had not even imagined them. Marx and his disciples speak as if science were socially important only because it helps men satisfy their needs by teaching them how to make or contrive what will satisfy them, forgetting that science creates needs as much as it satisfies them.

Considered in themselves, the pursuit of knowledge and the production of what satisfies material needs are different activities. True, they affect one another greatly; but they are also greatly affected by other things. It is odd, therefore, to lump them together as 'forces of production'. Marx and Engels do this only because their theory requires them to do it. They want to divide social activities into two main kinds, the economic and the rest, saying that the first kind determine the second. Science, they know, has had an immense influence on social change. They therefore cannot relegate it to the superstructure; they have to put it into the foundation, which means, in effect, that they have to treat it as a part of the productive process, since it very clearly is not a relation of production, no matter how we interpret that difficult phrase. They have to do this whenever they are directly faced with the question: Where does science fit into our division of society into a *base* and a *superstructure*? When they are not faced with the question, they ordinarily do not treat science as a part of production but as something different from it. Like the sensible fellows they are, they prefer to talk sense except when their theory impels them to do otherwise.

II. WHAT DID MARX AND ENGELS UNDERSTAND BY CLASS, CLASS CONFLICT AND CLASS INTERESTS?

1. *Class and Class Conflicts*

a. *Marxian Classes*

There are few social theorists who, having defined the terms they use, go on to use them consistently in the senses they have defined. Marx and Engels, as we should expect, use the word *class* in several different senses; but there is also a special Marxian sense of the word. In this special sense, two men do not belong to different classes because they do different kinds of work, nor even because they get widely different incomes. Salaried managers and manual workers do not belong to different classes merely because managers direct the work of others and manual workers work with their hands. In a classless society, if it were industrial, there would still be a need for managers, and if their salaries were then no greater than those of ordinary workers, it would be, presumably, because they were no longer working for private capitalists but for the community.

The class a man belongs to – in the special Marxian sense of class – depends on whether or not he owns property and on the type of property he owns. The proletarian does not own natural resources or instruments of production, but he does own his own labour; he has the right to sell his labour[1] to others and to withhold it from them; he even

---

[1] Marx says that what he sells is his *labour-power* (see especially *Capital*, vol. I, Part Two, ch. 6, and Part Three, ch. 7, pp. 270–306); but, for our purposes (since we are not concerned with Marxian economic theory), we can ignore Marx's distinction between *labour* and *labour-power*.

has the right to work for himself, though he cannot exercise it because he lacks the tools and natural resources he needs. The capitalist owns natural resources and instruments of production, which enable him to appropriate a large part of the product of other people's work; his income, as a capitalist, is not a payment for work done. The slave does not own even his own labour; for there is someone else, his master, who has the right to decide when he shall work and what he shall do. The serf differs from the slave and the proletarian; unlike the slave he is part-owner of his own labour, being obliged to work for his lord only at some periods, and he can even be said to have, unlike the proletarian (though Marx does not trouble to make this point), a limited right of property in land. The lord cannot deprive him of his land, even though he can divest himself of his rights over the serf in favour of some other person. The yeoman farmer or free peasant owns his own land and his labour; he has no rights of property in other people's labour, and lacks the means to hire much labour. The artisan is in the same position as the peasant, except that he owns a workshop instead of a farm. Tenants can be treated as a sub-class of the class of persons whose property they rent: if they rent a workshop or a farm to work in or on it themselves, they are a variety of artisan or peasant; if they hire labour to work on the property they rent, they are a variety of capitalist farmers or manufacturers or merchants.

The principle of this classification is clear enough, even though at times it may be difficult to decide to what class a man belongs. The yeoman or free peasant, if he hires any labour, is to that extent a capitalist farmer; but if he hires only a little, and most of the work on his land is done by himself and his family, we should still call him a yeoman or peasant rather than a capitalist farmer. So, too, the rights of the serf in his own labour and in the plot of land he cultivates to feed his family may be so diminished that we are at a loss whether to call him a serf or a slave. But the principle of the classification is none the less clear.

Bober says that Marx and Engels distinguish classes primarily in terms of the property they *own* and the extent of their personal freedom.[1] I do not quarrel with that, though I think that – using the word *property* in the broad sense in which Marx and Engels often use it – we can define personal freedom in terms of rights of property in one's own person or labour. The slave who has no right to marry or to cohabit except as his master directs cannot dispose of himself as a free man can. So, too, the serf who may not move from his village

[1] See Bober, Karl *Marx's Interpretation of History*, Part II, ch. v, pp. 96–100.

without his lord's permission can be said to lack certain rights over himself. If the serf is attached to the soil, it is chiefly in order that his lord should not lose his property in the serf's labour; if the slave may not create or refuse to create a family as he pleases, it is chiefly to ensure that his master has the supply of labour he wants. It is with the labour of his slaves or serfs, more than with anything else about them, that the master or the lord is concerned; and labour (or labour-power) is treated by Marx and Engels as a form of property, which may be owned, in whole or in part, by the labourer or by somebody else. To define classes in terms of the property they own is therefore quite in keeping with Marxian theory.

b. Class Inequality

Marx and Engels (and their disciples after them) speak as if – where there are classes in the Marxian sense of class – they must be unequal, and also as if – where there are no classes in their sense of the word – there can be no deep and self-perpetuating social inequalities. Again, they take it for granted that where there are classes, in their sense, there is necessarily exploitation of class by class. Now, none of these conclusions can be taken for granted. It is important to notice this, because many Marxian arguments are conclusive only if they can be taken for granted. The society divided into classes is, for Marxists, necessarily a society where there are deep and self-perpetuating social inequalities and exploitation, and the classless society (i.e. the society without classes in the Marxian sense of class) necessarily has neither inequality nor exploitation.

In any society – even the kind that Marxists would call classless – there is diversity of function, and there are differences in the rights and obligations which people have. Women have in all societies rights and obligations which men do not have; they have them no matter how strong the belief in the equality of the sexes. If only because the rôle of the mother in the bearing and rearing of children cannot be the same as that of the father, mothers have by custom and law duties and rights which fathers do not have. The greater the diversity of functions and the wider the variety of men's rights and obligations, the more different their positions in society.

It is only when the persons who occupy certain positions in society (that is to say, who have certain rights and obligations marking them off from other people) are held to be *superior* to others – not on account of personal qualities, but in virtue of the positions they occupy – that there is social inequality. They receive outward respect, which need not mean that they are liked or admired or even respected, but only that people behave towards them in a certain way because of their social position. This outward respect is not attached to certain positions merely by chance. It is attached to them, in the first place, largely because the holders of these positions have much more than ordinary power; because their recognized social function is to control, to protect and to advise;[1] or because their work is held to be in some other way especially useful to the community. This outward respect is also a source as well as an effect of power.

Superiority can long survive the causes that gave birth to it. A function which was once useful may become useless or even harmful, and yet the persons who perform it may retain the rights attached to it and receive the outward respect. They may have as much or more power than the early holders of their positions, but their exercise of it may now stand in the way of most people's realizing their aspirations, and in that sense may be against the common interest. Or they may have lost much of their power and yet continue to receive the old marks of outward respect.

In a tribal society where there are no slaves, and all of whose members are kinsmen – a society without classes in the Marxian sense of class – there can clearly be great social inequalities. Some men, in virtue of their position in society, can have much greater power than others and can receive much greater outward respect. Their power is not a mere capacity to get other people to do what they want, a capacity which a man may owe entirely to his personal qualities or to momentary circumstances; they owe it to their position in society, to the rights and duties which make it the position it is. Their power is a form of authority. Because of it they receive outward respect and are held superior to other people. Their position, moreover, may be hereditary, and it may entitle them or enable them to get many things that are withheld from ordinary tribesmen. All this is possible in a community of kinsmen, where there are no classes in the Marxian sense. No doubt, there may be classes in some other sense of the word, but that is here irrelevant.

Let us now consider the other conclusion of the Marxists – that, where there are classes in the Marxian sense, they must be unequal. We have seen that in all societies there is more than mere diversity of function, mere difference in rights and obligations; there is also social inequality, there are social superiors and social inferiors. But this is as true of societies which are classless, in the Marxian sense, as of those which have classes. It does not follow that, where there are

[1] Because, in other words, their power is authority – because they owe it, not primarily to their personal qualities, but to their social position.

social superiors and social inferiors in a society divided into classes, some classes are socially superior to others. It may often be so, but it need not be so always. Of course, if we define differences of class in terms of social superiority and inferiority, it follows that where there are social superiors and inferiors, there are unequal classes. But if we take the Marxian sense of class, it by no means follows.

In the Marxian sense of class, peasants who own their land and artisans who own their workshops belong to a different class from landless labourers and factory workers, but they need not be socially superior or inferior to them. They may be but need not be. A poor peasant is not socially superior to a landless labourer; he may be, even in his own eyes, socially inferior to the skilled men employed on a large estate. Rich and poor peasants belong to the same class, which is different from the class of well-paid but landless workers; but rich peasants may be socially superior to poor ones and the social equals of well-paid workers. People whose incomes consist mostly of rent or interest belong, in the Marxian scheme, to a different class from people whose incomes consist mostly of wages or salaries; but they need not be, and often are not, socially superior to them. Indeed, they are sometimes socially inferior, as many owners of slum property are to professional men. There can clearly be differences of class without social inequality – that is, if we take the Marxian sense of class.

But very often, when we speak of differences of income or power and not the various types of property that men own, and, since differences of income or power usually carry with them differences in outward respect, it is often true that, when two persons are said to belong to different classes – in this sense of class which is not the Marxian sense – it is implied that one is socially superior to the other. And that is perhaps still the most frequent use of the word *class*. Therefore difference of class, as ordinarily understood, often implies social inequality. This was even more so in Marx's time than now, and he was therefore disposed to take it for granted that what was true of class in a more usual sense of the word was also true in his special sense.[1] But whether it is so or not depends on whether or not differences in the types of property that men own correspond to differences in wealth and power. Though in some societies the

---

[1] He did not think that he was giving a new meaning to the word *class*; he supposed that he was giving the sense in which the word was ordinarily used. As a matter of fact the word was quite often used more or less in the sense which he and Engels stressed. It was also and even more often used in the sense which implies social inequality. These two senses were not clearly distinguished from one another, and there were also other senses. It is not to be wondered at that Marx and Engels should have been confused by these different senses.

correspondence is much closer than in others, in no society is it nearly as close as Marx and Engels supposed it was.

Just as there may be Marxian classes which are *not* unequal, so there may be two classes (in the Marxian sense) which are unequal though neither is exploited. The feudal nobles belonged to a higher class than the merchants and master craftsmen of the mediaeval towns, but they did not exploit them. There is exploitation, as Marx and Engels understand it, when some people get less than the value of what they produce because others appropriate the difference. If one man produces something which is worth one pound, or if his labour adds one pound to its value, and he gets only fifteen shillings, someone else getting the difference, he is exploited. There are difficulties to this notion of exploitation, some of which I shall have to discuss even though I have decided to let Marxian economics alone. I shall refer to them later in another connection. At the moment, I want merely to make the point that one class can be socially inferior to another without being exploited by it, or indeed by any other class; and by exploitation I mean here what Marx meant by it – the appropriation of surplus value.

It would not be difficult to quote passages from Marx and Engels to show that they admitted, at least indirectly, the three points I have made. They did not always speak of tribal societies as if there were no social inequalities within them; they did not speak as if peasants, no matter how poor, were socially superior to proletarians; they did not say that the feudal nobles exploited the mediaeval burghers, nor did they deny that they were socially superior to them. In this matter, as in so many others, we do not find them denying the obvious so much as ignoring its significance for their own theory.

c. Types of Classes

Marx and Engels do not confine themselves to using the word *class* in the sense which I have called Marxian; they also quite often use it in other senses. It would be sheer pedantry to object to their doing so, provided the context makes clear the sense they are using. For instance, they often apply the term *bourgeois* both to capitalists who own instruments of production and to what are called the professional classes, though these classes, like the proletarians, sell their labour. Of course, they charge more for it, and usually do not sell it by the week or the day or the hour, but by longer periods of time, or else by the piece or the visit, and not to one purchaser but to many, as the need arises.

Again, Marx and Engels do not always include the great landowners among the bourgeois, although their rights of property in their estates are essentially the same as the rights of factory-owners. The terms *bourgeois* and *capitalist*, as Marx and Engels use them, are by no means always equivalent, just as they are not so in ordinary speech. The French word *bourgeois*, when it does not just mean a town-dweller, has largely a cultural significance; it refers to anyone who lives in a certain way, though to live in that way he needs a larger income than the manual worker used to get until quite recently. It also often has this cultural significance for Marx and Engels.

We can discern, in their writings, two main types of social classi-fication, which, for the sake of convenience, I shall call *primary* and *secondary*. The primary classification is in terms of property rights, and gives us such major classes as slave-owners, feudal lords, capitalists, slaves, serfs, yeomen and proletarians; and also sub-classes of these major classes, as, for example, factory workers and country labourers – both of them proletarians – or industrialists, merchants, bankers and non-feudal landowners – all of them capitalists.

The secondary classification is into what I shall call *principal* and *subsidiary* classes. A principal class is a protagonist in the class struggle; in pursuing its class interests it either transforms society or is an obstacle in the way of progress. Its interests are decisive in determining the character of the class struggle. A principal class is always a major class or a sub-class thereof. A subsidiary class is not a protagonist in the class struggle; it may in fact take a prominent part in that struggle, but its interests are not decisive in determining its character. In the eyes of Marx and Engels, the professional classes are subsidiary to the capitalists. Since they get paid for their services, they are clearly not capitalists. Nor are they exactly proletarians, even when they have nothing to sell but their services; for normally they do not produce what the buyer of their services aims to sell at a profit. They are *sui generis*. Certainly, neither Marx nor Engels ever calls them proletarians, though in their time professional men still made a living by selling their labour mostly to the substantial propertied classes. It was the capitalists, and not the wage-earners or the peasants, who hired stewards, managers and lawyers, and who sent their children to schools and universities. Only the most poorly paid of professional men sold their services to the workers and peasants. The professional classes, sharing the culture and accepting the standards of the proper-ties classes, mostly followed their lead politically. Or perhaps it would be better to say that their political attitudes were largely determined by the interests of the propertied classes. In fact, as Marx knew and admitted, the actual rulers of a capitalist country are as much recruited from the professional as from the propertied classes. Yet he insisted that the political behaviour of these rulers is determined primarily by the interests of the propertied classes.

Marx and Engels also treat village labourers and even peasants who own their land as subsidiary classes. Hired labourers on the land are proletarians, but they are not destined to play a decisive part in the class struggle. When they come to know their true class interests, they will become the allies of the urban proletariat, but the lead in the struggle against the capitalists belongs to the urban workers and not to them. Again, Marx and Engels often call the peasants *petits-bourgeois*, not meaning to suggest thereby that they are capitalists in a small way, but that their interests are often in harmony with those of the capitalists. They are not protagonists in the class struggle; they are subsidiary allies of classes much more active, politically, than they are.

A subsidiary class may, but need not, belong to the same major class as the class to which it is subsidiary. Thus, if we consider the examples just taken, the village labourers belong to the same major class as the urban workers to whom they are subsidiary, but the same is not true of professional men or of peasants. Indeed, the peasants, though they usually follow the lead of the capitalists, may not always do so; they may sometimes side with the proletariat. Both Marx and Engels admit that they sometimes have done so. Thus the peasants can be subsidiary to either of the two classes engaged as principals in the class struggle; they can even be divided in their allegiance, some taking one side and some another. Though Marx and Engels make much less of these possibilities than Lenin was to do after them, they do admit them.

Neither Marx nor Engels speaks, as I have done, of major and sub-classes or of principal and subsidiary classes. I have invented these terms to help explain and criticize their views about the class struggle. I do not say that every group which they call a class falls into one or other of the categories I have defined. They often use the word *class* loosely, as we all do. Nevertheless, if we are to see clearly the merits and defects of their theory, we must make explicit certain distinctions which are only implicit in their writings.

d. Class Structure and Mode of Production

Sometimes, when they speak of the epochs into which they divide history, Marx and Engels refer to the tools and sources of power they suppose are characteristic of them. Thus we have such statements as the one often quoted from Marx's *Poverty of Philosophy*: 'The hand-mill gives you society with the feudal lord; the steam-mill, society with the industrial capitalist' (see p. 157, n. 1 above). But, though we are repeatedly told, as for example in the first volume of *Capital*, that 'it is not what is made but how, and by what instruments of labour, that distinguishes different economic epochs',[1] it is not after these instruments, but after the systems of property supposed to be peculiar to them or after the classes supposed to dominate them, that epochs are named. Thus Marx and Engels speak, not of the steam-and-coal or factory epoch, but of the capitalist or bourgeois epoch; they speak not of the hand-mill or workshop or strip-agriculture epoch but of the feudal epoch, having sometimes in mind the system of property in land and sometimes the dominant social class. By antiquity, they seem to mean all the societies on the shores of the Mediterranean until the fall of the Roman Empire. Though in this case the name does not indicate it, it is the division of these societies into masters and slaves which seems to them distinctive of the epoch; they say almost nothing of the tools and techniques peculiar to it. They do not seem to have enquired whether, in all or most ancient societies, the relation between masters and slaves was really the most important, whether most people belonged to the one class or the other, or whether there was a marked tendency for these two classes to increase in size and importance compared with others.

As Bober and other critics of Marxism have pointed out, neither Marx nor Engels made any attempt to show that slavery and serfdom arose out of or are connected with different methods or techniques of production. And indeed there is very little evidence that they did so arise, and much evidence that they did not. Bober, I think, exaggerates when he says that in antiquity and in the Middle Ages methods of production were very much the same. If by these methods we mean only tools and sources of power used, this is largely true. If, however, we include in them, as surely we ought, the way in which production was organized, we must admit that the mediaeval manor operated in many ways differently from, say, the Roman latifundium, even though much the same tools were used. Where you have serfs you cannot have agriculture organized as it can be where you have slaves. But this difference in methods of production is an effect rather than a cause of a difference in social relations.

It is therefore, in practice, much more in terms of the class structure than of the mode of production that Marx and Engels distinguish between different historical epochs and different types of society. They would no doubt say that it does not much matter which criterion you

[1] *Capital*, vol. I, Part Two, ch. 7, p. 286.

use, since class structure is determined by the mode of production. But this, as we have seen, is not true, and only wears the appearance of truth if we include in the mode of production the social relationships which are supposed to be determined by it – if we include in it not only (as we reasonably may) forms of co-operation actually involved in production, but also kinship and property relations. The distinction between the ancient and the feudal worlds, as types of society and not just as periods of history, makes sense (if it makes sense at all) only in terms of the moral and legal and political relations between men, or of the division of social classes arising out of these relations, and not in terms of the mode of production.

e. Class Conflict and Social Evolution

Marx and Engels say that 'the history of all hitherto existing society is the history of class struggles'.[1] By this they mean much more than that in all societies there have been classes and conflicts between classes; they mean that the political struggles of the past have been very predominantly class struggles. They believe that the transformation of society – of the system of property (or social 'relations of production') and the superstructure resting upon it – results from class conflict. The established social relations or system of property, together with the superstructure, are defended by the privileged classes, whose privileges depend on their maintenance, and are challenged by other classes as they come to find that their interests are incompatible with them. Thus the feudal system was undermined, partly because the serfs fled from their lords' estates or otherwise evaded or reduced their obligations to them, and partly because the mediaeval burghers, as they grew in number and in wealth, added to their privileges and strengthened the monarchy against the feudal nobles. The process was gradual, but it was, none the less, a social and a political revolution; it was a social revolution because it transformed the relations between classes, and a political revolution because it transformed the system of government. Or, to speak more accurately, in transforming the relations between classes, it altered their nature, making new classes out of the old. The serfs, in getting rid of their peculiar obligations, ceased to be serfs and became free peasants or tenant farmers or village-labourers when they did not go to the towns, and, when they did go, sometimes became capitalists or (and much more often) proletarians; while the craftsmen and merchants of the guilds became capitalists or sank into the proletariat.

[1] *Communist Manifesto*, sect. I, *Collected Works*, vol. 6, p. 482.

Although, when the requirements of their own theory are present to their minds, Marx and Engels affect to see, underlying this social transformation and causing it, a change in the mode of production, their actual account of it (if we examine it closely) suggests that it was more often the social transformation which made possible the change in mode of production. Nevertheless, it may still be true that important social and political changes – changes on such a scale that they deserve to be called *revolutions* – are usually effects of a struggle between classes. Clearly, the two assertions – that changes in the class structure are determined by changes in the mode of production, and that social and political revolutions are effects of class conflict – by no means stand or fall together. The second might be true even if the first were false. For my part, I believe that the second assertion comes nearer to being true than the first, though there are two large qualifications I should wish to make. Society can be transformed, socially and politically, by wars and conquests which are not themselves forms or effects of class conflict. Secondly, the classes whose conflicts bring about the transformations need not be (though in the past they often have been) classes in the Marxian sense of class; they need not be social groups having different kinds of property rights.

We cannot explain the social and political transformation of Western Europe resulting from the fall of the Roman Empire as an effect of class conflicts. There were no class conflicts weakening some classes and strengthening others in Western society to explain how it ceased to be what it was in Roman times and became what it was in the Middle Ages. Western society was transformed both by the conquest of the Roman Empire by the barbarians and by the spread of Christianity, and neither of these events can plausibly be taken to be bound up with the conflict of some classes or others. The German tribes pressed more strongly against the Roman frontiers because they were pushed forward by the movement of other tribes behind them; they were not urged westwards and southwards by any class conflicts inside them, for they were not, in the Marxian sense, class societies. The Roman Empire was growing poorer and losing population for a long time before it collapsed, but there is no evidence that this decay was due to class conflicts. Indeed, class conflicts had been much fiercer while Rome was creating her empire than when that empire was in process of decay. Moreover, even if the aggression of the barbarians and the decay of Rome had each been the effect of class conflicts in two separate societies, it still would not be true that the invasion of the West by the barbarians was itself a class conflict and that the type of society emerging from that invasion could be said to embody the gains made by some classes at the expense of others in conflict with them. What is true of Western Europe as it passed from Roman imperialism to mediaeval feudalism is equally true of Asia and Africa transformed by European penetration or conquest, and indeed of all great social and political revolutions brought about by foreign invasion and domination. Military conquest and other milder forms of invasion have been, historically, very important causes of social and political revolution. We can often, though by no means always, find class conflicts among their major causes; but they are not themselves class conflicts, even when they are partly caused by them. We cannot treat the social and political transformations resulting from them as advances and retreats in a struggle between classes.

Nor can we treat the conflicts between classes having different property rights as historically more important than conflicts between groups which are not classes in this sense of class. Conflicts between what we would call – using the terms we devised to help explain this part of Marxian theory – sub-classes of the same major class, or between one subsidiary class and another, or which involve social groups which are classes in some other sense, are just as important. The groups supporting Parliament and those supporting the King in the English Civil War were nearly all capitalist in the Marxian sense, for their property rights, whether in land or other things, were already more capitalist than feudal. The professional classes in France, especially the lawyers, played as large a part as any other group in strengthening the old French monarchy and later in conducting the French Revolution. In doing first one and then the other, they were promoting group interests which were often not in keeping with the interests of the capitalists. Again, wherever there is a vast apparatus of government, State officials are an important group, whose behaviour is often decisive in bringing about social and political transformation. The officials may be recruited from the humbler or from the upper classes, but in either case they acquire professional interests distinct from the interests of the classes they come from. The higher officials in eighteenth-century Russia and Prussia were largely recruited from a class of nobles who still – if we take into account their property-rights – were feudal rather than capitalist landowners. Can we plausibly treat State officials in Russia and Prussia as a class subsidiary to the feudal class? As a class which emerged primarily to satisfy the demand of the feudal nobility for certain services? Or as a class whose social function was to defend feudal interests? The higher State officials, though largely recruited from the feudal class, were not, as State officials, a sub-class of that class; they were not, as servants of the State, a variety of feudal landowners, as, say, farm labourers are one variety of proletarians and factory workers another. Their interests as State officials were not a variety of the interests of the feudal nobility. These men were both State officials and feudal nobles. The group interests and aspirations which they acquired in the service of the State were as powerful motives for their behaviour as the interests they shared with the rest of the class into which they were born.

There is a line of false reasoning which it is very easy to get into when we are discussing social groups and their group interests. We can divide society into groups in many different ways; we can make, so to speak, many different social maps of it. We can classify people according to their property rights, or the size of their incomes, or their religion, or their political rights, or in some other way. If, for any reason, we decide that one of these divisions – one of these maps – is more important than the others, calling it fundamental or primary, we fall easily into the practice of treating the group interests of any group on a secondary map as if they formed part of the group interests of a group on the primary map, whenever most (or perhaps only the most prominent) of the members of the first group also belong to the second. For example, if we decide with the Marxists that the division into classes according to property rights is the one that really matters, and we find that most seventeenth-century Protestants – or the most prominent among them – were capitalists, we easily fall into the practice of treating their interests as Protestants as if they were part of their interests as capitalists. Or if we find that the higher clergy who dominated the Church in the Middle Ages held fiefs as the lay nobles did, we are apt to treat the interest of the Church as if it were a variety of feudal interest. Or if we find that higher officials in Tsarist Russia were mostly recruited from the landowning class, we treat their interests as officials as somehow derived from their interests as landowners. We are not hard put to it to find them using their official position to promote the interests of landowners; we may even find them consistently preferring the interests of that class to those of other classes and groups outside the State administration. Their group interests as officials, or even their ambitions for the State they serve, we tend to forget, or to treat as unimportant, because officials are not what we understand by a class; and we have already made up our minds that only class interests matter 'in the long run'.

We tend also to forget that even a group which is not hereditary may last through many generations and have enduring interests, and also enduring ambitions for the State or other community they control

– ambitions which it is misleading to treat as merely the *interests* of that group, even if they are much stronger within that group than outside it. For example, in the countries they dominate, Communist parties have ambitions for those countries which, though they are often not shared by the people generally, cannot be treated as mere interests of the party. They are ambitions of the party for the country and not just for the party. The attempt to realize these ambitions constitutes one of the greatest social and political revolutions the world has ever known. The ambitions of the party are supposed by the party to serve the interests of the manual working classes. But this may be only the opinion of the party. What the party is doing may be understood and approved by only a very small proportion of the classes in whose name it is being done, which does not in the least prevent its being a revolution of tremendous importance.

f. The Marxian Model of Revolution

The social and political revolution which transformed the feudal into the capitalist system was, as Marx and Engels describe it, a class conflict very different from the class conflict which they believed would eventually put communism in the place of capitalism. The feudal nobility and the rising bourgeoisie, though their class interests conflicted, never stood to one another in the same relation as, according to Marx and Engels, the capitalists stand to the proletariat. The feudal nobility never exploited the mediaeval burghers as the capitalists exploit the proletariat; they exploited the serfs but not the merchants and craftsmen in the towns. The towns got their charters from the feudal lords – temporal and spiritual – whose interest it was to grant them, just as it was the interest of the townsfolk to receive them. As the towns grew larger and richer, they acquired the right to be represented in provincial or national assemblies; the burghers became an estate of the realm. Then (not always but often) they supported the monarch in his efforts to gain power at the expense of the feudal nobility. They also, by creating a predominantly money economy, helped to lighten or to break (though without intending to do so) the ties that bound the serfs to their lords. Without aiming at doing so, they helped to dissolve the manorial system.

The change-over from feudalism to capitalism was slow, and its significance was not understood by the classes involved in it. Sometimes the position of the feudal nobles was undermined by the activities of the burghers without the burghers knowing that it was so; and sometimes the burghers, by supporting the monarchy or by their explicit demands, consciously challenged the privileges of the nobility. Yet their actions, even when they knew them to be hostile to the nobles, were usually not thought of by them as a challenge to the established order. Not really until the end of the eighteenth century do we find them aiming at political revolution. But by that time the social revolution had largely come to pass; the old property relations had largely given way to new ones. The French Revolution removed only the last vestiges of serfdom, the remaining privileges of the nobility; it was aimed, as much against a bureaucratic but inefficient monarchy which the rising middle class had in the past helped to make strong, as against the nobles; it was directed as much against a system disliked by all classes as against any class. The bourgeois in France, like the classes represented in the English Long Parliament over a century before, wanted a larger share of political power at the expense of a monarchy which they had themselves until recently supported; if they were more consciously revolutionary than the Long Parliament, it was because they could not plausibly pass off their demands as traditional rights.

The class conflict of the future which is to put an end to capitalism and replace it by communism, is (as Marx and Engels imagine it) very different from this. It is a struggle of the exploited against their exploiters; and it is much more conscious, deliberate and sustained. The workers, even before they take political action, are directly engaged against the capitalists; they form trade unions to better their wages and conditions of work; they take strike action. As the workers see that there is a limit to the concessions they can extort from their employers by direct action, they come gradually to understand that they must themselves win political power and use it to change the social system – the relations of property – under which they are exploited. They therefore come to aim consciously at transforming the social system; they become, as the burghers never were, a consciously revolutionary class. They do not, as the bourgeois did in England and France, claim political power when the social revolution is largely over; and they cannot, as the English Parliamentarians did, put forward revolutionary political claims without admitting (even to themselves) that they are revolutionary. They make a political revolution not to complete but to begin a social revolution, and both as political and social revolutionaries they know what they are doing; they understand its historical significance.

There are only two conflicts between major classes – conflicts which transform society so deeply that the transformation is a passing from one historical epoch into another – of which Marx and Engels speak in sufficient detail to make a comparison between their accounts worthwhile. Comparing these two accounts we see how very different are the class conflicts they describe. I do not say this in criticism of Marx and Engels. If we hold that all great social and political transformations arise out of class conflicts, we are not bound to offer only one model of a class conflict. There is no reason why one major class conflict should not differ from another as greatly as the Hundred Years' War differs from Hitler's War. Rather than criticism, I should utter a warning. As Marx and Engels were much more interested in the struggle of the proletariat than of any earlier revolutionary class – a struggle in their time confined to Europe – their ways of thinking and speaking about class conflicts and revolution generally are very deeply marked by their conception of one particular struggle. This is still largely true of their disciples. When they speak of revolution and class conflict, they still have in mind the sort of action which Marx and Engels believed that the proletariat in the West were taking or must take to destroy capitalism. They still often take what the founders of Marxism believed was happening or was soon to happen in Europe as *the* model of revolution and class conflict – which means that the terms they use to describe these kinds of events apply without distortion much less widely than they suppose.

g. Class Consciousness

Marx and Engels often use the term *class-consciousness*. The French peasants, Marx suggests in the *Eighteenth Brumaire of Louis Bonaparte*, are not a *class-conscious* class. They have a way of life, a culture, and interests which mark them off from other classes, but their similar interests beget no unity; they do not work together to promote their interests, they have no organizations of their own to take political action on their behalf.[1] They are, no doubt, aware of themselves as a class different from other classes; they think of themselves and refer to themselves as peasants. They have class-consciousness in the same sense as people have national consciousness. But they do not have what Marx understands by class-consciousness because they do not act together to further their interests.

The bourgeois have class-consciousness; they work together to further their interests. They do not merely know what they want as individuals; they do not merely have personal ambitions. They have demands which they make in common; they know what they want done on their behalf as a class, or, if all of them do not know, they have leaders who do know, and whose leadership they accept.

[1] See Marx and Engels, *Collected Works*, vol. 11, p. 187.

They are organized to make collective demands, and could not even decide what demands to make unless they were organized. To act as a group – to be able to formulate collective aims and to pursue them – a class must be organized. Any class, to be actively engaged in a conflict with other classes, must be class-conscious in this sense.

There is also, I think, another sense which Marx and Engels give to the term *class-consciousness*; and in this sense of it, no class other than the proletariat need be fully class-conscious in order to make successfully the social and political revolution which they are destined to make. The bourgeois had to organize to promote their class interests before they could by their action gradually transform society; but they did not need to understand the historical significance of what they were doing. They did not have to see themselves as transformers of society in order to transform it. It was not necessary to their playing their part in history that they should consciously undertake the destruction of one social and political system and its replacement by another. But the proletariat, in order to accomplish their historic task, must understand its significance as a whole, for they are to be the *architects* of a new society as the bourgeois before them never were. They are to be revolutionaries in a deeper sense. They do not unwittingly change the system as they pursue their class interests; they see that it is their interest to change the system, and do not change it until they see that it is their interest.

I confess that I have never understood why this should be so. Of course, the study of history and the social studies, which hardly existed while feudalism was giving way to capitalism, were flourishing in the nineteenth century, and it was therefore much more likely that a group active in that century should entertain theories about its place in society and in history. These theories might have more or less of fantasy about them, but their power to influence action would presumably not depend on their truth. The very notions of a course of social development and of a transformation of society were unknown in Western Europe when the bourgeois embarked on the activities which helped eventually to bring feudalism to an end. They had to work in the dark because the light – that is, the serious study of history and society – came only when their task was almost done. The proletariat, starting upon their task already lit, can aim deliberately at the transformation of society. But this explains only why the proletariat *can* do deliberately what the bourgeois in their time did undeliberately; it does not explain why they *need* to understand their historic rôle in order to accomplish it. Yet Marx and Engels tell us in the *Communist Manifesto* that the Communists are 'the most advanced and resolute section of the working-class parties of every country, that section which pushes forward all the others . . . they have over the great mass of the proletariat the advantage of clearly understanding the line of march, the conditions, and the ultimate general results of the proletarian movement.'[1] It is clear from the context that Marx and Engels look upon this understanding as a condition of successful proletarian revolution, for the Communists must not keep it to themselves but must impart it to the class whose advanced section they are.

A class cannot be revolutionary unless it is class-conscious; but it can be revolutionary and class-conscious in one or both of two senses. It can be class-conscious merely in the sense that it is organized to pursue its interests, and revolutionary merely in the sense that, as it pursues its interests, it in fact transforms society; or it can be class-conscious also in the sense that it understands its historic rôle, and revolutionary also in the sense that it deliberately sets about accomplishing it. The bourgeois were revolutionary and class-conscious almost entirely in the first sense; the proletariat are or will be so in both senses.

The transformation of feudal into capitalist society was a long process; it was certainly not smooth but it was long. Political power did not pass directly from the feudal nobility to the bourgeoisie; there was no simple taking over the government of society by one class from another. The bourgeois at first supported the monarch against the nobles; they grew in numbers, wealth and influence under the wing of a more or less absolute monarchy which cannot (Marx admits) be fairly described as a political instrument of their class. They did not, as a class, begin to govern until long after the feudal nobility had lost most of its power. But the transformation of capitalist into socialist society, as Marx and Engels conceive of it, is to be very much more rapid. Control of the State is to pass quickly from the bourgeois to the proletarians. The building up of the revolutionary potential of the proletariat takes a considerable time; the workers acquire political experience in the course of a prolonged struggle against the dominant class; there are many assaults before the political hold of that class on society is loosened. But as soon as it is loosened, it is quickly lost. Not necessarily all at once, but within a short period of time. For the proletariat, ripeness is all. They must strike again and again, not so much to capture the citadel piece by piece, as to learn how to strike the blow which, when their hour comes, will deliver the citadel into their hands. Their political revolution will be a rapid and direct taking

[1] *Communist Manifesto*, sect. II, *Collected Works*, vol. 6, p. 497.

of power from the defeated class enemy, as the bourgeois revolution was not.

Marx and Engels had, I think, two reasons for believing this. They saw that as man's knowledge and his control over nature grow, the speed of social change quickens. Very reasonably, therefore, they expected the social revolution of the future to take much less time than the transition from feudalism to capitalism. But this alone does not suffice to explain why the political revolution of the proletariat – their taking over of the State power – should differ so much from the taking over of that power by the bourgeoisie. Here we must look for another explanation, and presumably it is this. The State power – the machinery of class oppression – controlled by the bourgeois is incomparably stronger than anything that the feudal nobles disposed of. The bourgeois are therefore better placed to defend their class interests intelligently and stubbornly. They also confront a revolutionary class whose interests are more and more clearly incompatible with their own. They too are affected by the study of history and society. Just as their class enemies are more self-consciously revolutionary than any revolutionary class before them, so they in turn, are more self-consciously a conservative class, a class defending a threatened social system, than any conservative class before them. Hence the special character of the political struggle between the bourgeois and the proletarians, making it probable that the proletarian capture of the State, when once it begins, will be rapid and complete. Though blood was often shed during the struggle of the bourgeois for power, there was no rapid unseating of a still completely dominant class, even during the great French Revolution; for the French nobles did not rule France just before 1789 and had already lost many of their privileges.

The proletariat are a revolutionary class in a special sense, and the proletarian revolution has a character all its own. But this does not mean that the proletarian revolution must involve the shedding of much blood, or indeed of any blood at all. Logically, violence, the shedding of blood, is no essential part of revolution as Marx and Engels conceived of it. True, they thought there would be violence when the proletariat took over power, in most countries if not in all. They even at times, I suspect, took pleasure in the thought that there would be. They were not very gentle persons; nor did they believe, as did certain other socialists and Communists of their day, that violence is wrong or that it corrupts those who use it. But all this takes nothing away from the point I am making: revolution, as Marx and Engels conceived of it, does not necessarily involve violence. A class may be consciously revolutionary, may aim deliberately at transforming the social and political system, and yet may be able to achieve its purpose without violence; just as it may not be consciously revolutionary (or indeed revolutionary at all) and yet may, in the pursuit of its interests, be very willing to use violence. No doubt, Marx and Engels believed that the proletariat, in the process of learning to take effective political action, would take many hard knocks from the police and the armed forces; but they did not exclude the possibility that, at least in England and the United States, the actual taking over of power by the working-class might be peaceful. Not that they thought that the bourgeois, moved by a sense of justice, would willingly hand over power to the workers, but they did for a time think it possible that they might in some countries, when the challenge came, surrender power to their class enemies without resorting to violence. Battles and even wars between nations can be lost and won almost without the shedding of blood. So why not also conflicts between classes? 'Force is the midwife of every old society which is pregnant with a new one',[1] Marx said. But what of it? Force also decides the issues of every military encounter, including the one at Yorktown, where the wise and humane Cornwallis surrendered to the Americans without a fight.

2. Class Interests, Irreconcilable Class Interests and Exploitation

Marx often remarks that the interests of certain classes are irreconcilable, that it is simple-minded to believe that they can be reconciled by an appeal to justice, and that therefore a conflict of interests of this kind can end only when one (or both) of the parties to it ceases to exist. When one class exploits another, the interests of the two classes are irreconcilable, and the conflict of interests cannot end while both classes remain in existence. Two classes can also have irreconcilable interests though neither exploits the other. The interests of the rising bourgeoisie were irreconcilable with those of the feudal nobles, even though the bourgeois were not exploited by the nobles. The two classes were never reconciled. The conflict between them ended only with the disappearance of the feudal nobility. This did not necessarily involve the ruin of particular families; the descendants of many feudal lords became capitalist landowners. They even intermarried with the newly rich, at first taking their well-supplied daughters, and afterwards, as they grew bolder, giving them their own daughters in return. Still, though many feudal families survived, they ceased to

[1] *Capital*, vol. I, Part Eight, ch. 31, p. 916.

be feudal; their class – as a class in the Marxian sense – disappeared. Or, to say the same thing in other words, the character of their class changed so profoundly that it ceased to be a feudal nobility, though the descendants of that nobility retained a social prestige on account of their descent.

What do Marx and Engels mean when they say that class interests are *irreconcilable*? What do they understand by *exploitation*? These two questions must be answered separately, for, as we have seen, there can be irreconcilable class interests even where there is no exploitation.

a. Reconciling Interests

Let us first see how we ordinarily speak of the reconciling of interests. John wants one thing and James wants another, and it looks as if both of them cannot get what they want. But, fortunately, means are discovered of giving them both what they want. Their interests are reconciled. This is the simplest case of all, where the reconciling of interests is merely the contriving that everyone gets what he wants. By simplest I mean the most easily explained – because the actual contriving, even when it succeeds, is often difficult.

It may, however, prove impossible to reconcile interests in this way. John wants several things and James wants several others, and there is no way of ensuring that they both get what they want. Their interests are incompatible in the sense that, if John gets all he wants, James cannot get all he wants; and the contrary is also true. Nonetheless, a settlement is reached between John and James giving each of them part of what he wants, and the settlement seems just to both of them. Their interests are reconciled; for though they may not be satisfied with what they get, they are satisfied that justice has been done between them. But suppose that James has been bullied into accepting a settlement which he thinks unjust. He then says (unless fear stops his mouth) that his interest has been sacrificed to John's. Though a settlement has been reached, interests have not been reconciled.

Though James has in fact been bullied, it may yet be that he and John have much the same standards of justice. This may be so, even if John has taken part in bullying James. In that case we can say that their interests, though they have not been reconciled, are in principle reconcilable, in the sense that, given the facts of the situation, there is a settlement which – by the standards of both parties to the dispute – is a just settlement. John may have so difficult a character that he refuses to accept this settlement; there may be no arguing with him because he refuses to listen to reason. It is in fact impossible to get him to accept what, by his own standards of justice – the standards he would apply impartially in a case in which he was not himself involved – is a just settlement. And yet we should say that his interests and James's are in principle reconcilable. They would be irreconcilable in principle only if there were no settlement which could be reached that would be just by standards common to both of them.

But standards of justice are not unchanging any more than are the demands men make upon one another. John and James have irreconcilable interests only as long as their demands are incompatible with one another and they have no common and relevant standards enabling them to reach a just settlement. If either their demands or their standards change, their interests may cease to be irreconcilable. And it is a matter of observed fact that people's standards and interests do change, and that they change in the process which adjusts demands to one another.

To get our bearings in this matter, we must distinguish between desires and interests; for as soon as we make this distinction we see that interests and standards are not related to one another as Marx believed they were. A child, before it has become a moral person, makes demands on the persons who look after it – demands as yet untouched by any idea of justice. But it soon discovers that there are limits to what other people will do, and that it must make concessions to them if it is to get what it asks of them. It must abate its demands to suit them, if its demands are to be met. As it learns that this adjustment – this moderating of demand – is required of everyone, and not only of itself, it comes to accept it, not only as expedient, but as just. It acquires notions of justice; it no longer demands whatever it desires but only what it feels entitled to. Indeed, its standards affect even its desires; it ceases not only to demand, but often even to desire, what it feels it is not entitled to. And because the child has some standards – because it is willing to take account of the claims of others – it can be reasoned with, it can be persuaded, and then it can be trusted as it could not be before it acquired them.

The child, having acquired standards, does not retain them un-changed throughout its life. As a moral and rational person, it is more than a mere subject of appetites; it has a 'place' in society and is aware that it has one; it has more or less settled preferences and ambitions. It has what most men (and Marx) understand by *interests*. And the closer it is to being an adult, the more this is true. But the standards of even an adult change. In pursuing its interests, it makes demands which others refuse to meet. If the demands are refused because the standards of the person who makes them differ from those of the persons upon whom he or she makes them, it is, for the time being, impossible to reach a settlement which seems just to all parties. Yet, eventually, such a settlement may be reached, because the parties to it have both abated their demands and modified their notions of what justice requires. If some of them have done only the first, the settlement will not seem just to them; it will seem just only if there has been a change in their ideas about what they are entitled to expect.

No doubt, grown-up persons do not change their standards easily; they are much more set in their beliefs and habits than children are. They are strongly wedded to their principles, and press their demands all the more obstinately because they find them just. Nevertheless, they do change their standards, as well as moderate their demands, though they often do so painfully and slowly, and often also without themselves being aware that they do so. As was understood by Hegel (whose writings Marx studied, though not always to good purpose), it is because men are self-conscious and self-critical creatures active in a social environment that they acquire standards of justice and other values, which are not unchanging, precisely because they are the standards and values of self-critical creatures whose need of one another is as deep as their need to assert themselves.

If this is true of individuals and their interests and standards, why should we suppose that it is not true also of classes and other groups? Since every large community consists of many smaller ones, and also of many classes and other groups, and since all these groups and communities are differently placed from one another, it is only to be expected that, at any particular time, there will be group interests and group standards which are incompatible. Therefore, at any one time, there will be irreconcilable interests in the large community, both between individuals and between groups. Men coming from different parts of the large community or belonging to different classes and groups inside it may be involved in disputes with one another and have no common and relevant standards enabling them to reach a just settlement, even when they agree about the facts. Their interests will then be irreconcilable. The same may happen with organized groups. They too may be involved in disputes of this kind, and therefore have irreconcilable interests. But, the more frequent these disputes, the stronger will be the need felt for standards making it possible to reach just settlements.

Since group and class interests are always changing and new groups and classes are always arising, there will always be *some* irreconcilable group and class interests, just as there will always be some irreconcilable individual interests. But those interests will remain irreconcilable only as long as the classes or groups or individuals persist in their demands and do not change their standards. When we say that interests are irreconcilable, in this sense, we say nothing about the chances that a just settlement will be reached. We make only a hypothetical statement. If these people persist in putting their demands and standing by their notions of what is just, we say that they can never reach a settlement acceptable to them all; *we do not predict that they will persist.*

But Marx and Engels, when they call the interests of certain classes irreconcilable, say more than this. They say that these classes, having incompatible interests and standards of justice, have no hope of reconciling their interests, which arise out of the social relations they stand in and are determined by how those classes are situated in society. Given the social situation of a class, its class interests are also given, and to the extent that it is aware of these interests, its standards are determined by them. It may, if it is an exploited class, be conditioned into accepting the standards of the class that exploits it, but those standards are none the less incompatible with its interests. As it comes to know these interests, it acquires the standards appropriate to them; it acquires the class morality which corresponds to its 'true' class interests. What a class is – its social situation – determines its class interests, which in turn, to the extent that the class is aware of them, determine its class standards. Therefore, if it knows its interests and they are incompatible with those of another class, the two classes are irreconcilable and must remain so.

This, presumably, does not mean that Marx and Engels deny that classes having irreconcilable interests do not also have common interests. Though they sometimes, perhaps inadvertently, speak as if they believed that, say, capitalists and proletarians have no common interests, this is not a point to be pressed against them; for their argument that no genuine compromise between the two classes is possible does not depend logically on their denying that they have common interests. Moreover, Marx and Engels do sometimes admit that there are or may be interests common to all sections of a community divided into classes.

Nevertheless, the doctrine that there are irreconcilable class interests, *in the form they give to it*, rests on mistaken opinions about how interests and standards are related to one another. If we take a man's interest to be, not his passing desires and demands, but the demands he makes (or which it would be reasonable for him to make) to preserve or improve his position in society, we can agree with Marx that what those demands are depends largely on his position in society. But we should insist against Marx that it also depends largely on his standards, on the moral and other values which he accepts. It is as a social and moral creature that he has interests. And what is true of the individual is true also of the group or class. The interests of a group or class are either the interests common to its members (which may be common to them even though they do not know that they are so and have to make the discovery before they become aware of themselves as a group having group interests), or they are the reasonable demands made on their behalf by spokesmen whose right to speak for them they recognize. No doubt, group interests differ in some ways from individual interests, but they do not differ from them in the respect needed to lend substance to Marx's doctrine that class interests are irreconcilable. For they too are interests which cannot be defined without reference to the standards supposed to be determined by them.

Therefore, though Marx was right to distinguish interests from mere desires and passing demands and to treat them as arising out of the social situation of the persons whose interests they are, he was wrong in assuming that they are prior to morality. What gives them a relative stability is that they are the select and persistent demands of creatures having a sense of values. He was wrong also in supposing that, where class interests diverge, no need is felt to reconcile them strong enough to cause both class interests and class values to change. Just as the still amoral child in learning to moderate its demands becomes a thoughtful and moral person having not merely appetites but interests; and just as grown men having divergent interests learn to reconcile them, even (if need be) by modifying, consciously or unconsciously, their moral standards; so too do classes and other groups continually modify both their interests and their values. The process of adjustment, with groups as with individuals, is unending, is both conscious and unconscious and often painful and sometimes violent. But it is as much a process of adjusting values to values as interests to interests, because the two are involved in one another. Interests are irreconcilable only while the values involved in them remain unchanged; but they do not so remain. This is a less exciting conclusion than Marx's, no doubt; it is also nearer the truth.

b. 'Objective' Class Interest

When Marx and Engels speak of classes knowing and not knowing their interests, they imply a distinction between the actual ambitions of a class – their interests as they or their trusted leaders would describe them – and their objective or true interests. Here we have, not a distinction between mere appetite or impulse and what is properly an interest, but between what people conceive their interest to be and what it really is. This distinction, too, has its difficulties, and we must examine them.

We make this same distinction when we speak of individuals. Someone wants something, but, we say, his true interest is that he should not have it. He is not moved by a momentary impulse or appetite; he has a settled purpose, an ambition. Yet we say that it is not his true interest that it should be satisfied. When we say this we are not passing a moral judgement on his ambition; we are not saying that he would be a better person if he did not have it. We are implying, rather, that if he gets what he wants he will be disappointed. If he gets what he wants, he will find he does not like it, or that he gets other things besides which he dislikes. He will be less contented with his lot for having it. So, too, we can say that a man's true interest is to have something which he does not want or even refuses. In saying this about him, we may take into account only what sort of man he now is, assuming that his character and situation remain more or less unchanged. Or we may also take into account the sort of man we think he will become and his probable future situation. We may say it is not his true interest to have this, because, though it will satisfy him for the time being, he will find as he grows older that he would rather be without it and cannot get rid of it, or must suffer if he tries to do so. This is the sort of thing that parents say when they suppose themselves to know better than their children what is good for them.

We pass these judgements on groups and classes as well as on individuals. But when we pass them on groups and classes – taking into account not only their present characters and situations, but also what we think they are likely to become in the future – they are far more hazardous than when we pass them on individuals. All men and all women, unless they die young, pass through the same phases of life: childhood, adolescence, maturity and old age. Each phase has needs and attitudes peculiar to itself. When, therefore, we say to a child, 'This may suit you now, but it won't suit you when you grow up', we may be talking excellent sense; and so, too, when we make a prediction about the old age of some man or woman in the prime of life. In more or less stable societies there is a variety of clearly defined occupations; there are typical careers, typical opportunities; there are ladders of promotion. Everyone's choice of occupations is limited, and, his occupation once chosen, there are limits to what he can do or become. If we know a boy's temperament and abilities, and the situation of his family, we can reasonably say that it is his true interest (though he may not know it) to choose one occupation rather than another; and of a man who has already chosen his occupation, we can say that his true interest – seeing that he is the sort of man he is – is this rather than that.

The same kind of judgement made of a group or class or nation is much more likely to be no better than a guess. Groups and classes do not have a normal span of life, passing through the same phases during the course of it. They do not have typical careers. There are not large numbers of them in similar situations with similar ambitions and with much the same prospects for the future. Judging by what has happened to other soldiers or coalminers or farmers, we can often make reasonable predictions about how this soldier or coalminer or farmer will be placed later in life if he persists in trying to get what he now wants, saying that he would be better off 'in the long run' (which in any case is not long) if he aimed at something else. But, judging by what has happened to other groups, and even to similar groups in other countries or in former ages, we cannot, with anything like the same chance of being right, predict the remoter consequences to this or that group of its persisting in one course or embarking on another. And when it is about classes – in the Marxian sense of class – that we make our predictions, we are even worse placed than when we make them about smaller and more homogeneous groups. Sometimes, no doubt, in a stable society, we can make more or less reasonable predictions for a few decades ahead. But what are a few decades in the life of a class?

An individual has a normal span of life, and often also a fairly stable environment. If the environment is not stable, judgements – his own or other people's – about the remoter consequences to him of his persisting in his present course are apt to be worthless. It is then almost impossible to discover his true interest, unless we take into account no more than a few months or even weeks ahead. In the summer of 1917 it was far more difficult to make reasonable judgements about the true interests of Russians than of Englishmen. But a class not only has no normal or predictable life-span; its social environment, even in a slowly changing society, is not stable. A class endures much longer than an individual, and the longer it endures, the more society changes.

It is odd to speak of the interests of classes over long periods of time for yet another reason. A class does not have an identity in the same sense as an individual has one. If you tell a young man that he will be better off in middle and old age for changing his present intentions, he has, if he believes your reasons are good, a strong motive for changing them. You may hope to persuade him that it is his true interest to aim at something different from what he is now aiming at. But in what sense could it be the true interest of the proletarians of one generation to work for a revolution which is not to happen until after they are dead? They may be better off if they do not work for revolution, even though the workers who come after them stand to lose by their indifference. If they are unwilling to make sacrifices for their successors, and yet are forced to make them, can we say that they are working for their own true interests? Surely, it makes better sense to say that they are being forced to sacrifice their own interests to those of future generations? Are they, then, working for the true interests of their class? But they belong to that class no less than their successors do, and what makes for their happiness is as much part of the true interest of the class as what makes for the happiness of their successors. Even if they are willing to make sacrifices for those who come after, it is only their true interest to do so if they are happier, or find life better worth living, for doing so.

The interests of a class are merely the interests common to its members; they are whatever satisfies the demands made by its members, or made on their behalf by their acknowledged spokesmen. Its true or objective interests are whatever makes for their enduring satisfaction – whatever satisfies their ambitions without stimulating in them ambitions which cannot be satisfied. If the class we have in mind, like the Marxian classes, lasts many generations, what are the interests common to its members? The situation of the class changes from generation to generation and so do its members, *and* the interests common to them, *and* what makes for their enduring satisfaction – their sense of well-being. What, then, are the true or objective interests of the class? John at seventy is the same person as John at seven. It makes sense to say that, given his character, his situation and his prospects, this rather than that was or is or will be his true interest – that, had he aimed at it, or were he to do so now or in the future, he would have been or would be the happier for it. But it hardly makes sense to speak of a class in this way, except for relatively short periods of time, while its situation and its members do not greatly change.[1]

---

[1] Of a corporate body whose functions are precisely defined, we can say that its true interest is whatever enables it to carry out those functions efficiently. But then its functions are defined without regard to the ambitions or happiness of its members. A class is not a corporate body. A profession may be so. In that case, we must distinguish between its true interest in the sense of what makes for its efficiency, and its true interest in the sense of what makes for the enduring happiness of its members.

c. Exploitation

The Marxian conception of exploitation is open to serious criticism on the ground that it treats only some kinds of useful work as creating value. There are functions which Marx and Engels do not deny are useful, and even necessary, but which they will not treat as productive labour, as creating value. The maintenance of order, for example. Unless order is maintained, production cannot go on smoothly; and it is illogical to treat only the work directly involved in production as productive if there are also other kinds of work which are conditions of efficient production. Exploitation, as Marx defines it, is the appropriation of surplus-value, the taking away from those who produce value of part of the value they produce; and exploitation is not theft because it is legal. Those engaged in non-productive (but not therefore useless) work are paid – so Marx would have us believe – out of the surplus-value appropriated from productive workers. They live on surplus-value just as much as people who do not work at all.

It is true that Marx and Engels predict the disappearance of the State,[1] but this, as we shall see later, does not involve the disappearance of all the functions now carried out by the State, but only of some. Therefore many functions which are not productive labour, as Marx defines it, will survive into the classless society, presumably because they are useful. It is odd to deny that useful, and even indispensable, services are forms of labour that create value.

Marx and Engels admit that the State is necessary in class societies, where its function is to keep the peace between classes whose interests are irreconcilable. They admit that peace is necessary to production, and that, in class societies, there must be a State to keep the peace. There appears to be here a contradiction in Marxian theory. The State is called oppressive, though its function is admitted to be necessary at a certain stage of social development. It would be absurd, Marx tells us, to try to set up a classless and stateless society where conditions do not allow it. The conditions that do allow it are high productivity and a high level of education in all sections of the community. Capitalism, as it develops, helps to create these two conditions. In that sense, it is progressive. But capitalist production could not go on unless the social order were maintained, which, in a class society, it cannot be except by the State. The State is therefore more than an unavoidable evil; it is a condition of progress. How then can it be merely oppressive? How

---

[1] Marx, for instance in the *Communist Manifesto*, sect. II, and in *The Civil War in France*, sect. III (*Collected Works*, vol. 6, p. 505 and vol. 22, pp. 332–3); Engels, most notably in his article 'On Authority' and in *Anti-Dühring*, Part III, ch. II (*Collected Works*, vol. 23, p. 422 and vol. 25, p. 268).

can we deny that those who carry out its functions are engaged in labour which creates value? True, they produce not goods but services; but services can have value as well as goods. Are indispensable services without value now because in the future they will be dispensed with? We might as well say that the services of a nurse are now without value because the child she looks after will not need them when it is older and more mature. The labour theory of value and the doctrine of exploitation derived from it rest on the paradox that not all services indispensable to society are labour which creates value.

A social system might give rise to activities which are unavoidable and yet harmful – activities not necessary to the proper functioning of the system or to its evolution towards something better. There might be, in this sense, some unavoidable but quite useless and even harmful activities. The persons engaged in them, since they consume the produce of other people's labour without doing anything useful themselves, might be called exploiters. They would be no less exploiters than the bone idle. Or a social system might give rise to activities which are necessary to its functioning and its evolution towards something better but which will disappear when that something better comes into the world. To call these last activities oppressive and the persons who carry them on exploiters is to misuse language.

The Marxian theory of exploitation lays so much stress on particular rights of property (e.g. the rights peculiar to capitalists) which make possible the appropriation of surplus-value that Marxists ordinarily deny that there can be exploitation where these rights do not exist; and since these rights are used to distinguish classes from one another, they also deny that there can be exploitation in a classless society. Thus, today, Marxists, if they wish to establish that there is no exploitation in the Soviet Union, set about showing that in the Soviet Union there are no classes. Exploitation, thus conceived, is both too wide and too narrow a concept. Sometimes it requires us to treat as exploiters people whose services are indispensable, and at other times inhibits us from treating as exploiters people who compel others to contribute to purposes they do not share but who do not, in the Marxian sense of class, belong to a different class from their victims.

There is, I believe, another important sense in which Marx and his disciples speak of exploitation. This sense has nothing to do with the appropriation of surplus-value. It is a sense which Marx does not define or distinguish from the other.

Acton says that *exploitation* is a moral term.[1] He means, presumably,

[1] See *The Illusion of the Epoch*, p. 243.

not merely that it is often used to condemn the activity it refers to, but that it is always so used. I believe that he is mistaken, and that it is important, if we are to do justice to Marx, to realize that exploitation is not always a moral term. No doubt, Marx condemned exploitation, both in the sense which involves appropriation of surplus-value and in other senses. But it is possible to apply a word to an activity usually condemned or praised without using the word to condemn or praise it. I usually condemn murder; but it does not follow that, when I say 'Yusupov murdered Rasputin', I am condemning Yusupov. I may be saying no more than that Yusupov killed Rasputin illegally, which is merely a statement of fact. The word *murder* is often used to condemn a killing and often to describe it; but surely, though the word has these two uses, we are not bound to make the first use whenever we make the second. The context reveals our purpose; and only when it does not do so need we take the precaution of saying 'illegal killing' instead of 'murder'.

Exploitation is a word like murder; it is often, but not always, a moral term. It refers to an activity which is against the law or which contravenes standards which men accept or might accept. But we can apply the term to an activity without ourselves accepting those standards; and, even if we do accept them, we can apply the term without ourselves invoking the standards. We may be speaking of someone in a society different from our own, and even of an activity which in our society is thought good, and we may call it exploitation, meaning that the activity is of a type which in that society is usually condemned; and we may also condemn it ourselves (because we prefer the other society to our own) without revealing that we do so by calling it exploitation.

We may also believe – and this, I think, brings us to the important sense of the world *exploitation*, which Marx sometimes used without defining it – that there are some things which all men would think desirable if they understood what sort of creature man is and what he is capable of. We may hold, as Hegel and others have done, that in a particular community men have the values and ambitions they do have only because their understanding is limited. If they understood themselves and the world more fully, they would have different values, and would be the happier for having them. We may find that certain activities which people engage in for their own advantage prevent other people getting this fuller understanding and thus acquiring the values which come with it. We may then call these activities *exploitation*, even though they are not condemned by either exploiters or exploited, who are equally ignorant of their consequences. For example, we may say that, in some societies, women are exploited, even though they are not dissatisfied with their lot. We need not be saying that by our standards they are badly treated, nor need we imply that our standards are better than theirs. We may be saying no more than this: by standards which they would accept if they understood human nature and human capacities better than they do, they are being badly treated. This, on the face of it, is not a moral judgement; it does not imply that the standards which come with a fuller understanding are higher than the standards they supersede. But, of course, if the judgement is not to be a moral judgement, the fuller understanding must not be what is sometimes called a deeper moral insight; it must be no more than a deeper understanding of the facts and possibilities, social and psychological. It must be an understanding which can be expressed without making any moral judgement. We then say only that, when persons come to have this understanding, they are disposed to accept these values, and to be satisfied in so doing because their circumstances are then such that they both desire to realize these values and are able to do so. There is attained a harmony of ambitions, resources and values.

Marx believed that men's values change as their understanding of themselves and their environment grows and also that eventually they will have values and resources enabling them to lead far more fully satisfying lives than ever before. He may have been mistaken in the latter part of his belief. For the moment, I am not concerned to argue that he was or was not. I want only to say that the assertion of this belief is not in itself a value judgement; it is merely a prediction which may be true or false. No doubt, if Marx had not been a moralist – if he had not himself accepted the values which he ascribed to the future communist society– he would not have made this prediction. It is the prediction of a moralist, but it is not a moral judgement.

Of course, I willingly concede that Marx and Engels did often speak as if the values that come with this understanding were higher than the ones they supersede, and also that they often use the word *exploitation* to condemn the activity they applied to it. Nevertheless, they were concerned to do more than just say that the values of the classless society are the highest; they also implied, firstly, that they are values which men in fact prefer to all others when they understand themselves and their environment, and secondly, that they are values in which alone men find enduring satisfaction.[1] If, then, some men

---

[1] Marx and Engels imply this when they speak of the morality of the future classless society as if it were somehow more human than the morality of their day, and also when they speak of *alienation* – of which more later.

use other men in ways which make it more difficult for them to get this understanding and these values, they are exploiting them; they are helping to prevent their getting what they may as yet have no idea of, and therefore do not want, but would prefer to their present condition if only they knew about it. If this is exploitation – and it is, I think, what Marx *sometimes* meant by it – then the word is not always a moral term.

That is not, surely, an unusual use of it. It is often part of what we mean when we say that children or other more or less ignorant persons are being exploited. Admittedly, it is not often the whole but only part of our meaning, the other part being a moral judgement. That is to say, even when we speak of children and ignorant persons being exploited, we ordinarily use the word to condemn as well as to describe an activity. Nevertheless, it is not merely a moral term, and we can use it, if we take the trouble to make our purpose plain, to describe without condemning.

III. WHAT DID MARX AND ENGELS MEAN BY IDEOLOGY? HOW DID THEY CONCEIVE OF ITS FUNCTION IN SOCIETY?

Often, when a commentator sets about explaining a theory, he makes it out to be simpler and neater than it is in order to make better sense of it. It is a temptation sometimes difficult to resist; it appeals to the love of order if not to charity in him. Several critics of Marxism have succumbed to it. Among the social activities and features of social life which Marx puts into the *superstructure*, which he distinguishes from the economic *substructure* of society, are law and government and also what he calls the social forms of consciousness. Marx says of these forms of consciousness that they are *ideological*. It might seem, then, that he distinguishes, within the superstructure, between what is ideological and what is not.

No doubt, it would better if he had done what some of his critics assume he has done; for then one important part of his theory would be clearer and sounder than it is. But, unfortunately, the matter is not as simple as that.

1. Marxian Uses of the Word 'Ideology'

There are at least three different senses in which Marx and Engels use the word *ideology*, though they do not distinguish between them.

Sometimes, when they speak of *ideology*, they seem to have in mind the entire system of ideas which men use to describe the world and to express their standards, feelings and purposes. This is so when Marx and Engels are most self-consciously materialists, when they are concerned to show how men come to have ideas at all. That – perhaps the most obscure sense of the three – is also the least interesting to the social and political theorist. Though not exactly taken from Hegel, it is an adaptation of an idea central to his philosophy. Hegel had spoken of Spirit, of the Real, as essentially active and as coming to know itself through its activities. Spirit is what it does, and by doing acquires self-knowledge. Marx speaks of man as essentially practical, and as coming to understand himself and the world through what he does to satisfy his needs. Men are active in a natural environment which they adapt to their needs, and by their actions they create a social environment which deeply affects them. They learn to think – they acquire a coherent picture of the world and of themselves in it – as they strive to satisfy their needs. But Marx and Engels are not content merely to say that men learn to think in the process of acting to satisfy their needs. They go further than this; they say that how men conceive of the world and themselves is determined by their needs and what they do to satisfy them – by *social production*. They speak as if this conclusion followed, granted that men learn to think in the process of satisfying their needs.

Yet they do not deny that all social activities, not excluding production, involve the use of ideas. Thus they seem to be saying that certain activities – which are basic in relation to all others – determine men's ideas, and yet seem also to be willing to admit, at least tacitly, that even these basic activities involve the use of ideas. All social activities are rational, in the sense that they involve the use of ideas, and yet some – the ones that are basic – determine what ideas men use. If this is a position that Marx and Engels take up – and it has been argued, not implausibly, that they do adopt it – then it is, so it seems to me, untenable. Even if we allow that men acquire language and the use of concepts as they co-operate to satisfy their needs, it does not follow that we can treat this co-operation – this social production – as a factor which determines what concepts they have and how they use them.

So far, we have been considering only one Marxian sense of the term *ideology*, and that the least important to the social and political theorist. There are two other senses, a wider and a narrower. The wider treats as ideology all theories and doctrines which are not scientific, and also all normative concepts. It marks a retreat from the extreme position which I said was untenable; its use is a tacit recognition that the ideas used to describe the world, whether at the level of ordinary common sense or at the level of science, are not determined by what men do to satisfy their needs, even though they are the ideas of creatures who would never have sought to understand the world if they had not had needs to satisfy. The narrower sense treats as ideology, not all normative concepts, but only those which serve the interests of some class or group, and also all theories and doctrines which are not scientific. This sense is prominent when Marx or Engels is trying to explain the behaviour of social classes.

Critics of Marxism who take it for granted that Marx and Engels make a clear distinction, within the superstructure, between law and government, on the one hand, and what they call 'the social forms of consciousness', on the other, imply that it is in what I have called the narrower sense that the two masters ordinarily use the term *ideology*. Indeed, these critics sometimes imply that they use it in an even narrower sense, to refer only to theories and doctrines which are not scientific. But this is not true. Marx and Engels often use the term in ways which suggest that all normative concepts are ideological, and they seldom use it in ways which suggest that none is so. When, for example, they speak of law and morality as part of the 'ideological superstructure', they clearly imply that all important normative concepts are ideological; they are speaking, not just of theories about law and morality, but of legal and moral rules and of the concepts they embrace.

For example, in the Preface to *A Contribution to the Critique of Political Economy*, Marx, having spoken of a conflict between the *forces* and *relations* of production, invites us to distinguish between the 'material transformation of the economic conditions of production' resulting from this conflict and the 'legal, political, religious, artistic or philosophic – in short, ideological forms in which men become conscious of this conflict and fight it out'.[1] This passage, no doubt, is multiply obscure; it casts shadow upon shadow. Marx seems to be saying both that there are two types of conflict and that there is only one: that there is conflict within the economic substructure giving rise to conflicts within the superstructure, and also that the conflicts within the superstructure are merely ways of being aware of, and carrying on, the conflicts within the substructure. But, fortunately, there is no need for our present purpose, to try to dispel the manifold obscurities of this often-quoted and therefore familiar statement. For

[1] Marx and Engels, *Collected Works*, vol. 29, p. 263.

the statement, highly obscure though it is, does at least plainly suggest two things: that there is nothing ideological about the activities which belong to the economic *substructure*, and that the entire *superstructure* is ideological. In this statement, therefore, we see Marx using the word ideological in the wider of the two senses of which the social and political theorist need take notice.

I have said that Marx and Engels were sometimes moved by their *materialism* to speak as if all ideas were determined by social activities prior to them, as if how men think about the world and speak about it to one another were determined by how they co-operate to produce what satisfies their needs; and I have said also that they could not abide by this position – that they had to admit, at least by implication, that all social activities, not excluding production, involve the use of ideas. Yet their materialism, though it did not prevent their admitting what was too obvious to be denied, did move them to use the word *ideology* in as wide a sense as possible. They felt that their materialism required them to treat *all* ideas as determined by activities more fundamental than they are – activities whose function is to satisfy needs. They could not in practice, without patent absurdity, do what their materialism seemed to them to require, but they went as far as they could towards doing it.

I now want to show, if I can, that their bias towards including as much as possible under the heading of *ideology* drives them to include more than is consistent either with what they suggest is the primary social function of ideology or with the most striking characteristic they ascribe to it. If not always, certainly very often, they speak as if the function of ideology were to promote or challenge the interests of social classes or groups, and especially of dominant and revolutionary classes. And they say of ideology that it is illusion, or even, as Engels very occasionally remarks, *false consciousness*.[1] I shall argue that not everything which serves this function is false consciousness, and that not everything which is false consciousness serves this function. In the Marxian doctrine of ideology we have a medley of ideas not properly sorted out. It is an extraordinarily confused doctrine, and yet also important and suggestive.

I have said that Marx and Engels use the term *ideology* in too wide a sense for their own purposes, and also that they use it in two senses interesting to the social theorist. Evidently, it is the wider of these two which is the less suited to their purposes; but the narrower is also not

---

[1] See especially Engels to Franz Mehring, 14 July 1893, in Karl Marx and Frederick Engels, *Selected Correspondence* (Moscow 1956), p. 541.

well suited to them. It, too, is too wide, for it cannot always be said of it that it refers to false consciousness or to what serves or challenges class or other group interests. Nevertheless, it is the narrower sense which is the more important and suggestive. There are – buried in the morass of the Marxian doctrine of ideology – ideas well worth extracting for their usefulness as tools of explanation.

But before I attempt this extraction, let me give examples to show how easily Marx and Engels could pass from one sense of ideology to another without being aware that they had done so. Though they pass from one to the other unconsciously, they do not do so at random but as serves the need of the argument. They create confusion and exploit it unwittingly, as social theorists so often do.

My examples come from *The German Ideology*. In one place we read the following statement:

> Conceiving, thinking, the mental intercourse of men at this stage still appear as the direct efflux of their material behaviour. The same applies to mental production as expressed in the language of the politics, laws, morality, religion, metaphysics, etc. of a people. Men are the producers of their conceptions, ideas, etc., that is, real, active men, as they are conditioned by a definite development of their productive forces and of the intercourse corresponding to these, up to its furthest forms. Consciousness (*das Bewußtsein*) can never be anything else than conscious being (*das bewußte Sein*), and the being of men is their actual life-process. If in all ideology men and their relations appear upside down as in a *camera obscura*, this phenomenon arises just as much from their historical life-process as the inversion of objects on the retina does from their physical life-process.[1]

In this passage there is an oscillation between at least two senses of *ideology*: the sense which includes all ideas used in mental intercourse, the widest sense of all; and the sense which includes only normative concepts and theories and doctrines which are not scientific. This second sense is suggested by the singling out of the language of *politics, laws, morality, religion* and *metaphysics* – for these languages do not include all ideas but only those involved in the activities relegated to the *superstructure* – and perhaps also by the assertion that *in all ideology men and their relations appear upside down*, for presumably they do not appear so in science or in the 'mental intercourse' actually involved in production. This often-quoted passage is not obscure in any ordinary degree, nor is it an empty darkness; it is the darkness of the womb concealing what is already alive but still only half-formed.

In another place we read,

[1] *The German Ideology*, I, *Collected Works*, vol. 5, p. 36.

The individuals composing the ruling class possess among other things consciousness, and therefore think. Insofar, therefore, as they rule as a class . . . they . . . rule also as thinkers, as producers of ideas . . . thus their ideas are the ruling ideas of the epoch. For instance, in an age and in a country where royal power, aristocracy, and bourgeoisie are contending for domination, and where, therefore, domination is shared, the doctrine of the separation of powers proves to be the dominant idea and is expressed as an 'eternal law'.[1]

Here the ideas referred to do not include all normative concepts; they include only concepts and doctrines which favour the interests of a class.

2. Moral and Legal Concepts

Marx calls ideology *illusion*, and Engels also calls it *false consciousness*. I take it that these two expressions have much the same meaning. Now, it makes no sense to treat legal and moral concepts – concepts used to invoke rules of conduct and to make value judgements – as illusory. We may have illusions about them; we may believe that, when we use them, we are doing something different from what we really are doing. Let us suppose, for the sake of argument, that when we use these concepts we are merely invoking rules of conduct or giving vent to our feelings about types of behaviour. Then, if we believe that we are doing more, if we believe that we are describing men's motives or actions, if we believe that we are referring to qualities inherent in their motives or actions, we are under an illusion. But merely to use the concepts to invoke rules and give vent to feelings is not to be under an illusion. Even if we do not know that that is what we are doing, even if we cannot correctly describe it, we are under no illusion. Any more than Monsieur Jourdain, when telling his servant, Nicole, to bring him his slippers, is under an illusion because he does not know that he is and has always been speaking prose.[2]

It may be that the effectiveness of rules and moral judgements depends largely on men's being under some sort of illusion about them. It may be that if they did not believe that the judgements referred to qualities inherent in human actions and states of mind, or that the rules followed from the essential nature of man, or were commands of God, or were accepted by all men everywhere, or were adaptations to circumstance of natural or divine or universal law, they would be less moved by the judgements and less disposed to obey the

[1] Ibid., p. 59.
[2] See Molière, *Le Bourgeois gentilhomme*, Act II, scene iv.

rules. It may be that in all societies men have had, and have needed, some such illusions. I think it probable that Marx and Engels believed that it was so. If they were right, and if ideology is false consciousness or illusion, we can say that there have been ideologies attached to all moral and legal and political systems. Most of these ideologies have not been explicit or elaborate or precise theories and doctrines; more often than not they have been vague though powerful beliefs varying considerably from person to person. Thus there can be ideology even in the most primitive – the least articulate and sophisticated, the least dogmatic – society. But, though it is important to notice these accretions to morality, law and government, it is no less important to notice that the concepts actually involved in the making of moral judgements, in the invoking of rules of conduct, and in the forms of social intercourse which constitute government, are different in kind from them. It makes no sense to call these concepts 'ideological', if ideology is false consciousness or illusion. There is here an important distinction which Marx and Engels failed to make. It also makes no sense to treat these concepts as 'reflections' or 'reflexes' (whatever that may mean) of social relations, no matter how basic the relations are supposed to be; for there are always moral concepts, if not legal ones as well, involved in the very having of social relations. They are of the essence of all important forms of social intercourse.

There is another reason – apart from their being used in normative statements which those who make them mistakenly believe to be statements of fact – that disposed Marx to treat moral and legal concepts as ideological. He believed that the function of ideology, or false consciousness, is usually, if not always, to support or to challenge the position or pretensions of some class or other. Ideology, for him and for Engels, is above all class ideology. Now, rules of conduct and moral judgements do sometimes serve to support or challenge the position or pretensions of a class; they can do so just as much as theories and doctrines can, just as much as theology or ethics or social and political theory. Although there must be rules and values which do not serve this purpose (because all social relations involve rules and values, and society is therefore always a moral order, and classes can arise in it only because it is one), yet there are also rules and values which do serve it.

Marx saw that there are rules and values which support class interests; but, unfortunately, he too often lost sight of the fact that there must be others which do not serve this purpose if there are to be communities within which classes can arise. He was therefore sometimes tempted to speak as if concepts involved in rules and value

t accepting the truth of Marxism and fighting hard against the
etariat, striving to put off the evil day for as long as possible.
re are perhaps some men in the world who will fight the harder
ast something for being told that its victory is inevitable. But the
t majority of mankind are not like that.

arx and Engels did not deny that their theory was favourable
he interests of the working class; they even gloried in the belief
it was so. Yet they did not call it a class ideology, presumably
he ground that it was a serious attempt to explain the facts.
logy, as they conceived of it, has two essential properties; it is
consciousness or illusion, and it gains currency because it serves
ests, especially class interests.[1]

Marx and Engels had been concerned merely to give notice how
intended to use the term *ideology*, there would be no point in
relling with them. But in fact they wanted to do more than this.
y often spoke about ideology in such a way as to suggest that
theory which gains currency because it serves interests is false
ciousness, containing a large element of fantasy. The suggestion
lse. Admittedly, they expected their own theory, which they
ved was scientific and not fantastic, to gain currency because it
in line with the interests of the proletariat. But their hopes for
own theory are not in keeping with their account of ideology.

is also important to notice that even a theory which explains
t society ought to be like – a theory which is frankly utopian –
not be a form of false consciousness or illusion. Indeed, if the
ry is frankly utopian, if the maker of it is perfectly aware that he
scribing an ideal, it cannot be a form of false consciousness. It
be fantasy, but it is not illusion.

he fantasy may, of course, be unrealistic. It need not be but
be. The maker of it may have illusions about human nature
bout the course of history or about God's purposes for man, and
antasy may be related causally to his illusions. It may be true
unless he had held these false beliefs, he would never have been
ed to construct that particular fantasy. It may be that, misled by
e beliefs, he is convinced that his ideal will be realized or could
ealized, when in fact it will not be or could not be. But he need
no such false beliefs; he may know that his ideal is unrealizable, or
hay have good grounds for believing that it could be realized.

arxists nowadays will often admit that Marxism is a class ideology. Yet they
ll insist that it is scientific. Thus (though they may not know it) they use the
ord ideology in a different sense from Marx's; a theory is ideological, in their
nse, if only it gains currency because it serves interests.

judgements – concepts which are normative but which those who use
them are apt to think are descriptive – were illusions serving to support
(or challenge) class interests. It came easily to him to treat moral and
legal concepts as ideological in a double sense: as serving class interests
and as being forms of *illusion* or, as Engels puts it, *false consciousness*.

3. Ideology as False Consciousness

If ideology is false consciousness, moral and legal concepts used
merely to invoke rules and to make value judgements cannot be
called ideological. What then can be plausibly so called? Presumably,
such things as theology, metaphysics, ethics, or social and political
theory. I am not saying that they always are forms of illusion but
only that they may be. They may be – they sometimes have been
– fantasies whose purveyors have put them forward as true accounts
of some aspect or other of reality. It makes sense to say of them that
they are forms of false consciousness or illusion. The assertion may
not always be true, but at least it is not absurd, as it is to say that
moral and legal concepts are so.

When Engels calls such theories and doctrines *false consciousness*, he
does not mean that they are sometimes mistaken. Scientists too make
mistakes and sometimes very big ones. Yet science is not ideology.
What, then, is the difference between them? The scientist confines
himself to explaining the facts of experience; his explanations, his
hypotheses, can be tested by an appeal to the facts. As new facts are
discovered, or come to be taken into consideration because they are
seen to be relevant, old explanations are discarded and others thought
to be more adequate take their place. Disputes between scientists can
be settled; scientists use, to test their hypotheses and to establish what
the facts are, methods which rest on assumptions that they all make.
The ideologist, though he claims (and usually sincerely believes) that
he is explaining some aspect of the real world, does not confine himself
to accounting for the facts; he does not test his hypotheses by an appeal
to facts. The primary function of ideology, according to Marx, is not
to explain the world but to support interests. The important question
to ask about an ideology is not 'Is it true?', or 'Does it accord with
the facts?'. It is, rather, 'Who benefits from it?'. We can also usefully
ask 'How did it arise?'. The answer to this second question often
throws light on the first, and the answer to the first on the second.
An ideology is a more or less fantastic theory that promotes beliefs
which are to the interest of some class or other. This is what Marx and
Engels often seem to be saying, though, as we shall see, not always.

'The ideas of the ruling class', we are told, 'are in every epoch the ruling ideas', for it is the ruling class who 'regulate the production and distribution of the ideas of their age'.[1] When the position of the ruling class comes to be challenged by another class, there arises a revolutionary ideology; there arise theories and doctrines serving the interest of the revolutionary class. All these ideologies, conservative and revolutionary, put forward the interest of a class as the common interest; they do not openly justify the existing order or challenge it on behalf of a particular class; they justify or challenge it ostensibly for the common good. The function of ideology is to induce as many people as possible to do what it is the interest of some class that they should do; and clearly it cannot carry out this function unless that interest is put forward as the common interest. Yet the makers and purveyors of ideology are not hypocrites; they do not consciously present class interests as the common interest. They are usually sincere in their belief that what they are arguing for *is* in the common interest.

I have put Marx's position briefly but I hope not unfairly. There is, I think, a considerable measure of truth in it. Many theories – especially theories about man and society, about God and God's purposes for man, and about the universe as a whole tending towards some end – have been largely speculative, or, as some people would put it, have been fantasies. And many of these fantasies have served the interests of some class or other. But there are two observations that I would make: first that theories which do not rest on illusion can serve class interests as well as theories which do; and, second, that theories which are speculative or fantastic, when they do serve interests, do not always, or even usually, serve class interests.

4. Ideology and Class Interests

To establish my first point, let me take social theory as an example. A social theory may seek to explain how society functions, or how it ought to function, or both the one and the other. If it seeks to explain how society functions, it may take serious account of the facts. No doubt, being a social theory, it is likely to be confused and to contain grave errors. It is likely to be confused because of the looseness of the terms used to describe social phenomena, and it is likely to contain grave errors owing to the difficulty of getting at all the relevant facts and assessing their importance. However impartial the social theorist may be, however eager to discover the truth, however cautious and modest, he is apt to lose his way and commit blunders as the physicist

[1] *The German Ideology*, I, op. cit., p. 59.

or biologist is not. He has to cope with difficulties
worry the natural scientist. Yet he may be, by tempe
an impartial seeker after knowledge as any natural
may be very much aware of the difficulties peculiar
study. If that is so, then his confusions and errors, n
they are, cannot properly be called fantasies or false co
more than can the confusions and errors of the natural
may be bigger mistakes, but they are still only mista

Now, a theory produced by such a theorist mig
serve the interests of some class or section of the co
there might be no good reason for believing that i
only because of the confusions and errors it conta
often as useful as error, even to the most self-centr
groups. Let us suppose that Marxism is a theory of
honest, intelligent, impartial attempt to explain the fac
by two men conscious of the shortcomings of all social t
their own and determined to do their utmost to avoid
us suppose also that Marxism happens to favour the i
manual working class. We can suppose, further, though
sake of argument, that Marxism never pleads for that cla
any other class. The theory, on this supposition, favour
of the manual workers only in the sense that it predicts
in a struggle against another class, and so encourages the
and discourages their opponents. The theory may bec
precisely because it does this; it may owe its popularity
people's being impressed by its intelligence, honesty and
than to their liking what it predicts. In that case, what mak
is that it favours the interests of the working class, and no
qualities as a social theory. Does that make it ideology? If
is not necessarily false consciousness. If this is ideology, th
or doctrine – no matter how scientific – is ideological
gains currency primarily because it serves interests.

Marx and Engels believed (much of the time, if not al
their social theory aimed primarily at explaining how societ
and develops, including (among other things) how classe
interests arise. Perhaps they were mistaken about their theo
have been less scientific, even in intention, than they honest
it was. But, granted that they were not mistaken, it still re
that their theory, even if it does not seek to justify claims
or on behalf of the working class, does predispose people w
it to take up these claims and to work for their realizatio
not commit them logically to doing so. There is nothing

We must distinguish, as Marx fails to do, between theories and doctrines which contain false beliefs, and theories and doctrines which rest on false beliefs. To illustrate my meaning, let me take the doctrine of the rights of man as it was put forward in the eighteenth century. In so far as this doctrine does no more than make certain claims on behalf of all mankind, there is nothing illusory about it; it merely asserts that all men have certain rights, which is a way of saying how they ought to be treated and what they ought to be allowed to do. The illusion, if it exists, is not in putting forward the claims; it is in the statements made to support them. These statements may be about human nature, or about what has to be done to make good the claims, or about something else; and they may be false. Or they may be so vague that it is impossible to discover whether they are false or true. And yet the claims may be accepted largely because the statements used to support them are accepted. Certainly, there were many illusions connected with the eighteenth-century assertion of the rights of man. Yet to call that assertion a form of false consciousness does not really make sense.

As a matter of fact, Marx himself believed in the doctrine of the rights of man. If he had been asked whether men ought to enjoy these rights, or whether they would eventually come to enjoy them, he would have said that they ought and would. He did not always reject even the assertions about human nature used to support these rights; he sometimes spoke as if he believed that men, by reason of their humanity, ought to have such rights. He merely thought that – society being what it was in the eighteenth and nineteenth centuries – only the property-owning classes could in fact enjoy them. These classes, though often willing to concede that all men should enjoy the rights of man, were determined to preserve a system of property which, in Marx's opinion, made it impossible for most men to enjoy them. As he saw it, they falsely believed that those rights could be enjoyed by all classes in a class society, whereas the truth was that they could be enjoyed by all men only in a classless society.

5. Class Ideology and Religion

Marx was concerned with religion as a psychological and social phenomenon before he took to economics or thought of history as a succession of conflicts between classes. He read Feuerbach's *Essence of Christianity* and was deeply excited by it. In that work, Feuerbach argues that religion is a fantasy which compensates man for his sense of his own inadequacy, his sense that he is in fact greatly inferior to what he might be. Into his notion of God, man projects his idea of what he aspires to and cannot yet attain; he creates God in his own image, or rather in the image of himself as he unconsciously desires to be. His life to come, in the company and love of God, is the dream in which he seeks the satisfactions still denied him in the world. The idea of God expresses man's sense of his own worth, of the worth of his fully realized self. As his understanding and his opportunities increase, as he comes nearer to being able to live the sort of life which seems to him worthy of his kind, he will give up seeking in fantasy the satisfactions which he will at last be able to get in the real world. The need for religion will pass away. Man will come into full possession of his humanity and will dispense with the illusion of God. Religion is a product of man's immaturity, of his not yet having learnt to live in ways satisfying to himself.[1]

This idea of religion Feuerbach took from Hegel. Where Hegel speaks of Spirit, Feuerbach speaks of man. Reality, for Hegel, is Spirit, and Spirit is essentially active; it is an activity which culminates in complete self-knowledge and satisfaction; it is a process of self-realization. But before Spirit is fully self-realized, before it has attained self-knowledge, it feels itself a stranger in the world as it actually is, even though that world is merely a projection of itself; and it seeks compensation for this sense of self-estrangement in the idea of another world in which it is fully at home and satisfied. Now, for Hegel, Spirit at its higher levels, at the levels at which it is self-conscious, is manifest in the activities of finite rational selves – of men, and in the communities formed by them. Thus, if we eliminate the notion of Spirit and speak only of finite selves – of men – we pass easily from the conception of Hegel to that of Feuerbach.[2] Man aspires to full self-realization, to the full exercise of his capacities, which is possible to him only when he has attained self-knowledge and knowledge of the world – when he has come, morally and intellectually, to maturity; and in the meantime, while he is not yet what he aspires to be, while he is frustrated and unsatisfied, he projects his sense of what he has it in him to become and to enjoy into the ideas of God and of an after-life.

---

[1] See Feuerbach, *The Essence of Christianity*, trans. George Eliot (New York 1957), especially chs. i and xviii, and appendix, §§ 1 and 22.

[2] While Feuerbach treated religion as sheer fantasy, Hegel did not do so. He said that religion expresses the truth about the world figuratively, while philosophy does so literally; he spoke of Christianity as the highest form of religion, and of his own philosophy as saying literally what Christianity says figuratively. There is no question but that Feuerbach was an atheist, but with Hegel the matter is not so simple.

This was the account of religion which first excited Marx. But, whereas Feuerbach was concerned primarily with the psychological state of the believer, Marx soon came to take an interest in the social conditions of belief. Religion is the fantasy of man afflicted by the sense of his own inadequacy and will disappear when he is no longer afflicted. But why is he so afflicted? He is so because he lives in a social environment which does not allow him to realize his potentialities. He is the victim of circumstances which, though they are effects of human activities, he cannot control. He is the victim of forces which he has himself produced, though he does not know how he has done so. He engages in production to satisfy his wants, but the system of production is such that he is impelled into courses which do not satisfy him. Only when man ceases to be the victim of the productive system and the money economy brought into being by his efforts to satisfy his needs will he be able to live a fully satisfying life. Only then will he cease to be a frustrated, a deprived, creature, and have no need to resort to fantasy.

Religion, thus explained, is false consciousness; it is ideology.[1] But it is not obvious that it is class ideology. And yet both Marx and Engels sometimes spoke of religion as if it were class ideology. What had they in mind when they did so? Though Marx and Engels, in their views about religion, were more deeply influenced by Feuerbach and Hegel than by anyone else, these were not the only influences working upon them. There were older ideas about religion which also, no doubt, affected their thinking.

Ever since political theorists had taken to considering religion as a social phenomenon, they had noticed certain things about it. They had noticed that its beliefs and ceremonies serve to strengthen the ties which hold communities together. They strengthen these ties because religious beliefs provide men with powerful motives for carrying out obligations necessary to the social order, and because religious ceremonies express and magnify feelings which attach men to one another and to the community.

They had also noticed that religion allays men's fears, especially the fear of death, and comforts them when they suffer. And in this idea of religion as a comforter, we can see one of the roots

---

[1] In the introduction to his *Contribution to the Critique of Hegel's Philosophy of Law [Right]*, Marx speaks of religion as '*inverted world-consciousness* . . . . the fantastic realization of the human essence because the *human essence* has no true reality' (*Collected Works*, vol. 3, pp. 175); in *Anti-Dühring*, Part III, Engels remarks that 'all religion . . . is nothing but the fantastic reflection in men's minds of those external forces which control their daily life, a reflection in which the terrestrial forces assume the form of supernatural forces' (*Collected Works*, vol. 25, p. 300).

of the conception common to Feuerbach and Marx. The believer takes comfort in religion and also knows that he does so. As he sees it, religion is comforting because it is true. But to the sceptic contemplating the situation of the believer, religion is comforting to the believer because he believes it is true, whether or not it is so. It is, in the eyes of the sceptic, a consoling fantasy; and the idea that it is, or may be so, is, of course, much older than Feuerbach. Feuerbach, inspired by Hegel, adds to this idea two others: the idea of a process of moral and intellectual evolution which first creates the need for such fantasies and then later dispels that need, and the idea that these fantasies express man's sense of his own inadequacy and his largely unconscious aspirations for himself.

The rationalists of the eighteenth century had spoken of religion as if it were a kind of substitute for knowledge. Men are full of curiosity even when they are still ignorant, and therefore put questions which they lack the knowledge to answer. They therefore invent the answers and easily persuade themselves that those answers are true; for they do not yet know how to test them, how to distinguish truth from fantasy. Mind, like nature, abhors a vacuum; where knowledge is out of its reach, it makes do with something which is not knowledge, but which it takes for such. It makes do with theology. But as men acquire knowledge, and above all as they learn to distinguish between true and false knowledge – between what is clearly demonstrated, or well attested, by the facts and mere fantasy – they come to be satisfied only with knowledge and put fantasy away. It is the opposite of Gresham's law that operates here: it is not bad money that drives good money out of circulation but good money that drives out bad.

True, the more knowledge accumulates, the smaller the proportion of it that any one man can acquire. Even the most learned man will know only a small part of what is to be known, and all men will be more keenly aware of the extent of their ignorance. But more and more of them will be imbued with the scientific spirit, and will know what it is to have true as distinct from counterfeit knowledge. Religions and other fantasies are taken for true not so much because every man's ignorance is great (which it always must be) as because most men do not know how to distinguish genuine from spurious knowledge. Thus it is that the progress of the sciences undermines the old religions. Perhaps the best eighteenth-century account of how this progress loosens the hold of religion is to be found in Condorcet's *Sketch for an Historical Picture of the Progress of the Human Mind*.

It is a theme repeated by Saint-Simon and linked by him with an account of how in the course of social evolution one class supersedes another. In the Middle Ages society was dominated by a feudal class – a class of warriors – and by a Church which preached a body of doctrine well suited to hold together a society of unequals in an unscientific age. But now a new class – the producers of wealth – are coming to dominate society, and their rise to dominance coincides with the disintegration of the old theology and the substitution for it of science, of genuine knowledge. Though Saint-Simon does not call religion *the opium of the people*, he does say that theology flourishes while men are still incapable of explaining the world and themselves scientifically and that it holds together a society in which an unproductive ruling class live off the labour of others. Of the early socialists none had a greater influence on Marx than Saint-Simon.

In the eighteenth century, sceptics who felt that they could themselves do without religion often thought it a good thing for the poor and the ignorant, partly because it helped to keep them obedient to the laws and partly because it consoled them in their sufferings. They believed, most of them, that inequality was inevitable, and they conceded that its being so was more obvious to the rich than to the poor. That the social order was in the interest of all classes might be true, but unfortunately it was a truth not equally apparent to all classes; and therefore it was good that the classes least able to appreciate this truth should find in religion a guide and a consoler. So thought the sceptics who were also conservatives. They too did not call religion the opium of the people; but they agreed with Marx and Engels about its effect on the workers and differed from them only in approving the social order which they condemned.

Though the Marxian account of religion owes more to Feuerbach and Hegel than to anyone else, it also bears the mark of other doctrines and attitudes. Neither Hegel nor Feuerbach treats religion as class ideology, and if we want to discover the beginnings of this conception of it, we must turn to French rather than to German thinkers.

If we take religion in the broadest sense, we can hardly call it class ideology. For there have been, and indeed still are, primitive tribal communities without classes in the Marxian sense of class; and these communities are not without religion. But it may be that Marx and Engels, when they speak of religion as if it were a form of class ideology, do not have in mind the kind of religion which flourishes in very simple communities. It may be that they have in mind, not fetishism and magic, but religion which is properly theological, which explains the world as created or governed by a God or a hierarchy of gods. Such a religion is dogmatic and systematic; it embodies a more or less coherent conception of the world, a *Weltanschauung*. This is the kind of religion of which it can most plausibly be said that it forms the faith of alienated man – the religion in which he expresses his sense of what he might be and is not, his aspirations and his sense of present inadequacy.

In the Marxian attitude to religion we can discern two elements. The first and simpler is no more German than it is French or Italian or English; it is the belief that religion flourishes because men are ignorant and will die away as knowledge accumulates, as science destroys illusion. This belief figures more prominently in the writings of Engels than in those of Marx. The second and less simple is German, coming from Feuerbach and from Hegel; it is the doctrine that religion is the fantasy of alienated man, the fantasy in which man, unable to live a full and satisfying life, seeks compensation for his incapacity. This doctrine, though there is more to it than the age-old belief that religion consoles men for the frustrations and sufferings of this life, has clear affinities with that belief.

Neither of these doctrines – that religion is the child of ignorance and curiosity, and that it is a fantasy of alienated man – in itself implies that religion is class ideology. Yet both doctrines are compatible with the belief that it is so. For religion, on either of these views, can be held to be a cement holding society together; and if society is divided into classes, some of which exploit others, it is a cement which helps to make this exploitation possible. For religion to be class ideology, it is not necessary that only the exploited should believe it, that it should be propagated among them by unbelievers to keep them docile. All classes may accept it, and yet, if it serves to hold together a society in which class exploits class, and tends to disappear as the conditions – social and cultural – of the classless society come into being, it is class ideology, as Marx and Engels understood that term.

Marx and Engels did not believe that the mere progress of science would destroy religion; they believed that the root cause of religion – the alienation of man or his incapacity to live a full and satisfying life – would disappear only in the classless society, the society without exploitation, the society in which men would cease to be the victims of their environment and would become its masters. And yet they too saw a close connection between the progress of science and the decay of religion. Progress in the natural sciences had helped to bring into existence the industrial system which had created the proletariat, and progress in the social sciences will eventually ensure the proletariat's becoming the pre-eminently class-conscious class, the class fully aware of its historic rôle, which is to bring to an end the exploitation of class by class, the system which makes alienation possible. Moreover, though Marx and Engels did not believe that the mere progress of science would destroy religion, they did share the belief, already prominent in the eighteenth century, that science and religion are incompatible.

Today, even when we are not believers, it seems less clear to us than it did to sceptics of the eighteenth and nineteenth centuries that science and religion are incompatible. Condorcet and Saint-Simon took it for granted that dogmatic theology is a substitute for science, that it is a premature attempt to answer questions which men are still unable to answer, though they do not recognize their incapacity. Therefore, as they learn how to answer these questions, how to distinguish true from false answers, they discard the false answers; they discard theology and take to science.

It is true that the questions which science and religion claim to answer have something in common: they are not questions about the use of words or concepts, and the answers to them purport to give us information about the world. Nevertheless, science does not claim to answer the same questions as religion. Science seeks to explain only how things happen in the world. It does not pretend to answer such questions as 'Is there an Intelligent Being in control of the world?' or 'To what end are we in the world?'. Like theology, it aims at a systematic explanation of the world, but it is explanation of a different kind. Science does not take the place of theology; it does not do more adequately what theology claims to do. The view that it does – prominent in the writings of Condorcet and Saint-Simon and still discernible in those of Engels and even of Marx – is clearly false.

But the sceptics who proclaimed the incompatibility of science and theology held other beliefs less simple than the one I have just discussed. They also believed that, as knowledge accumulates, men come to understand that some questions which theology claims to answer are not properly questions at all, being unintelligible, and that others are unanswerable. The progress of knowledge, as conceived by Condorcet, consists largely in learning how to put genuine questions and how to find answers to them. It is, I think, implicit in his conception of progress that all intelligible questions can be answered, just as it is in the conception of Marx and Engels. But this does not mean that Condorcet and Marx had any very clear ideas about the criteria to be used to decide whether a question is intelligible or answerable. For this is a matter which has received a great deal of attention since their time.

Perhaps many philosophers and scientists would today agree that there are questions about the world which are intelligible, involving

no misuse of language or confusion of thought, that science cannot
answer. The answers to these questions, though not amenable to
the tests which scientists use, are not mere value judgements but
are also statements about the world, statements which are true or
false, though science cannot show them to be the one or the other.
And these questions, which science cannot answer, are still supremely
important to persons who understand science and its methods as well
as anyone does. Today there are many people without religion willing
to admit all this, but Marx and Engels would probably not have done
so. Religion, in their eyes, is ideology or 'false consciousness', and
therefore incompatible with science.

Beliefs can be incompatible either logically or psychologically. They
are logically incompatible when, if some are true, others must be false;
and they are psychologically incompatible when men who accept
some of them are disposed to reject others. Clearly, beliefs can be
incompatible in one of these senses without being so in the other.
Those who, like Engels and Marx, take it for granted that science
undermines religion do not trouble to distinguish between these two
senses.

Theologians have certainly made some assertions which must be
false if the findings of science are true. And clearly, it would be
unreasonable to accept these findings on all relevant occasions except
when they conflict with theology. But theology has made other
assertions which are intelligible and also untouched and untouchable
by science. The logician has not shown that they are empty or
confused, and the scientist has not shown – and indeed cannot show
– that the world, as he explains it, is such that they cannot be true.

If these assertions are not logically incompatible with science, are
they so psychologically? Is it true that the more people accept the
findings of science, the more they are inclined to reject such assertions?
Does the spread of science incline men to reject all assertions about
the world which are not verifiable, even though they are logically
compatible with the findings of science? Marx and Engels, like so
many other rationalists of their day, seem to have taken it for granted
that it does. But it is not immediately obvious why it should do so.
If it is true that theology claims to answer questions of a type which
science does not put, it is not clear why men should be inclined to
reject the answers on the ground that they cannot be tested as the
hypotheses of the scientist can. It is surely not unreasonable to accept
unscientific answers to important questions of a type which science
does not put and cannot answer. Nor is it unreasonable to *put* such
questions merely because science cannot answer them. If the questions

are important – if they matter greatly to the persons who put them – they will accept unscientific answers to them.

Can we then say that the questions which theology purports to answer cease to be important to men as science progresses? Marx and Engels apparently believed that they do, and this for two reasons. They took it for granted, as sceptics so often do, that men, as they become imbued with the scientific spirit, come to be indifferent to theology. Believing, as they did, that questions about the world which science cannot answer are either empty or unanswerable, it seemed to them that men who have come to understand what science is all about must soon lose the taste for them. They took for granted what had seemed obvious to the materialists of the eighteenth century. They took it for granted that science and religion are incompatible, without making it clear in quite what sense they are so.

But they also, as we have seen, had another and more plausible reason for believing that men lose interest in religion as science progresses. They do so, not because science and religion are incompatible, but because religion is a need of alienated man, and the social evolution which involves scientific progress brings this alienation to an end. Thus it is not the mere spread of science which destroys religion; it is rather the transformation of society, a transformation closely connected with the progress of the sciences, natural and social.

Logically, we can accept this second reason even if we concede more than Marx and Engels were willing to do – even if we concede that religion provides intelligible answers to important questions which science does not put, answers which science cannot show to be false. If we accept this second reason, we do not have to attack religion on the ground that all, or even most, of its doctrines are logically absurd or inconsistent with science; we can confine ourselves to saying that men will come to do without religion because the questions it claims to answer will eventually cease to be important to them. The need for religion will disappear. This account of religion goes deeper than the eighteenth-century conception of it as the product of ignorance and curiosity which disappears with the mere spread of science. It is not open to the same objections.

But there are objections to it. Even if we do not (for the moment) question Marx's conception of what religion essentially is – even if we allow that it is a response to a need rooted in man's sense of his own inadequacy – why should we suppose that the need will be weaker in the future than it was in the past? Why should we suppose that this sense of inadequacy and the need for a compensating fantasy will disappear in the classless society in which all men are educated and enjoy a high standard of living, material and cultural?

The sort of religion which Marx has in mind when he speaks of it as the fantasy of alienated man is not the animism and magic of the simplest societies; it includes a dogmatic theology and flourishes in relatively sophisticated societies. Such evidence as we have suggests that, in societies of this kind, dogmatic theology has often (though not always) been the religion of the privileged and the educated, of those enjoying the widest opportunities. We must not allow ourselves to be deceived by appearances. It is easy to make a misleading contrast between ages of faith and ages of scepticism. In the Middle Ages, most people who were called, or who called themselves, Christians were ignorant and illiterate; and it is improbable that many of them understood what the religion they adhered to was about. They were churchgoers and partakers in ceremonies rather than persons having definite beliefs. We ought surely to say of them, as of illiterate peasants in the Balkans and the southern parts of Italy as late as our own century, that they did not challenge the doctrines of the Church, and not that they accepted them. Where orthodoxy is unchallenged, nothing more is required of most people than outward conformity, and orthodoxy is never less challenged than when the vast majority are illiterate, or almost so, and are incapable of either accepting or rejecting the doctrines which are orthodox. Do we really know that true believers were a larger proportion of the population of Christendom in the thirteenth century than they are now? That the authority of the Church was then less challenged than it is now is not in itself enough to show that they were. The religion of the illiterate, of the oppressed, of the deprived, is in practice often very different from the religion officially established, even in so-called periods of faith. And yet it is established religion, elaborate and sophisticated, which seems to answer to Feuerbach's and Marx's conception of it rather than the practices and beliefs of the ignorant and oppressed, which often retain about them much of the spirit of primitive religion, of animism and magic.

No doubt, theocentric religion, as distinct from animism and magic, flourishes in relatively complex societies; and nearly all such societies have so far been class societies, in the Marxian sense of class. They have also been literate and sophisticated societies – that is to say, there have been literate and sophisticated classes in them, even though most people remained illiterate. In societies of this kind the sense of deprivation among men – the sense that they are not what they aspire to be, the sense of frustration and inadequacy – may be much greater than in primitive societies. In them the ideas of all classes about what is desirable, what is worthy of a creature like man, are deeply influenced by the values and the opportunities of the privileged. Thus the unprivileged are apt to feel deprived because the opportunities of the privileged are denied to them; and it may well be that, sometimes, when they see that they can do nothing to improve their lot, they become resigned to it and seek compensation in some image of the world which religion presents to them. The spread of Methodism in England during the industrial revolution has been explained in these terms, and there are, no doubt, other examples. But if we look at the records, we see the spread of Methodism described as the bringing of Christianity to classes which until then had been only nominally Christian. These were classes rapidly becoming more literate – classes becoming more sophisticated, morally and intellectually – than their ancestors had been, and therefore able to get from such a religion as Christianity what, according to Feuerbach, it is the function of religion to provide. This, I suspect, was not the condition of serfs in the Middle Ages, just as it was not the condition of most peasants in eastern and southern Europe in quite recent times.

Theological religion – the type presented to us by Feuerbach and Marx as the religion of alienated man – is the religion of the sophisticated. It has been most fully accepted by the educated and the privileged. I would not deny that it has also been, genuinely and not merely nominally, the religion of the unprivileged, especially at times when the unprivileged have been gaining in sophistication. Among the unprivileged, it has served sometimes to reconcile them to their lot and sometimes to justify revolt.

At this point, it may be objected that to call religion the fantasy of alienated man is not to imply that it is the fantasy of the unprivileged rather than the privileged. This is certainly true. Though Marx speaks of exploitation and oppression in class societies, and of the degradation of the worker under capitalism, he does not say that only the exploited are alienated. It is man, and not just the exploited worker, who is alienated, who is frustrated and incapable of realizing his potentialities, who is the victim of his social environment.

To this objection, there are two answers. The first, and less important, is that Marx, though he speaks of alienated man and not just of the alienated worker, also sometimes speaks as if the exploited were more alienated – further from self-realization, more the victims of their environment – than the wealthy and the privileged. The second answer is that, if we take all men in a class society to be alienated, it is difficult to be clear just what alienation is.

Alienated man is man who has not realized his potentialities. But what are we to understand by his potentialities, seeing that there are so many things that man can become? What men aspire to depends on the values they accept, which vary from age to age and society to society. In all class societies there are some values accepted by all classes and others which are peculiar to this or that class; and, presumably, by the values common to the whole society, it is the privileged classes who are best able to live well. They are the least deprived classes. If this were not so, they would not be held by the other classes to be privileged but merely to be different. If the idea of the full or satisfying life, the life worthy of such a creature as man, differs according to the values generally accepted in a society, it would seem that, in class societies, it is the privileged who have the largest opportunity to live up to the idea. We can then say that, if the other classes had the same opportunities (that is to say, if society were classless), there would be less deprivation, less alienation. But in saying this, we tacitly make an assumption which may be false; we assume that the values generally accepted – the values by reference to which men construct their idea of a full and satisfying life – will not have changed as a result of society's becoming classless.

On the other hand, if we construct our idea of the full life in some other way, we still cannot conclude that, when society becomes classless, men will be able to lead full and satisfying lives. We can, of course (as Rousseau did), so define our idea of the full (or good) life that society's being classless is a condition of its being realized; but we still have to show that in a classless society men would in fact accept this idea. Without making it clear what a full and satisfying life is, we cannot – as Marx and Engels do – simply take it for granted that in the classless society men will be able to live up to their idea of it. We cannot take it for granted that in the classless society man will not be alienated.

I would not deny that the sort of religion which is a cosmology – which ascribes to man a place in the world – can serve to compensate him for a sense that he does not live a worthwhile life, or for frustrations deeply felt and whose causes are not understood, though they lie in the social environment. Nor would I deny that these causes, when they come to be understood, can be removed. But I suspect that the frustrations which arise because the social order is such that man cannot live what seems to him a worthwhile life are only some among the causes of religion. And by religion I mean what Feuerbach and Marx meant by it; I mean a cosmology which presents the world to man as a theatre in which are unfolded purposes larger than his own. Religion, thus understood, is not less, but perhaps even more, attractive to those who enjoy most fully the opportunities which a complex and highly cultured society has to offer, than to the socially deprived.

According to Feuerbach and even Hegel, religion springs from man's need to feel 'at home' in the world. I would not quarrel with this opinion, which only repeats in rather different words what some of the most deeply religious men have said. The fear of insignificance, of purposelessness, is one of the most terrible to which sophisticated man is liable. But is it a fear which arises in men because they cannot live satisfying lives in society as they find it? Is it a fear that would cease to plague them in a society offering to all men the opportunities which only the most favoured now enjoy? Is it not as true that men are unsatisfied because they have this fear as that they have it because they are unsatisfied? No doubt, the need for a religion which is a cosmology is a need of sophisticated man, and not all sophisticated men feel this need. But what reason is there for believing that, as society grows wealthier and more egalitarian – as it makes more abundant provision, culturally as well as materially, for all its members – this need will disappear?

If you want to understand what religion is, even though you are moved only by curiosity, it is not wise to pay exclusive attention to writers whose purpose is to show that it is a passing need. Marx was too much impressed by the arguments of Feuerbach and the materialist philosophers of the eighteenth century. If he had paid more attention to religious writers – if he had tried in imagination to put himself into the state of mind of a Luther or a Pascal – he might have remained a staunch atheist and yet have understood better than he did what it is that makes men turn to religion.

6. The Theory Tidied Up

To extract from the writings of Marx and Engels a clear, coherent and useful conception of ideology – a conception which helps to explain important aspects of social life – we have to eliminate what makes for confusion and what is inconsistent with the facts. If we do that, we are left with this residue: a theory or opinion which purports to describe some aspect of reality, or a moral or legal rule, or a concept used to express such a rule or to encourage obedience to it, is *ideological* when its function is to maintain or challenge some part of the social order or (as Marx might have put it) of the system of social relations; and a theory or opinion is *ideological* also when it serves to allay fears and create hopes. A descriptive theory or opinion may be fantasy or 'false consciousness' or it may not be; but what makes it *ideological* is that it is widely accepted, not primarily because there is good evidence of its truth, but because it serves to maintain or challenge the social order, or to allay fears and create hopes, And a moral or legal rule, though neither it nor the concepts used to express it or to encourage obedience to it can be 'false consciousness', is *ideological* in relation to some part of the social order provided it is not included in that part and serves to maintain or challenge it.

I have already insisted that moral and legal rules (and therefore also moral and legal concepts) are part of the very stuff of social relations – that to stand in a social relation to someone involves recognizing that you ought or are required to conform to certain rules in your behaviour towards him. Every form of social intercourse involves accepting some rules and using some normative concepts, and it therefore makes no sense to say that these rules and concepts are determined by the nature of the intercourse; they are an integral part of it. But we can distinguish rules and concepts *involved* in the having of certain relations from rules and concepts *serving to strengthen or undermine* those relations. Co-operation is possible, for example, even among people who have no *esprit de corps*, who feel no loyalty to the group they belong to, who, for one reason or another, merely conform to the rules involved in the co-operation, approving conformity and condemning non-conformity. But out of this co-operation there may (and usually does) arise a group loyalty expressed in rules and concepts not involved in the actual co-operation but helping to strengthen it. These secondary rules and concepts we could call ideological. Marx called them so, and we may take issue with him, not for giving them that name, but for failing to distinguish them from the primary rules and concepts which are an integral part of the co-operation.

The practice of these secondary rules is itself a form of social intercourse, but it is intercourse different from the intercourse it helps to maintain. Provided it serves to strengthen the primary intercourse and not to undermine it, it can be called, in the parlance of Marx, a *superstructure* upon it. In every army, and in many other types of social organization, there are practices whose function is to make subordinates more readily obedient to their superiors; there are also practices, which Marxists are more prone to ignore, making superiors more attentive to the needs of their subordinates. These practices are distinct from the proper work of the organization; they are not part of it but serve only to make it smoother. The rules which these practices embody and the concepts used to express the rules and to encourage conformity to them are therefore ideological in relation to the work, but are not ideological in relation to the practices serving to make the work go smoothly.

Ideology, thus defined, is a really important aspect of social life. There are theories and opinions by which men set great store and which they take for true because they feel the need to do so, and these theories and opinions have a large influence on their behaviour. But this type of ideology is not always, nor even usually, class ideology. There is no reason to believe that, even in societies divided into classes, class ideologies are the most important. They are, no doubt, characteristic of class societies; and if we want to distinguish one kind of class society from another we can point, among other things, to differences in their class ideologies. But *characteristic* and *most important* are not equivalent terms; we may not conclude that class ideologies, because they are peculiar to class societies, are, even in these societies, more important than others.

Nor must we imply, as Marx does, that the only function of ideology is to support or challenge the social order, the system of social relations. Religion can, and often does, strengthen men's motives for doing what they are required to do; it can be, and often is, a set of beliefs helping to preserve the social order. It can also help to undermine it. If the social order favours some classes more than others and religion serves to maintain that order, it can be treated as a form of class ideology. But it is always more than that. It is more than class ideology, and more even than an ideology preserving the social order for the benefit of all classes. It serves another function besides strengthening (or weakening) men's motives for doing what their neighbours require of them; it also allays fear and instils hope in them. This fear and this hope are the fear and the hope of rational creatures whose reason has developed in society. The need which religion satisfies is, in this sense, a social need; it is the need of rational and moral creatures that life should seem worth living; it is, as Hegel saw, the need of a self-conscious being, aware of its mortality and fearful of solitude, to feel at home in the world. That all men do not turn to religion to satisfy this need is no proof that it is not an important function of religion to satisfy it.

Nor must we, as Marx and Engels do, call morality and the law ideological. We must distinguish between the moral and legal rules and concepts actually involved in the social relations we have in mind, on the one hand, and the rules and concepts which serve to strengthen or undermine those relations, on the other; we must call only the second, and not the first, *ideological*.

Marx and Engels also set too wide a gulf between science and ideology. They were too much inclined to believe that theories and opinions which gain currency primarily because people feel the need to take them for true are false or fantastic. Even if we agree with them that most social and political theories prior to their own, to the extent that they aimed at explaining the facts, were further from the truth and took less notice of what they purported to explain than their own theory, we may set this down chiefly to greater ignorance. If the makers of these theories had been better informed, or had known better how to use what information they had, they might have produced theories equally attractive to upholders or challengers of the social order and also much nearer the truth. The more people know the facts and the better they understand how to use them to test the truth of explanations, the more carefully social and political theorists must construct their theories if they are to gain currency.

Theology and metaphysics, since they claim to transcend experience, need take much less notice of the facts. In spite of their close connection, historically, with social and political theory, they are intrinsically different from it. Taken in themselves, they rarely serve either to preserve or to challenge the existing social order; they only seem to do so when a show is made of deriving social and political conclusions from them. I doubt whether Christian theology favours one type of social order more than another; I doubt, for example, whether the democracy and liberalism we adhere to today are any more in keeping with Christianity than was the feudal order of the Middle Ages. We like to make a show of deriving our political principles from our religious beliefs; and yet persons who agree in their religion but disagree in their politics make equally plausible attempts to show how the second follows logically from the first. But social and political theory, being necessarily much more concerned than is theology with what happens in this world, is also closer to being scientific. I suspect that, among the theories that Marx would call ideological because they serve group interests, those which are nearer to being scientific are also nearer to being class ideologies.

7. Ideology as a 'Reflection' of Something Else

Marx says that ideology *reflects* social relations or conditions, and also that it *reflects* class interests. I have already argued that some forms of ideology – with religion the most important of them – do very much more than serve class interests or support or challenge the social order; I have argued that Marx neglects their more important for their less important functions. Nevertheless, there are ideologies which support or challenge the social order, and there are also class ideologies. I want therefore to consider in what sense, and to what extent, ideologies serving these purposes *reflect* social conditions or class interests. Let me take the first point first. What can be meant by saying that an ideology *reflects* social conditions?

When people who work or live together acquire a sense of community and group loyalties, the rules and attitudes which embody this sense and these loyalties, together with the beliefs which sustain them, can be said to arise out of their working and living together. They serve to make the collaboration and the living together easier, and their character varies, more or less, according to how men collaborate and how they live together. When we say that an ideology *reflects* social conditions we mean presumably that it helps to support them, that it would not arise unless a need were felt for this support, and that what it is – its character – is largely determined by its function. But, if this is what is involved in an ideology's *reflecting* social conditions, how can we say that a revolutionary ideology reflects them?

Some concrete examples may serve to illustrate my meaning. Marriage is one of the most important of social relations, and differs greatly in different societies. If we take any form of marriage, we can distinguish between the rules and attitudes inherent in it, making it the kind of marriage it is, and the ideology which builds up around it, owing its existence and its character to it. In so far as the aspirations of the men and women bound together by this kind of marriage are affected by that ideology, they are aspirations in keeping with the marriage, and are satisfied in this kind of union, provided it is a normal union of its kind. The Bantu woman who is married after the fashion of her tribe, and whose attitude to what is required of her as a wife is in line with what is thought and felt about marriage in her tribe, will presumably be satisfied with her marriage; or, if she is not, it will be for some other reason than because it is that kind of marriage.

Let us now take another example. To the extent that a slave's attitude to his servile condition arises out of that condition, being in harmony with ways of thinking and feeling which build up around it, he is satisfied with it. But if he wants to be free, his aspiration to freedom must come of his having ideas incompatible with his condition. No doubt, he would not want to *become* free unless he were a slave. But a free man also puts a value on freedom; if he does not want to *become* free, he wants to *remain* free. The slave's wanting freedom does not spring from an attitude to servility which arises from his being a slave; it springs from an attitude to servility which he acquires by adopting for himself the ideals of the free man. It is paradoxical to say that a revolutionary ideology *reflects* the social conditions which it aims at destroying. If we admit this paradox, we must, I think, concede that both an ideology and its opposite can reflect the same social conditions. Let us suppose that the slave's beliefs and values make him contented with his servility, that he knows his station and is happy in it, that he has an ideology in keeping with his station. We can hardly refuse to say that this ideology reflects his social condition. If, then, we go on to say that the beliefs and values which make him loathe his condition also reflect it, we are bound to conclude that two opposing ideologies reflect the same condition. No doubt, a master and slave can have different beliefs and values arising out of the social relations between them; but that is because their social conditions differ, because the master is not related to the slave as the slave is to the master. The master and the slave, though each of them is content with his condition, will have different ideologies *reflecting* their different conditions, but neither ideology, if it reflects its possessor's social condition, will be revolutionary.

It is also paradoxical to say that the ideology of a revolutionary class reflects the interests of that class. How can people having a given social status come to have interests incompatible with that status unless they acquire an ideology which is also incompatible with it? So long as what they strive for is in keeping with their status, they seek for nothing which is to be had only by destroying that status. As a matter of fact, no class has an ideology entirely in keeping with its status; even a ruling class is never completely conservative and contented, for it too has aspirations, and therefore also interests, which cannot be satisfied while existing social relations remain unchanged. But it has an advantage denied to the other classes; it can change the social order to suit its interests much more easily than they can. It feels the need to do this precisely because no class ideology, not even the ideology of the ruling class, merely reflects the social condition of the class whose ideology it is.

We cannot say that the feminism of the early nineteenth century *reflected* the interests of women at that time. For generations before the rise of feminism, women had accepted a social status in many ways different from, and in some ways inferior to, the status of the other sex. While they accepted that status, they had interests and ideologies in keeping with it. If their interests – their ambitions and aspirations

– changed, it was largely because they acquired ideas which women before them did not (except rarely) have.

Instead of saying, as Marx does, that class ideologies reflect class interests, we should say rather that the interests and ideology of a class, to the extent that they are in keeping with its social condition, reflect that condition, and that the interests of a class, to the extent that they are not in keeping with its social condition, are affected by an ideology which does not reflect that condition. This conclusion, though it does not square with what Marx says about how class ideologies, class interests and social conditions are connected with one another, is entirely in keeping with what he says about the political rôle of ideology.[1] A class, he tells us, becomes class-conscious in the process of learning what its interests are and what it must do to promote them; and he says also that, as it becomes class-conscious, it elaborates its ideology. True, even a class which is not class-conscious has some kind of class ideology; it has prejudices and values peculiar to itself. But, as it becomes class-conscious, it acquires opinions about its position in society and what needs to be done to preserve or change that position; it acquires a more elaborate and sophisticated ideology. It acquires this ideology as it comes to recognize its interests and learns to work for them and becomes a political force to be reckoned with. Learning to recognize its interests and acquiring a sophisticated ideology and becoming politically formidable are all, for Marx, parts of the same process. If we look at this process, even as Marx imagines it, we see that ideology affects interests and social conditions just as it is affected by them. We see that Marx's own account of what classes do politically, especially when they are revolutionary classes, gives the lie to the famous sentence so often quoted: 'It is not the consciousness of men that determines their existence, but their social existence that determines their consciousness.'[2] 'Consciousness' or ideology has a profound effect on social being, on the most important social relations. Indeed, if it were not so, there would be no point to the class conflicts and revolutions in which Marx believed so strongly. If it were really true that class ideologies only *reflect* class interests and do not also powerfully affect them, Marx would not be nearly as important a figure in world history as he actually is.

[1] We have here yet another example of something we have already come across several times in the writings of Marx and Engels: the generalizations they make, about how certain aspects of social life are connected, are contradicted by their accounts of actual processes in which these aspects are involved.

[2] Preface to *A Contribution to the Critique of Political Economy*, op. cit., p. 263. Cf. *The German Ideology*, I, op cit., p. 37.

CHAPTER FOUR
Marx and Engels   II

I. WHAT DID MARX AND ENGELS THINK IS THE FUNCTION OF THE STATE IN SOCIETIES DIVIDED INTO CLASSES, AND WHAT DID THEY PREDICT WOULD DISAPPEAR IN THE CLASSLESS SOCIETY?

1. The State and Social Classes

a. Three Views About The State

There are three assertions about the State characteristic of Marxism: that the State arises when society divides into classes, that the State is an instrument of class rule, and that when society becomes classless there will be no need for a State. Marxists, and Marx and Engels also, sometimes speak as if these three assertions stood and fell together. We shall see that they do not.

Though Engels tells us that in tribal societies there is no need for a State, he does not deny that in such societies there is a need for authority. In the tribe, as in the State, there are persons admitted to have a right to give orders and to interpret rules, and there are also customary rules which impose obligations or confer rights – that is to say, there are, in the broad sense of the word, laws. Those who have authority inside the tribe owe it, not merely to personal qualities giving them an exceptional influence over their fellows, but to status, to the position they occupy in the tribe. They are not leaders whose authority rests on mere strength of character; they are rulers who come by their authority in traditional ways. In saying that there is no State in tribal societies, Engels does not mean to deny that there is in them a structure of authority resting on customary rules. Sometimes he even speaks of the rudiments of State power in tribal societies. In saying that there is no State in such societies, he means, I take it, that in them the business of declaring the rules and enforcing them is not recognized as a special function. Society is not yet clearly divided into rulers and ruled. The authority of the chiefs is quasi-paternal; it is clear who has it, but it is not clearly defined. Exercising authority is only a part of what the chiefs do; the extent of their authority varies with the circumstances, and there is almost no hierarchy of rulers. Authority is exercised as the need is felt for it.

When the State appears, the business of declaring what the rules are and applying them becomes the full-time activity of some persons; it becomes, more and more clearly, a separate function, a political function, and elaborate procedures are evolved for carrying it out. There arises an organized hierarchy of government, with superiors and subordinates, and there come to be more or less definite rules limiting their competence. The sanctions that maintain social discipline are no longer the same: in place of the rebukes of elder or chief, the pressure of public opinion or the fear of magic, there are courts of law using a settled procedure to establish responsibility and to impose penalties or remedies. The political function, as it becomes a distinct and elaborate activity, also becomes coercive; a person who infringes an important rule is no longer exposed to private vengeance or to the mere displeasure of his community; his offence is investigated and he is liable to fines, imprisonments, whippings or even death at the hands of a public executioner. This, I take it, is what Engels, like most other political theorists, has in mind when he speaks of the emergence of the State.

Both in *Anti-Dühring* and in *The Origin of the Family, Private Property and the State*, Engels says that the need for the State arises as the division of labour increases and society divides into classes.[1] In tribal societies the division of labour is still relatively simple; it does not divide society into classes, and the maintenance of social discipline – the seeing to it that people carry out their customary obligations and that disputes between them are settled peacefully or in a way that does as little harm as possible to the community – is still too simple a business to require that it should be the full-time occupation of a hierarchy of persons clearly marked off from the rest of the community as its rulers. The need for the State arises from the increasing size of the community and from the extended division of labour inside it.

---

[1] See Engels, *Anti-Dühring*, Part II, ch. IV, in Marx and Engels, *Collected Works*, vol. 25, pp. 168–70, and *The Origin of the Family, Private Property and the State*, ed. E. B. Leacock (London 1972), ch. ix, pp. 228–32.

That the need for the State arises in this way is not to be disputed. It is what Plato said at the dawn of political theory, and what has often been repeated since. But it is important to notice that the increasing division of labour does not of itself divide society into classes – at least not unless we so define or use the word *class* that differences of occupation are differences of class. And this, as we have seen, is not how Marx and Engels define or use it. Though tinkers and tailors have different occupations, they do not therefore belong to different classes, in the Marxian sense of class. The increasing division of labour, making the clan or tribe no longer self-sufficient, breaks up the old social order. As the clan or tribe disintegrates into many smaller independent families, communal ownership of land and cattle gives way to private ownership, and the father of each small family becomes the only possessor of the land cultivated and the animals used by his family. Whether we regard the break-up of the clan or tribe as the cause or effect of this change in the system of property, or as partly the one and partly the other, does not matter when we are considering the emergence of the State. Nor does it matter that property in workshops and tools increases in importance with the greater division of labour.

The point to bear in mind is that all this could conceivably happen without society being divided into classes, in the Marxian sense of class. Instead of the extended family or clan enjoying common rights over large pieces of land, we might have the fathers of small families enjoying private rights over smaller pieces of land, and we might have artisans and traders owning other kinds of property than land or cattle. We might have all this, without masters or slaves, without feudal lords or serfs, without capitalists or proletarians. We might have a society as classless – in the Marxian sense of class – as tribal society. And yet the task of maintaining discipline inside it would be quite different. The need for forms of authority different from those which sufficed to keep the peace and to enforce obligations in tribal society would still be there. We should then have a classless society giving birth to the State.

No doubt, with the break-up of the tribe and the emergence of a new system of property, classes in the Marxian sense soon arise. I am not concerned to deny it. I say only that, even if they did not arise, there would still be a need for forms of authority which tribal society could do without; there would still be a need for the State. In a boarding school children are kept in order by different methods from those found sufficient inside the family. It may be that children who are sent to boarding schools become more troublesome for being sent there; but, even if they did not, they would have to be under a form of discipline different from that of the home. The full-time occupation of their masters is to teach them and keep them in order, and their relations with their masters are different from their relations with their parents. This must be so, no matter what happens to the children as a result of their being sent to such schools; it must be so even if they become quieter and more amenable to reason.

The larger the community and the more diverse and specialized the occupations inside it, the more elaborate and precise the rules needed to control the behaviour of its members. There must be forms of contract unknown to tribal society which have to be interpreted and enforced. There is room for many more and far more varied disputes, and therefore a need for more regular and more elaborate procedures for settling them. It is not just a question of finding other people to do what the chiefs and elders did in tribal society; there is a need for authority of a different kind, and therefore for different relations between those in authority and the persons subject to them. Of course, Engels does not deny this; he insists upon it. But he does not see that the need would exist even if there were no classes in the Marxian sense. He sees the need arise and also the classes, and therefore takes it for granted that the classes create the need.

The truth is that Engels, when he says that the division of society into classes makes the State necessary, is not using the word *class* in the same sense as when he speaks of class exploitation or calls feudal lords or capitalists a class. He is treating as separate classes groups whose interests diverge because their occupations differ, and is saying that their interests cannot be reconciled by the methods open to the old tribal authorities, so that a new structure of authority – the State – emerges. He calls the interests of these groups irreconcilable, presumably because they cannot be reconciled by the old methods, and then goes on to say that it is the function of the State to keep the peace between groups having irreconcilable interests. He does not trouble to ask himself what is meant by calling the interests irreconcilable if the State is able to keep the peace between the groups having such interests. There is here, surely, an odd line of reasoning: an increased division of labour gives rise to groups with divergent interests leading to disputes which cannot be settled by the old methods, and therefore the groups are called *irreconcilable*; there then emerge new methods of settling disputes used by a new type of authority – the State – whose function is therefore said to be to keep the peace between irreconcilable groups. But why, if the peace can be kept between the groups by these new methods, should it be said of them that they are *irreconcilable*?

241

Engels speaks of the groups as separate classes. But in what sense are they classes? Even in tribal societies there are different occupations; the division of labour in them may be rudimentary, but still it exists. And in all societies, tribal or otherwise, persons with different occupations have interests which often diverge. Engels admits that there are no classes in tribal societies. It would seem therefore that persons having different occupations and divergent interests do not, for those reasons alone, belong to separate classes. Do they, then, belong to separate classes because disputes between them can no longer be settled by the old methods? Or, rather, because the disputes can only be settled where there is a structure of authority of the kind we call a State? If we say this, then we do not use the word *class* to refer to groups which are distinct from one another because they have different property rights. Two groups are then separate classes, not because their interests diverge or their social positions differ, but because disputes between them (or, rather, between persons belonging to them) can only be settled by a certain type of authority.[1] But if this is so, it is by no means obvious that where private property in the means of production is abolished, society is made classless and the need for the State disappears; it is by no means obvious that, where this type of property ceases to exist, there is no need for the State to settle disputes.

Engels, having first explained how an increased division of labour produces groups whose divergent interests lead to disputes which can only be settled by the State, then goes on to show how out of these groups there emerges, in the course of time, a society whose members have different property rights. Of course, as soon as that happens, we have a society divided into classes, in the specifically Marxian sense of class. And, no doubt, these classes, as much as the groups out of which they arise, are involved in disputes which cannot be settled by the old tribal methods. Thus, because the process which first produced groups whose disputes could not be settled in the old ways later produced classes, in the Marxian sense of class, Engels slips easily into calling these groups *classes*. He does not notice that he is using the word *class* alternately to refer to two quite different things: to groups having divergent interests arising directly out of the division of labour – interests which cannot be reconciled by the old tribal authorities – and to groups whose property rights differ and who therefore have divergent interests for quite other reasons. There are

---

[1] Engels does not distinguish disputes between individuals which need a new type of authority to settle them because the individuals belong to groups having divergent interests, from disputes between these groups. He probably has in mind both kinds of dispute.

here at least two movements of thought which are logically unsound but which easily escape notice: the movement from interests which cannot be reconciled in the old ways to interests which somehow remain irreconcilable even though new ways are found of settling the disputes they lead to, and the movement from groups arising directly out of the division of labour to classes in the Marxian sense.

As the extended family disintegrates, as land and cattle and other forms of property are divided at a father's death between his children or his sons, so that each becomes the separate owner of what passes to him; as the division of labour expands and the use of money comes to be general, it becomes much easier for some persons than for others to grow rich, acquiring more property than they can cultivate or use profitably. While they grow rich, others fall into debt and lose their property, and are obliged to hire themselves out as labourers or even to sell their liberty. Given a fast expanding division of labour and new systems of property and inheritance, society, as Engels saw, is soon divided into classes, in the Marxian sense of class. Keeping the peace in society may then be even more difficult, and make more urgent the need for strong government. Engels was impressed by the quarrels between rich and poor, between creditors and debtors, in Athens and in Rome. He saw struggles between classes almost destroying these two States: he saw compromises reached between the classes when Solon reorganized the Athenian state and when the office of tribune was instituted at Rome. Though he was candid enough to admit that these compromises set limits to the oppression of the poor by the rich, he nevertheless insisted on seeing in them evidence that the function of the State is to keep the peace between irreconcilable classes. No doubt, where there are classes and they are in conflict, it is the business of the State to keep the peace between them. And it may be that conflicts between classes in the Marxian sense are apt to be more bitter than most other conflicts. All this we can admit without also admitting that to keep the peace between classes is ever the sole or even the most important business of the State.

We can also admit that the form of the State often depends considerably, though never entirely, on how society is divided into classes. The class structure in turn depends partly on the division of labour and partly on the system of property. Given the division of labour, several different systems of property are possible, and therefore also several different forms of class structure. Though the need for the State arises in the first place from an extended division of labour, the way the State is organized depends only in part on the extent of that division; it also depends on the class structure, and no doubt on other things as well. Engels mistakenly supposes that to say that the need for the State arises from an extended division of labour which eventually gives rise to classes is equivalent to saying that it arises from the division of society into classes, and that therefore how the State is organized depends *primarily* on the class structure. And yet, though this extreme position is mistaken, it is certainly true that the form of the State is often deeply affected by the class structure. Thus we have here an important truth, and we owe our firmer grasp of it mostly to Engels and to Marx. Others before them had said that the rich use the State to oppress the poor, but they were the first to insist strongly that how the State is organized depends largely on how society is divided into classes. They exaggerated the dependence, no doubt, but they put forward an hypothesis which is plausible and has proved fruitful. They brought into prominence a matter neglected before their time.

b. *The State And 'Irreconcilable' Classes*

Very sensibly, Engels admits that the persons who perform the tasks of government, as those tasks come to be more clearly marked off from others, can (and usually do) become a distinct class. They use their political power to acquire forms of property which put them in a class apart from other classes. Engels does not say that these forms of property are acquired only by the use of political power. They can also be acquired in other ways. But he does admit that the use of political power is one of the important ways of acquiring them.[1] Those who win power usually accumulate wealth the more quickly for having won it.

This wealth, acquired by those who have political power and also by others, makes the possessors of it not only a distinct, but an exploiting, class. They have more land than they can cultivate themselves; they employ labour. They also acquire, in various ways, rights of property in other people's labour; they acquire slaves or serfs. Therefore the exploitation of class by class arises, at least in large part, as a consequence of the emergence of the State. It is sensible of Engels to admit this because there is much evidence that it is so. But the admission, as we shall see, is not consistent with other things that he says about the State.

Not only do those who wield political power use it to acquire wealth which puts them into what Marx and Engels call an exploiting class; they also make it easier for others who have no political power to acquire wealth enough to become exploiters. One of the important

[1] See Engels, *Anti-Dühring*, Part III, ch. II, op. cit., pp. 268–9, and *The Origin of the Family, Private Property and the State*, ch. ix, pp. 230–2.

ways in which the rich get their wealth in primitive societies where the State has recently emerged is by acquiring the properties and even the persons of debtors. Another way, also important, is by making slaves of prisoners captured in war. The importance of both these methods is acknowledged by Engels. But a man is no richer for what is owed to him unless his debtors, when they prove unwilling, are coerced into paying their debts. If they are required to surrender everything that is theirs, including the free disposal of their labour, the chances are that they will be unwilling. Prisoners captured in war, if they are to be enslaved, must be distributed among the victors and kept properly subservient. All this, Engels admits, is scarcely possible, or at least cannot go far, where there is no authority strong enough to enforce it. The emergence of the State is therefore a condition of society's becoming divided into unequal classes, some exploiting others. It may not be a condition of the extended division of labour which first breaks up tribal society, nor yet of the rules of property and inheritance which first supersede the tribal rules; but it is a condition of these things leading eventually to the division of society into unequal classes, exploiting and exploited.

If all this is admitted – and I think it is admitted by Engels either in *Anti-Dühring* or in *The Origin of the Family, Private Property and the State* – what can we make of the famous sentence in the second section of the *Communist Manifesto* that 'political power. . .is merely the organized power of one class for oppressing another'?[1] This sentence suggests that the State arises as a result of the division of society into unequal classes. Yet Marx and Engels are ready to admit that there cannot be class oppression, at least on any considerable scale, unless there is a State. Where there is no apparatus of power controlled by one class to the detriment of others, there cannot be much class oppression. Yet nearly always – except when Engels is actually describing how, in his opinion, the State arises – they speak as if the division of society into unequal classes happened independently of the emergence of the State. This does not imply that these two processes – the appearance of unequal classes and the appearance of the State – do not overlap, but it does suggest that the first is the cause of the second, and not the other way about. It suggests what Engels implicitly denies when he describes in detail the origins of the State. That description, obscure though it often is, attributes the division of society into unequal classes in large measure to the emergence of the State. True, it does not suggest that the rise of the State is the sufficient cause of class

---

[1] *Collected Works*, vol. 6, p. 505.

inequality, but it does suggest that it is a necessary condition. Here, as in other parts of their social theory, we find that what Marx and Engels say about the connections between two social processes does not accord with their actual descriptions of those processes. They tell us that one process determines another, and then, when they come to describe one or other of the processes, they admit (though more by implication than in so many words) that each has a powerful influence on the other.

Though Engels says that the State arises to keep the peace between classes whose interests are irreconcilable, he does not trouble to explain why they should be irreconcilable. The expanded division of labour which breaks up the old tribal society is presumably in the general interest; and so too, at least to begin with, are the rules of property and inheritance which replace the old tribal rules. Certainly, Engels says nothing to suggest the opposite. These rules may not be the only ones compatible with the increased division of labour, but they are compatible with it. Only after the division of labour and the new rules have been in operation for some time does society become divided into classes, in the Marxian sense of class. This happens for a variety of reasons: because families differ in size and some men get much more by inheritance than others, because debtors forfeit their properties and even their persons to their creditors, or because some people work harder or are abler or more lucky than others. Not until there are classes can there be *irreconcilable* class interests; and the rise of the State is, as we have seen, as much a cause as an effect of the emergence of classes.

It may be that, when tribal society breaks up, disputes are less easily settled than they used to be. It may be that the new methods evolved for their settlement do not reconcile the parties to the disputes as well as the old tribal authorities did. Within the kinship group, the authority of the chief is almost paternal; his business is as much to restore amity as to adjudicate claims or punish wrong-doers. He wants to change people's attitudes towards one another, restoring good feeling between them. The judge or arbiter in the State is perhaps not a restorer of amity in the same way; he is a maker of judicial decisions, a settler of claims, a dispenser of punishment. When he settles a dispute, the parties to it may or may not find the settlement just. If they do not, they may still accept it because they cannot safely do otherwise or because they recognize in general the need for courts of law. Accepting the decision from such motives as these, the parties to the dispute are not fully reconciled.

It may be that it is much more usual for men to feel aggrieved about professional judges in a political society than about chiefs or patriarchs in a tribal society; and it may be that this is one reason among others why force or the threat of it has to be used to back up judicial decisions more often than to back up the decisions of tribal chieftains. Fear of the consequences of disobedience may be a more frequent motive for obedience in the State than in the tribe, and respect for the wisdom and good will of the arbiter a more frequent motive in the tribe than in the State. If that is so, then parties to disputes are less easily reconciled in the State because the social relations between them are different. Perhaps Engels had this also in mind. He may have confused a greater intransigence, a lesser docility, between disputing parties whose social relations are no longer those of the tribe, with a clash of irreconcilable interests between classes. He may also have believed that, when society divides into classes, parties to disputes are even less easily reconciled, so that it is more than ever necessary to use force and the threat of force for the settlement of disputes.

Therefore, even though we disagree with Engels that the State arises to keep the peace between *irreconcilable* classes, we may still agree with him that it arises to settle disputes less easily settled than they used to be, because the parties to them are no longer socially related as they were. We may agree, too, that the settlement of disputes in the State often does not reconcile the parties to them, and that the causes which produce the State help to divide society into unequal classes, thus making it yet more difficult to settle disputes and to reconcile the parties to them.[1]

There is yet another possibility; it sometimes happens that, as class divisions deepen, the settlement of disputes becomes easier, even though the parties to them are less often reconciled. The privileged classes may be so powerful that the others quickly accept the settlements forced on them. They may think quick submission less dangerous than resistance; they may even, from prudence or timidity, refrain from making claims which they are legally entitled to make. Not long ago, in most parts of Africa and some parts of the United States, disputes between white and coloured persons were often settled more quickly than disputes between white persons; but this is no evidence that the parties to the disputes were reconciled.

It could also happen, where the *ideology* of the privileged class is accepted by all classes, that parties to disputes are reconciled almost as easily as disputes are settled. If the socially inferior classes accept

---

[1] By the settlement of a dispute I mean the reaching of a decision which puts an end to it, and by the reconciliation of the parties I mean their accepting the decision as just.

their position, if they are resigned to it, if they think it the work of Fate or Providence, it makes no sense to say that their class interests are irreconcilable with those of their exploiters – unless we can make the distinction that Marx and Engels wanted to make between actual aspirations and *true* interests, which I think we cannot make for the reasons already discussed.

But, though I say that it *could* happen that – in a society divided into unequal classes – parties to disputes were reconciled almost as easily as disputes were settled, I think it most unlikely. I very much doubt whether, where class divisions are deep, the poor and the powerless do accept the class ideologies of the rich and the powerful. They may not reject them consciously; they may not even know what they are. They may put up with the system without understanding it and without producing theories to condemn it; but I suspect that very often, in their disputes with their so-called 'betters', they feel themselves to be victims of injustice.

Marx and Engels sometimes weaken their own case unnecessarily. They are much too ready to concede that ideas which suit the special interests of the privileged classes are accepted by the whole of society: 'The ideas of the ruling class are in every epoch the ruling ideas. . ... The class which has the means of material production at its disposal, consequently also controls the means of mental production, so that the ideas of those who lack the means of production are on the whole subject to it.'[1] This is not true, or is so only in part. No doubt, where the privileged classes are firmly entrenched, the ideas and theories serving to strengthen their position are much the most important, and, even when not produced by the privileged, they flourish and are respectable because they serve their interests. They are taught in the schools and are printed in books. They loom the largest in men's conscious minds; they are the most paraded and the most discussed. Therefore, we can say that, in a stable society divided into unequal classes, most *theories* which are class ideology favour the ruling or privileged classes, if only because it requires trained minds and a large expenditure of mental energy to construct such theories. A stable society with unequal classes is stable only while the ascendancy of the privileged is not seriously challenged. Thus it is true almost by definition that the prevailing ideology of a stable society which is also a class society is the ideology of the ruling class.

But not to challenge the ascendancy of a privileged class is by no means the same thing as to accept its ideology. In societies where there

[1] *The German Ideology*, I, *Collected Works*, vol. 5, p. 59.

are deep divisions, whether between classes in the Marxian sense or between races or religious groups, the ideology of the ruling class or race or group may have very little influence on the thinking of their 'inferiors'. This is all the more likely when the 'inferiors' are poor and illiterate. As often as not, the ideology of the ruling class or group serves much more to hold that class or group together and to justify the social order in the minds of those who benefit from it than to reconcile the subject classes or groups to it by persuading them that the social order is just. The ruling ideology in Ireland in the early part of the eighteenth century was that of the Protestant and privileged minority, and it was probably not shared to any but a small extent by the Catholic majority. Yet Ireland, at that time, was nearer than she had been in the seventeenth century, and than she was to be in the nineteenth, to being a stable society divided into unequal classes.

It does not always, nor even often, happen that, where some classes dominate others which accept their inferior position, the thinking of the inferior classes is moulded by the ideology of their superiors. No doubt, where classes are very unequal, the intellectual life of the community is confined to the superior classes; but that life consists of much more than class ideology, so that, if other classes come later to share in it, it is not the class ideology of their superiors which they imbibe so much as a cultural inheritance which is classless even though hitherto confined to only some classes. Marx and Engels were too much inclined to speak as if socially inferior classes, until they acquire a revolutionary ideology to challenge the ideology of the socially superior, accept the ideas which it suits those who are set above them should be in their heads. There is plentiful evidence that this has not always, nor even usually, been so, at least in Europe.[1] We have evidence that the serfs often resented the grievous burdens placed on them, which they could hardly have done if their ideas of justice had been moulded by the ideas of their masters. And yet, most of the time, they had nothing worth calling an ideology of their own to set against the dominant ideology; they had no ideas and no principles coherent enough to draw them together to resist their masters or to reform the social order. They could not do battle on the intellectual front and, with rare exceptions, felt no need to produce a theory to justify the resentment they felt. And yet they often felt resentment, and often saw themselves as the victims of their superiors or of circumstances.

Marx and Engels were intellectuals, and were prone to a mistake

[1] And in Asia and Africa, where European rule has been widespread and the influence of European ideas immense, no ideology favourable to that rule has been successfully purveyed to the subject peoples.

often made by intellectuals; they took it for granted that persons not equipped by education to challenge the ideas of those who dominate society mostly accept them or at least do not condemn their masters. If they had looked more closely and with greater sympathy at the peasants, whom they despised for their ignorance and boorishness, they might have seen how wide of the mark they were.[1]

I am not now going back on what I said before; I am not arguing that there are, after all, classes with *irreconcilable* interests in the sense which I denied earlier. I am saying only that, if the poor and unprivileged feel oppressed, as they often do, it is because, even when they are not class-conscious and revolutionary in the Marxian sense – even when they do not challenge the established order – their ideas of what is right and just are much less affected by the class ideology of their social superiors than Marx supposed.

It may even be that the unprivileged have beliefs favourable to the interests of the privileged but which do not come to them from the privileged and which are compatible with a deep hatred for them. The unprivileged may believe that the social order is unchangeable; they may accept it from mere habit or because it has never occurred to them that there is anything they can do to improve their lot. This belief that society is unchanging and unchangeable is ordinarily an effect of habit and illusion; men take for granted what they are accustomed to, and therefore have no idea either that it changes or that it can be changed. There is always some change from generation to generation in all societies, even the most primitive or the most stagnant, but it may not be noticed because it is slow and there are no records kept of the past, or because such as are kept are too meagre to destroy the illusion that there is no change. This illusion, shared by all classes, favours the interests of the privileged; and yet it is not class ideology. It arises because society changes slowly and imperceptibly; it arises as readily in classless societies as in those divided into classes; it is not an illusion produced, deliberately or unconsciously, in the unprivileged by the privileged, nor does it arise to consolidate the position of the privileged. The socially inferior may hate the classes above them, they

[1] In a society where there are great inequalities, the 'lower orders', when they speak to their 'betters', often speak as if they shared their beliefs, and yet speak quite differently among themselves. Their 'betters', if they catch them at it, condemn their hypocrisy, but to the 'lower orders' this hypocrisy is a necessary precaution of the weak in their dealings with the strong. The socially weak are apt to imitate the socially strong when actually in their presence, sometimes from the desire to placate or deceive, and sometimes from a sense of their own inadequacy. No doubt, the imitation also springs at times from a conviction that the manners and beliefs of their superiors *are* the best.

may have notions of justice moving them to condemn the behaviour of those classes, they may be almost untouched by whatever, in the views of their superiors, can be plausibly treated as class ideology; they may be all this, and still be long-suffering and make a virtue of their patience. They may be resigned to their fate.

Or, if they are not exactly resigned to it, they may lack the ideas which would give them social cohesion and make them politically formidable. In that case, they put up with their lot indefinitely, not because they have been touched by the ideology of their masters, nor because they do not hate and condemn them, but because they do not know how to set about putting an end to the oppression they suffer from. Perhaps the serfs felt like this in the Middle Ages in the West, or in Russia in the seventeenth and eighteenth centuries. Occasionally they rose in revolt, but they did not know how to change their social condition, and most of the time they merely put up with it as they did with their natural environment. Did religion make them more docile than they would have been without it? Who can tell? But, for my part, I doubt it. What did Christianity mean to the mediaeval or the Russian serf? How much of it did he imbibe? How differently did he understand it from his master? How much was his Christianity mixed up with pagan beliefs?

It may be that Christianity has served as much to make the oppressed rebellious as to make them docile. That the promise of a life after death reconciles the humble to their lot in this life is by no means obvious. Nor is it obvious that, when they are told that all men are equal in the sight of a God who is in Heaven, they are the more willing to be treated as inferiors in this world by their fellow-men. We know that the privileged classes, when the classes beneath them become restive, have used Christianity to try to calm them and make them more docile, but this is no proof that Christianity usually has the effects they hope for.[1]

c. Instrument or Condition of Class Domination?

Though Marx and Engels often speak of the State as an organ or instrument of class rule, they by no means do so always, even when they are speaking of long-established States in class societies. Almost as often they speak as if the State, merely by helping to maintain the

---

[1] There is good evidence that the spread of Methodism in England during the Industrial Revolution helped to dissuade the poor from resorting to violence to alleviate their miseries, but we must not generalize from one example. Besides, in the long run, Methodism may have added to the discipline and effectiveness of the poor in their struggle for greater equality.

social order, makes the exploitation of class by class possible. But this is to say only that the State is *a condition of class exploitation* and not that it is *an instrument of class rule*. Yet Marx and Engels treat these two quite different assertions as if they were the same. In this they are followed by more than their disciples; they are followed even by some of their critics.

If we are to see both the weak and the strong points of the Marxian theory of the State, it really is important to notice that the two assertions are not the same. It is important as much in order to do justice to Marx and Engels as for any other reason. For, though neither of these assertions is true, one is much nearer being true than the other. It is nearer the truth to say that the State is a condition of class exploitation. But the Marxian doctrine about the eventual disappearance of the State rests on the second of these assertions and not on the first; it rests on the one which is the furthest from the truth. If, then, we treat the two assertions as equivalent, we treat evidence which bears out the first as if it also bore out the second, and we are disposed to accept the doctrine which rests on the second. We are disposed to treat evidence which goes to show that the State is a condition of class exploitation as if it supported the conclusion that in a classless society there is no need for the State. Or else, if we find the conclusion too extravagant to be accepted, we question the evidence on which it is supposed to rest; we are then too apt to deny that the State is a condition of class exploitation.

To call the State an instrument of class rule is to suggest that, if there were no unequal classes, with the superior among them needing to use force to maintain the social conditions of their superiority, there would be no State. The system of property being what it is, society is divided into exploiting and exploited classes, and the State is used by the exploiting classes to maintain the conditions of exploitation. There is no need to deny that the State also keeps the peace; but the implication is that it would not be needed to keep it, if there were no exploitation of class by class. This is what the founders of Marxism and their disciples mean to suggest when they call the State an instrument of class rule.

But, as we have seen already, Engels – though he does not know it – gives us a description of the rise of the State which does not square with its being an instrument of class rule. He says that it arises to keep the peace between irreconcilable classes, without troubling to notice that the classes which emerge with the division of labour that breaks up tribal society are not classes in the Marxian sense of the word. They are groups owning different sorts of things, but they do not have different property rights in the sense needed to make them different classes, in the Marxian sense of class. Farmers own land, cattle and agricultural implements; wheelwrights own workshops and the tools of their trade, which differ from those of the smiths and the potters. But these differences in the kinds of things that are owned are not enough to divide society into separate classes. It is not until later, when more and more people have forfeited to others their property in their means of production, and even in their own labour, that classes, in the proper Marxian sense, arise – which they can hardly do except where there is a State to enforce the rules whose enforcement enables them to arise. It is only after classes have arisen within the legal order protected by the State that some of them, the exploiting classes, can win control of the State and use it to protect their interests more effectively than it could do when it merely enforced the rules enabling them to rise superior to the rest of society; it is only then that the State can become an instrument of class rule. In order to become an instrument of class rule, it must first be a condition of class exploitation.

I have tried to explain how Engels' account of the rise of the State gives the lie to the assertion that the State is merely an instrument of class rule. How could what seems obvious to us not be so to him? How was it that he did not see the significance of his own account of the origins of the State? I think he failed to see it partly because he failed to distinguish between two different senses of the term *a system of property*; in one sense it refers to rules of property, and in the other to the distribution of property. He failed to distinguish between the rules, customary or legal, governing the use of things and their transference, and the way in which things that are owned are distributed among their possessors. Two countries might have much the same rules of property, and yet property might be much more evenly distributed in one country than the other. We have seen, in considering Engels' account of the rise of the State, how the rules of property which superseded the old tribal rules were, when they first arose, in the common interest; and how in the course of time they led, for a variety of reasons, to a very unequal distribution of property, enabling a few people to live luxuriously on the labour of others who lived miserably. There was no need to change the rules to get the inequality; all that we needed was that the rules should go on being enforced after they had ceased to be in the common interest. If there had been no State, the division of society into unequal classes might never have gone as far as it did, because the poor might have refused to pay their debts when they found that, by paying them, they would be left without property. Rules which began by being generally convenient might have ceased to be obeyed when they ceased to be convenient except to a part of society. But, fortunately for that part, fortunately for the rich, the State was there to enforce the rules. It was there to serve their interest, though it arose in the first place, not for their benefit, but to enforce rules which could not be enforced by the old tribal authorities – rules which affected a much wider area of transactions, that is to say, transactions more varied in kind and involving a much larger number of persons more remotely related to one another.

Since Engels and Marx, and also their disciples and critics, use such expressions as *relations of property* and *system of property* to mean indiscriminately the rules governing the use and transference of things and the way such things are in fact distributed, they fail to make a distinction which needs to be made if we are to see clearly how different these two assertions are: that the State is a *condition* of the exploitation of class by class, and that the State is an *instrument* of class oppression. If the State is a condition of the exploitation of class by class, then, although it follows that where there is class exploitation there must be a State, it does not follow that where there is a State there must be class exploitation. It is only if the State is defined as an instrument of class rule that it follows that, where there are no unequal classes and no class exploitation, there is no State.

Of course, it might be true that most States, at one time or another, have been instruments of class rule – that they have been controlled by exploiting classes. It might even be true that most States, more often than not, have been instruments of this kind. If Marx and Engels, in calling the State an instrument of class rule, had meant to say no more than this, we might be content to let the statement pass, leaving it to the historians to contest it if they felt so inclined. But that is not what they meant by it; for they drew from it the conclusion that, if there were no class oppression, no exploitation of class by class, there would be no need for the State. Now, clearly, even if it were true that most States most of the time have been controlled by oppressing classes, it would not follow that, if there were no class oppression, there would be no need for the State.

In *The Origin of the Family, Private Property and the State*, Engels says that the State arises to keep the peace between classes having irreconcilable interests.[1] But we have seen that the classes which exist when the State arises are not classes in the Marxian sense of class;

---

[1] See *The Origin of the Family, Private Property and the State*, ch. ix, p. 229.

they are merely groups engaged in different occupations and having divergent interests. Therefore, if Engels is right, it follows that there can be irreconcilable interests even where there are as yet no classes in the sense in which he uses the word *class* when he calls the State an instrument of class rule or a condition of class exploitation. The division of labour breaks up the old tribal society and creates groups with irreconcilable interests; then the State arises to keep the peace between these groups; then, within the social order maintained by the State, there emerge classes in the proper Marxian sense; and gradually the exploiting classes gain control of the State and shape it to suit their peculiar needs. I put this forward as a revised version of Engels' account of the origins of the State, and I call it a revised version precisely because it adds nothing substantial to the original; it merely refrains from drawing, from his account, the conclusions which Engels drew, and does so on the ground that they do not follow from it. If what Engels says about the origins of the State is true, it follows that the State is *not* an instrument of class rule in the sense which requires that where there are no classes there is no State; and it also follows that the State is a condition of class exploitation.

d. *States not Controlled by any Class*

Though Marx and Engels speak of the State as an instrument of class rule, they are willing to admit that there have been States not controlled by any class. I have in mind here something more than Engels' saying that the State first arose to keep the peace between irreconcilable[1] groups which he calls classes, although they are not so in the specifically Marxian sense. I have also in mind what Marx says in *The German Ideology* about absolute monarchies in general, and what Engels says in *The Origin of the Family, Private Property and the State* about absolute monarchies in the eighteenth century – that they sometimes, at certain periods, have appeared to be uncontrolled by any class.[2] If the French monarchy before 1789, in particular, was not so controlled, then presumably most of the other absolute monarchies in Europe were not so either, for they, like the French monarchy,

---

[1] I argued earlier that there are no *irreconcilable* interests in the sense imagined by Marx and Engels. I am not now retreating from that position; for that sense, I tried to show, rests on a false theory about how interests are related to values. But I also said that there might be conflicts which could not be settled in a way that seemed just to the parties to them while they retained their notions of justice unchanged. Conflicts *irreconcilable* in this weaker-than-Marxian sense can arise between classes and also between groups that are not classes.

[2] See Marx, *The German Ideology*, III, op. cit., pp. 194–5, and Engels, *The Origin of the Family, Private Property and the State*, ch. ix, p. 231.

ruled over societies in which the feudal nobles were fast losing ground and the middle class were still too weak to take over the State. The First and Second Empires in France were also not States controlled by either the decayed nobility or the rising bourgeoisie. It is the parliamentary form which Marx treats as *par excellence* the bourgeois form of government; and that form has been the exception rather than the rule in the West since what Marxists call *capitalism* began to replace the productive system prevailing in the Middle Ages.

How is it that Marxists, who so confidently speak of the State as an instrument of class rule, are so ready to admit that this or that State is not controlled by any class? I suggest that their readiness is due to a mistaken belief that the State's being a condition of class exploitation, is equivalent to its being an instrument of class rule. If this equivalence is taken for granted, it comes much easier to say that the State is an instrument of class rule and at the same time to admit freely, whenever the facts warrant the admission, that the French or some other State is not in fact controlled by a class. For, clearly, the State could be a condition of class exploitation, without being controlled by a class; it could maintain a legal system enabling one class to exploit another, without actually being in the hands of the exploiting class or of their agents. This mixture of candour and paradox is typical of Marxism. It is also useful; it enables the Marxist to stick to his assertion in spite of the evidence against it. Indeed, it enables him to do better than this; it enables him to use the evidence against his assertion as if it were in favour of it.

It might be objected, in favour of Marxism, that this criticism is of small importance and scarcely worth making. No doubt, if the exploiting class or classes do not control the State, it is not literally true that the State is an instrument of their rule. But if those who control the State, whoever they may be, maintain a legal system which allows some classes to exploit others, it is surely not seriously misleading to call the State an instrument of the exploiting classes. Those who rule may not be their agents, but they maintain a system favourable to them, and so in practice act pretty much as they would do if they were their agents.

This objection is not sound. Admittedly, if those who rule, though they are not agents of the exploiting classes, maintain a legal system favourable to those classes, they act pretty much as they would do if they were their agents. But, since in fact they are not their agents, there is no ground for believing that they will continue to maintain the legal system favourable to the exploiting classes if, for any reason, it should happen to become their interest to change it for the benefit of other classes. Perhaps Marx and Engels believed that this was most unlikely to happen; perhaps they believed that, in a society divided into classes, those who govern, even when they are not agents of any class, always have interests more in line with the interests of the exploiting classes than with those of the exploited; perhaps they believed that, since the form of government varies with the class structure, it follows that, however little the rulers may be directly controlled by the exploiting classes, they will always find it their interest to maintain the legal system favourable to those classes. If they held these beliefs – and they often spoke as if they did hold them – they were mistaken.

Even where they admit that the State is not controlled by any class, Marx and Engels still insist that the form of the State depends largely on the situation of the classes inside it. The old French monarchy and the First and Second Empires were not States controlled by the exploiting classes. Neither the nobles nor the bourgeois actually ruled France. Yet the Bonapartist type of absolute monarchy differed from the Bourbon because, as a result of the French Revolution, the relative positions of different classes had changed. The old nobility had been greatly weakened, the peasants had rid themselves of their remaining 'feudal' obligations, the bourgeois were richer and more influential than they had been. The two Napoleons relied, much more heavily than the Bourbons had done, on the loyalty of the peasants and of the lower middle class. They respected the property rights of the capitalists, thus maintaining the conditions of exploitation from which the bourgeois profited; they kept the urban workers down. A Bonaparte on the throne was security against the re-establishment of the old order, which had kept the rich bourgeois socially inferior to the nobles and had put restraints on their money-making enterprises. But the Bonapartes also used the loyalty of other classes to make themselves politically independent of the bourgeois. Like the Bourbons, they played class off against class – though the game in their day was different. The devices used by those who have power to keep it vary with the ways in which society is divided into classes, with the sorts of classes there are and with their relative size and importance. Thus, even where the State is not controlled by any class – even where it is not literally an instrument of class rule but only a condition of class exploitation – the structure of the State depends largely on the class structure.

This is perceptive and true, but it is only part of the truth, and a small part, if we use the word *class* in the Marxian sense. The structure of the State depends also on other things besides the class structure thus understood; it depends on whether or not the country is industrialized, on whether the people are mostly illiterate, on whether the rulers enjoy the people's support or can rely on their acquiescence. Marx, no doubt, would say that these other factors are closely connected with the class structure. When a country becomes industrialized, it acquires (he thought) a capitalist and a proletarian class. We cannot blame him, writing at the time he did, for thinking so. But we can now see that it need not be so. Industrialization can be brought to a country by its government, even where there are no capitalists, or very few, as it was in Russia. Although industrialization, when it comes, must transform the social order, it can do so without creating capitalists and proletarians. The Soviet Union is, in the Marxian sense of class, a classless society. It may well be divided into groups whose interests, if they were free to push them openly, would prove just as near to being irreconcilable as the interests of classes in Western Europe in Marx's time. It may, in some other sense of *class* which is just as usual and important as the Marxian sense, be divided into classes as jealous of one another as any in the West. The enormous power that has been wielded, often most ruthlessly, by the government in the Soviet Union suggests that the State is as much needed there as anywhere to keep the peace between groups with divergent interests. Nevertheless, the Soviet Union, in the specifically Marxian sense of class, is a classless society, or is much nearer being one than any Western country. It is therefore misleading to say that the form of the State *depends* on the *class* structure; much better would be to say that it *varies* with the *social* structure.

Marxists might claim that the two statements come to much the same thing. They do not. When we speak of the social structure, we refer to the division of society into groups, whether or not they are classes in the Marxian or any other sense; and when we say *varies* instead of *depends*, we allow that the form of the State and the policies of its rulers may powerfully affect the social structure, as they clearly have done in Russia and elsewhere.

Neither Marx nor Engels denies that the rulers of the State, whether or not they are the agents of a class, have their own group interests which differ considerably from the interests of all classes. They also admit that organized bodies like the Army and the Church, which are not classes in their sense of the word, have their own corporate interests. We should expect to find that, in a class society, the officers of the Army, the higher clergy and senior State officials are mostly recruited from the privileged classes. We should expect to find them favouring those classes against others. Yet they also have their own professional interests, and they are powerful in the State. They are powerful in it even when the State is controlled by a class, and are only the more powerful when it is not. I take the Church and the Army for examples because they were important in Europe in Marx's day; but they are not the only examples.

If we allow, as I think we must, and as both Marx and Engels sometimes do,[1] that in the State there can be powerful bodies with interests peculiar to themselves – bodies which are not mere class organizations even when their leaders come mostly from the same classes – we must also allow that the interests of these bodies may clash with the interests of the classes from which their leaders come. Now, if this is so, why should it never be the interest of these bodies to side with the unprivileged against the privileged classes, or at least to pursue policies which in the long run strengthen the unprivileged classes? Why, as the relative strengths of the classes change, should not these groups find it their interest to support the classes that are growing stronger against the classes that are growing weaker? Why should we suppose that these bodies, when they have to choose between their corporate interests and the interests of the classes from which their leaders are mostly recruited, will ordinarily choose to sacrifice their corporate interests? Marx and Engels make an assumption which is by no means obviously true: that class interests always, or nearly always, take precedence over the interests of bodies or groups which are not classes. Of course, while the senior ranks in these bodies are recruited mostly from the upper classes, they will favour the interests of those classes against other class interests, provided their corporate interests do not move them to do otherwise. But if their corporate interests do so move them, why should we assume that they will sacrifice them to their class interests? And why should we assume that these two types of interest will never diverge so widely as to move the corporate body to do what undermines the position of the class?

Marx and Engels believed that, as the machinery of government grows more massive – as more and more people take a full-time part in one capacity or another in the business of government – the State acquires, as they put it, a certain 'independence of society'.[2] The persons who exercise political authority, as they grow in number and in power, come to think of themselves as raised above the rest of society. That is only another way of saying that government, as it grows bigger and more active, becomes more bureaucratic. The larger

[1] See especially Marx, *The Eighteenth Brumaire of Louis Bonaparte, Collected Works*, vol. 11, pp. 139, 185–6 and 191–2.
[2] Above all, in *The Eighteenth Brumaire of Louis Bonaparte*, ibid., pp. 186–7.

and more active a group becomes, the greater its social importance, and the more its group interests count as against other interests. This is as true of those who take part in government as of any other group, and perhaps even more true. Therefore, the mere increase in the size of the government machine creates an enormously powerful group, which is not a class, and which, precisely because it is so powerful, is unlikely to be controlled by any class. That is, I think, what Marx and Engels admit when they speak of the State rising above society and becoming a parasite upon it.

But they admit that without seeing the implications of what they are saying. If the State can do this, it may become its interest to put an end to the exploitation of class by class. And yet it may still deserve to be called a parasite, for it may be as oppressive as any class ever was. Yet it may be impartial as between the classes; it may be the sole oppressor. It may care no more for one class than another, and yet be as little public-spirited as any class government; it may be as ready to sacrifice any interest, even the public interest, to its own. An entirely selfish bureaucracy could be so placed that it was its interest to deal impartially with all classes and groups subject to it except when their interests conflicted with its own; which of course they often would do.[1]

It is a pity that Marx, who was one of the shrewdest of political observers, did not see more clearly the light that some of his own observations shed on his theory of the State. *The Eighteenth Brumaire of Louis Bonaparte*, though spoilt by violence and diffuseness, is essentially right in many of its judgements. Louis Napoleon was an adventurer surrounded by others of his kind; he owed his success largely to the support of the lower middle class, envious of its social superiors and contemptuous of the workers, and also to people whose class allegiance was uncertain, the *déclassés*. No one at that time understood better than Marx a phenomenon which, in its later and much grosser form, has come to be known as Fascism. Far be it from me to suggest that Bonapartism was ever as cruel and unprincipled a movement as Fascism has been in our day. In political nastiness we have outdone our ancestors. Nevertheless, Bonapartism and Fascism have more than a little in common. Neither is really a class movement; they both play upon the fears and jealousies of all classes, and their leaders are mostly adventurers – persons who, for one reason or another, are

---

[1] A government as completely selfish – as completely indifferent to the public interest – as this is doubtless most unlikely; but a government habitually impartial as between the classes subject to it might be as much disposed to selfishness as any class government. That is the point I wish to make.

déclassés and therefore not inhibited by ordinary loyalties. The Fascist Party in Italy and the National Socialist Party in Germany were not class organizations. They got control of the State in order to bend all classes to their will – or, rather, they got control of it in order to satisfy ambitions which could not be satisfied except by the sacrifice of class interests. This, of course, was much less true of Bonapartism in Marx's day; Louis Napoleon was kinder to the propertied classes than were Mussolini and Hitler, and also less anxious to flatter and to soothe the industrial workers. That was partly because his ambitions were more modest and his political weapons weaker, and partly because the industrial workers in France were still a small and unorganized class. In Bonapartism we find only the meagre beginnings of a new kind of illiberal and popular Caesarism which is neither bourgeois nor proletarian.

No one was shrewder than Marx in describing these beginnings, and it is therefore all the more to be regretted that he did not see more clearly their significance for his theory. He saw that classless adventurers could, by playing off the classes against one another, capture the State and use it to promote interests which were not class interests. He also saw, sometimes at least, that modern bureaucratic government, owing to its very size, can rise superior to all social classes. What he did not see is that the modern State, when classless adventurers get control of it, can be used to make society classless, in the Marxian sense of class, without in the least diminishing the oppression of man by man. No doubt, the State could conceivably also be used to reduce oppression, for it might be the interest of those who took over the government to remove class exploitation in the Marxian sense, without putting other forms of oppression in its place.

If by a classless society we mean a society in which there are no classes in the Marxian sense of class, we have to admit that in such a society there can be just as much oppression as in any class society, and also that there can be groups with interests just as difficult to reconcile as the interests of different classes. The modern State, as it grows larger and more enterprising, reduces the importance of classes, as Marx understood them, and adds to the importance of other groups. This is proved as much by what has been happening in the West in the last hundred years as by the history of the Soviet Union. It is a truth which strikes at the roots of the Marxian theory of the State, and Marx himself was among the first to get an inkling of it. We can often appeal to Marx against Marx; and, when we do so, it is by no means in order to score at his expense. For we appeal to his perspicacity. It is a tribute to him even more than a criticism to say, as I do now, that we learn too much from him to be able to accept some of his most famous doctrines.

2. The Disappearance of the State

If we define the State as an instrument of class rule, or if (more cautiously) we say that its essential function is to keep the peace between irreconcilable classes, in the Marxian sense of class, we have to conclude that, if society becomes classless, the State will disappear. But our conclusion is then a mere tautology. We know only that there will be no State, as we have defined it, if there are no classes, as we have defined class. We do not know that, where there are no classes, there will be no parliaments and law-courts, no civil servants, no police, no armed forces. Nor do we know that, where there are no classes as we define class, there will be no groups with interests as difficult to reconcile as class interests.

Now, Marx and Engels were not uttering a tautology when they predicted the disappearance of the State; they really believed that, where there were no classes in their sense of the word, there would be no need for many of the institutions of what we ordinarily understand by the State. I say *many* advisedly, and not *all*; for they did not deny that there would always be a need for administration. Wherever there is organization on a large scale, as there must be in every industrial society, there is always the need to allot work and to see that it is done, and also the need to make rules and to see that they are observed. Marx and Engels, like Saint-Simon before them, made a distinction between *government* and *administration*, predicting the disappearance in the classless society of only the first.[1] Though they did not, as I shall try to show, make it clear just what this distinction amounts to, they seem to have included in administration some of the activities usually called governmental. We therefore put, and try to answer, two questions: What is it that they thought would disappear with the disappearance of the State?, and what reasons are there for believing that the institutions whose disappearance they predicted are needed only where there are classes?

a. No More Organized Force
The answer to the first question is not easy. Or perhaps I should say that part of the answer is easy and part is not. The easy part of

---

[1] See especially Marx, *The Civil War in France*, sect. III, *Collected Works*, vol. 22, pp. 331–3, and Engels, *Anti-Dühring*, Part III, ch. I, *Collected Works*, vol. 25, p. 247.

the answer is *organized force*. In the classless society, it will not be necessary to use force to get people to carry out their obligations. I take it that this does not mean that there will never be disputes about what people's obligations are; I take it that it means that where there are disputes, the parties to them, if they cannot settle them amicably, will always submit them to arbitration and loyally accept the decisions of the arbiters. Men will be so much in agreement about essentials, and will have methods for settling disputes which seem to them so just, that they will readily accept the decisions they are required to accept. If anyone should not accept them in this spirit, the pressure of public opinion will ordinarily be enough to induce him to do so. Crime – the doing deliberately of what is known to be against the rules – will be virtually unknown, or at least so rare that there will be no need to organize the use of force to prevent it. The motives for crime will be less urgent and less frequent, and the criminal will be more easily brought to his senses by the need to regain the good opinion of his neighbours. The assumption is that he lives in a society which is not divided, where men are not one another's victims, where no man is an outcast or an inferior merely in virtue of his position in society. In a society of this kind, crime is much more clearly irrational, much more clearly against the interests of the criminal; it is an aberration, and the criminal, when the mood which led to the crime has passed, sees it as such. He then wants to make amends. He is in a society which seems just to him, he is provided for, he is a man among equals, he is a man who counts; he is not the victim of society, and is therefore not its enemy.

These are the reasons which the anarchists gave, and which the founders of Marxism shared with them. They are part of a stock of ideas common to all the communists of the last century who denounced the State as an instrument of class rule. Marx and Engels were not anarchists in the ordinary sense. They did not want, then and there, to get rid of the State; they wanted the workers to capture and transform it so that they could use it to destroy the social relations and attitudes of mind of bourgeois society. But, in another sense, they *were* anarchists: they wanted the workers to use the State to destroy the social conditions which made it necessary to have a State; they shared the belief common among anarchists that class privilege and State power are corrupting.

The defenders of the capitalist system which Marx attacked were sometimes given to expatiating on the dignity of labour. Hard work, they said, is good for men; it gives them self-discipline. Labourers compete with one another for work, and this competition makes for self-reliance. Marx felt only contempt for this line of argument, treating it as a form of hypocrisy. He held that in capitalist society labour is monotonous and degrading. Men are forced to work long hours to earn the necessities of life; the work they do is not creative; it does not call forth their powers. They work, not for the enjoyment they get from what they do, but only to get a wage. Their labour is a commodity which they sell on the market to the highest bidder; it is not something they do because it absorbs them and gives them a sense of achievement. It takes up most of their waking hours and most of their strength, and yet in itself means nothing to them. They use up their lives and their strength in the effort to keep alive, and have neither time nor energy left over to enjoy life by making an ample and free use of their talents. Their labour, as Marx puts it, is *alienated*; it is a commodity sold to others and not a form of self-expression. And the capitalists, in their competition for profits, also lead unsatisfying lives; they chase the outward marks of success. They are driven to it by the system they are involved in. Both workers and capitalists are slaves of the system in the sense that it impels them to pursue ends which cannot satisfy them; it prevents their living fully human lives. This distortion and crippling of human nature is an inevitable consequence of a system which makes a fetish of production, driving men to behave as if it mattered more that goods should be produced and profits made than human needs satisfied. Crime flourishes under capitalism because of what capitalism does to human nature.

In the classless society of the future, the social and psychological causes of crime will disappear, and therefore it will not be necessary to use force to maintain obedience to social rules. Men will be richer than ever they were before; productive techniques will be so efficient that there will be much less time spent on producing the necessities of life and much more on creative and satisfying activities. There will be plenty for all, due partly to the much greater efficiency of production and partly to men's not wanting things merely to impress their neighbours. There will be neither poverty nor ignorance in the classless society, and there will be leisure to lead a full life. There will be no rebelling against a system of law and morality that cripples human nature; there will be little or nothing to move men to crime. They will obey rules which serve the common interest because they see that the rules in fact do serve it.

The easy part of the answer to the question, What is involved in the disappearance of the State?, is organized force. The less easy part is, a hierarchy of persons, *separate* from the rest of society, managing its common affairs. This is what Engels tells us comes into existence when the State appears, and it is presumably what is destined to wither away when the State disappears. But what this can be is not as easily understood as what organized force is. How must we interpret Engels' meaning? Is he saying that in the classless society there will be no administration other than business management? That there will be no need for any decisions to be made except about the assignment of work and the use of resources? Or is he saying that, though there will also be a need for decisions of other kinds, they will be taken by the workers themselves or by part-time officials whom they appoint? Or, lastly, does he allow that the work of administration will be done by full-time professionals, insisting only that those who do it will be very closely responsible to those affected by what they do? I do not believe that the texts make it possible to decide roundly in favour of any one of these three interpretations, though I suspect that the first two come closer than the third to giving us Engels' meaning. I shall consider all three, including the one which seems to me the least likely, for I am less interested in weighing the evidence in favour of this or that interpretation of Marxism than in seeing what can be said for and against such views as Marx and Engels held.[1]

b. No More Alienation

But before I consider these three versions of what is involved in the disappearance of a hierarchy of persons, *separate* from the rest of society, managing its common affairs, I want to go back for a moment to the prediction that in the classless society there will be no need to use organized force to get men to carry out their obligations. Such force will be unnecessary because there will be no more *alienation*. Society will no longer produce in us the motives that lead to crime, to the deliberate flouting of the rules which we are required to obey.

The Marxian doctrine of *alienation* bears a strong likeness to Rousseau's doctrine that society corrupts man. Marx and Rousseau agree that it is in society that man becomes moral – a maker of claims and a recognizer of obligations, a rule-prescribing and rule-respecting animal – and that it is also in society that man acquires the motives impelling him to break the rules. That, at bottom, is what is wrong with society; it sets up standards and at the same time produces in men

---

[1] When two or more versions of some doctrine of theirs are put forward, I am less concerned to argue that one version comes closer to their meaning than the others, or to explain how they shift from one to another, than to consider what is to be said for these different versions. There is a good deal of ambiguity in all social and political theories, and it is less important for my purpose to decide what their authors can most plausibly be held to have meant than to consider how much truth there is in the doctrines attributed to them.

passions which move them to reject those standards. The remedy for this condition is a society which so acts upon its members that they willingly do what is required of them.

Marx's doctrine of *alienation*, like Rousseau's doctrine of social corruption, rests on this assumption: Given men's natural capacities, there is a form of society whose discipline is pre-eminently acceptable to them, because in it their environment creates in them the motives which make them willingly obey the rules needed to hold society together. This is the just society, the social and moral order in conformity with human nature. In bourgeois society, men acquire values in which they cannot find satisfaction; they are frustrated, and are therefore prone to actions which are wrong or illegal according to the moral rules and laws which embody these values. The morality of bourgeois society is not a truly human morality; it does not allow men to make the most of their natural capacities.

Leaving aside this condemnation of bourgeois society, we may agree that a community can be so organized as to dispose many of its members to break the rules which it requires them to obey. Communities do vary greatly in what, for want of a better word, I shall call cultural solidarity. In some communities people find it easier and more satisfying than in others to live up to the standards expected of them. But the doctrine of *alienation* or *social corruption*, which is sociological and psychological as well as moral, has never, to the best of my knowledge, been put clearly and adequately; it has never been put in a way which is intelligible and which also seems to account for the facts. I suspect that it is a doctrine containing a large measure of truth – though just how large, I do not know.

What evidence is there that *alienation* is peculiar to societies divided into classes, in the Marxian sense of class? Marx seems to have believed that alienation is an effect of poverty and of man's being somehow the victim of his social environment. Man is helpless in bourgeois society; he is pushed by forces he does not understand and cannot control into courses which restrict and stultify. Though some countries are much richer now than they were in Marx's time, they seem to be afflicted as much as ever they were by what Marx calls *alienation*. Crime flourishes even where the extremes of poverty have disappeared. Britain, Russia and the United States are, in the Marxian sense of class, much less class societies today than they were in the mid-nineteenth century; the rights of property which distinguish the privileged or 'exploiting' classes have been greatly curtailed, while the workers who have nothing to sell but their labour are much more sure of a market for it and are able to sell it at a better price. No doubt, new kinds of inequality have arisen; but the kinds that go along with class divisions as Marx understood them are much less important than they were. Yet there is little evidence that men feel less helpless, less lost, in society than they used to do, or that they are less driven by passion than they used to be to flout social rules.

Marx was so certain that *alienation* springs from the division of society into classes – from the pursuit of profit, from unrestricted competition, from the treatment of labour as a commodity – that he never stopped to enquire how far it was due to the scale and complexity of industrial society. Men can no longer rely, as their ancestors could, on custom and tradition to guide them; for they live in societies which are swiftly changing as well as immense. Whether the societies they live in are bourgeois or proletarian, men are still apt to lose their social bearings, to feel isolated and rootless, to feel themselves impelled into courses of action which do not satisfy them. It may be possible to save them from these feelings which (as Marx saw) move them to crime. But it seems that it cannot be done merely by abolishing social classes and exploitation as Marx understood them.

Given a certain definition of class, a society becomes classless as soon as there are no groups inside it falling under the definition. Marx disliked the division of society into classes, and he also disliked inequality. Unfortunately, he took it for granted that where there were no classes there would be no inequality. He never asked himself whether society, even though it should become classless, might continue to produce inequalities leading to *alienation*. He disliked capitalism, and took it for granted that, when it disappeared, the harmful effects of competition and the division of labour would disappear as well; he never enquired whether they might survive in a socialist society which was also industrial.[1] He believed that *alienation* is in large part a result of using money. The pursuit of profits is the pursuit of money, and under capitalism the measure of a man's success is the amount of money he can make. Money is only a medium of exchange, but the capitalist economy drives men to pursue it as if it were worth having for its own sake. This attack on money is an old theme of the moralists to which Marx adds twists of his own. He is eloquent and ingenious. But to quite what purpose?

[1] Some socialists have so defined a socialist society that it is by definition very little competitive. But a classless society in which there is no private property in the means of production can be intensely competitive and can induce in those who are outdistanced a sense of failure that is deeply frustrating. The Soviet Union is as fiercely competitive as the United States.

Will there be no money in the classless society of the future, which is to be as industrial and enterprising as bourgeois society? Is not the use of money, in some form or other, essential in every society in which there is a great division of labour? And must there not be such a division wherever modern techniques of production are used? And even should the coming of plenty make the pursuit of money pointless, will not men compete for other things to prove their superiority over one another? How are we to distinguish between the kinds of competition that produce *alienation* and the kinds that produce cultural solidarity? How can we know that the disappearance of classes as Marx defines them will leave us with only the kinds that produce such solidarity, so that organized force is no longer needed to maintain order?

c. Management and Hierarchy

Can we suppose, as Marx and Engels seem to do, that, in the classless society, administration will consist only of business management and the adjudication of disputes? The classless society is to renounce none of the benefits of large-scale industrial production. It must therefore have a highly complicated economy. What exactly are the workers to take over? Are they to take over each separate factory and enterprise and to run it as they think fit? If they do that, the economy, considered as a whole, will be just as little managed as it was under capitalism in Marx's day. There will be competition and the risk of economic anarchy. Are the workers to take control of the entire economy? But if they do that, they undertake much more than mere business management.

We must not be the dupes of words. The control of a factory or farm is essentially different from the control of an entire economy. To call both these activities business management or administration, and to leave it at that, is to mask, or at least to play down, the differences between them. The manager of a business organizes production for the market; the controller of an entire economy plans over-all production for the benefit of every section of an immense community. If administration is taken to be the sort of thing that the manager of a business does, and if government is taken to be (as it often was in Marx's time) the keeping of order and the settling of disputes, then the running of an entire economy for the benefit of all concerned is neither administration nor government. It is a kind of activity with which we are now familiar but which was much less known in Europe a hundred years ago. This activity – since it is primarily concerned, not with increasing profits and lowering costs, but with reaching goals which are not commensurable, and are not to be understood apart from accepted notions of justice, decency, dignity and freedom – clearly comes closer to being *political* than *economic*, as those terms were understood long before Marx's day and are still understood in our day; though it may be that in Marx's time the term political, owing largely to the influence of the *laissez-faire* economists, was used more narrowly than either before or since.

But the word we choose to describe this activity does not much matter. What matters is that the activity is vast in scale and many-sided, involving not only hierarchy and desk-work, but the making of decisions different in kind from those made by the manager of a business. It calls for special training, great experience and, at the upper levels of the hierarchy, uncommon talents. It cannot, as Marx and Engels sometimes imply, be a part-time activity of the workers. It is full-time work for men who make such work their profession.

Of the three versions of what is involved in the disappearance of a hierarchy of persons, *separate* from the rest of society, managing its common affairs, only the third is at all realistic, though what Marx and Engels say suggests that it is the one they had least often in mind. This version makes *separate from* the rest of society equivalent to *not closely responsible* to it. If we accept this version, then, in the classless society which is also highly industrialized, the management of common affairs, though it is a massive and diverse undertaking and the full-time occupation of thousands, will be the work of persons closely responsible to the rest of society.

But how is that to be contrived? This is a question never really faced by the founders of Marxism. How, in a large and complicated society, can persons whose full-time occupation is the management of common affairs be made closely responsible to the people, who can spare only a little time to consider these affairs? How can the great majority, who are inevitably largely ignorant, control the actions of a minority much more knowledgeable than they are?

If we retain Rousseau's model of democracy – if we think in terms of a *will of the people* put into effect by their agents – we cannot solve this problem. As Rousseau saw, his model can apply only to a small and simple community whose citizens themselves constitute the legislature. In an advanced industrial society, where the important decisions, even when they are made by an elected assembly, are made by a body tens of thousands of times less numerous than the people on whose behalf it takes them, there is no *will of the people* as Rousseau understood it. The people do not decide the great issues of policy, and then appoint agents to carry out their decisions; at best, they merely choose the persons who are to make the decisions, having only the vaguest ideas about what those decisions should be. If we are to speak realistically of representative democracy on a vast scale, we must use another model than Rousseau's. We must speak of organized bodies whose function is to define and promote the interests of all important sections of the community; of the freedom to form such bodies; of the need to ensure that they are so organized as to be highly responsive to the demands and feelings of their members; of the need for procedures enabling these bodies to compete fairly for the attention of the government and to reach settlements which seem just to them; of the need to ensure that governments lose power when they lose the people's confidence. We have to ask, as Marx and Engels did not ask, What institutions and what rules of political conduct best serve these needs?

I suspect that Marx and Engels accepted, for the classless society of the future, something not unlike Rousseau's model of democracy. Of course, they did not accept, as he did, the enduring need for organized force, and they did not want a simple society; but they did share his belief that, in the community of equals, the deciding of important public issues is the part-time occupation of all the members of the community. It is their business to decide in principle what shall be done, though they may appoint agents to execute their will and even to take minor decisions of policy.

I think it probable that Marx and Engels were victims of their own phrases. Having called the State an instrument of class rule, they were disposed to take it for granted that the enormous machinery of the modern State is needed because that State is the most repressive of all forms of organized force or because the task of repression is now more difficult than it used to be. To keep scattered and illiterate serfs in order, there was no need for such massive organs of repression as are now needed to hold down a proletariat congregated in large towns and fast growing in literacy and political intelligence. The modern State is a heavier lid on a pot boiling more furiously than ever.

One after another, the organs of the nineteenth-century State, authoritarian or liberal, are dismissed as serving the interests of the exploiting class. There would not be large armies were it not that the class structure of bourgeois society makes the bourgeois State aggressive, and were it not also that armies are needed to supplement the police in maintaining domestic order. If it were not for the division of society into classes, there would be no huge departments of State, no courts with professional judges and lawyers, and no assembly elected at long intervals, ostensibly to represent the people, but actually to increase the pressure on the executive of the wealthy and exploiting classes.

It is taken for granted that these organs, because they are often used for the benefit of some classes against others in a society divided into classes, will disappear in a classless society. But why should that be so? Are not some of them needed in any large industrial society? What evidence is there that classless societies are less aggressive than others, and that therefore, in a world consisting only of classless societies, there would be no need for armies? Are the proletariat less inclined to war than other classes? If there is more pacifism in the world today than there was in Marx's time, is this because the workers now have more influence than they had or because war has changed its character and is much more to be feared?

d. The Paris Commune and the Soviets

Marx admitted that, in the modern State, power grows at the higher levels at the expense of the lower levels of government. Sometimes he welcomed its doing so. The revolutionary State of the Jacobins was stronger and more centralized than the old French monarchy, and it needed to be so in order to destroy the remains of feudalism. Marx derided the German liberals of 1848 for wanting to give Germany a federal constitution. What Germany needed was a strong central government to do for her what the Jacobins had done for France. About the Paris Commune of 1871, which he hailed as the first proletarian government, he spoke equivocally: although it wanted to dissolve France into a loose confederation of communes, he defended it by denying that it wanted to do what in fact it did want to do – which was to destroy the power of the centralized State.[1] Marx seems to have believed that the modern State, bourgeois or proletarian, must be strong at the centre to carry out its class purposes: to destroy the vestiges of feudalism and to defend capitalist social relations in the bourgeois State, or to destroy the vestiges of capitalism in the proletarian State.

Marx's defence of the Paris Commune is a defence of proletarian government, of a form of the State. We cannot infer from it how he conceived that *administration*, as distinct from *government*, would be organized in a classless society. We know that he thought proletarian government the most popular of all forms of government, and the institutions of the proletarian State the best adapted to serve the interests of the great majority. Proletarian government, if we take the Paris Commune as an example (however imperfect) of it,

[1] See *The Civil War in France*, sect. III, op. cit., pp. 333–40.

271

is, though democratic, neither parliamentary nor presidential. The legislative assembly is elected annually, deputies can be recalled if they displease their constituents, and the executive is elected by the assembly. Parliamentary government, in the eyes of Marx and Engels, is essentially bourgeois, and so too is the separation of powers as we find it in the United States.

We cannot know how Marx and Engels imagined that the classless society would be administered. They reveal their minds so little that it would be foolish to attribute definite opinions to them. I shall therefore confine myself to considering the possibilities.

The Communards in Paris, though Marx pretended otherwise, wanted to destroy the power of the central government in France. Many of them were very much influenced by the teachings of Proudhon, who was a kind of anarchist. They believed, as Marx did, that in the society of equals there would be no centralized State and eventually almost no need for the use of force to keep order. They wanted the smallest administrative unit in France, the commune, to be sovereign, being responsible to its members alone for how it managed communal affairs. Matters common to a district larger than the commune were to be settled by delegates chosen by all the communes in the district, and the delegates were to be bound by their instructions; and matters common to a region larger than a district were to be transacted by delegates from all the districts in the region, also closely bound by their instructions. This gives us a pyramidal structure rather like the Russian system before the Stalin Constitution – that is, like the Russian system, not as it really was, but as it was supposed to be by its apologists. This Russian system was said by its champions to be more truly democratic than any other then existing; it was alleged in its favour that it made government at every level more closely responsible to the people than any Western parliamentary government. It made all public officials mere agents of the people or of their representatives.

This Russian system, as it was described by its champions, as it was on paper, did not really correspond to the system which Marx insisted that the Communards had wanted to establish in France; but it did correspond rather more closely to the true aspirations of the Communards. In other words, the illusions of its apologists about the Soviet system before the Stalin Constitution came closer to the real aspirations of the Communards than to the aspirations attributed to them by Marx; whereas the Soviet system, as it really was, came closer to being what Marx mistakenly believed the Communards had wanted for France.

Certainly, the Communard Constitution – *as it really was* – was not in the least a suitable model for the proletarian State, as Marx conceived of it; for the rôle assigned to that State by Marx was to use force boldly to establish its authority and to destroy the vestiges of the old order. And nobody was more convinced than Marx that a revolutionary State carrying out such a rôle would need to be highly centralized. Indeed, it was because he was convinced both of this and of the proletarian character of the Paris Commune that he was so strongly impelled to misinterpret the Communard Constitution.

But it may be that Marx – though he would not have accepted the Communard Constitution, as it really was, as a model for a proletarian State – might have thought it well suited, with certain modifications, to serve as a model for the administration of a classless society. I do not say that he would or that he would not; I say only that it is a possibility not excluded by anything that he or Engels says about communist society. The Communard Constitution was a scheme inspired by anarchists as certain as Marx ever was that in the classless society, the society of equals, there would be no need for the State, no need for government as distinct from administration. And Marx, though he differed strongly from the anarchists about how the transition to the classless society should be made, was yet considerably influenced by their ideas; he looked forward to anarchy, if not as lovingly, at least as confidently, as they did, and what hints he gave as to what the society of equals would be like suggest that his image of it did not differ greatly from theirs.

The Communards, many of them disciples of Proudhon, looked upon the French State of their time as an instrument of class rule; they saw and disliked in it all the features which Marx and Engels said were characteristic of the State. They intended, in their projected constitution for France, to abolish the old State and to put in its place an administrative system suited to the needs of a society of equals. The scheme they put up for France to adopt was inspired by just the same doctrine about the State as the one which caused Engels to predict that, with the coming of the classless society, the State would *die out* or *wither away*.[1]

Now, this scheme can be shown to be unworkable. It can only give the appearance of working when it is controlled by some body which decides beforehand what decisions shall be taken at each level of the pyramid. The bodies lower down the pyramid are busy, most of the time, discussing their own affairs, which are in many ways different

---

[1] See *Anti-Dühring*, Part III, ch. II, op. cit., p. 268.

from the affairs of the bodies higher up. The affairs of a village are not the affairs of Normandy or of France. If the persons elected by the lowest bodies to the bodies immediately above them are mere delegates bound to carry out their instructions, how can the higher bodies reach any decisions? Suppose that each of twelve delegates gets different instructions from the others. How is a decision possible? There can be no decision unless at least seven of the delegates reach agreement, which requires that six of them, if not all seven, agree to something which does not accord with their instructions. Those who vote against the decision can remain true to their instructions only at the cost of being out-voted. But if each delegate is merely told that his electors have certain preferences, and is instructed to vote for whatever proposal has a chance of acceptance and accords best with these preferences, he ceases to be a mere delegate. What proposal is accepted cannot be inferred from the instructions given to the twelve delegates; it depends on the trend of the discussion between them. The supposedly mere delegate becomes in fact a representative.

The lowest bodies, moreover, cannot be sovereign. If the system is to work at all, they must abide loyally by the decisions reached at higher levels, whether they like those decisions or not. In a highly industrial society, the decisions they take must in practice be closely limited by the decisions taken by the bodies above them. Their own decisions are not the most important, and their influence on other decisions is the smaller the higher up the pyramid we go. By the time we get to the top, the instructions given to the delegates chosen by the lowest authorities have little bearing on the decisions actually taken. They are too remote and too irrelevant.

Logically, it is possible for all decisions reached by a higher body to be referred back for approval to the lowest bodies within its region, the supposedly sovereign bodies. But what rule should govern this process? Should each lowest body be bound by a decision reached at a higher level only if it votes in favour of it? That rule alone preserves its sovereignty. But there are many decisions not worth anyone's acting upon unless all whom it concerns are bound by it. Or should the rule be that all the lowest bodies are bound by decisions endorsed by a majority of them? In that case, it is no longer true that each lowest body is sovereign.

Even if the second rule is adopted, the process is absurdly cumbersome. It can be made to appear to work only where all the bodies at the lowest level are in fact controlled by one party or organized group ensuring that compatible decisions are taken quickly at that lowest level, and therefore also at all levels above it. But this remedy takes the life out of the system, reducing it to make-believe. It is what happened in Russia with the soviets almost as soon as they were established. The country would have been ungovernable if the soviets at the lowest level – in the factories and villages – had really been sovereign, and if the soviets above them had consisted of mere delegates. The country was saved from chaos because all the soviets at all levels were controlled by the Bolsheviks, who saw to it that they took the decisions which the party decided they should take. The chaos that threatened Russia was ascribed to the illiteracy and political inexperience of the people. No doubt, they were illiterate and without experience. But that was not the only cause of confusion and disorder. The system was unworkable. The pyramid of soviets was not a possible structure of administration; it could only be a screen to hide the real structure from view.

Where in an industrial society there are many units and several different levels of authority, the units at the top (or at the centre) will be responsible to the people only if they are elected by them. Not everyone who has authority at the centre need be directly elected, but those who take the important decisions, the policy-makers, must be so. The central legislature must be directly elected, if the central government is to be democratic. If the legislature is elected indirectly, at several removes from the people, there may or may not be chaos but there cannot be democracy. The more industrial a society, the more the really important decisions must be taken at the centre. Therefore, if the society is to be democratic, the persons taking these decisions must be directly responsible to the people. There must be a periodic and free judgement passed by the people on the central legislature and executive. That is precisely what the systems called 'bourgeois' by the Marxists provide for – whether, as in Britain, the same election produces a legislature and an executive, or whether, as in the United States, there are separate elections for the two branches.[1]

This does not mean that local autonomies are not worth preserving or enlarging, that the trend towards centralized administration ought not to be resisted, that devolution is undesirable. The more active your lesser authorities within the spheres of their competence, the better for democracy. No matter how industrial, how closely integrated, your society, there are always many decisions which are best not

[1] There are, of course, other models than the British and the American. A general election need not be a virtual choice of government, as it is in Britain; it may merely decide that governments are to be taken from one part of the legislature rather than another. But where the people come to believe, as they did in France under the Fourth Republic, that how they vote has little to do with deciding how they are governed, or by whom, democracy is in danger.

taken at the centre, and others which need not be taken there. The democrat will be rightly concerned that decisions which can be taken locally should be so taken. But this does not affect the point at issue. However desirable it may be that local autonomies should be preserved or enlarged, the fact remains that, in industrial societies, many – indeed most – of the important decisions must be taken at the centre. Therefore, unless the persons who take them are directly responsible to the people, the society, no matter how impressive its pyramidal structure of administration, has gone only a little way towards being democratic.

Often, in a pre-industrial society, where villages are almost self-supporting and small towns depend for their living on the districts immediately surrounding them, there can be really considerable local autonomies, even though authority at the centre is quite irresponsible. And the local authorities can be democratic, though in fact they have more often been aristocratic or oligarchic. What they are depends on local circumstances rather than on the character of the central government. Thus, there can be autocracy at the centre and aristocracy or even democracy at lower levels of government. Yet the power of the central government, great though it is on paper, is in fact much smaller than it appears. The central government must in practice respect the rights of the authorities subordinate to it. But, in an industrial society, the power of the central government is necessarily much greater. Therefore, where the central government is not democratic, it is most unlikely that the authorities in fact subordinate to it (whatever their rights on paper) are so. It is not impossible but is unlikely – except where there are good grounds for believing that the central government is intent upon setting up democracy among a backward people and is making a beginning at the lower levels. In that case, we must look at the record of the government and of the party that controls it. We must enquire what they have done to justify the belief that they honestly desire to establish democracy, and whether they know how to set about achieving their purpose.

e. Conflicts in the Classless Society

Marx and Engels were precluded by their own theory about classes and the State from considering the group conflicts that might arise in a society which was classless in their sense of class. They set a fashion which their disciples have followed. They made a number of statements about conflicts between classes, and said that the State is needed because there are these conflicts. They never stopped to enquire whether such conflicts could arise between groups which were not classes in their sense. Wherever they looked they saw only what they wanted to see; they saw only class conflicts. This was so partly because they looked most closely at the societies and epochs which came nearest to bearing out their thesis; they looked at the history of Western Europe from the fifteenth century onward, and at the periods of Greek and Roman history when class conflicts were most bitter. It was so also because, without knowing that they did so, they used the word *class* in other senses than the sense they defined; they spoke of class conflicts when the groups in conflict were not classes in their sense. This is what Engels did when he spoke of classes with irreconcilable interests arising at the break-up of tribal society and the emergence of the State.[1]

Conflicts are difficult to settle for one or both of two reasons: because there is no procedure generally accepted for their settlement, or because the parties to them have widely different conceptions of justice and honour. These two reasons are closely connected: where there is an agreed procedure, there tend to be the same conceptions of justice and honour, and, where these conceptions are the same, there is usually an agreed procedure, or it is easy to set one up where it is lacking. Not all conceptions of justice and honour need be the same or closely similar; it is enough that the relevant ones should be so. Two countries with different conceptions of justice and honour in family life do not therefore find it difficult to have pleasant relations with one another.

As far as I can see, there are no grounds for believing that in a society without classes, in the Marxian sense of class, these two reasons making difficult the settlement of disputes will not operate. No doubt, in a society which is classless in some other sense, they may not operate. We can even define a classless society as one in which there are no groups having widely different conceptions of justice and honour or different ideas about how disputes should be settled. I suspect that Marxists sometimes – perhaps often – when they speak of a classless society, have this also in mind. I should not quarrel with them for using the phrase in this sense; I should quarrel with them

---

[1] As Engels describes it, the break-up of tribal authority involves a change in the system of property. Common ownership gradually gives way to private property, and this transformation is accompanied by the rise of groups with 'irreconcilable' interests. But, as we have seen already, these groups with 'irreconcilable' interests are not, *to begin with*, different classes in the Marxian sense, though Engels calls them classes; they do not differ in their rights of property, and yet they have 'irreconcilable' interests in the sense of divergent interests leading to disputes which require a new type of authority – the State – to settle them.

only if they took it for granted that a socialist or communist society must be classless, if that is what classless means.

3. 'Backward' Societies and Their Political Problems

a. Two Assumptions

When we call society *backward* we make either or both of two assumptions: that there is a normal course of social evolution, or that some social forms are more desirable than others. Logically, if we make one of these assumptions, we need not make the other; and it has often happened that only one has been made. But in the nineteenth century it was usual for radicals to make both, and in this respect Marx and Engels followed the common example.

Their assuming that there is a normal course of social change did not prevent them from allowing exceptions. Though they predicted that socialism would come to most countries after a violent revolution, they allowed that in Britain and the United States it might come without violence; and Marx at one time thought it possible that the proletariat might first get power in Germany, though Germany was then more 'backward' than either France or England; and later he thought it possible that the revolution bringing socialism might even break out in Russia, which he took to be the most backward of the great European Powers. But, though Marx and Engels were willing to admit that there might be exceptions, they were never moved to examine critically their assumption that there is a normal course of social change.

I have tried to explain elsewhere what is peculiar about this assumption.[1] A biological organism which grows or has a normal course of change and span of life can be easily identified; it develops in a more or less stable environment, and its growth is not affected by the growth of other organisms. But what is the subject of which we predicate a normal course of *social* change? Whatever principle we adopt to classify societies, we find few societies belonging to any one type, and we find great differences even among those few. How, then, can we speak of a normal course of change for any one type of society, not to speak of all types? And what is to constitute a single society for this purpose? Can we treat a community like England as a single society? Clearly, Marx did not do so. He had in mind, not independent States, but large populations with broadly similar productive methods and social institutions. The society whose evolution is described in

[1] In my *German Marxism and Russian Communism*, ch. 5, pp. 76–81.

Capital is not England or France or Germany but Western Europe from the later Middle Ages to the nineteenth century. But what exactly were the confines of this society? Where did it end and other societies begin? To what extent was it one society distinct from others?

If people having similar institutions constitute a society, we can divide mankind into separate societies in more than one way, depending on the institutions we choose to take into account. If we take some into account, France and England are parts of the same society; if we take others, they are separate societies. We have here, moreover, not only the difficulty of deciding into what class to place a thing, but the further difficult of locating the thing we want to classify – the difficulty of separating it from other things. The entomologist may be puzzled as to whether the insect he is examining belongs to one species or another, or even as to whether it is an insect or some other form of life, but at least he knows it as a specimen separate from all others. He can distinguish it from its environment. It is a distinct individual in the animal kingdom. There may be other systems of classification than the one he uses, and, if another were used, his specimen would be differently classified. But it would be put entire into a different class.

A population, however, which is the whole of a society of one type may be only a part of a society of another type, and may contain several societies of a third type. Or again, people living within a given area who at one time belong to the same society because they share certain institutions may at another time belong to different societies because they no longer share them. I must not elaborate on these points, which I have discussed at greater length elsewhere. I repeat them only to show how improbable it is that mankind can be divided into societies following a normal course of change.

When we speak of a normal course of social evolution we use ideas taken from biology to explain social change, and we use them improperly. Perhaps because society consists only of persons, we are tempted to apply to it ideas which apply to its constituents; man has a normal course of maturation and senescence, and a normal span of life. We see society as man writ large, as the macrocosm of which he is the microcosm. Sometimes, since man is a contriver, a mechanic, we see society as his product, as the instrument he has devised to attain his ends. But, if we look more deeply, we see that society is not deliberately man-made; we see that, though it is the product of his activities, it is an unintended product. We see also that man is deeply affected by his social environment, and differs greatly from one society to another. And so, forced to admit that society is not made by man, we are tempted to speak of it as if, like man, it grew – as if it followed a normal course of change determined by what it is. Change which touches us so nearly, if it is not contrivance, must be growth. We do not like to admit that it is neither the one nor the other.

It is true that not every normal course of change known to us is biological, consisting either of organic growth and decay or of a course of mental evolution closely connected with organic change. We can speak of a normal course of moral or cultural change, which may differ considerably from society to society, though the individuals subject to it are biologically the same. This course of change is much more difficult to observe and to measure than organic growth, and more difficult even than the psychological change connected with that growth. Yet we can sometimes construct a realistic model of normal cultural or moral development because, in a given social environment, we can find a large number of persons exposed to fairly similar social influences. We can speak plausibly enough, for example, of a normal course of moral or cultural development for an English child born into the professional class or into the manual working class; we can even speak of a normal course of cultural development for the child born in the West or in a Westernized community. The more we know about how social environments differ and about the children born into them, the more we can distinguish what, in a child's moral and cultural development, is common to societies of many types from what is peculiar to one type and therefore normal only inside it.

Here we are considering only individuals. There are many of them in every more or less stable environment, and so, by taking a random sample, we can construct our model of a normal course of change. But we cannot do it as easily with communities – not even where we are able to identify them in their separateness. For communities differ from one another much more than individuals do, and their social environments are much less similar. It is far more difficult to find many communities of much the same type and exposed to much the same external influences, and to show that they have changed in much the same ways. No doubt, there are many towns and villages in Europe and Asia which have existed for centuries as separate and self-conscious units. They are the most easily identified, and they were, until the rise of the nation-state, perhaps the most sharply self-conscious of communities. But we can hardly speak of a normal course of change, even for English villages, so greatly have they differed from one another in size and structure, and so enormous the variety of influences that have touched them. Or, if we do speak of it, we are immediately aware that this is merely a device of explanation, and we heap one qualification upon another in the attempt to get closer to the truth. The shorter the period we take and the smaller the area, the more confidently we speak. This, we say, is what was happening to the villages along the Welsh borders in the second half of the fifteenth century. But we would not presume to speak so confidently of a course of change undergone by the villages of England from the fifteenth to the nineteenth centuries. If we cannot speak in this way of the most compact, easily identified, and numerous communities, how can we do so of the loose and shapeless giants whose limits in space and history we are hard put to it to determine? To construct a model of a normal course of change we must have many specimens, easily discerned and closely similar in structure, from which we can take a representative sample.

b. Two Types of 'Normal' Evolution

There are thus two kinds of *normal evolution*, which we are apt to call *organic change* or *growth*, though one differs profoundly from the other. How a plant or an animal evolves, from the moment at which it acquires a separate identity, depends on what sort of plant or animal it is. The seed of a rose will not grow into a lily. Provided its physical environment is suitable, the seed, being what it is, will grow into a rose bush. This is the properly organic change. But the cultural development of a child depends on the social influences to which it is exposed in a quite different way from that in which the growth of a plant depends on its physical environment. No doubt, unless the child were, biologically and psychologically, the sort of creature it is, these influences would not affect it as they do. Yet the influences are not conditions of organic growth; we cannot say of them that they must be present to allow of a course of change determined by the structure of what changes. If an English child were exposed to other social influences, it would still develop culturally, but the development would be very different. It is therefore improper to call it organic. And yet we can properly call it normal, where there are many children exposed to much the same social influences. So also, though much more cautiously, we may speak of a normal course of evolution for communities of the same general type exposed over a certain period of time to the same external influences.

Neither Marx nor Engels troubled to distinguish between these two types of a normal course of change. Does that mean that we cannot say whether they had one or other of the two in mind? I do not think so. For, like most of the philosophers and historians of their day who spoke of a course of social evolution in the West, they thought of it as almost untouched by external influences. They spoke as if how society evolves were determined by its structure, by the complex of operations which it is; or, at least, they came closer to this way of speaking than to any other. They took man's nature and physical environment for granted, and sought the cause of social change in the nature of changing society. We may therefore say that the normal course of social evolution which they had in mind, most of the time if not all of it, was organic.

Yet they could not ignore the fact that societies – even the vast and amorphous society they had in mind when they spoke of a normal course of social evolution – can deeply affect one another. Though they took almost no notice of external influences on the West, they often insisted that the influence of the West on other parts of the world was profound. They could not shut their eyes to the obvious: that countries poorer and less powerful than the great Western Powers were exposed to their influence, and were therefore, by reason of that exposure, differently placed from the Western countries. Can the course of social change in a 'backward' country, deeply influenced by a country more 'advanced' than itself, be the same as the course in the country that influences it? Marx and Engels did not exactly address their minds to this question. They may even perhaps have unconsciously turned away from it because of the difficulties it creates for persons committed to such a theory as theirs. But they could not avoid it altogether. When Marx, towards the end of his life, considered the impact on 'backward' Russia of Western techniques and ideas still unknown to the West at the time when it was at roughly the same stage of evolution as Russia then was, he could not deny that Russia's advance towards socialism might be different from that of the West.

But, though we can sometimes notice, in the writings of Marx and Engels, a certain awareness that 'backward' societies deeply affected by 'advanced' ones are placed as the 'advanced' societies never were, they do not appear to have given much thought to the matter or considered its implications for their theory. The 'advanced' societies of the West contain only a minority of mankind. Must we therefore conclude that the social evolution of only a minority is normal? But the West, too, has been deeply influenced in the past by other societies. How, then, in a world in which every society has, at some time or other, been deeply influenced by other societies, can there be a *normal* course of social evolution? Is it the course that a society would follow if it were never influenced by other societies, or never deeply influenced by them? But how can we discover what that course would be?

We have seen that Marxism, like other theories of its kind, makes two assumptions: that there is a normal course of social evolution, and that some social forms are more desirable than others. Thus, one society may be more 'advanced' than another in either or both of two senses: it may be further along the normal course or it may have social forms which are more desirable. Usually, but not always, Marx and his disciples speak as if a society were necessarily more advanced in the second sense when it is more advanced in the first. Serfdom belongs, they think, to a later stage of social evolution than slavery, and is also a milder form of exploitation; and they speak of the proletarian, who belongs to a still later age, as freer than the serf. Since they in fact condemn exploitation and approve of freedom, we can conclude that, by their standards, it is better to be a serf than a slave, and better to be a proletarian than a serf. But they also admit that in tribal societies there is greater equality than in the societies coming after them, and they sometimes speak as if exploitation must grow worse as capitalism grows older.[1]

Apart from these two assumptions, there is another which Marx and Marxists ordinarily make; they take it for granted that when an 'advanced' society impinges on a 'backward' one, it hastens its progress, moving it more quickly along the normal course and bringing it nearer the desirable goal; or else that, if it deflects it from the normal course, it does not push it onto another course which takes longer to reach what is ultimately desirable or which leads away from it. Their usual assumption is that the progress of 'backward' societies is quickened by the impact upon them of the more 'advanced', and they take little account of the possibility that the progress of the more 'advanced' may be retarded. Admittedly, Marx and Marxists do not say this in so many words, but it is not, I think, unfair to them to say that they often take it for granted.

c. The Impact of 'Advanced' on 'Backward' Societies

In only one of his writings does Marx take serious account of the effects on a 'backward' society of the impact upon it of a more 'advanced' one. In the 'Address to the Communist League' he admits that Germany is more backward than France or England, and yet expects the German Communists – the members of that league – to take an active part in the coming revolution, exhorting them,

---

[1] There is a certain ambiguity here. What comes after may, in itself, be worse than what went before it, and yet may be more desirable as bringing us closer to the best, which comes last.

so far as they can, to control its course. He sees Germany as a still partly 'feudal' country where the bourgeois have yet to make, or to complete, the revolution which their class have already made in England and France.[1] When the bourgeois in those two countries made their revolutions, there was no scope for the sort of activities to which Marx urged the German Communists in the 'Address'. England and France were not influenced by countries more advanced than themselves. But the situation in Germany in 1848 was different. Socialist ideas had penetrated into that country while it was still partly feudal, and had attracted many of the workers in the towns. Marx believed that Germany, though she had still to complete her bourgeois revolution, already had a proletariat capable, if properly led, of acting independently of the bourgeois; whereas in France, during the great revolution, the workers in Paris had been the tools of the bourgeois. If in Germany in 1849 the workers need not be such tools, it was presumably because socialist doctrines and proletarian organizations were already developed enough to enable them to know their own class interests and to act decisively to promote them. Though Marx advised the League and the workers to co-operate with the bourgeois parties to complete what he called *a democratic petit-bourgeois revolution* – that being the unavoidable next step in the advance towards communism – he also told them to mistrust their bourgeois allies, and to harass and frighten them into making as many concessions as possible to the workers. He even believed that the Communists and workers, if they used the tactics he advised, might stampede their bourgeois allies into converting the great 'feudal' estates and larger industrial undertakings into public property, thus making easier the eventual passage from a capitalist to a socialist economy.

Though Marx believed that Germany's situation in 1849 was unlike that of France in the 1790s – though he saw her progress towards socialism as different in important respects – he did not see Germany as moving on a widely different course. A bourgeois revolution in which the workers take an independent and decisive part is, of course, different from one in which they do not, and has different and important consequences. If those to whom Marx gave his advice had been able and willing to take it, Germany after her 'bourgeois revolution' would have been different, in important respects, from the France of the first Napoleon and the restored monarchy. But the difference would not have consisted in events happening in Germany

---

[1] See the 'Address of the Central Authority to the League' ['Address to the Communist League'], in Marx and Engels, *Collected Works*, vol. 10, pp. 281–7.

which had never happened or never would happen in France; it would have consisted merely in events happening in Germany simultaneously or hard upon one another's heels which in France had been, or would be, separated by considerable intervals. There would have been a telescoping of events in Germany which would even – so great were Marx's hopes at that time for his own country – have put her in some ways ahead of countries until then in all ways ahead of her. Though socialist ideas and proletarian organizations were more widespread and stronger in France and England than in Germany, the bourgeois were also stronger and more firmly in power; and so 'backward' Germany had in 1849 (in Marx's eyes) an opportunity to take a leap forward which would put her, in some respects, in the van of progress.

There is no trace, in Marx's 'Address' of a fear that the Communist League and the workers, by trying to force the pace towards socialism, might set going a train of events which would lead Germany away from it. Though the passage from capitalism to socialism might be different in Germany from what it would be in England or France, it was still inevitable. Marx could conceive of a society which was part capitalist and part socialist just as he could conceive of one which was part feudal and part capitalist. He could see that 'backward' countries deeply affected by countries more 'advanced' than themselves might have mixed economies and mixed political systems of a kind that the 'advanced' countries had never had. But it never occurred to him that the countries he called 'backward' might move along courses quite different from the one he took to be normal, because England and France had already moved some way along it; it never occurred to him that these 'backward' countries might acquire social and political systems to which the categories familiar to him did not apply. It never occurred to him – any more than today it occurs to his Russian disciples that the country they govern is no more socialist than capitalist in the senses in which those terms were used by Marx.

So, too, it never occurred to him that the 'advanced' countries might be so deeply affected by their increasingly close ties with the rest of the world as to develop quite differently from how they would otherwise have done. He did suggest that the exploitation of colonies and dependent territories might delay the collapse of capitalism in the West, but he went no further than this. We can conclude, from his rather scanty references to the impact of 'advanced' and 'backward' countries on one another, little more than this: that he was very sure that the effect of 'advanced' on 'backward' countries was to hasten their progress and might sometimes even give them an opportunity of taking a lead, and that he took some notice of the possibility that the effect of 'backward' on 'advanced' countries might be to retard their progress. All countries, he thought, must travel what is essentially the same road; their influence upon one another cannot divert them from it but can only increase or slacken the speed at which they move along it.

The later German Marxists were not much interested in the effects of 'advanced' and 'backward' countries upon one another. They discussed, in much greater detail than either Marx or Engels had done, what they called the later stages of capitalism; they discussed such topics as the increasing concentration of capital, international finance, the failure of the capitalist farmer to displace the peasant on the Continent as he had done in England, the growth of vast working-class organizations in the West able to exert a strong pressure on bourgeois governments. They refined upon the doctrines of the two masters and sometimes revised them. They were the most learned, the most thoughtful, the most intellectually fertile of the disciples of Marx. But only when they discussed imperialism did they turn their minds to the problem of the relations between 'advanced' and 'backward' countries. They were interested in them only from the point of view of the 'advanced' countries, confining themselves to little more than the elaboration of Marx's suggestion that the exploitation by the West of the rest of the world slowed down the trend towards falling profits and thus delayed the collapse of Western capitalism.

As might be expected, the Russian Marxists were much more interested than the Germans in the impact of 'advanced' societies on 'backward' ones. But they, like Marx, assumed that it could serve only to increase the rate of progress in 'backward' countries. Though they criticized the Populists for teaching that Russia might become socialist without ever passing through industrial capitalism as the West knew it, they were, for obvious reasons, eager to see as many signs as possible of quick progress in their own country. They took the fullest advantage of any hint they could find in the writings of Marx to justify their belief that Russia, though backward, was destined to play a major part in the coming triumph of socialism in the world. The doctrine of the 'uninterrupted revolution', as we find it in the writings of Trotsky and Lenin,[1] is merely an application to Russian

---

[1] The phrase is drawn from Lenin's 'Attitude of Social-Democracy Towards the Peasant Movement'. I do not deny the great historical importance of this doctrine, which I have discussed elsewhere when it seemed relevant to do so (see my *German Marxism and Russian Communism*, ch. 10, pp. 227–40); but in this book, which examines doctrines not because they are historically important but because they enlarge our understanding of society and government, I feel no need to discuss it.

circumstances of ideas to be found in the earlier pamphlets of Marx, above all in the 'Address to the Communist League'.

The Russian Marxists, though sometimes bold, were seldom deep or rigorous thinkers. It would be absurd to say that they were timid in their interpretations of Marxism, that in the realm of doctrine they only followed and never led; for they sometimes drew astonishing conclusions from familiar texts. They were adroit and resourceful. But they were not much concerned with consistency. This is especially true of Lenin and the Bolsheviks. Though they felt – more even perhaps than the German Marxists – the need to be orthodox, to support their policies by copious quotations from Marx and Engels, their concern for orthodoxy was not concern for consistency. The Bolsheviks took from the treasure house of Marxist doctrine whatever they needed to justify what they thought it necessary to do; their skill and audacity were remarkable. What mattered to them was that they should always be able to get support from the same sacred source; it did not matter nearly so much that their various policies should be in keeping with one another or with an internally consistent body of doctrine.

That is why the Bolsheviks or Communists, in spite of the ingenuity and audacity with which they have adapted Marxism to their needs, have never been impelled to think deeply about it, to subject it to rigorous criticism or to revise it drastically to make it more consistent in itself or with the facts. That is why, as social and political theorists, they have been as shallow as they have been bold. It is only the thinker that cares deeply for consistency and adequacy who, when he is bold in action, feels the need to reconcile his policies with the body of doctrine he adheres to. It is not enough for him to quote texts in his own favour; he feels the need to show that the policy he proposes really is in keeping with the doctrine he holds. He is therefore moved to think the doctrine out afresh, to reinterpret it; and if he cannot, when he has done that, show that the policy is in keeping with the doctrine, he will be impelled either to change the policy or to revise the doctrine, or both together. But if he cares greatly for orthodoxy and little for consistency, he is easily satisfied, provided he can find in the sacred texts the quotations he needs. Though he is bold in action and even in thought, producing new doctrines when he needs them with just enough ingenuity to persuade himself that they are in line with the old, he is never moved to reinterpret or to revise the old body of doctrine systematically. Indeed, it would be fatal to him if he did so, for he would undermine the faith on which his energy and courage largely depend.

Thus the Communists – though they have been the Marxists most concerned with applying the doctrine in countries which, in the Marxian scale, are 'backward' – have never been moved to reconsider that doctrine in the light of the problems they have faced. They have been too busy getting and using power to think deeply and rigorously about the faith to which they appeal to justify their having it.

d. The Bolshevik Predicament

Marx and Engels believed that the proletarian revolution, though it might start earlier in one country than another, and even perhaps earlier in a less than in a more 'advanced' country, would quickly spread to all the great industrial countries – the countries dominating the world economically and politically. They believed that the proletarian revolution would be, or would quickly become, a 'world revolution'. This does not mean that it would affect, either simultaneously or in quick succession, all or even most of the countries of the world; it means only that it would spread so quickly among the most 'advanced' countries as to become irreversible. With the workers firmly in control of the industrially more powerful countries, the forces of reaction elsewhere would be too weak to dislodge them. An isolated and premature[1] attempt at proletarian revolution, like the Paris Commune of 1871, might be quickly put down, but a revolution which spread to the whole industrial West would not be at the mercy of forces outside the West. Provided the revolutionaries were strong enough to put down all domestic attempts at counter-revolution, they would be safe in a world where the most powerful countries were controlled by them.

Marx and Engels never considered what would happen if the proletarian revolution did not spread quickly to all or most of the powerful industrial countries; they never contemplated the situation of a country ruled by the industrial workers surrounded by other

---

[1] A revolution which is premature in the sense that, given the situation in which it is made, the revolutionaries can neither succeed in their purpose nor retain power, is not necessarily a revolution which ought not to have been attempted. Marx believed (not altogether accurately) that the Paris Commune *was* a proletarian revolution, an attempt by the workers to seize power in Paris and in France, and he thought it premature because the workers were not strong enough to retain control of Paris, let alone to win control of France. But he did not therefore condemn the attempt. Some defeats, though inevitable at the time, help to bring nearer the ultimate victory; others do not. It is sometimes wise to refuse a fight when you have no chance of victory; and at other times it is unwise, the failure to fight being even more demoralizing than defeat. Though Marx exhorted the workers to prepare carefully for the class war – though he condemned recklessness, though he spoke of *premature* revolution – he never said that it is always a mistake to fight when defeat is certain.

countries, not less powerful, ruled by the bourgeois. They therefore never put to themselves the question, What will the workers' State – the dictatorship of the proletariat – be like in a country surrounded, perhaps for decades, by capitalist countries industrially as powerful as itself? Nor did they ask what would happen to the State in such a country if, when it became classless, it was still surrounded by capitalist Powers. If the State is defined as an instrument of class rule, there can be no State where there are no classes. But where a classless society is surrounded by class societies hostile to it, it must be organized for defence; it must be able to wage war on a much larger scale than a mere tribe can wage it. It must have a military organization as formidable as the armies of the States which surround it. It must have at least some of the attributes which are ordinarily considered attributes of a State.

The Bolsheviks, before they seized power in Russia and retained it for years – before they had reconciled themselves to the idea that their country might be surrounded by capitalist Powers for a long time to come – had been as indifferent as Marx and Engels were to these questions. They too had never contemplated the possibility of a proletarian country isolated for decades in a bourgeois world, or of a classless society obliged to organize its defence against external Powers. They had taken it for granted, as all Marxists had done, that when an industrial society – an 'advanced' society – became classless, there would be no question of its having to wage war against foreign enemies as powerful as itself. Lenin had justified his intention to make what he called a 'proletarian revolution' in backward Russia by arguing that it would spark a world revolution; the example set by Russia would be quickly followed by the Western Powers. The industrially most advanced countries, whose collective power was overwhelming, would soon be proletarian and socialist, and there would be no prolonged isolation of a workers' State in a predominantly bourgeois world. It was only in the years after 1917 that the Bolsheviks, slowly and reluctantly, made some show of facing the problems created for Marxists by the West's remaining obstinately 'capitalist' and 'bourgeois'.

To justify their retaining power, they could not indefinitely use the argument which they had used to justify their seizing it. They could not say that they were touching off in backward Russia a world proletarian revolution which would be successful because it would spread quickly to the most advanced countries – the countries where the 'objective conditions' of socialism and proletarian rule already existed, and whose resources were great enough to enable them to help the workers in more backward countries to create those same conditions. They could not say that a revolution, which would be premature if it were confined to Russia, was not premature because it must soon spread to countries riper for it. They therefore argued that the proletariat, even in a backward country like Russia surrounded by capitalist countries industrially more advanced, could create a socialist society.

The argument is a denial of a basic tenet of Marxism – that socialism can only be established where certain economic and cultural conditions are present. These conditions are developed under capitalism, and so it is impossible to set up socialism successfully where capitalism has not prepared the 'objective conditions' of it. Marx, as we have seen, does not forbid the proletarians from attacking the bourgeois before the time is ripe for their final victory; he does not advocate their doing nothing until the capitalist economy is sufficiently developed to allow the establishment of socialism. The workers must acquire discipline, class solidarity and political experience before they can defeat the bourgeois and set about creating socialism. He foresees a political struggle starting long before the time is ripe for final victory – a struggle in the course of which the workers sustain many defeats, a struggle which is necessary because it prepares the way for victory. The time is not ripe for socialism unless the workers are politically mature, no matter how developed the capitalist economy. But, though he does not put off the proletarian struggle whose goal is socialism until the economy is ripe for socialism, Marx does hold that the struggle will not bring victory until that point is reached; he does not envisage the workers getting political power in the infancy of capitalism and using it to establish the economic and cultural conditions of socialism.[1]

Yet this Bolshevik argument, though it denies a principle basic to Marxism, may well be true. Even if we admit that industrialism and widespread literacy are conditions not only of socialism but of aspirations to socialism, we need not agree that a country must have an industrial economy and a literate working class before it can have a government capable of establishing socialism within it. No doubt, Marx was right in believing that, before the rise of industrial society, socialism, as he and the other socialists of the nineteenth century understood it, was inconceivable – that before men could

[1] This statement needs to be qualified. The advice that Marx gives in his 'Address to the Communist League' does indeed suggest that the workers can use political means to create the economic and cultural conditions of socialism; that is not what he actually says, but it is a fair conclusion from what he does say. Nevertheless, the implications of the advice given in the 'Address' deny a doctrine basic to Marxism.

have such aspirations and could conceive of ways to achieve them, it was necessary that there should be industrial production on a large scale. We can admit this and yet hold, quite consistently, that a devoted minority can use political methods to create the economic and cultural conditions of socialism where they do not exist. Though we admit that the minority would not have acquired socialist aspirations had there not existed somewhere in the world 'the objective conditions' of socialism, we are not bound to concede that men who get their socialist convictions from abroad cannot deliberately create these 'objective conditions' where they do not exist. Indeed, it might be true – I do not say that it is but only that it might be – that, though aspirations to socialism could only have arisen in an industrial society, once they have arisen, it is easier to achieve them in countries on the threshold of industrialism than in countries which are industrially 'mature'. Or if we grant that socialism can be achieved only in an industrial society, we may hold that it is more easily achieved in a country whose industries are the creation of the State than in a country which has become industrial as Britain or France has done. For where there have never been great industrial enterprises in private hands, certain powerful interests strongly opposed to socialism do not exist.

Of these possibilities Marx took no account. Except on rare occasions and almost inadvertently, his doctrines suggest that a country must be already industrial before socialists can hope to gain control of it in order to make it socialist. But this is not to be taken for granted. Though what Marx calls the 'objective conditions' of socialism (conditions as much cultural as economic) are not to be created in a backward country by such methods as the Bolsheviks and their imitators have used, it may be that they could be created by other methods. There are doubtless peculiar and great difficulties facing a government seeking to establish socialism in an economically backward country, but other difficulties, different in kind and perhaps as great, face a government intent upon establishing it in an advanced country. It may be that the difficulties facing the first government are greater than those facing the second; I am inclined to believe that they are, but I am not certain of it. And yet, even if they are greater, it does not follow that the first government cannot succeed in its object.

There is another argument which Marxists have used to show that the attempt to establish socialism in a country isolated in a capitalist world must fail. This argument, unlike the one we have just considered, applies as much when the country striving for socialism is industrially advanced as when it is industrially backward. According to this argument, the governments of the capitalist countries fear the attraction to the classes they exploit of the example of successful socialism; they therefore combine to suppress any government which aims at creating socialism, as soon as it looks as if it might succeed. The class struggle takes the form of hostility between nations, and the nation aspiring to socialism is much weaker than the nations combined against it.

The argument is defective because it is unrealistic. Countries are seldom dominated by classes having well-defined class interests, and it is therefore by no means certain that the governments of the countries called 'capitalist', whose ambitions differ greatly, will want to combine to suppress the dangerous example, or will even agree that it is dangerous. In several, if not most, of the 'capitalist' countries, the workers and socialists are likely to be organized and powerful, and some of their aspirations are likely to be recognized as just by all parties with a hope of forming a government. Socialism will therefore be held by many to be a respectable creed even in the capitalist world. There may well be widespread sympathy in the encircling States for the lone government aspiring to full socialism.

I have no wish to argue in defence of the Bolsheviks, and especially not in defence of the Stalinists. I am not more certain of anything political than that socialism – as Marx and Marxists understood it before 1917 – cannot be established in any country by the methods used by the Bolsheviks. But that has nothing to do with the issue I am now discussing. If we look at the course of events in Russia during the decade before and the decade after the Bolshevik seizure of power, we can see how it came about that the Bolsheviks used the methods they did use. We can see how their party acquired, before 1917, the temper which made it possible for them to resort to such methods, and we can see how, in the situations which arose after 1917, it seemed to them in their own and the country's interest to use them. Perhaps, given the conditions in which they seized power – given the exhaustion and confusion of Russia – they could not have maintained their power except by using methods whose use precludes the creation of a socialist society.[1]

But we must not generalize from the example of Russia. We are not bound to hold that any government aspiring to socialism in an industrially backward and largely illiterate country must either despair

---

[1] It could be argued that, though some of the more brutal methods they used were not needed to maintain their power, others probably were. I think it could also be argued that, long before the October Revolution, the Bolsheviks had become a group unlikely to use methods which could bring socialism to a 'backward' country.

of achieving its object or must, in the endeavour to retain power in order to achieve it, be driven to methods which make it impossible of achievement. There very probably are, as Marx said there were, economic and cultural conditions of socialism; and there are also, as the Bolshevik example teaches us, political methods which must be avoided if socialism, as it was understood by Marxists and by most other socialists before 1917, is to be successfully established in any country, whether it is industrial and literate or not. The temptation to resort to such methods may be unusually great in backward countries, but there were also conditions peculiar to Russia making it difficult for the Bolsheviks to retain power unless they resorted to them.

The Bolsheviks say, and perhaps believe, that they have achieved socialism in Russia, but they can do this only by shutting their eyes to the immense differences between the system they have established and socialism as it was understood before they seized power. Their example is attractive to other 'backward' peoples, partly because they are impressed by the power of Russia and partly because they are not aware of how far what Russia has become under the Bolsheviks falls short of the ideals proclaimed by Marx. It may be easier to achieve what the Bolsheviks have achieved in Russia than what all Marxists before 1917 understood by socialism, and it may be a great temptation to the weaker and poorer nations to try to follow the Russian example, now that Russia has come to seem so formidable to the world. I do not deny this. I am concerned to say no more than that socialism, as the world knew it before the Bolshevik revolution, is an ideal which can reasonably be pursued by a resolute, intelligent and humane minority even in a country which is industrially weak and where most people can neither read nor write. Such a minority would do well to study the activities of the Bolsheviks in Russia, not in order to follow their example, but to learn to avoid their mistakes. And they would perhaps have a better right than the Bolsheviks to call themselves Marxists, for, though they too would be attempting what Marx said was impossible, they would at least be striving for what he thought desirable.

4. The Marxian Ideal

The idea of a normal course of social change, allowing us to call some countries more 'advanced' than others because they are further along it, must be rejected. It may serve to excite people to move more quickly in the direction desired by the exciter; it may be a useful trick of propaganda. But if we try to use it to explain how society changes, we involve ourselves, as Marxists and others have

293

done, in spurious or insoluble problems. No community, no matter how large or small, has ever, during the periods when it could be readily distinguished from other communities, been free of external influences, and we cannot know how it would have evolved if it had been free; and no two communities, except for short periods of time, have been exposed to the same external influences. Untenable also is the conception of the State as an instrument of class rule destined to wither away when society becomes 'classless'. It is by using these ideas, and others equally defective, that Marxists have been caught up in unprofitable[1] disputes about whether it is possible to establish *socialism* in a *backward* country isolated in a *capitalist* world, or about the survival of the *State* in a country which is *socialist* and *classless* but still has to reckon with the enmity of other countries as powerful as itself. It is not difficult, if we follow these disputes at all closely, to uncover the confusions of thought and the contradictions of the persons engaged in them – persons making use of such loose notions as those I have put into italics.

But let us not allow the defects of Marxian theory – defects which have led to such loud and sterile controversy – to blind us to its merits. Some of these merits I have already tried to explain. Marxism is one of the richest and most suggestive of social theories, and is worth careful scrutiny. It has been exciting in two quite different ways: it has deeply moved the radical, dissatisfied with the world as he finds it and in quest of a philosophy to guide his endeavours to change it; and it has stimulated the curiosity and the imagination of the student whose object has been, not to change society or to prevent its changing, but to enlarge our understanding of it.

There is an idea, common to both Hegel and Marx, which – even if it should prove unacceptable in the forms which they give to it, or should need to be greatly qualified – has had a deep influence on many liberal and radical thinkers. This idea is not peculiar to them, though their versions of it, for all their obscurity and elusiveness, are among the most elaborate and most suggestive. It is the idea of *perfectibility*, which receives at their hands dimensions unknown in the eighteenth century, because Hegel penetrates more deeply into the human mind and Marx into the social processes affecting that mind. Though their versions of this idea may be open to criticism on other grounds, they are hardly touched by most of the criticisms levelled more broadly at the Hegelian and Marxian social philosophies. It would be a pity if

[1] I mean intellectually unprofitable, for the disputants have often raised these issues as a manoeuvre to get power or to confound rivals. From their point of view, the disputes have sometimes been immensely profitable.

this idea, so largely and rightly associated with them, were lost in the general condemnation of their systems. It is an idea which deserves to be extracted from those systems and to be considered on its own merits.

It is the idea that men – in the process of coming to understand themselves and their condition as self-conscious creatures living in a coherent world which can be rationally explained – come in the end to acquire a set of values more *adequate* to their nature and condition than any they had before. This idea, as I have now briefly formulated it, cries out for elucidation; but, before I endeavour to make it clearer, I must insist that it is not just another version of the old Stoic and Christian idea of an eternally valid moral law, a law of reason, likened by those who seek to expound it to the axioms of mathematics – a supposedly self-evident law which anyone capable of understanding and defining human nature can see, in his dealing with other persons, applies to all mankind. Even if we should hold, with Hume and with many contemporary philosophers, that moral rules differ in kind both from statements of fact and from the propositions of mathematics and logic, and even if we agree that an *ought* cannot be derived logically from an *is*, we need not reject this Hegelian and Marxian idea.

Admittedly, Hegel's views about statements of fact, mathematical axioms and moral rules differ greatly from Hume's; while Marx, even if we suppose that he had (in the privacy of his mind) views definite enough to deserve consideration, never succeeded in communicating them to the world. After all, Marx was not, in the same sense as Hume and Hegel, a philosopher, a systematic critic of the ideas we use to explain the world or to act in it. But this does not touch the point I am making. No matter what we believe to be the correct explanation of moral rules and value judgements, we are not thereby inhibited from agreeing with Marx and Hegel that men gradually acquire rules and values adequate to their nature and social condition only in the process of coming to understand that nature and condition – a process enduring through many generations in the course of which it modifies its objects. What we come to understand has been altered by the process of our coming to understand it. Rules and values are *adequate* to human nature and the human condition whenever men are so placed, psychologically and socially, that their desires and ambitions are in keeping with one another and with the rules and values they accept, and the means are not lacking to realize them.

Rousseau held that man's usual condition in society is such that there arise in him passions incompatible with one another and with the rules and values he is taught to accept. He therefore only half accepts them;

he is by no means free of their influence, and yet he cannot in practice live by them because of his passions. Both the passions and the values are social products, being what they are because human nature and man's social condition are such and such and not otherwise; they are also human products, effects of man's activity, for society is no more than the living together of men. But they are such that man cannot live a satisfying life – a life in which his passions and his values are in harmony and he is able to fulfil and realize them. Rousseau condemned nearly all human societies for precisely this reason, because they make it impossible for man to live a satisfying life, or, as he put it, 'a life according to nature'. He imagined an ideal society free of the defects of actual society. No doubt, he claimed to understand man's nature and his social condition; he would have agreed that without this understanding he could never have imagined the ideal society. But he was very far from believing either that the coming of the ideal was inevitable or that knowledge is the cure for man's ills.

It is here that Hegel and Marx differ from him; they both imagine – each in his own way – a long process of social, intellectual and moral change leading man steadily but inevitably to the condition where he understands himself and the world, which is also the condition where his passions are in harmony with his values and his most cherished ambitions can be realized with the means at his disposal. In this condition, man is at long last no longer 'alienated' but is at peace with himself – is 'whole' and morally secure in his 'wholeness' – because he is 'at home' in the social world which is both the product and the sphere of his activities.

If we deny – and most critics of Marxism do deny it – that there is any such steady and inevitable process, we are not bound in logic also to deny that there is a set of rules of conduct, a moral code, which all men would accept if they understood man's nature and social condition – a code in keeping with the passions and aspirations which would be strongest in them if they all had that understanding. We may admit this possibility, though we are at pains to insist – against the Stoics and even against Rousseau – that there is no eternally valid moral law in the sense of a set of moral rules which can be derived logically from a true description of human nature or of the divine purpose for man. We can also hold, quite consistently, both that there is a moral code which men – having reached the condition, social and intellectual, enabling them to conceive of it – can see is the most fully adequate to their nature and condition; *and* that all other moral codes – though each is received while social conditions are propitious to it – are inadequate in the sense that men, in those conditions, acquire passions and ambitions difficult or impossible to satisfy and not in keeping with the moral code they accept. In other words, we can, without logical inconsistency, accept *both* the moral relativism of Marx *and* his belief that there is a morality more adequate than the others because it is what men are moved to accept when they have come to understand themselves and the world, when they have taken their own measure and have cheerfully assented to it – a morality they are unlikely to abandon because the understanding which brings it in its train also educates their passions and ambitions to conform with it.

There may have been primitive communities in which men's passions and values were so much in harmony that there was almost no trace of what Marxists call *alienation*. We should have to say of such communities that, in them, moral and cultural values were adequate to human nature and man's social condition, as they then were; and, unless we postulated certain absolute values, we should have no ground for treating them as inferior to more sophisticated communities where the same condition holds. But such communities, if ever they existed, no longer do so now, and are not attractive to civilized peoples, especially when they bear in mind what they would have to forgo in order to re-establish them. Or, if they are attractive, they are out of reach; they cannot be deliberately created. Like innocence, once lost they are never to be recovered.

Rousseau and Hegel both suggest that men, when their passions and values are not in keeping with one another, are profoundly unhappy: they are, as the common phrase has it, 'untrue to themselves'; or, as Rousseau puts it, 'outside themselves'; or, as Hegel says, *alienated*. They are in a painful condition possible only to rational creatures, and only reason can find a remedy for it. As Hegel sees it, men, when they reflect on this condition, strongly desire to change it; they strive, at first confusedly but more deliberately and hopefully as their understanding grows, to set themselves and society in order. They make their way slowly to a condition in which their passions and values are in harmony with one another – where their ambitions are within their powers, where self-respect is possible, where life, though strenuous, seems worth all the effort it calls for, where men need look for nothing outside themselves and the societies they have created to console them for being alive. Rousseau describes the evil but suggests no practicable remedy for it; Hegel has more to say than Rousseau about its social and historical causes and makes bold to predict an inevitable remedy. Rousseau's pessimism is excessive, being as much an effect of temperament as supported by cogent argument; and Hegel's optimism is no better grounded. But it is, or may be, more useful; it is encouraging and perhaps also, to some extent, a guide to action. Though we do not believe that what Hegel predicts must come true, we may – in so far as we find it good, sharing his idea of freedom – strive to make it come true.

Marx, like Hegel, is an optimist, but, in at least one respect, he is more plausible than Hegel. He foretells great social and political changes before what he thinks desirable can come to be – before there can be a morality adequate to man's nature and his social condition. Man is still *alienated*; he is still so situated – socially and culturally – that he is impelled to strive for what does not satisfy him, living, not as he would live if he knew how, but as the market requires. He may not accept wholeheartedly the values of bourgeois society, but, unless he is consciously a revolutionary, he does not reject them either; and if he is revolutionary, he cannot live by the values he accepts, for society will not let him. Man in bourgeois society, as Marx depicts him, is still short of the knowledge and self-knowledge needed to put an end to *alienation*; he has still to make great changes in society and to be himself greatly changed before his condition is such that what he strives for is within his reach and seems to him fully worthwhile – before he sees himself and his situation as they really are, and wants what he can get and what will satisfy him. Though Marx says too little about the society of equals to make it clear just how he conceives of the freedom which is (so he thinks) the condition of men's living truly satisfying lives, he does not find his ideal, as Hegel does, fully realized in the nation-state of his own century. He is, in this, both truer to the ideal which he shares with Hegel, and more realistic. For their ideal is also, at bottom, the ideal of Rousseau and Kant: that no man should be the mere instrument of other men, and that all men should be able to live in accordance with principles they inwardly accept. They differ from Rousseau in being altogether free from parochialism and obscurantism, and from Kant in the interest they take in the cultural and social conditions of freedom. Marx is truer, I think, to this ideal than Hegel – not in giving a clearer account of it, not in speaking more profoundly about freedom and equality and how they stand to one another, but in refusing to admit that it could be achieved in the kind of social and political order which satisfied Hegel. There existed in Hegel's time and in Marx's – as there still exists today – a widespread desire for greater freedom and greater equality, a widespread striving after an ideal which was deeply attractive though not clearly defined; and there was also a strong belief that freedom could not be much enlarged unless there were greater equality. Though Hegel spoke more eloquently and even perceptively of freedom than Marx ever did, it is not too much to claim that Marx held the more firmly of the two to the common ideal.

Whether or not this ideal, suitably elaborated, is the morality adequate to men's nature and condition (if, indeed, there is such a morality[1]), it is most improbable that it came anywhere near being realized in Hegel's Europe. In spite of his great hopes for the future, Marx was quite free from complacency; he saw men, even in the society which he considered most advanced, as still very much in the throes of a social and moral revolution nowhere near completed; he saw them striving to make real an ideal seen only fitfully and confusedly, an ideal about whose social conditions they were still largely ignorant. Perhaps it is a mistake to suppose that revolutions are ever completed, that there is ever a final passing from stormy seas into calm waters, a consummation of human effort. If this is a mistake, then Marx made it no less than Hegel. But at least he could never have brought himself to believe that in the Europe he knew – with its poverty, illiteracy, oppression and war – man had already almost attained the goal he strove for.

---

[1] Hegel and Marx both assume that most men would be rational and moral in the right social environment, that the causes of *alienation* are mostly social and will eventually disappear; they do not consider the possibility that there are many men who are *born* to alienation, i.e. who have inherited qualities making it unlikely that they could in any society acquire passions and ambitions in keeping with values they wholeheartedly accept and which society approves or tolerates. But I am not concerned to argue that their ideal is beyond criticism; I want only to say that we can reject their accounts of social evolution, and still accept their ideal or be strongly attracted to it. We can also conclude, quite rationally, that the ideal, though never to be realized completely, is worth striving for.

CHAPTER FIVE
The Idea of Progress

Man cannot help but see himself a traveller, and can change his mind only about the road he is taking. He cannot be aware of himself as a person, cannot know that he is alive, without looking back to a past and forward to a future. Whoever can put to himself the question, 'What am I?' will also be tempted to ask, 'And where am I going?'. Again, man knows himself as one among others of his kind, as a member of society, as an heir and an ancestor, and so passes easily from seeing himself to seeing his kind as a traveller. From the beginning, the philosophical student of politics has been interested in the course of social change. Aristotle imagined the *polis* growing out of the village, and the village growing out of the family; and, since he called man a *political animal* – a creature whose nature it is to create a political community and to realize itself in so doing – he saw the movement from family to *polis* as a movement in a desirable direction, as progress. But he imagined nothing better than the *polis*, and did not ask himself what might come after it to take its place. When he looked to the future, he apparently expected nothing more of it than had happened already. The more hopeful among the ancients, those with the most robust faith in their own civilization, confined their hopes to maintaining in the future what had been achieved in the past; and the less hopeful expected decay. Some believed in a progress whose highest point was reached already, others in a golden age in a remote past, and still others in a perpetual movement repeated over and over again, through the same stages. There will always be men with a future, with a life to live, a journey to make from birth to death, from a beginning to an end; but mankind have reached the end of the journey, or are moving away from a perfection they once knew or are passing ceaselessly through a cycle of change.

In the Middle Ages, both journeys, of the individual and the species, were conceived differently. There was a destination which the individual might reach, though it was not in this world; for he passed through this world only on his way to something incomparably better or incomparably worse. He could earn his reward or his punishment in this world, but would get his deserts after he had left it. As for the species, its days also were numbered in this world. It was to endure for a time, and to achieve nothing while it endured; it moved neither forward nor backward, nor in circles. In the mediaeval view of the world, humanity, as distinct from the individuals who composed it, had neither destiny nor history; it merely occupied the space and time allotted to it by God. There was nothing for mankind to accomplish or to live through and be affected by – no course of change, social and cultural. There were no achievements, no endeavours, no failures to be attributed to mankind: there were only the efforts of men. The mediaeval view of the world was dramatic, but there was no collective actor on the stage; there were innumerable actors, each a soul making its own way to salvation or perdition.

Belief in progress, as the modern world has known it in the last two or three hundred years, was unknown in antiquity and in the Middle Ages. Yet we find, in Aristotle and in others, the idea of a course of change – social and cultural – determined partly by man's nature and partly by his environment, and we find in the Middle Ages the idea of a journey still uncompleted and leading (at least for a happy few) to a condition infinitely better than the present. If we add to these two ideas two more – that man's knowledge and power over nature increase indefinitely, and that this knowledge and power bring worldly happiness – we have the modern belief in progress. My purpose is not to examine how this idea arose (except to the extent that to do so serves to bring out more clearly what it is), nor yet to examine particular examples of it; for some of the best known among them have been examined elsewhere together with the social philosophies which embody them. I shall discuss only three matters: what is involved in the idea of progress; the rôle of the individual in social evolution; and the belief that the expansion of knowledge leads to increasing happiness.

I. WHAT IS INVOLVED IN THE IDEA OF PROGRESS

1. *Before the Age of Science*

To believe in progress is to believe that there is or can be movement in a desirable direction. But men find many things desirable, and movement towards one or more of them may mean movement away from the others. Getting more of some things thought desirable may involve getting less of others. Differences of opinion about whether there has been or will be progress may be due to several causes: men do not find the same things desirable, or they do not have the same preferences among the things they find desirable, or their estimates differ about the extent to which the things they find desirable are compatible with one another. Some who have believed in progress have not believed that happiness has increased or will do so: they have set a higher value on freedom than on happiness, and have believed that men are freer than they were, even though not more content. Others have believed that happiness cannot be measured while freedom can, and so have thought it reasonable to aim at increasing freedom rather than happiness. Virtue, knowledge, freedom, happiness, justice and 'self-realization' have all often been held to be desirable in themselves, though some of them have also been held to be valuable only as means to other ends. The Utilitarians have said that nothing is desirable for its own sake except happiness. Nevertheless, all these things have been held by some people to be intrinsically desirable. Those, moreover, who have said that happiness alone is to be desired for its own sake have not always agreed about what happiness is: some have sought to reduce it to a mere sum of pleasures, but the greater number have spoken of it in ways which suggest that it includes some of the things which they have also said are to be desired only as means to it.

No doubt, it has been widely assumed that the things desired for their own sakes are closely connected. Widely and perhaps not unreasonably. Let us consider for a moment two of these things: virtue and happiness. We have to allow that men, taken individually, are not always the happier the more they are virtuous; and yet we may reasonably argue that the connection between virtue and happiness, though by no means simple, is close. We may argue, with the Utilitarians, that behaviour comes to be thought virtuous because its general tendency is to increase happiness and to decrease unhappiness; or we may argue that men obtain happiness by getting what they strive for and that their ideas of what is worth striving for are affected by what they see praised or blamed, admired or despised. Whichever of these two explanations we accept, it would seem that virtue and happiness are so connected that they flourish and decay together, if not in each individual, at least over an entire community. So, too, if we take justice and happiness, or 'self-realization' and happiness, or freedom and happiness, we can argue, plausibly, that they are closely connected. The freedom which is precious to man is not mere absence of impediment; it is the opportunity to do what he thinks worthwhile, and he finds his happiness in doing it. He also 'realizes himself' by becoming what he aspires to be and what he claims the 'freedom' to become; and his idea of what makes for his happiness depends on his aspirations. We may explain the connections in these ways or in others: there is room here for a wide diversity of opinions. And yet, diverse though these opinions are, they all affirm the closeness of the connections which they explain so differently. The moralists of Greece and Rome, of the Middle Ages and of our own era seem to be agreed in seeing here a closely related family of ideas, even though their descriptions of the family vary widely.

They also agree, for the most part, that knowledge is a means to these desirable things. Man, if he is to be securely free or virtuous or happy, must understand himself and his circumstances; he may, if he is lucky, be happy without this understanding, or without much of it. He may acquire tastes and habits suited to his condition, and his condition may not change. But, if his happiness is to be secure – if he is not to lose it as soon as his circumstances change – he must be adaptable; he must know himself and his limitations and must also know something of the 'world', of the chances and changes to which men are liable. If he has this knowledge, he will be more free, less the victim of change and better able to make decisions and carry them out; and he will also acquire a clearer understanding of the principles on which he acts. If they are good principles, he will be the more virtuous for having them, for he will not conform thoughtlessly to convention. From Socrates to Kant, nearly all the great moralists have seen a close connection between knowledge and virtue or happiness, or whatever else they have considered desirable for its own sake. Even Rousseau, who deplored the 'progress' made in the arts and sciences, saw it.

Long before the modern faith in progress was born, it was conceded that knowledge could make for happiness, or for the greatest good otherwise conceived, and that it could do so in two ways. It could help the individual to attain that good whatever his social condition, and it could guide the ruler in his efforts to improve society. The Stoics set a high value on knowledge mostly for the first reason, and Plato for both the first and the second. So, too, Rousseau valued it for both reasons: Emile, to be capable of virtue and happiness in a corrupt society, had to acquire self-knowledge and had to learn how to live; and society could not be cured of its ills unless these ills were correctly diagnosed and a social and political order suited to man's nature discovered. But Rousseau, though he believed that knowledge is or can be a means to virtue, freedom and happiness, denied that the accumulation of knowledge tends to make men more virtuous or more happy or more free. He denied what philosophers had seldom affirmed before the eighteenth century, though it was then beginning to seem obvious to them. That knowledge is a means to the good was an opinion which nearly all moralists had shared since the time of Socrates. That the accumulation of knowledge increases or enhances the good was an opinion hardly worth denying before the eighteenth century, for almost no one held it.

Yet the idea that knowledge accumulates is much older than the eighteenth century. The Greeks, at times, were acutely conscious of having added to the store of knowledge inherited from their ancestors; they were aware that later thinkers had built upon the achievements of their predecessors. The Epicureans believed that there had been progress in knowledge, which they valued for its own sake as well as for some of its effects. They welcomed the decline of superstition and also a variety of useful discoveries and institutions. But, if we compare them with the Utilitarians of the eighteenth century, who, like them, were conspicuous hedonists and enemies of superstition and prejudice, we see how much weaker was their belief in a connection between increasing knowledge and increasing happiness. No doubt, any Greek or Roman who was attached to his community, who believed that it was better than what it had grown out of, believed in progress; he believed that there had been progress and also a considerable increase in knowledge. The citizen of the *polis* or the Roman citizen, proud of his condition, no doubt thought himself more favoured than his ancestors, and believed that his advantage rested in large part on greater knowledge. But he did not believe that there would be progress in the future; he did not believe that the condition of his descendants would be better than his own. Or, if he did believe it, it was because he believed that his community was in decay, having declined from some better condition to which it might in the future be restored. The best condition had already been achieved, either now or in the past; and the future, though it might offer something better than the present, would offer nothing better than both the present and the past.

Such knowledge as was needed to live the good life existed already; it was not to be added to, but merely imparted. Yet the Greek or the Roman, who saw progress entirely in the past and not in the future, did not see this because he believed that men already knew all that they could or were likely to know. Though he did not share the modern belief that the accumulation of knowledge would go on indefinitely, his lack of faith in future progress was not rooted in a conviction that there would be no further increase in knowledge. He merely took it for granted that any such increase would not add to man's capacity to live well and be happy. The civilized man, the partaker in the life and culture of the *polis*, the citizen of the republic, was better off than the primitive man, possessing knowledge which that man lacked. Such knowledge had not been acquired separately by each of its possessors; it had been accumulated over generations. But it was now all that it needed to be; it was an immutable store of wisdom, entire and sufficient. Any man, to be able to live well, must make it his own; and some men might have a better opportunity than others of doing so. Or it might be that some men were unfitted by nature to profit by it. Or the community might be corrupted and not provide the education needed to impart it. For a variety of reasons, the knowledge conducive to the good life might be less or more entirely possessed by the individual, less or more widely spread in the community; and therefore there could be either progress or decay. It was reasonable to try to improve education or to reform the community. But, though there could be progress, it was not progress as the eighteenth century conceived of it; for there could be no surpassing the best already achieved. And progress was held no more probable than decay. As the ancients saw it, the knowledge needed for the good life was, in at least one respect, like the grace of God; it was an unchanging and inexhaustible treasure offered to any man capable of receiving it.

This knowledge was usually spoken of as if it were all of one kind, all knowledge in the same sense, though it consisted partly of factual knowledge, partly of skill and partly of what is best called wisdom. It was acquired by getting information, by learning how to do things and by learning to value things at their 'true worth' – or, to use language less out-of-fashion today, by acquiring the preferences needed to lead a satisfying life. It was assumed that these were the same in all societies.

Rousseau's attack on the arts and sciences would have seemed as extravagant to the Greeks and Romans as it did to his contemporaries; they set a high value on knowledge generally, both as a means to other things and in itself, and they did not see the evil effects which he claimed to see. Yet they took for granted what also seemed obvious to him: that the accumulation of knowledge, beyond a certain point, does nothing to increase freedom, virtue or happiness. They put a higher value on knowledge than he did (though he valued it more highly than he sometimes pretended), but at bottom he and they were agreed about how knowledge is connected with other things thought to be desirable.

In the Middle Ages, knowledge was less esteemed both in itself and as a means to the good life than it had been in antiquity. It was also more often condemned as a source of pride. The idea that there had been progress in the past, and the preference for a civilized over a primitive life, disappeared almost entirely. The faith necessary to salvation was not knowledge which men had acquired by their own efforts over many generations, an intellectual inheritance which they must make renewed efforts to preserve; it was a gift of God (through the Church) which the humblest and most ignorant were as well placed as any to receive. The sense, moreover, that knowledge had accumulated in the past and might continue to do so – which had been strong in some circles and periods before Christianity took a large hold – was quite lost. It did not become important again until the Renaissance.

Its renewed importance came long before the modern belief in progress. Machiavelli believed that he lived in a more enlightened age than Italy had known since the fall of the Roman Empire. He believed that knowledge lost or neglected for centuries had been recovered. But he also believed that Italy was decadent; he expected no increase in freedom, virtue or happiness from the recovery of what was lost. Bodin was more impressed even than Machiavelli with the knowledge recovered or acquired in his own age, which he thought fully the equal of any age before it. He would not have accepted that his own age was morally inferior. He believed in the progress and decay both of knowledge and of other things. But he saw no connection between the accumulation of knowledge (which, like the Greeks, he valued for its own sake) and other forms of progress. True, he did not foresee a continuous increase in knowledge; but he also said nothing to suggest that, if he had foreseen it, he would have looked forward to men's becoming indefinitely more virtuous or more happy.

2. In the Scientific Age

In his book, *The Idea of Progress*, J. B. Bury claims for Francis Bacon that he was the first great philosopher to preach the doctrine that the accumulation of knowledge is desirable because it puts it in men's power to increase their happiness.[1] The Greeks had valued knowledge primarily for its own sake, whereas Bacon urged men to obtain it so as

[1] See Bury, *The Idea of Progress* (London 1920), ch. 2, p. 52.

to use it for their own benefit by increasing their power over nature. He saw knowledge as a means to power, and power as a means to happiness. Bacon also differed from the Greeks about how knowledge is to be obtained; he advocated, as the Greeks had not done, the use of the experimental method.

This, no doubt, is important; but to point to it, as Bury does, distracts attention from what is common to Bacon and modern believers in progress. Though important experiments had been made before Bacon wrote a word about the experimental method, and though his account of it was not altogether accurate, his advocacy of it encouraged its use and so quickened the increase of knowledge. But to say this is not to explain what Bacon contributed to the idea of progress; it is to explain only what he contributed to the increase of knowledge. Since, for the moment, our concern is with the idea of progress, it is more important to notice how Bacon differs from the Greeks about the kind of knowledge which makes for happiness. In their opinion it consists in self-knowledge, in knowing how to behave, and in what the French call *savoir-vivre*. But the knowledge which Bacon recommends as useful is 'natural philosophy'. The greater men's understanding of the material world and the greater their ability to harness nature to their purposes, the better for them. The Greeks, said Bacon, had excelled in morals and politics, but had not gone far in studying nature as he wanted it studied; and it was on this study – on the natural sciences – that he grounded his hopes for mankind. Bacon, as Bury points out, did not foresee an indefinite extension of knowledge; he believed he was living in the old age of mankind. But he gave clear utterance to a belief which is at the root of the faith in progress; it is a belief in the utility of a kind of knowledge not thought particularly useful by philosophers before his time – the kind that was later denounced as harmful by Rousseau.

Bury is right when he argues that faith in progress rests partly on the belief that knowledge will grow indefinitely, and that this belief was not strong and widespread until men had learnt to distinguish knowledge from opinion – until they had acquired clear ideas about how opinions are to be tested to establish whether they are true or false. It was in the seventeenth century that such ideas were acquired; it was then that philosophers turned their minds once again to questions long neglected: What is knowledge? How is it to be increased? Though, no doubt, they learnt a great deal from the Greeks, who had put these questions before them, they gave answers different from the old ones. The seventeenth century did more than make scientific discoveries; it discovered science; it made explicit the assumptions on which science rests and defined the methods it uses. Bury sees this as above all the achievement of two men, Bacon and Descartes; he might have added a third, Galileo, who had clearer ideas than Bacon of what is involved in the experimental method. Of course, these men did not say the last words in such matters, but they did say the decisive ones. They produced a solid faith in methods of explanation and discovery which have enormously increased man's power to predict and to control the course of events. Bury rightly sees in the idea of science a necessary, though not a sufficient, condition of the idea of progress – of the idea of progress, not as the ancients sometimes knew it, but as we have come to know it in the last two to three hundred years.

To use the language of Hegel, science first became, in the seventeenth century, *for* itself what it was *in* itself: scientists were aware, as they never had been before, of how their activities, their methods and explanations, differed from those of theologians and other builders of theories. It was also in the seventeenth century that it first came to be widely accepted that knowledge tends to increase steadily, if no calamity occurs to prevent its doing so. It was not forgotten that barbarian invasions had destroyed the Roman world. Yet comparisons were made between antiquity and contemporary Europe; and it was both widely asserted and widely denied that the moderns had surpassed the ancients. Those who claimed superiority for the moderns rested their claim above all on the recent achievements of science. But even the most ardent champions of the moderns did not yet claim for them that they were more virtuous or more happy than the ancients. They felt themselves superior only because they had more knowledge or (less often and less confidently) because they had gone beyond them in the arts. They made no claim which Rousseau would have been concerned to deny: he did not contest that there had been 'progress' in the sciences and the arts – that knowledge had increased greatly and that artists had extended their powers, giving vivid and delicate expression to a wider range of feelings. He said only that progress in the sciences and the arts had been bought at too high a price in virtue and happiness. In the seventeenth century nobody was much concerned with this price: the belief which Rousseau denied – that progress in the arts and sciences makes for happiness – was as yet seldom asserted.

Not till the late eighteenth century did it come to be widely believed both that knowledge would increase indefinitely and that happiness would increase with it. It was then argued that the invention of printing had diffused knowledge more widely than ever before, and so made it unlikely that a calamity would destroy it, as the barbarians had destroyed the accumulated knowledge of antiquity. Moreover, there probably would be no such calamity, for the European peoples were so much stronger than the others that they could not be conquered by them unless the others acquired the sciences and the skills of Europe. Peoples who had made progress could no longer be conquered by peoples who had not made it, and so the conquest of some peoples by others would no longer destroy what had already been achieved or seriously retard further progress. It was also argued that knowledge stimulates curiosity – that the more widely it is diffused, the more minds there are able and willing to add to it. The more men know and the more men there are who share the knowledge, the faster knowledge accumulates and the less likely that something will happen to slow down the rate of accumulation. There is a natural tendency for knowledge to accumulate, because men are endowed with memory and can keep records and so make a store to which they can add continuously, and the greater that store the more unlikely its destruction. Knowledge – like man, its possessor – is more vulnerable in infancy, and becomes the less so the larger it grows. This was the faith of the philosophers of the eighteenth century, of the Enlightenment – the faith which finds clear, confident and classic expression in Condorcet's *Sketch for an Historical Picture of the Progress of the Human Mind*. Or, rather, it was part of their faith, the part that Rousseau was not concerned to deny; the other part was the belief which to him seemed certainly false – that as knowledge increases so too does happiness.

Bury makes this claim of the idea of progress before the nineteenth century:

> It had waited like a handmaid on the abstractions of Nature and Reason; it had hardly realized an independent life. The time had come for systematic attempts to probe its meaning and definitely to ascertain the direction in which humanity is moving. Kant had said that a Kepler or a Newton was needed to find the law of the movement of civilization.[1]

Though Bury's book is an excellent example of its kind, it is sometimes misleading. The search for a 'law of progress' belongs, he says, to the nineteenth century, and the earliest would-be Keplers were such men as Saint-Simon and Comte. Bury is right in suggesting that the theories of progress of Saint-Simon and Comte differ radically from earlier theories, but he does not (so it seems to me) make it clear just where the difference lies.

[1] Ibid., ch. 15, p. 278.

What are we to understand by 'a law of progress'? It was often asserted before the nineteenth century – as Bury himself admits – that, given man's natural capacities, his living together with other men, and his physical environment, wealth and knowledge will accumulate if nothing happens to prevent their doing so. It was conceded that in the past the accumulation had not been smooth, and that sometimes, when disaster supervened, what was slowly acquired over generations was quickly lost. Yet the tendency to accumulate was often asserted. Was not the assertion a putting forward of a law of progress? Was it not an assertion of what would happen, *ceteris paribus*? Was it not as much a *law* as the laws of the classical economists? As we have seen already, the men who, before Saint-Simon and Comte, asserted and explained this tendency also gave their reasons for believing that the causes which had impeded its operation in the past would not do so in the future.

Or are we to understand by 'a law of progress' a law asserting a set course of change, a passage from stage to stage, in a definite order? If that is 'a law of progress', then such a law was asserted (to take account of France alone) by at least three important writers before Saint-Simon – Fontenelle, Turgot and Condorcet. Fontenelle argued that scientific knowledge, as it accumulates, must do so in a certain order: some discoveries presuppose others; some sciences can come to birth only after others have made considerable progress. True, Fontenelle did not say that progress is inevitable, and spoke only of scientific progress, without affirming or denying that it conduces to progress in other directions. But he clearly implied that, unless something happens to prevent its doing so, knowledge will accumulate, and argued that, if it does accumulate, it must do so in a certain order.

According to Turgot, given man's natural capacities and the nature of the world in which he lives, all societies, as they change, tend to pass through the same stages; though, from a variety of causes peculiar to this or that society, all societies do not pass through these stages at the same speed. Some make progress more quickly than others and some stagnate, and there are also other differences between them due to their different circumstances. But, where there is progress, the order of it is determined in a general way by two factors: by human nature and by what is broadly similar in man's natural environment in all parts of the world. Though Turgot, like Fontenelle, paid special attention to the accumulation of knowledge, he conceived of progress more broadly, as Saint-Simon and Comte were to do after him.

Where Turgot saw only three stages of progress, Condorcet saw ten, which he described in considerable detail. He, too, was interested in more than the accumulation of knowledge, believing that men, as they come to know themselves and their environment better, grow in virtue and happiness. Like Turgot, he saw in the accumulation of knowledge the prime cause of other kinds of progress; but then so too did Saint-Simon and Comte.

How, then, do Saint-Simon and Comte differ from Condorcet and Turgot? In asserting the *necessity* of progress in some sense in which Condorcet and Turgot did not assert it? I doubt it. Do they not all four agree that, given the capacities peculiar to us and what is common to our environment everywhere, mankind will move in a certain direction, unless something happens to prevent its doing so, and will pass from stage to stage in a given order? And, if Saint-Simon and Comte believed that nothing would happen to prevent it, can we not say the same of Turgot and Condorcet? We have seen already that it was widely held, in the eighteenth century, that 'progress' had gained such momentum that what had stopped it in the past could stop it no longer. Mankind had made progress and would almost certainly continue to make it. This was what Turgot and Condorcet believed. Did Saint-Simon and Comte believe more than this? Did even Marx do so? I doubt it. Nineteenth-century believers in progress do not, I suspect, differ from earlier ones in asserting the *necessity* of progress in some sense in which it was not asserted before, though they do assert it more loudly and more often.[1] They differ, rather, in having a more unquestioning faith in progress, no longer troubling to argue that what had stopped progress in the past would do so no more.

And yet Bury is not wrong in suggesting that the theories of progress of Saint-Simon and Comte differ greatly from those of Turgot and Condorcet. He merely fails to explain the difference. Turgot and Condorcet say only this: It is not mere chance which causes men to make some discoveries before others, for there is a necessary order in the accumulation of knowledge, later achievements presupposing earlier ones. Knowledge is not acquired as pebbles are collected on a beach, as the whim takes the collector. Creatures capable of acquiring a comprehensive understanding of the world (and not just bare facts) and who of necessity acquire it little by little must do so in a certain order; they cannot begin anywhere and then go on from there in any direction. There is a natural beginning and an orderly course.

---

[1] Hegel and the Hegelians are a special case; for, according to them, it follows from the very nature of Spirit, which is all reality, that it moves inevitably to a consummation. Here we have a properly metaphysical conception of progress. But Saint-Simon's and Comte's conception of it was no more metaphysical than Condorcet's.

If men's capacities and their situation were different, the beginning and the course might also be different; but, given their capacities and situation, they must begin where they do and move forward as they do. If we suppose that the needs and motives which cause them to begin to acquire knowledge do not cease to operate after they have made a beginning, we must conclude that the accumulation of knowledge will continue indefinitely, unless something happens to put a stop to it. And we know from experience that these needs and motives do not cease to operate, for the speed at which knowledge accumulates increases with the amount accumulated. If we suppose further, as both Turgot and Condorcet do, that the growth of knowledge brings other benefits to man, we naturally conclude that it is the source of progress in a larger sense.

But Turgot and Condorcet, though they take it for granted that the growth of knowledge affects other sides of man's life in society, do not assume that all social activities are so closely connected that they all change in a fixed order; they do not assume that there is a set course of *integral* social change. Thus, if we make only the assumptions which they make, we are not at a loss to explain either social stagnation or how it is that countries can be very similar in some ways and yet differ greatly in others. The acquisition of knowledge is only one of man's social activities, and it does not determine but merely affects the others. Though there is a tendency for science to make quicker progress the greater the progress it has already made, there may arise *within society itself* obstacles to that progress.[1] It need not be so but it may be. It is true that Condorcet, when he speaks of obstacles to progress, has in mind natural disasters and barbarian invasions as much as internal obstacles, and that among *internal* obstacles he takes account only of the Church. But we are not here discussing his particular beliefs so much as his assumptions and what follows from them. He asserts a law of progress: he says, firstly, that knowledge

---

[1] Those who, like Saint-Simon, Comte or Marx, assume that there is a fixed order of *integral* social change must hold (if they are to be consistent) that obstacles to progress which arise within a society are merely temporary. Their assumption rules out the possibility of some aspects of social life developing in ways which stop the progress (or set course of change) of the others; whereas Condorcet's assumption does not rule this out. Yet their assumption still allows that an *external* cause (e.g. a natural disaster, or the impact of another society on this one) may put a stop to progress. I dare say that those who made one or other of these two assumptions did not understand what they were committed to by so doing. Indeed, they seem hardly to have been aware that these are in fact two different assumptions. Some writers (Saint-Simon perhaps?) may even have vacillated between the two. But this makes it only the more important to distinguish between them and to consider their implications.

will increase, provided that nothing happens to prevent its doing so, and secondly that, if it increases, it must do so in a certain order. But he does not assert a law of integral social change.

Now, this is precisely what Saint-Simon, and Comte do assert, and so too does Marx. The difference between the earlier and the later writers is not what Bury takes it to be; it does not consist in the later writers saying that progress is *necessary* in some sense in which the earlier ones do not say it. Saint-Simon, Comte and Marx do not hold, with Hegel, that progress is necessary in the sense that it could not conceivably be otherwise; they hold, rather, with Condorcet and Turgot, that it will continue if nothing happens to stop it, and they take it for granted that nothing will happen. The later writers differ from the earlier ones in assuming that all aspects of social life are so connected that they pass from stage to stage in a fixed order, though some move forward sooner than others. They make a more complicated and less plausible assumption. To sustain it, they use stranger arguments and take more frequent refuge in ambiguity. It is they, rather than Condorcet and Turgot, who produce a Procrustean bed on which to stretch the facts of history. I have no wish to belittle the difference between them and their eighteenth-century precursors, but only to say that it is not what Bury says it is.

Saint-Simon, Comte and Marx differ from Condorcet and Turgot in yet another way; they speak as if how men behave in society were determined by the social and cultural order. Or, rather, though they do not deny that there are certain natural functions which men would exercise much as they do now, even if they were subject to no social influences, they speak as if the rest of their behaviour – if it is important, if it is of the kind that the historian or the social theorist takes notice of – were socially determined. There are some things which men would do even if they were not social creatures – even in a hypothetical state of nature – and some of these things are no doubt important since they satisfy biological needs; and there are also forms of behaviour peculiar to this or that person, which are unimportant, except to the person himself and to those close to him. But men have capacities which are developed in society, by social intercourse with other men, and their properly social activities consist in the exercise of these capacities. It is the system of these activities which constitutes the social system, and it is these same activities which determine how the system changes. In other words, the behaviour which brings about social change is itself socially determined.

This doctrine, which is common to Saint-Simon, Comte and Marx, I shall call *social determinism*. Many writers on society and politics have found it attractive, though they have also felt the need to qualify it. It has seemed to them to give proper weight to important truths unknown or neglected before the nineteenth century. Yet the doctrine is more obscure even than most of its critics have noticed, as I shall try to show later. It contains important truths but fails to put them clearly, and in the meantime suggests a good deal that is false. It is a difficult and a slippery doctrine; those who accept it do not know quite what it is that they are accepting, and are apt to abandon it (without noticing that they have done so) when to adhere to it would put them in a false position. It is a doctrine loudly proclaimed to which even its loudest champions are frequently disloyal.

3. Rousseau's Denial

Rousseau denied what Condorcet affirmed; he did not believe in progress. Yet he too, in his *Discourse on Inequality*, described a course of social change. Though he reached conclusions different from Condorcet's, their conceptions of social change were not dissimilar. He too argued that, men's capacities being what they are, human societies evolve as other animal communities do not. Much less versed than Condorcet in the sciences, he could never have shown how the scientific spirit emerged or how one science prepared the way for another. Yet the course of change which he envisaged was not fortuitous, though he admitted that his description was conjectural; it seemed to him, as it did to Condorcet, that some achievements presuppose others and therefore necessarily come after them. His method also was deductive; he argued to his conclusions largely from two assumptions: that certain capacities are peculiar to man, and that what first brought men together was the need to co-operate for the better satisfaction of their wants.

The account of man's evolution which Condorcet gives in his *Sketch* is more elaborate and perhaps also more lucid than Rousseau's in his second *Discourse*, and he comes much closer than Rousseau to formulating a 'law of change'. Rousseau saw himself merely as a reconstructor of the past, explaining in broad outline what must be presumed to have happened to a creature, endowed by nature as man is, to bring him to his present condition, whereas Condorcet saw himself more clearly as the discoverer of a fixed course of cultural change. But though, of the two, Condorcet used history the more copiously to illustrate his theme, they were both more concerned to explain what must have happened than to establish what in fact did happen. And if Rousseau never assumed an integral course of social change, or what I have called social determinism, neither did Condorcet. In spite of the great differences between them, in several important respects they are alike. The claim which is implicit in the *Discourse* is made explicit in the *Sketch*: given the capacities peculiar to man and the fact of social intercourse, there are certain developments to be expected if nothing happens to prevent them.[1]

Yet Rousseau denied what Condorcet affirmed; he denied that there is progress. He did not, as we shall see, deny progress in all the senses in which Condorcet affirmed it, but he did deny it in the most important sense. He denied that the increase of knowledge makes eventually for greater happiness. I shall discuss, in the third part of this chapter, the belief affirmed by Condorcet and denied by Rousseau; but before I do that, I want to examine certain objections to the doctrines of an integral course of social change and social determinism.[2]

II. INTEGRAL SOCIAL CHANGE AND THE INDIVIDUAL

I discuss elsewhere certain difficulties about the conception of a set course of integral social change.[3] What is it, exactly, which is said to

[1] Rousseau, less lucid and elaborate than Condorcet, had perhaps a deeper sense of what social intercourse does to man, forming his character and making a moral person of him. Condorcet was mainly concerned with the intellectual achievements of man, and Rousseau with the effects of the social environment on the *psyche* of the individual.

[2] A fear, now very present to us, that the increase of knowledge and of power over nature may lead to the destruction of mankind, was unknown to the eighteenth and nineteenth centuries. The pessimists then predicted, not destruction, but misery and corruption; and they mostly did not trouble to describe in detail the long course of deterioration which they foresaw. Even Rousseau, the arch-pessimist, attempted only a rough outline. It was not the pessimists, not the Rousseaus, but the optimists – the believers in progress in some larger sense than the mere increase in knowledge and wealth – who were tempted to map the future. There are two forms of pessimism in Rousseau: there is the belief that man is deteriorating morally, becoming feebler and more confused in his passions; and there is the belief that, as society grows more complex, man's problems pile upon him so fast that he cannot keep pace with them. Whoever holds the first belief is often inclined to hold the second, seeing a connection between the state of society and the decline of man; but the converse is not true. Today, the second belief is probably more widely held than the first: there are many who see no reason for holding that men are feebler than they were but who doubt men's ability to remedy the evils and avoid the dangers which their achievements have brought on them. To them, the first belief is sheer prejudice, the product of depression or misanthropy, while the second looks reasonable.

[3] In treating of the social theories of Hegel and Marx (see especially pp. 54–60, 90–93 and 277–94 above).

change? How can there be a set course of change when societies are continually affecting one another? In just what sense of the word is the supposed law of social change a *law*? It is quite unlike any *law* of the natural sciences; it does not say what will happen to anything of a given kind under such and such circumstances. Nor does it describe a course of change normal to members of a species who are clearly distinct from one another and from their environment. A law of social change is a pronouncement *sui generis*: it refers to groups of individuals and to relations and attitudes of mind which individuals have as members of groups. These relations and attitudes give to the groups their identity, and the law asserts that they change in a fixed order. Wherever men stand in social relations to one another, these relations, together with the modes of thought and feeling which 'correspond' to them, will change in this order, so long as there is no breach of continuity – that is to say, so long as each generation can pass on to their successors the wealth, the knowledge, the skills and the values they have acquired either by inheritance or in their own generation. The peculiarity of a statement of this kind – the extent to which it differs from a *law* of the natural sciences (not excluding biology) – is masked by the practice of speaking of groups of men socially related to one another and of their *social posterity* (those to whom they pass on what they have acquired) as if they were organisms. Clearly, men are not just externally related to one another; their 'nature' is modified by the relations they stand in to other men, other creatures of their kind. To express their sense that this is so, social theorists have used conceptions taken from biology, which are useful in some ways and misleading in others.

Statements of this kind are shielded from criticism by their very obscurity, and they are obscure because it is uncertain both what they refer to and what they say of it. Indeed, these two uncertainties go naturally together. Where a word is used in several senses, we get the particular sense in which it is being used mostly from knowing what it is being applied to. But, unfortunately, it is by no means easy (perhaps not even possible) to identify a society of the kind said to be involved in a set course of change.

It is sometimes astonishing how little men know what they are about when they speak of social change or social *evolution* in the grand manner of a Comte or a Marx. Marx has been called the *Darwin* of the social sciences. Some who have called him so have meant only that he put forward ideas which, in their own way, have been as revolutionary as those of Darwin; but others have spoken as if they had in mind something more. Presumably, they have known that Marx was not the first to say that there was a set course of social change or evolution. What then have they meant to convey about Marx by calling him the Darwin of the social sciences? Have they meant that his conception of social change, as compared with earlier conceptions, is more like Darwin's idea of evolution? But this is absurd; for the idea of evolution, as we find it in Darwin, makes no sense whatever if we apply it to a course of social change. Neither Marx nor anyone else has ever come near to so applying it. Darwin never spoke of a set course of change, of a normal course of evolution, of a fixed order of stages through which a species must pass unless something extraneous prevents its doing so; he never spoke of any species as if it were an individual, going through a course of change peculiar to its kind; and the species of which he spoke were not social groups. Evolution, as Darwin conceived of it, differs *toto caeolo* from the course of social change as Marx explained it. To the extent that Marx used ideas taken from biology to expound what he meant by social change, they were ideas as old as biology itself, as old as Aristotle.[1] Marx was no more 'Darwinian' than was Condorcet.

But I must not repeat what I have said elsewhere. I shall confine myself to defending such theories as those of Comte and Marx from some of the charges brought against them, and to making one or two criticisms of my own, which come more naturally here than in the chapters dealing with Hegel and Marx.

1. Social Change and Individual Freedom

It is often objected to such theories as Marxism that, if they were true, men would have no freedom of choice; and the objection is made even by persons who accept full determinism, who believe that acts of choice are like other events in the sense that, given the circumstances in which they happen, they must happen. But the truth is that these theories are no more and no less a denial of freedom than determinism itself. If freedom is compatible with the doctrine that acts of choice are no less caused than are other events, then it is compatible with Marxism. It is important to see why this is so.

Such theories as those of Comte and Marx are theories about what men do, about how they behave; they are not theories about what happens to men no matter what they do. The activities they discuss

[1] Of course, he did not use even these ideas consistently; for, after all, social change is not like organic development, and it is beyond the powers of even the most Germanic system-builder always to speak of something as if it were what it obviously is not.

are peculiarly human in the sense that they involve deliberation and choice. To say that such activities are *socially determined* is no more to deny their peculiarly human character than to say that they are determined in some other way. It may be a false statement, and it might still be false even if determinism, taken generally, were true; but, true or false, it is not a statement about what happens to people no matter what they do. Therefore criticisms of Marx or Comte which imply that their theories commit them to statements of that kind quite miss the mark. I have in mind such criticisms as this: 'It is absurd of Marx to exhort men to action, for he holds that what will happen must happen, whether or not they choose that it shall.' But here, surely, it is not Marx but his critic who is being absurd. Marx does not say that the proletarian revolution will happen, no matter how men choose to act; he says that it will happen because men will choose to act in certain ways. Their choice, he thinks, will be determined; and among its causes there will be exhortations such as his. And the exhortations in their turn are determined. Both the decisions of the revolutionaries and the exhortations belong to the course of events which Marxism purports to explain.

When they speak of *deliberation* and *choice*, determinists – whether or not they also believe in a law of social change – mean by these words pretty much what indeterminists mean by them. They do not deny that men take stock of the situations in which they act, that they consider the courses of action open to them, and then decide upon one course in preference to the others. They do not play down the importance of reason and deliberate choice in human affairs; or at least they are not committed by their doctrine to doing so. If the determinist who does not believe in a law of social change has no commitment to playing down reason and choice, then neither has the determinist who does. The importance of an event depends on its consequences; and if an event is an action of a kind of which human beings alone are capable – if it involves deliberation and choice – it is none the less important for being determined.

No doubt, Marx and others who believe in a set course of social change often speak carelessly, and they sometimes speak as if it did not matter what men choose to do. They sometimes speak as if 'social forces' were not human activities, and therefore as if there were something which was at once social and different from human behaviour which determined that behaviour. And it may be that this is due to more than carelessness. Marx and others who have thought as he did have not been remarkably lucid; they have put together elaborate and obscure theories and have often been entangled in coils of their own making. They often have not seen precisely what was implied by their own doctrines. There are, no doubt, passages where they speak of men as if they were puppets pulled hither and thither by social forces – laws of social change external to them, as if the course of history did not consist merely of what men do but were a kind of stream into which they are plunged and which carries them along with it until death throws them out of it. But these are aberrations due either to carelessness or to confusion of thought; they do not follow logically from the doctrine that there is a set course of social change. That doctrine is, I think, unacceptable, but not because it commits those who hold it to this kind of absurdity.

Not only social theorists but also natural scientists sometimes speak, carelessly and improperly, as if the laws formulated by them were causally related to the events they apply to; as if the causes of events were not other events but laws. When a physicist or biologist speaks in this way, as if there were something external to events causing them to happen as they do, we are not offended, for it does not matter to us that what is merely physical, what is altogether different from the actions peculiar to us, should be 'subject' to 'forces' external to it. Yet this way of speaking, though it is only sometimes offensive, is always misleading unless it is seen for what it is – as a way of speaking which may be convenient but must never be taken literally. There are no forces external to events determining their order in the physical world any more than there are in the social world.

We can, of course, often say, without absurdity, that some things will happen to men no matter what they choose to do. We can say, for example, that they'll die. Their deaths and such events as these are natural and not social, and social theorists are not much interested in them. We can also, without absurdity, make predictions about what men and women will choose to do; we can say, for example, that seven out of ten persons now between the ages of twenty and thirty and still unmarried will get married within the next ten years. They will not get married unless they choose to do so, and yet the belief that marriage depends on choice does not lessen our confidence in our prediction. Nor does confidence in the prediction weaken our belief that marriage depends on choice.

Although those who say that there is a set course of social change which determines how men act, think and feel are not, except when they are being careless or confused, saying that there are forces external to men causing them to act as they do; although they are aware, in their more lucid moments, that what they refer to as 'social forces' or 'the course of events' consists only of human activities, they are nevertheless, for reasons which I shall discuss later, saying something which, if we consider it carefully, can be seen not to make sense. But, before I go on to discuss these reasons, I want to defend holders of this doctrine from another charge sometimes made against them.

It has seldom been made against them indiscriminately, but more against some than others, and most often against Marx and his disciples. The charge, this time, is not that they speak of 'social forces' external to men moving them to act as they do, but that, by implication, they deny the importance of 'great' men. It is not easy to assess the exact nature of this charge. It would seem absurd to bring it against, say, Hegel or Saint-Simon. For Hegel spoke of *World-Historical Individuals* and was full of admiration and respect for great men, and Saint-Simon, though his manner was different, was scarcely less so; he made heroes of the great scientists – of Galileo and Newton. Yet Hegel and Saint-Simon also believed that the course of history is necessary; and Hegel believed it in an even stronger sense of necessity than did Marx. How, then, does their position differ from Marx's? In their not believing, as he did, in economic determinism? But this, surely, is not relevant. If he and they are agreed about what, say, Newton achieved, we cannot say that they estimate the importance of his achievement differently merely because they disagree about how such achievements are determined.[1] They all three hold that the opportunities open to great men – be they men of action or men of thought – are determined by the situation, social and cultural, in which they find themselves; they disagree only about how the factors in that situation are related to one another.

To say, as Marxists have done, that if Newton had not discovered what he did someone else would have done so is not to detract from the importance of Newton. For whoever else had done it would have had a mind of Newton's quality, and his achievement would have been no less admirable and important. Marxists need not deny that some men are immensely more gifted than others, and that men as gifted as Newton are wonderfully rare. It is perfectly consistent to

---

[1] This is not to deny that economic determinism has difficulties peculiar to itself. Marx was (or sometimes passed himself off as being) an economic determinist, holding that men's ideas about the world and themselves are determined by how they produce goods and services to satisfy their needs. Since production is an activity involving the use of ideas and is also deeply affected by science, Marx could not in practice do what he sometimes thought he was doing; he could not explain the course of social change on the assumption that how men think is determined by how they produce what satisfies their needs. But, peculiar though economic determinism is, its peculiarities are irrelevant when we are discussing the Marxist attitude to great men.

hold both that, if Newton had not done what he did, someone else would have done it, and that the history of mankind would be vastly different if there were no geniuses among men. Just as it would be vastly different if men generally had other capacities than they do have, or if men and women were not born in roughly equal numbers. The Marxist need not deny this. He need not say that the course of history would be the same no matter what men were like. Nor need he say that the course of history depends only on capacities common to all human beings. It depends on the bearing of children, and only women, who are not the whole of mankind, can bear them. It depends also on capacities which are incomparably more rare and which we call genius. No doubt, Marxism and other such theories assume some kind of 'uniformity' in human nature; but they need not assume either that all human beings are born alike or that how they differ is socially and historically unimportant. They assume merely that the important natural differences between human beings remain much the same in degree and extent from generation to generation; they assume that the incidence of genius or talent does not differ greatly from age to age.

There have been Marxists who took it upon themselves to reduce great men to ordinary proportions. Perhaps they believed that historical materialism required them to do so. If this was their belief, they were mistaken. Or perhaps their motive was quite different; perhaps they were proclaiming a faith in equality without quite knowing what kind of equality they had faith in. That, too, is possible.

2. Of What is Social Change Predicated?

There is another, and more serious, objection than these to such theories as those of Comte and Marx – an objection which I have already touched upon but which I now want to consider from a rather different point of view. When Comte and Marx spoke as if there were a set course of social change, they presumably were not thinking of all mankind as one society, for they found some peoples more advanced – further along the course – than others. Nor did they have in mind either a natural or a 'civil' community (i.e. one involving regular administration); they did not mean a family or class or tribe, nor yet a collection of persons under the same government, however wide or narrow the function of that government. A kinship group has definite limits; and so too has what I have called a 'civil community', using that term because I want to put into the same broad category both States and other associations in which there is a regular control by some persons over others, in which a distinction is made between those who act on behalf of the community and those who do not. What makes a community identical over the years differs not only as between natural and civil communities but also as between different species within each of these two kinds. For example, a civil community may be reckoned to be the same over a long period of time because, throughout this period, its rulers have authority over all persons within a given territory; or because, though its members have moved into another part of the world, it consists of the same natural communities having a common government; or because authority has passed from ruler to ruler by a fixed rule; or because recruitment has continued uninterruptedly. There are many criteria used to establish the identity and continuity of communities, and especially of civil ones. The Church of Rome, the Royal Society, and the French State have existed for a long time, and we use different criteria to decide whom they include and exclude. Yet these criteria, though sometimes far from simple, can be more or less precisely defined.

Comte and Marx (and others of their kind), when they speak of a course of social change, are not speaking of changes of which anything thus easily identifiable is the enduring subject. True, they do not know this; they often speak as if there were societies distinct from one another which must all pass necessarily from stage to stage in the same order if nothing happens to destroy them. Yet they speak improperly, though they do not know it. There is nothing which retains its identity as it changes in the ways they describe; there is only a course of events. There are men who are born and live and die, and among whom certain modes of action, thought and feeling endure for a time and then give way to others. What, then, are we to understand by a necessary course of social change if we refuse to follow those who speak as if there were an enduring subject of it?

To say that there is a necessary course of social change is, presumably, to say at least this: Wherever there is social intercourse between men who are able to pass on to their successors the fruits of their labour and experience, social modes of behaviour (i.e., those modes which do not come 'naturally' but are acquired in social intercourse) will change in a fixed order provided that no extraneous cause intervenes to prevent their doing so.

Now, this statement is not analytic; we can establish its truth or falsity only by appealing to the facts. In order to test it, we should have to locate in history several quite separate courses of social change, and see whether and to what extent they were similar. But this we cannot do. Wherever we look, we cannot find even one region or one people (let alone several) in which or among whom there has been a long course of social change unaffected by what went on elsewhere.

The modes of behaviour here in question are neither natural nor idiosyncratic; they are not acquired in a process of physical and psychological maturation independently of social intercourse, and they are not peculiar to this or that person. They are conventional; they are acquired by the individual as he learns to live with his fellows, as he becomes aware of himself as a man among men, as he enters into social relations with them. What, then, causes these modes to change? They are conventional; there is nothing about them which explains why they should change. Modes of behaviour have no inherent tendency to change; they are not organisms. If they do change, it is presumably because men, for some reason or other, begin to act differently, because they break with convention, because they deviate from the normal. What, then, causes them to break with convention? Presumably, it is not convention itself. Presumably, it is not established modes of behaviour which themselves produce the behaviour that alters them. Nor can it be mere 'human nature', the inborn capacities common to all men or distributed among them in much the same proportions from generation to generation.

Custom, convention and received opinion may set limits to the kinds of behaviour which depart from them; we should not expect to find the innovations of the nineteenth century in the thirteenth. Nonetheless, established modes of behaviour do not determine what innovations there shall be; they do not produce what causes them to change. We cannot, given 'human nature' and the modes of behaviour established among a body of men (the modes which make of these men a society having a distinct character or 'structure' of its own), predict that particular behaviour which will cause those modes to change. But, unless we can do this, how can there be a necessary course of social change?[1]

If we deny social determinism and a set course of social change, we need not deny determinism in general; we need not deny that the behaviour which alters established modes of behaviour has its sufficient causes. We deny only that this behaviour is determined

---

[1] Elsewhere in this chapter I speak of a *set* course of social change, and in the last section of the second chapter on Marx and Engels I speak of a *normal* course. I use the three words, *set*, *normal* and *necessary*, in the same sense in this context – to refer to a course which moves from stage to stage in a given order, unless something impinges on it from outside to prevent its doing so. Though most of the theorists asserting such a course did not trouble to qualify their assertion in the way I have done, it is not obvious that they would have refused to qualify it, if invited to do so. In any case, the criticisms made here apply to the assertion whether or not it is qualified in this way.

by the very modes which it alters – by the institutions and culture which give to a society its distinctive character. We say no more than that these things, though they deeply affect the behaviour which alters them, do not make it what it is. To speak as if the behaviour which changes the social order were itself the mere effect of that order is absurd, true though it is that such behaviour always occurs in a social context which sets limits to what it can be.

If this argument is contrasted with another, the point of it may become clearer. Bury accuses Comte of failing to grapple with a 'fundamental' question, the question of *contingency*. He speaks of 'the collision' of two 'independent causal chains', meaning by one of them the 'course of history', which Comte and others say is necessary, and by the other any series of events which interferes with that course. For example, Bury says that Napoleon's existence was due to an 'independent causal chain' having nothing to do with 'the course of political events', and then goes on to say that 'the course of history' was profoundly affected by what Napoleon did. This action of Napoleon upon the course of history was contingent in relation to that course, and (so Bury tells us) 'the whole history of man has been modified at every stage by such contingencies'.[1]

This line of argument looks odd because it seems both to affirm and deny that there is a 'course of history' in the sense envisaged by Comte or Marx. Bury speaks as if there would (or might) be a set course of change, were it not that it was continually interfered with by such actions as Napoleon's – actions whose causes are contingent in relation to that course. But it makes no sense to treat the course of history as an 'independent causal chain' with which other such chains are perpetually colliding. True, we can distinguish various kinds of events from one another; and we can give a name to each kind to mark it off from the others, calling one kind *economic*, another *political* and a third *cultural*, and so on. But if events of these different kinds continually impinge upon one another, we cannot treat any one kind as an independent causal chain. No doubt, there are innumerable 'causal chains' which are, over considerable periods of time, independent of one another. What Jones does may not affect Smith, nor what Smith does affect Jones, for days or weeks on end; and then one of them may impinge on the other. We should then, presumably, have what Bury calls two 'independent causal chains' coming eventually into 'collision'. We need not deny that there are, at any one time, many such 'chains' and also frequent 'collisions'. But there is still no 'course

[1] See *The Idea of Progress*, ch. 16, pp. 303–4.

of history', no central causal chain, in relation to which those events of Napoleon's life which are not political or military – which are not to be included in 'the course of history' – are contingent. To base an argument against Comte or Marx on a distinction between 'a course of history' and actions which are contingent in relation to it is to build on shifting sand.

But we can distinguish between conventional modes of behaviour and the behaviour which causes these modes to change, and we can see that the modes do not determine (though they set limits to) the behaviour which changes them. Therefore we can see that there can be no set or necessary course of social change.

3. An Effect of Science and History

It has been said that belief in a necessary course of social change was a substitute for older beliefs in a Divine Providence or in final causes – beliefs weakened by the intellectual revolution of the seventeenth century, in which Descartes was the chief actor. According to Descartes, the universe is a system in which everything that happens does so according to some unchanging law. There is movement and change in every part of the universe, but the system, as a whole, does not change. The astronomers describe movements which are repeated again and again, the stars and the planets remaining physically the same, and in the vegetable and animal kingdoms, though individuals are born and grow and die, the species do not change. So, too, the political theorists described a stable order. Doubtless, they would not have asserted that the social and political order, as they knew it, had been as it was from the beginning; nor would they have denied that it differed considerably from part to part of the world. Nevertheless, when they put together their theories, they took little notice of changes in the past or of present differences.

Later, when the study of history flourished, they could no longer ignore the course of change which had made the present what it was and had made it different from place to place. The historians brought it home to them, as never before, that the social and political order, though it formed a more or less coherent whole and was the product of human activities, was yet not the deliberate creation of man. Men had not decided how it should be, though it was the consequence of what they had done and was fairly well adapted to their needs. How then had it come to be what it was, coherent and useful? It seemed obvious that it could not have become so merely by chance. Burke suggested that God, working through men, had made it what it was, and Hegel put Spirit in the place of God. But what could be done by those who wanted, without benefit of theology or metaphysics, to explain how society had come to be an elaborate structure adapted to men's needs and attitudes of mind? It seemed to them that they must offer a 'scientific' explanation, and also that no explanation could be properly 'scientific' unless it postulated a 'law of social change'. Thus respect for science inspired an enterprise unknown to any of the authentic sciences: the attempt to formulate a law explaining, not any event of a given kind, but a whole course of events. Yet respect for science alone could not have inspired an enterprise so alien to the scientific spirit. The desire to explain the whole course of history sprang from a need much older than the century which saw the triumph of the scientific spirit: the human need for assurance that man is moving in a definite and desirable direction. It is this same need which has given birth to religion. But, though the need is at bottom the same, these new doctrines meet it differently. Religion gives this assurance conditionally and to each man separately. It assures him that there is a destination which he can reach provided he deserves to reach it, whereas these doctrines give the assurance unconditionally and to mankind in general. And yet the assurance, to whoever can bring himself to accept it, is worth having, because, though he may not himself reach the promised land, the movement towards it gives dignity and importance to his efforts, which form part of the movement. He strives for the species, seeing it as an enlargement of himself.

III. HAPPINESS AND THE EXPANSION OF KNOWLEDGE

1. Error and Vice

Bacon and the abbé de Saint-Pierre valued knowledge for its usefulness. They held that men, by extending their knowledge, increase their power over nature and their ability to satisfy their wants, and by satisfying their wants increase their happiness.[1] Bacon had a larger view than Saint-Pierre of the utility of knowledge; he would never

---

[1] That doctrine, in this rather crude form, has been so much and so severely attacked that it no longer appeals to intellectuals; but it is still widely popular. It is implicit in many contemporary arguments which take it for granted that men are the better off for the spread of industry.

have put the inventor of a useful machine higher on the roll of honour than a Newton or a Leibniz. Yet he, too, set store by knowledge chiefly because it increases man's power over nature; he agreed with Saint-Pierre about the way in which knowledge is useful to man and differed from him only in seeing more clearly how what is not useful immediately may be so in the long run.

Nobody – not even Rousseau – would deny that the expansion of knowledge increases man's power over nature. But Rousseau (and many others) would deny what both Bacon and Saint-Pierre take for granted – that man is the better for increasing this power. As man's power to satisfy his wants increases, those wants change. Why should we believe that his power more than keeps pace with his wants? Why should we even believe that the wants he acquires must be such that he could satisfy them, provided his power increased sufficiently? Why should we take it for granted that we are faced here with a problem of the kind to which economists seek a solution – a problem of ensuring that, given men's wants, what is needed to satisfy them is produced as efficiently as possible?

But there are less simple views than these about how knowledge makes for happiness. There is the doctrine that the expansion of knowledge changes man's conception of himself and his environment in ways which make him more capable of happiness, putting him out of reach of what has hitherto led to unhappiness. Hegel is perhaps the boldest and the most exciting exponent of this doctrine. As I have already discussed his theory at considerable length, I shall not return to it here. I shall take other examples of this doctrine; I shall discuss it in the forms given to it by Condorcet and Comte. Not that I am concerned with their theories for their own sake; I consider them only because I want to examine certain assumptions and lines of argument. Assumptions and arguments very like theirs can be found in the writings of Saint-Simon and Marx, and if I choose to examine these particular versions of them, it is only because they are more coherent or are less mixed up with other things. Condorcet and Comte are more systematic than Saint-Simon, and they do not make the excessive demands on the reader made by Hegel and Marx.

Condorcet and Comte were not primarily interested in man's increasing power over nature. They by no means neglected it, but they did not insist upon it. Technological progress was of only secondary importance to them. They were concerned, above all, with how man sees himself and the world he lives in; they were more interested in the nature of science, of man's vision of the world, than in scientific discoveries which have practical effects.

Condorcet believed that vice is grounded in error – not that it is error but that it proceeds from it.[1] And by vice he meant either conduct which is harmful or the motives which ordinarily produce such conduct. Creatures capable of knowledge are liable to error, but are also able to correct their errors. Hence vice is the product of reason and knowledge; or, rather, it is the product of bad reasoning and half-knowledge, and is eliminated as men learn to reason correctly and acquire sounder knowledge. Yet error tends to perpetuate itself for two reasons: because men are attached to their prejudices, to opinions received in childhood, which they do not easily discard even when all the truths needed to destroy them have been discovered; and because, as soon as there is a large store of what is taken for knowledge to be passed on from generation to generation, those whose profession it is to pass it on – the teachers – find it their interest to make a mystery of their supposed knowledge and to use it to get power over the taught. These 'groups or families of charlatans and sorcerers' form priestly 'castes',[2] whose organized imposture is a powerful cause of unhappiness and an obstacle to progress. But the motives which cause men to seek knowledge continue to operate, and eventually error is dissipated and imposture exposed.

If we consider Condorcet's account of how organized imposture arises, we see that it does not arise from error alone, but from error and the desire for power. And the error consists, not so much in the particular beliefs propagated by the teachers, as in the belief that those who teach are not impostors – a belief which may be confined to the taught or be shared as well by the teachers. Before the imposture can be brought to an end, the 'authority' of the impostors must be destroyed, and it cannot be destroyed until men have learnt to distinguish truth from error. Or, to say the same thing differently, it cannot be destroyed until men have learnt what knowledge is – until they have learnt what tests to apply to discover whether a belief is true

---

[1] At times Condorcet speaks as if vice were a kind of error, as, for example, when he calls cruelty towards enemies an error (see his *Esquisse d'un tableau historique des progrès de l'esprit humain*, ed. O. H. Prior and Yvon Belaval [Paris 1970], première époque, p. 17). But at other times he speaks as if the two were different, as if vice proceeded from error. As this second is the more plausible doctrine and is as well suited as the first to his theory of progress, I shall assume that it represents what he really believed.

[2] Ibid., troisième époque, pp. 38 and 43. Though from time to time Condorcet admits that the 'impostors' deceive themselves as well as their victims, he usually speaks as if they were deliberate deceivers. The 'imposture' he has chiefly in mind is organized religion. But, even if the deceit were not deliberate, his general argument would remain what it is.

or false. More important therefore, in Condorcet's opinion, than any particular discoveries is the discovery of what constitutes knowledge. Errors will continue to be made, even after this discovery, but those who challenge the errors will be able to do so to good effect.

Condorcet does not explain exactly how vice springs from error. But if we look at the examples he gives, it would seem that ignorance and error do not merely cause men to act harmfully but also affect the motives from which they act. What he calls 'imposture' thrives on ignorance and error, though not on them alone, for it is kept alive by the desire to dominate others. He does not speak as if – were ignorance and error to disappear – this desire would remain as strong as ever and would merely cease to have harmful effects; he speaks as if the desire would evaporate. The kind of domination exercised by impostors over their victims would no longer be possible, and would eventually cease to be desired. Though men might still wish to be important in the eyes of their fellow men, or to be admired by them, this wish would no longer give birth to a lust for power. So, too, envy, jealousy and malice would be greatly weakened, if men understood themselves and the world better than they do. These motives may arise out of passions which are part of man's 'enduring nature', either because he is born with them or acquires them in any social environment; and yet the motives are not the same as the passions from which they arise. A creature incapable of desiring the good opinion of others might also be incapable of envy or malice; but envy and malice are not the same motives as desire for good opinion, though they may be casually related to it. Nor are they distinguishable from it merely by their effects. Men's motives are changed by the situations in which they find themselves and by the opportunities open to them; and these situations and opportunities are in turn changed by how they see themselves and others and the world. Where men see things as they really are, their situations and opportunities produce (or strengthen) virtuous motives in them and not vicious ones. This, I think, is how vice and error, virtue and knowledge, are connected in Condorcet's opinion; for though he does not trouble to explain these connections, that is the explanation most in keeping with what he says.

Comte, though he expresses himself differently, holds what is at bottom much the same opinion. If he does not say, in so many words, that vice is an effect of error, he does suppose that men will become more sociable (that is to say, better able to live happily together) as their understanding is improved. Man, by extending his knowledge, comes to have needs which he can satisfy and learns to adapt the world to his needs. As he acquires a coherent and adequate knowledge of the world, he comes to have needs which are compatible with one another and with the needs of his fellows. The process which is a learning to get what he wants is also a learning to want what he can get; and the process which is a learning what he is and how he is situated is also a learning to be satisfied with his situation. 'Man', Comte tells us, apart from society, is 'an extremely sterile, or, rather, thoroughly defective, abstraction of our psychologists or ideologists, discarded by the positive spirit. The systematic propensity of that spirit. . .finally achieves its full importance; gaining within [the collectively developing individual] the philosophical foundation of human sociability, so far at least as sociability depends upon the intellect, whose capital significance. . .is incontestable'.[1] By the positive spirit Comte means the scientific spirit, which is the faith that everything that happens in the world can be explained in terms of laws whose truth is established by an appeal to the facts, by observation and experiment. It is part of that faith that all these laws form a coherent system; and this is what Comte has in mind when he speaks of the 'systematic propensity' of the 'positive' or scientific spirit. He says of it that it 'constitutes the logical unity of each individual mind', and also that it is 'the philosophical foundation of human sociability'. He means, presumably, that the knowledge provided by the sciences, being systematic, affects those who acquire it in such a way that they not only see the world as a coherent whole but come to have moral principles and needs which enable them to live together in peace and amity. Comte speaks of the great 'intellectual communion' upon which all 'true human association' rests, and says that it must go along with what he calls 'conformity of feeling' and 'convergence of interests'.[2] Though he does not, I think, make it clear precisely how these things are connected, he does say enough to show that, in his opinion, the more systematic and adequate men's understanding of the world, the more they will have the feelings and interests which enable them to form a 'true human association' or, in other words, a harmonious society.

2. Knowledge, Virtue and Happiness

There are two respects in which Condorcet and Comte differ from many present-day philosophers. They take it for granted that there are moral truths which are *true* in the same sense as the discoveries of

[1] Comte, *Discours sur l'esprit positif* (Paris 1905), I.ii.1, § 21, p. 40.
[2] Ibid., p. 41.

'science'; and they do not treat the hypotheses of the natural scientist as propositions different in kind from the axioms and theorems of the mathematician. Condorcet speaks of the discovery of the 'true rights of man' as if it were in the same sense an advance in knowledge as the discoveries of Newton or Galileo, and he also says that these rights 'can all be deduced from the single truth that man is a sentient being, with a capacity to reason and to acquire moral ideas'.[1] Comte speaks as if ethics were a science in the same sense as physics or biology; and he takes it to be a branch of sociology. He admits that hitherto moralists have not been scientific; they have been untouched by the 'positive spirit'. For that spirit does not direct human curiosity from the beginning, and it does not pervade all branches of study at the same time. Some branches become scientific before others, and the last to do so is the study of man. But Comte predicts that 'unimpeachable demonstrations, confirmed by the immense experience which mankind now possesses, will determine exactly the real influence, direct or indirect, private or public, of each act, each habit, each inclination or feeling. From such demonstrations there will naturally follow, as so many unavoidable corollaries, the general or special rules of conduct most in accordance with the universal order – rules which, consequently, will usually be found conducive to individual happiness'.[2]

We may reject both these views – that moral principles can be deduced from the capacities peculiar to man, or that they can be discovered by seeing what rules of conduct accord with 'the universal order' – and still hold that the expansion of knowledge leads to greater virtue and happiness. It is no argument against the belief in progress that men's tastes and preferences and their moral principles change. For we can still hold that men are the more virtuous the more they live in accordance with their principles, and we can say that they are the happier the more they have the feeling that life, as they live it, is worth living. If then we can show that, the greater men's understanding of the world and themselves, the more likely it is that they will live according to their principles, we can show that the expansion of knowledge leads to greater virtue. Again, if we can show that, the more men live according to their principles, the more they have the feeling that life, as they live it, is worth living, we have established a connection between virtue and happiness.

No doubt, if we put these propositions into the singular, there is

---

[1] Condorcet, *Esquisse des progrès de l'esprit humain*, neuvième époque, p. 149.
[2] Comte, *Discours sur l'esprit positif*, II.iii.3, § 53, pp. 110–11.

evidence in plenty that they are not true. We cannot plausibly say that, the greater any man's understanding of the world and himself, the greater the likelihood that he will live up to his own principles; for it may be that his principles are difficult to live up to because his neighbours are less enlightened than he is. Nor can we say that the more any man lives up to his own principles, the stronger his feeling that life, as he lives it, is worth living; for the attempt to live up to his principles, albeit successful, may exhaust him or cause him to be hated by his neighbours. The virtuous are often reduced to despair, and the intelligent often lack the courage to do what they believe to be right. Yet these propositions, though false in the singular, may be true in the plural. It may be true that the more men in general understand the world, the more likely it is that they will have principles which they can, and will in fact, live up to; and it may also be true that the more men in general live up to their principles, the more widespread and deeper the feeling among them that life, as they live it, is worth living. It may even be true that men will be the more free, the more they are virtuous. This may be so, even though freedom is not defined as the ability to live up to one's principles – even if it is defined as the ability to indulge one's tastes and preferences. For it may be that the more men live up to their principles, the more likely it is that they will have tastes and preferences which are mutually compatible and can be easily and safely indulged. Thus it may be that knowledge, freedom, virtue and happiness are, as Condorcet believed, so connected with one another, that, if we take society as a whole and not individuals separately, the first brings the other three with it.

The four may not increase *pari passu*. It may be that, from time to time, the increase of knowledge reduces freedom or virtue or happiness. And yet it may be that, in the long run, it increases them. This was the faith of Condorcet, and it could, without absurdity, be shared by someone who denied that moral principles can be deduced from the capacities peculiar to man or that they can be shown to be 'true' in the manner proposed by Comte.[1] No doubt, whoever shares that faith asserts that at least one of these three things (happiness, virtue or freedom) is desirable for its own sake, but this he can do without claiming that the assertion is true in the same sense as are the laws of either the mathematician or the natural scientist.

---

[1] Condorcet set great store by freedom, whereas Comte did not; but this difference between them, important in other connections, is not so in this.

3. *Reason and Understanding*

Condorcet says that 'nature has set no term to the perfecting of human faculties'.[1] He has in mind, above all, two capacities, which he does not distinguish from one another: reason and understanding, the ability to make inferences and the ability to explain and predict. We 'reason' (so he implies) better than our ancestors did and also have greater understanding than they had; and, as we surpass them, so our descendants will surpass us. But we do not walk or run much better than they did. The expansion of knowledge improves our mental abilities as it does not our physical ones. Logic improves our reasoning powers, and science improves our ability to explain and predict; but science does not improve our bodily powers to anything like the same extent. The *perfectibility* of man, as Condorcet conceives of it, is primarily intellectual and secondarily moral. Man improves his ability to reason, to explain and to predict, and, as he does so, strengthens in himself the preferences, tastes and motives which make for happiness.

But, surely, reason is not susceptible of indefinite improvement in the same sense as understanding is. We can never say of any scientific explanation that it is incapable of improvement; we can only say that, in the present state of our knowledge, it is the best available. But we can say of an argument that it is logically impeccable; that, given its premises, its conclusion necessarily follows. If we should venture to say that the ancient Greeks understood both nature and man less well than we do, we need not imply that the ability to reason was less developed in them than in us. It may have been more developed, even though logic has made progress since their time. For, though our modern logicians may offer us better explanations than we can find in Aristotle of what is involved in reasoning, it does not follow that we reason better than did Aristotle and his contemporaries. This is not to deny that the study of logic improves our reasoning powers; it is to say only that both science and logic can make progress without our reasoning powers being improved. No doubt, these powers *can* be improved; for, though an argument which is impeccable cannot be bettered, it is possible to ensure that we argue better about more and more things. It is also possible to ensure that, given the knowledge available to us, we more often make reasonable assumptions.

Let us distinguish, rather more carefully than Condorcet troubled to do, between *reason* and *understanding* – between knowing how to

[1] *Esquisse des progrès de l'esprit humain*, avant-propos, p. 3.

333

use certain methods and being able to give explanations acceptable to anyone who knows how those methods should be used. And let us understand by reason, not only the ability to make correct inferences, but also the ability to make reasonable assumptions – that is to say, the ability to make assumptions which are borne out by the 'available and relevant' facts. This, admittedly, is a rough definition of reason, if only because the words *available* and *relevant* call for further elucidation; but it may be good enough for our purpose, which is merely to examine what Condorcet meant by perfectibility and not to discuss matters better left to the logician. Given this sense of reason, an assumption which is perfectly reasonable at one time, in the sense that it is borne out by such relevant and well-authenticated facts as are available, may not be so at another. Again, an assumption which might be reasonable if more were known than is known – if relevant facts not yet available were available – may be unreasonable at the time it is made. Thus, one man might be nearer being right than another and yet be the less reasonable of the two; he might be so either for the reason just given or because, by making faulty inferences from the same assumptions, he reaches a conclusion later seen to be nearer the truth.

Now, in theory, it is quite possible that, after a certain period, man's reasoning powers should have become perfect – that he should have acquired, as fully as he ever can acquire them, certain skills, that he should have mastered certain methods. This need not mean that logic, understood as the study of these methods, has no further progress to make; it may mean only that what further progress it does make does not improve man's ability to reason correctly. Thus it may be that logicians will offer better explanations of what is involved in the making and testing of hypotheses than any they have offered so far; if they do, they will improve our understanding of scientific method. But this they may do without in any way increasing the competence of scientists. Scientists may be as fully masters of scientific method as ever they will be. That is not to deny that they may improve their experimental techniques; it is only to suggest that their grasp of the essentials of their method (as distinct from their capacity to explain those essentials, which is the business of the logician and not theirs) is already perfect.

Condorcet spoke not of perfectedness, but of perfectibility. Yet he also spoke as if, in the seventeenth century, owing largely to the work of Bacon, Galileo and Descartes, science had come to maturity – as if, at that time, men had at last grasped the essentials of certain methods of enquiry and explanation which enabled them to distinguish, as never before, knowledge from mere opinion, and therefore also enabled them to measure progress in knowledge. If he was right, then by the seventeenth century reason was already, in one sense, perfected, even though in later centuries logicians improved their understanding of scientific method and scientists improved their techniques. Thus, though Einstein's theory is an improvement on Newton's, each may be perfectly reasonable, given the facts available when it was produced. To say this is to imply that no improvement in Newton's understanding of logic or scientific method would have made it more reasonable for him, given the facts he had available, to put forward other hypotheses. On the other hand, a theory constructed before science came to maturity might be less reasonable than Newton's, even though the maker of it was as gifted as Newton and made as good a use as could be made of the methods available to him. It might be just as intelligent a theory, just as well constructed, just as perfect in its kind, given those methods; and yet it would be less *reasonable* in the sense of the word implied by Condorcet when he took it for granted that an explanation, to be fully reasonable, must be scientific.

Condorcet sometimes spoke as if explanations constructed by the proper method must endure forever – as if progress in knowledge consisted in a steady increase in the number of 'truths' acquired once and for all rather than in the repeated supersession of less by more adequate explanations. He took it for granted that science, as it progressed, would not shake the 'truths' discovered by a Newton but would merely add other truths to them. Yet he did not always speak in this way. For example, he said that 'methods which lead us to discoveries can die out, so that science is somehow forced to stop, unless new methods arise to provide genius with a new instrument, or to facilitate the use of those which it could no longer employ without too much waste of time and energy'.[1] From the context it would appear that what he had in mind here was not a drastic change in men's ideas about what constitutes knowledge and about how knowledge is to be tested – not a change of method of the sort that would interest the logician, but the framing of new hypotheses. An hypothesis, when its implications have been worked out, may be said to be 'exhausted', and further progress may require the framing of a new hypothesis, which can be properly tested only if new instruments and techniques are devised. Science has its technology, just as production has – and a technology which changes with time, even though the essentials of the scientific method remain the same.

Therefore, if we understand by the improvement of knowledge,

---

[1] *Esquisse des progrès de l'esprit humain*, neuvième époque, p. 191.

not only the extension of a certain type of explanation more and more widely, but also the substitution of more for less adequate explanations of that type, we do not exactly part company with Condorcet; we merely choose, of two positions which he adopted, the one which is the less prominent and the less clearly put. Again, in distinguishing between knowledge thus understood – knowledge which can always be improved upon[1], and reason – which may be impeccable – we make a distinction which Condorcet did not make but which is implicit in some aspects of his theory of progress.

Once men have mastered the methods of enquiry and explanation which are 'rational', they can apply them more and more widely, more and more successfully. One branch of study after another can become scientific. There is therefore a sense in which reason, the successful use of these methods, can make progress indefinitely – a sense in which reason always has further conquests to make and is never in complete and secure possession of men's minds. In one sense, reason, unlike understanding, can be perfect; and yet, in another, it too is always imperfect. Men will always adopt some irrational opinions and put forward some irrational explanations, and what they take for science will never be wholly scientific. By this I mean, not that new theories will take the place of old ones as men become better acquainted with the relevant facts, but that there will always be current among them theories which are not borne out by such facts as they have available. No matter how great men's ability and willingness to construct rational explanations, it will always be possible to make them greater; and this is the sense in which reason is indefinitely 'perfectible'.

4. Knowledge as a Means to Happiness

In the *Sketch*, Condorcet considers the triumph of reason only in the sphere of theory, of general explanation. One branch of study after another becomes scientific, and men come to know the natural world, society and human nature more and more as they really are. This increase in knowledge is the progress of science, and it is how Condorcet and Comte see that progress. But how exactly, we may ask, is such progress connected with the increase of happiness? Granted that happiness depends, in some way, on understanding, it is by no

---

[1] The knowledge here in question – the knowledge susceptible of improvement – is not mere acquaintance with facts, a mere knowing that something is or was the case; it is knowledge of causal connections.

means clear how it depends on the kind of understanding which is science. No doubt, there are illusions about himself and his situation which can make a man deeply unhappy. If he is to gain happiness, he must be rid of these illusions; he must acquire knowledge which he lacks. But this knowledge is not general; it is not science; it is particular, though it may, of course, involve the use of science.

There are several questions which we must put, of which neither Condorcet nor Comte took notice. Granted that there are illusions which make for unhappiness, will men be less prey to them the greater the progress of science among them? Are there not also illusions which make for happiness and which science dispels? May it not be true that, as science progresses, illusions making for unhappiness actually increase in number and in strength? Even though science, in itself, is the enemy of all illusions, whatever their effect, it may still happen that scientific progress brings along with it changes which make men more inclined than they were to harbour dangerous illusions. Even though science produces the knowledge which could be used to dispel these illusions, the ability and the will to use that knowledge may be lacking.

Knowledge can be a means to happiness in two ways. Where what men aspire to makes them happy if they get it, knowledge can help them to get it; and where they aspire to what does not bring happiness, it can explain to them both what will happen if they persist in trying to achieve what they aspire to and how they come to aspire to it. If what they aspire to brings them happiness, then they may need very little knowledge in order to be happy. They may be living in a simple society, and their understanding of the world and themselves may be slight, and yet they may be happy if what they aspire to can be achieved and they know what to do in order to achieve it. They may have illusions and still be happy, even though their aspirations and illusions are closely connected. Provided that what they aspire to is attainable and they know how to attain it, they may be happy. Indeed, they may be happy even if part of what they aspire to – and that part the most precious – is not attainable; for they may aspire to a life after death, and there may be no such life. But their aspirations for this world, which they think of as a preparation for the next, may be attainable and satisfying. If they lacked the knowledge to attain what they aspire to in this world, they would be less happy; but they would also be less happy if they lost their illusions.

Clearly, the connections between knowledge, illusion and happiness are less simple than Condorcet supposed. Men may have little knowledge and be happy, or they may have much knowledge and be unhappy. They may have strong illusions and be happy, or they may have no illusions and be unhappy. Or the illusions which make for happiness may be more easily dispelled by science than the illusions which make for unhappiness. For the illusions which make for unhappiness may be much less the sort of theological and metaphysical beliefs which science undermines than the misconceptions about himself and his situation which a man can easily retain in a society where the prestige of science is immense. Science could, of course, help him to get rid of these misconceptions if he applied the findings impartially to his own case, but this he might not be able to do, even if he were himself a scientist.

Still, unhappiness, like everything else, has its causes, which can be discovered. As science progresses, society may change in ways which multiply the causes of unhappiness, but science may discover these causes. As society becomes more complicated and its members more sophisticated, it may be that happiness is both more precarious and more within men's reach. Just as civilization, by herding men together in large towns, may expose them to risks of infection unknown in simpler societies, and may yet contrive to keep them in better health, so it may also add greatly to the risks of unhappiness and yet contrive to make them more happy. The happiness which in simple societies costs so little may require a much greater exercise of will and intelligence, a much larger use of knowledge, in sophisticated societies. For worse and for better, the old innocence (such as it was) has been lost. True though it may be that civilization brings great evils with it, we can only hope to cure those evils by using the knowledge which it also brings. If Condorcet and Comte had said merely this, it would be easy to agree with them. But they said much more; or, if they did not say it, they implied it. They implied that, as knowledge increases, so too does the likelihood that men will use it to remove the causes of unhappiness.

Nearly all believers in progress have been willing to admit that it brings great evils with it. Even Condorcet admitted that, when knowledge begins to accumulate, there arise in society bodies of teachers who pass on from generation to generation what has been acquired – bodies whose interest it is that the doctrines they teach should not be challenged. These bodies arise before men have learnt how to test what passes for knowledge in order to see whether or not it is genuine; and they therefore teach false doctrines as well as true. They perpetuate error and impede the further advancement of knowledge. Comte was less inclined than Condorcet to speak harshly of these bodies. Far from deploring the errors and illusions which flourish when men make their first attempts to explain the world systematically, he spoke charitably of their purveyors, because it seemed to him that men, as soon as their faculties begin to develop, need assurance that the world is a coherent whole and that there is a way of life proper to creatures of their kind. They need assurance that the world as a whole, including their place in it, is understood – if not by themselves, then at least by teachers and guides whom they trust. They need the assurance long before it can be well grounded, and therefore the bodies that create it, though purveyors of error and illusion, perform a useful task. Yet he too believed that these errors and illusions – the effects of early progress – eventually become obstacles to further progress. He believed also that, after the inevitable ruin of such illusions, there must ensue a period of moral and spiritual anarchy until men can get from science the assurance which the purveyors of illusion had earlier given them.

Neither Condorcet nor Comte denied that the increase of knowledge brings evil with it. But they affirmed or implied that this increase, if it continues (and they were certain it would continue), must eventually cure these evils and others also. It never occurred to them that the knowledge needed to cure these evils might be available and yet not be used. Man, they thought, desires happiness. Therefore, if he is unhappy and can discover the causes of his unhappiness and how to remove them, it is highly probable that he will make use of this knowledge for his own good. Unfortunately, that argument is not as convincing as it appears; but, before we examine it more closely, there is another matter that needs discussing.

5. Condorcet and Depth Psychology

We have seen that, in Condorcet's opinion, vice, which is the chief cause of unhappiness, springs from error. But Condorcet did not confuse vice with error. Properly speaking, it is only our motives and the actions which proceed from them, and not our beliefs, which can be vicious; and if we call beliefs vicious, it is because they are inspired by or encourage vicious motives and actions. The doctrine that vice springs from error asserts no more than this: that men would not acquire vicious motives unless they had mistaken beliefs. But, in order to be vicious, a man need not be mistaken about the situation in which he contemplates action; nor, in order to be virtuous, need he be free of mistakes about it. Condorcet has been called a 'rationalist', and this doctrine – that vice springs from error or ignorance – has been called a 'rationalist fallacy'. It is therefore well to remember that the doctrine is not quite as simple or simple-minded as it is sometimes made out to be.

To see more clearly both the strength and the weakness of Condorcet's doctrine, let us compare it, for a moment, with what is called depth psychology, which seeks to explain how character is built up out of primitive urges or desires (sometimes called the *libido*), as those urges are transformed and the child learns to control them or contrives to ignore them by thrusting them into the 'unconscious'. Though the depth psychologist is not concerned, as Condorcet sometimes was, to pass moral judgements, though he seldom speaks of vice or virtue, he does attempt to explain how men come to have passions harmful to themselves and to others – passions which most people, including Condorcet, would call vicious. These passions, he says, are acquired in early childhood; and though he does not see them as effects of error, of mistaken judgements, he does see them as arising, at least in part, from a failure to understand. A child's character can be deeply affected by what happens to it before it has learnt to think – before it is able to pass judgements, mistaken or otherwise. No doubt, when it is able to pass judgements, it will make mistakes; it will believe what is false, and these beliefs will give rise to anxieties and other feelings which are harmful. The psychologist does not neglect or belittle the bad effects on a child of false beliefs, especially of false beliefs about its parents' feelings towards it. But he does allow that its character can be damaged before its intelligence is developed enough to enable it to pass judgements, and therefore to make what Condorcet understood by errors; and he also allows that true beliefs may be damaging to it. Not all children who believe that their parents do not love them or may hurt them are mistaken, and the belief is not the less damaging for being true.

And yet, unless I have misunderstood them, such psychologists do imply that the damage to the child's character is due in large part to a failure of understanding. The child has a painful experience about which it may still be incapable of passing any judgement, false or true; or it may pass judgements some of which are false and others true, or all of which are true. But, even if they are all true, they express only a partial understanding of what has happened, an understanding which is insufficient to prevent the misdirection of 'psychic energy', the emergence of harmful passions. And these passions, even when they are not themselves effects of false beliefs, may be fertile sources of error. Fear, jealousy, anger and envy, which move men to hurt themselves and one another, are as much producers as they are products of false beliefs. Thus, if we follow these psychologists, we can deny that the passions ordinarily called vicious always, or even generally, spring from error, and yet also insist that they would not arise in us, or would be much weaker, if we had a better understanding of the situations in which they do arise. If we had been able, at the time, to see those situations as they would appear to a perceptive, calm and intelligent adult, they would not have affected us as they did. But we were children, and could not see them as they were. Thus it is that, before we are old enough to understand them, we can have experiences which bewilder and hurt us, and are too painful to recall. We come to be so ashamed or frightened of certain of our passions that we refuse to admit, even to ourselves, that we have them, resorting to false beliefs to help us avoid the shame we should feel if we saw ourselves as we really are or were. From a failure to understand due to ignorance and incapacity – that is, to our faculties not yet being sufficiently developed – there arise in us feelings which inhibit our use of those faculties when they are developed. Because of what happened to us when we were still incapable of understanding, when reason was defective in us, there are now things which we dare not understand even though we are intellectually mature, even though we have learnt to think. And because we dare not see ourselves as we really are or were, we construct a false picture of ourselves and our situation as a protection against the truth; we feel the need to assert ourselves, to make ourselves felt in the world, in ways which are harmful, or else we are tempted to withdraw from it, refusing to deal with the problems that face us. We are apt to be either a menace or a burden to others and ourselves.

The depth psychologist also believes, although not quite in the same way as Condorcet, in the corrective and curative use of knowledge. Though most of us never get rid of the harmful passions produced in us by experiences which we could not understand when we had them, we do, to a greater or lesser extent, learn to keep them under control. We come, more or less, to understand our environment and to have coherent and attainable purposes; we acquire a measure of self-discipline and some capacity to play a part in society which affords us self-respect and the respect of others. This is the corrective use of knowledge. But our harmful passions may be so strong that, when they are upon us, we cannot control them; they may make us incapable of self-discipline, incapable of sustaining a respectable social rôle which can satisfy us. Yet even then we are not without a remedy, for we may be able to weaken these passions by reliving in memory the experiences which produced them. In 'reliving' an experience we see it, for the first time, in perspective; we understand it as we could not do at the time we had it. We put it, as it were, in its proper place. But that we cannot do unaided; we need the help of the psychoanalyst who possesses special knowledge and skills. This is a curative use of knowledge.

The depth psychologist has more elaborate and, no doubt, more profound ideas than any eighteenth-century philosopher about how understanding and passion are connected in the human mind and about the kind of self-knowledge which serves to weaken harmful passions. Condorcet seems to have thought that science alone could weaken them – that it was enough for men to understand the working of the mind, as the psychologist strives to understand it, for them to cease being subject to such passions. It seems not to have occurred to him that a man might have a deep knowledge of psychology without being able to apply this knowledge to himself – that he might even be able to pass shrewd, severe and true judgements on himself and still not know that about himself which a man needs to know if he is to exorcize or weaken his harmful passions. His severity might even serve to protect him from this knowledge; he might castigate himself ·for faults which are trivial (though he pretends to think otherwise) or which in him are small (though he insists that they are not) to turn his mind away from others which he dare not look at. He might even in some moods, when he can speak of himself as he would of another man, bring himself to admit that he has certain passions, and yet be unable to recognize them when they are actually upon him or have moved him to action.

There is a great deal in recent psychology unthought of or only lightly touched upon by Condorcet. Yet this psychology does suggest that our harmful passions (those which Condorcet would call *vicious*) are often produced in us by something closely akin to error, by a failure to understand; and it does agree with Condorcet that knowledge can cure us of these passions, or at least can greatly weaken them in us. But, we may ask, why should this be so? Why should the light of understanding take life or strength from some of our passions and not from others? Why should our coming to understand what has made us jealous, envious or cruel weaken jealousy, envy or cruelty in us when our coming to understand what has made us affectionate or generous does not weaken our love or generosity? Presumably, because we are social as well as rational creatures – creatures whose happiness depends upon being able to inspire and to feel affection and respect. We aspire to a happiness whose character is determined, not merely by our desires, but by how we see ourselves and the world. To be happy is to be satisfied with a way of life, which only a rational creature can be:

that is to say, a creature capable of systematic thought, and therefore of seeing itself as having a life to live. If that creature is also social, its happiness will depend upon how it feels towards others and itself, and how others feel towards it. If, given its capacities and environment, it is to be happy, some of these feelings (which are the feelings of a being that thinks) must be strong and others weak. Therefore such creatures, to be securely happy, need to know more than what to do to satisfy their actual desires; they must, if their desires stand in the way of their happiness, change themselves, which they cannot do effectively unless they know what they are and how they come to be as they are.

The depth psychologist differs conspicuously from Condorcet; he does not treat error or false belief as the sole, or even the prime, cause of harmful feelings, and he sees in these feelings a source of false beliefs peculiarly difficult to eradicate; he has a subtler understanding of what is involved in self-knowledge and considers the curative use of only that one kind of knowledge, whereas Condorcet can hardly be said to consider self-knowledge at all, for he does not distinguish it from the science of psychology. By man's knowledge of himself he means only scientific knowledge, the apprehension of general propositions about man; he does not mean a particular man's seeing himself as he is or was. He thus has no conception of the curative use of a self-knowledge which is not psychology, though psychology may be a means to it. The false beliefs he has in mind when he speaks of the errors from which the vices spring are about the world or society or human nature; they are not false beliefs about unique individuals and particular situations. They are therefore beliefs which are dissipated by the mere dissemination of scientific knowledge. Condorcet does not even seriously enquire whether it is more difficult or more important to dissipate some kinds of error than others. There are many and large differences between Condorcet and the psychologists I speak of – between the rationalists of the century before the last and the men of our day who are supposed to have shown how small a part reason plays in human behaviour; and, no doubt, if we follow Condorcet rather than these men, we are apt to cherish much larger hopes of moral improvement and increasing happiness resulting from the progress of science. Nevertheless, there are also important similarities, which we ought to bear in mind, if only to preserve ourselves from some of the criticisms still levelled at the 'shallow' rationalism of the eighteenth century.

Condorcet has almost nothing to say about how the growth and dissemination of knowledge weaken the vicious passions and increase happiness. Believing that vice, which makes for unhappiness, is rooted in error, he takes it for granted that scientific progress, since it dissipates error, strikes at the root of unhappiness. He is therefore much more concerned to show how science progresses and why it is likely to do so indefinitely than to explain how it weakens vice and makes for happiness. But Comte has more to say.

Hitherto, Comte tells us, science has confined itself largely to explaining the physical world; the sciences which have made spectacular progress have been the 'natural' sciences. But already the scientific or positive spirit – the search for uniformities of behaviour rather than teleological and theological explanations – is prominent in the study of man and society. When the positive spirit has triumphed in all branches of study, when what is taken for authentic knowledge (other than mere acquaintance with particular facts) consists only of abstract principles of reasoning and calculation (logic and mathematics) and of empirical laws supported by observation and experiment, then men will understand for the first time the manner of beings they are and the world in which they live. They will know how to organize their lives for happiness; and with such knowledge there will come the will to use it. In a society where the positive spirit prevails, though no man possesses all the knowledge useful to mankind, most men are willing to defer to those whose knowledge is greater than their own. That is to say, where the knowledge needed for happiness is available, there are men able and willing to use it to that end, while those who lack this ability recognize it in those that have it and look for guidance from them.

This, I admit, is not quite what Comte says, but it does, I think, put into words what he implies. For he takes two things for granted: that, when the study of man and society has become positive or scientific – when it has produced 'authentic' knowledge – that knowledge will be used for the common good; and that the knowledge will not be possessed by all men but by an élite to whom other men will defer. And, presumably, this knowledge will not be possessed entire by every member of the élite; it will be knowledge which they have between them. Therefore, there will be deference to superior knowledge both within the élite and from the rest of the community towards the élite. But Comte goes further even than this; he speaks of a need for a spiritual authority, for an organized body to do for the society of the future what the Church attempted in the past, before science began to undermine theology. This body must have all knowledge for its province, making a system of it; its pronouncements must be authoritative. It must be the overseer of society. And Comte does not merely proclaim the need for this spiritual authority; he implies that, as knowledge increases, the need will be felt and met. The progress of science, of positive knowledge, will so affect men that there will arise among them the spiritual authority required to ensure that knowledge is used for their good.

6. The Uses of Science, Natural and Social

Knowledge can be used to dissipate harmful passions in two ways: it can be used to create a social environment unpropitious to these passions, and it can be used to increase the individual's self-control and self-knowledge. For the sake of convenience, let us call the first use *indirect* and the second *direct*. The second may be either *education* or *therapy*: it may consist in teaching the individual to behave well, or it may consist in improving his physical and mental health. Both Condorcet and Comte had chiefly in mind the indirect use and the direct use which is education. Of therapy, as the psychiatrist now understands it, they, of course, knew nothing. They believed that men, as their knowledge grew, would use that knowledge to create a social order making for virtue and happiness and would so educate the young that they would accept this order. Though that belief was expressed more elaborately and explicitly by Comte than by Condorcet, it was common to them both.

Condorcet and Comte also believed (though this time the belief was stronger in Condorcet than in Comte) that, to cure men of error and prejudice, little more is needed than to bring the truth to their notice. If the truth is brought to them and they do not accept it, this is because, through indolence or inattention or defective intelligence, they have failed to understand it. That a man should resist the truth and fear it; that he should argue himself into rejecting it, even when he has intelligence enough to understand it; that he should attend to it as to an enemy, using his reason to persuade himself that it is not true, even against the weight of the evidence: that he should do all this was a possibility that Condorcet never took into account. He admitted that truth might be impeded because some men had an interest that it should be; but he believed that these very men, if they were educated and intelligent, could not attend to the truth and reject it *in foro interno*. If, then, having attended to it, they denied it, they must be impostors. Comte saw rather more deeply than Condorcet into the social causes of false beliefs, and was more willing to allow that these beliefs had been useful while the truth was still undiscovered; but he also was too apt to believe that the soundest arguments convince. The psychological causes of irrational beliefs – of beliefs inconsistent with one another or held against the weight of evidence easily accessible – were less understood (or, at least, less discussed) in their day than they are now.[1]

But the optimism of Condorcet and Comte is to be discounted for other reasons than their exaggerating the persuasive power of sound argument. They did not see that the increase of knowledge and the technical progress resulting from it might have social consequences which would prevent men so using their knowledge as to increase happiness. So far, I have attended more to Condorcet than to Comte, but now, if I am to make this point clear, I must attend more to Comte.

Comte emphasized, more strongly even than Condorcet, that in the earlier stages of 'progress' men's understanding of the physical world grows much more rapidly than their understanding of themselves and society. With the increase of knowledge, society grows more elaborate, but the knowledge whose use makes society more elaborate does not enlarge men's understanding of the social order or their power to adapt it to meet their needs. Physics, chemistry and biology make possible the use of methods of production, war and coercion which convert small and simple societies into large ones, but add nothing to men's understanding of themselves and their social environment. It is not until much later that men address themselves to the scientific study of the human mind and social institutions. They want, no doubt, to increase their power over nature the better to satisfy their needs, but they soon acquire a curiosity about the world which moves them to push their enquiries much further than is needed to solve their practical problems. Hence the bold theories, theological and metaphysical, which often change profoundly their conception of the world, without deeply affecting their material way of life. As rational creatures who need to feel that they are living in a tidy and intelligible world, men produce these vast intellectual systems into which they pour such little genuine knowledge as they possess. They create in themselves the illusion that they understand

---

[1] Long before their time, Pascal was aware how strong men's motives might be for fearing the truth and resisting it. He was aware, too, that the ability to reason and irrationality are closely connected in more than the obvious sense that only creatures capable of reasoning are capable of false reasoning. He was aware that truth might be unbearable to such a creature because, being able to think conceptually, it could be an object of thought to itself, and therefore a victim of ambitions and fears unknown to creatures lacking that ability. He understood, as Condorcet and Comte never did, the need for self-deception peculiar to the mind capable of reasoning.

all aspects of reality long before they come anywhere near doing so. Their curiosity about themselves and society and their need to explain them systematically arise as early as their curiosity about the external world. But the ability to explain them *scientifically* comes to them last of all. Precise observation, measurement and experiment are easier in the natural sciences than in psychology and the study of social institutions. Therefore the knowledge which increases men's power over external nature comes to them earlier than the knowledge which increases their power over themselves.

There is more to it than just this. For the use of the first kind of knowledge changes men and their social environment; and, since they still lack the second kind (though believing they have it), it changes them in ways they do not understand. When society is stable or changes slowly, men need not understand it to be on good terms with themselves and their neighbours. It is enough for them to follow ancestral ways, to do what is expected of them, and to accept the philosophy whose function is to assure them that there is a scheme of things in which they are important. But when society is changing fast, largely as the result of the use of the first kind of knowledge, this type of philosophy can no longer give men the assurance it once gave. Therefore, they are at sea until the study of man and society has also become scientific, until they have acquired the second kind of knowledge. They can then discover what are the conditions of happiness for creatures like themselves, and can set about creating those conditions.

Thus Comte, while he agreed with Condorcet that some sciences necessarily appear long before others, had a much sharper sense that this might be the cause of great suffering. Science deprives men of a faith they can live by long before it provides anything fit to take its place, and in the meantime men are lost and unhappy. The complaint so often heard today that some kinds of knowledge can greatly outrun others, to the detriment of mankind, was one with which Comte, like his one-time mentor Saint-Simon, would certainly have sympathized. Yet he took it for granted that the increase of knowledge must eventually remove whatever evils it has brought with it. The knowledge that comes first without the knowledge that comes after may have consequences that are harmful, but the later knowledge will come in its turn and whatever harm has been done will be undone. If we grant that men desire happiness and can discover its conditions, social and psychological, must we not admit that, having discovered them, they will create them? It seemed obvious to Comte that we must.

7. *Knowledge and the Opportunity to Use It*

It seemed obvious to him, perhaps, because he did what we all do for the sake of convenience, because he spoke of mankind as if it were one man – as if all the knowledge acquired by mankind were the possession of one possessor. If a man desires happiness and knows what to do to obtain it, will he not use that knowledge to get what he wants? If it is objected that he may suffer from defects which stand in the way of his using it, the answer is that, *ex hypothesi*, he also knows how to get rid of the defects, to cure himself. Provided that the desire for happiness is not destroyed or greatly weakened in the very process of acquiring the knowledge needed to satisfy it, how can it be doubted that the knowledge, once acquired, will be used for the purpose it was sought?

But this argument is plausible only if it refers to one man having all the knowledge he needs to ensure his own happiness. Even if we grant that a man who strongly desires happiness and knows how to get it will almost certainly use that knowledge to get what he wants, it does not follow that a large number of men, who *between them* have that knowledge, will so use it. They may or they may not. All that needs to be known to make men happy may be known by some member or other of a community, all of whose members strongly desire happiness, and yet there may be little chance of this knowledge being put to good use. Clearly, there is a great difference between two communities, of which one is so organized that the knowledge available inside it is likely to be put to good use and the other is not; and yet the knowledge of how a community should be organized to make the best use of what knowledge is available inside it might be as great and as widespread in the second community as in the first. The increase of knowledge may have profound effects on society without ensuring that it is so organized that good use is made of the knowledge available inside it. Have any people in our time been more learned than the Germans? Has their superiority been less marked in psychology and the social studies than in the natural sciences? What people have had a greater respect for learning? The knowledge useful to the social reformer and the educator has been as abundant and as widespread among them as among any other people. Yet the Germans have never been more dangerous to themselves and their neighbours than during this period of their intellectual pre-eminence.

The increase of knowledge makes possible technical changes which transform the economy and the social structure. Men must, if they are to earn their livings and achieve their ambitions, acquire skills and knowledge unnecessary to their ancestors; they must become literate and learn a great deal from books. There must be, in a complicated industrial society, a wide and varied dissemination of knowledge. Yet the transformation of society may strengthen harmful passions or otherwise create conditions making it unlikely that knowledge will be used for the common good, though it is used abundantly to attain a much greater variety of goals than are known to simple and illiterate communities. The kind of knowledge which to Comte seemed the most valuable of all – the understanding of man and society, the knowledge needed for moral progress (as he conceived of it), for individual happiness and social harmony – may be available, and yet the persons who have it may have neither power nor influence. There may be theoretical knowledge and practical ability in plenty, and yet the two may seldom come together for the common good.

No doubt, in every technically advanced society, knowledge and skill are held in high esteem. Men in high positions are expected, much more than in simpler societies, to be efficient, and efficiency depends on knowledge. Not only children, but adults too, spend long hours acquiring knowledge and skill. And this knowledge and skill are doubtless, in the economist's sense, useful, not only to their possessors but to others as well. For those who acquire them perform services which are marketable, which have a price; and their having a price is a mark of their utility. There is an effective demand for these services; there are persons willing and able to pay for them. But if, like Condorcet or Comte, we have in mind utility in a sense different from the economist's, we cannot conclude that whatever is marketable is useful, let alone that its price is a measure of its utility. Those who attain the highest positions, who make the most successful careers, who acquire the largest shares of power and influence, may owe what they get to proven competence, and not to birth or patronage; and their competence may be rare, requiring a degree of knowledge and skill to which few can aspire, no matter how great their opportunities. But this knowledge and skill, though useful for certain purposes, may not be used for the purposes which, in the eyes of a Condorcet or a Comte, are the most important. The politician, the businessman, the civil servant or the teacher, to rise to the top of his profession, may need rare abilities useful to his party or his business or his profession, or even his country; but his having these abilities is no warrant that he has others needed for the common good.

In short, as society accumulates the products of men's muscles and their brains, it may come to have the knowledge and skill required for moral progress – for movement towards some desirable condition of man and society – as well as the knowledge and skill required for the making of successful careers and the acquisition of power; but, unless the makers of successful careers and the acquirers of power also have the first kind of knowledge and skill, or are able and willing to make use of those who do have them, society will make no progress, though it has the means to do so. Knowledge, power and will are closely related to one another, and related in many ways, both in the individual and in society. Unfortunately, they are not so related that we can assume that, as knowledge accumulates, it will be so distributed among men that it comes to those who have the power and the will to use it for the common good. But this is precisely the assumption tacitly made by Condorcet and by Comte, as by so many other believers in progress.

The uses to which men put their knowledge often have harmful consequences which they do not foresee, and which it takes time for them to understand and to learn to avoid. Therefore, it can easily happen that, before they have understood them and discovered remedies, such passions have been aroused that it is unlikely that those who know the remedies will be in a position to apply them. It can easily happen, for example, that, as a country grows rapidly industrial, the crowding of people together in enormous towns, the great mobility of labour, mass unemployment, the weakening of family ties and other causes, will generate such passions that power and influence come easily to the fanatical or the unscrupulous. The 'masses' subject to these passions are not more ignorant or more mistaken than their ancestors. On the contrary, they may well have a larger understanding as well as a greater variety of skills. And yet it is because they have these passions and because their understanding is defective that they can be made use of by the fanatical and the unscrupulous. It requires greater understanding than either they or their leaders possess to find a remedy for their condition. Their ancestors, living in a simpler society and relying on tradition, could make do with less understanding, but *they* need more. Thus, we may say of them that they are victims of the use of one kind of knowledge who can be saved only by the use of another kind. But the evils which knowledge brings may grow faster than the knowledge required for their remedy, or may prevent the effective use of that knowledge when it comes.

Condorcet valued both freedom and happiness, as liberals still do in the West. He even believed that the two go together – not that any man will be the happier the freer he is, no matter what the condition of other men, but that men generally will be the happier the freer they are. The more resolutely men claim for themselves and respect in others the rights of man, the happier they will be; and the greater their knowledge, the greater their attachment to these rights and their capacity to realize them. Condorcet was so much struck by the idea (which is partly true, though it needs to be qualified) that the harmful passions are rooted in error and ignorance, that he failed to notice that the use of knowledge can create conditions which encourage ambitions destructive of freedom and happiness, even where the knowledge needed to remedy those conditions is not lacking. Not lacking, but unlikely to be used.

Comte valued happiness more than freedom, and his ideal was a society ruled by an educated and public-spirited élite. He saw that the prestige of science had increased and was increasing, and that the study of man and society was beginning to rely, as never before, on observation. The purveyors of fantasy were losing ground to the discoverers and disseminators of authentic knowledge. He saw, too, that the rôle of the managers – the administrators, the directors of effort on a large scale – was greater than it had ever been, and that the activities of man in society were both more diverse and more tightly connected. It was easier than it had been for a group of men working closely together to control a vast community. Never before had there been such opportunities for the enterprising and competent few. No doubt, Comte was right; but the few most likely to take those opportunities were perhaps not the sorte of élite he had in mind.

Neither Condorcet nor Comte saw the real point of Rousseau's indictment of modern society: that the increase of knowledge has social consequences which strengthen the harmful passions. This might be true even though the men best able to discover that knowledge or to master it were less a prey than others to these passions. The scientists and inventors whose achievements make possible a great expansion of trade and industry, the philosophers, artists and poets who help to form men's tastes and their values, might be morally, as well as intellectually, among the best of men, and yet society be the worse for what they do. Sometimes Rousseau spoke as if the corrupters of society, the scientists and artists whose achievements seem so admirable to believers in progress, were themselves the worst corrupted; but he need not have done so, and in his more sober moments did not do so. For example, in the *Letter to d'Alembert* he condemned the theatre without condemning the men who wrote for it or belittling their talents.

Rousseau would probably not have denied that it was largely to the Enlightenment, which believers in progress valued so highly, that he owed his own insight into the social evils of his day. He might even have agreed – since he believed that the arts and sciences corrupt society – that only a corrupt society produces the knowledge needed to cure its ills. For he believed himself to possess some part of that knowledge; he did not confine himself to making a diagnosis, but also suggested remedies, though without much hope that they would be taken. What he despaired of was not so much men's acquiring the knowledge to cure social and moral ills, as their making use of it for that purpose. *Si jeunesse savait, si vieillesse pouvait!* We have only to amend this to read *Si innocence savait, si corruption pouvait!*, to get the gist of Rousseau's pessimism.

I would not say that his pessimism is better founded than the optimism of Condorcet or Comte. But at least it is not worse founded. And just as we can say of them that their faith in knowledge was not so simple-minded as some have taken it to be, so we can say of him that his attack upon it was not so perverse. Both he in his fears and they in their hopes were extravagant; they all three spoke as if they knew much more about the effects of knowledge than in fact they knew.

It is more reasonable, perhaps, to follow neither him nor them, but to say, in the spirit of Pascal, that we blame equally those who are sure of the coming of what they think desirable, and those who despair of it, and the indifferent, and approve only those who hope and who strive for what they hope.

Further Readings

A list prepared by Robert Wokler

CHAPTERS 1-2 THE SOCIAL AND POLITICAL PHILOSOPHY OF HEGEL

Shlomo Avineri, *Hegel's Theory of the Modern State* (Cambridge 1972). A subtle treatment not so much of Hegel's doctrines as of the problems of political and social theory he addressed, pointing to his acute appreciation of the achievements and limitations of the modern age.

Jürgen Habermas, *Theory and Practice*, trans. John Viertel (first published in German in 1969, London 1974). A collection of essays in sociology, the philosophy of history and the history of ideas, obliquely addressed to mysterious problems in the interpretation and legitimation of social action, with particular emphasis on Hegelian and Marxist doctrines.

Jean Hyppolite, *Studies on Marx and Hegel*, trans. and ed. John O'Neill (London 1969). A commentary on dialectical themes in Hegel's philosophy, and particularly the *Phenomenology of Spirit*, joined to a reading of Marx, including *Capital*, in an attempt to show that Marxian economics owes much to a still essentially Hegelian theory of alienation.

Alexandre Kojève, *Introduction to the Reading of Hegel: Lectures on the 'Phenomenology of Spirit'*, assembled by Raymond Queneau, trans. James H. Nichols, Jr., (ed.) Allan Bloom (New York and London 1969). A boldly original and illuminating interpretation of Hegel's *Phenomenology of Spirit*, including a particularly influential discussion of the dialectic of master and slave.

353

Karl Löwith, *From Hegel to Nietzsche: The revolution in nineteenth-century thought,* trans. David E. Green (first published in German in 1941, London 1965). A sweeping, lofty and learned commentary on nineteenth-century German Idealism, embracing the Hegelian reconciliation of philosophy with the State and Christianity, the Nietzschean transcendence, and the subjectivity of Christian truth in a bourgeois world.

Maurice Mandelbaum, *History, Man & Reason: A Study in Nineteenth-Century Thought* (Baltimore 1971). An energetically grand survey of ideas and doctrines, including historicism, organicism, the belief in man's malleability and in laws which govern the direction of history, put to rest by the advent of an age which has lost faith in progress.

Herbert Marcuse, *Reason and Revolution: Hegel and the Rise of Social Theory,* 2nd ed. (first published 1941, London 1963). A provocative study of the social and political dimension of Hegelian and Marxian dialectics, each motivated by a conception of the negative character of reality, for Hegel in the context of an ontological idea of reason, for Marx as an historical method.

Z. A. Pelczynski, (ed.), *Hegel's Political Philosophy: Problems and Perspectives* (Cambridge 1971). A notable collection of essays by thirteen leading contemporary scholars on central and controversial issues, including Hegel's conception of the State, his philosophy of history and his theory of punishment.

Raymond Plant, *Hegel* (London 1973). A subtle analysis of Hegel's political thought in connection with the metaphysical and especially religious doctrines that shape and inform it, embracing above all his critique of the fragmentations of Christianity and his vision of man rendered whole in an integrated political community.

Judith N. Shklar, *Freedom and Independence: A Study of the Political Ideas of Hegel's 'Phenomenology of Mind'* (Cambridge 1976). An illuminating commentary on Hegel's most difficult and influential contribution to the history of political thought, emphasizing the polemical tone of the work and the significance of passages pertaining to Greek philosophy and drama, around its central theme of freedom as a dynamic process tending towards the identity of personal and public goals.

Steven B. Smith, *Hegel's Critique of Liberalism: Rights in Context* (Chicago and London 1989). A sympathetic reading of Hegel's conception of the State as a meeting of minds on the part of rational citizens, whose shared articulation of the public interest provides a communitarian alternative to the morally deracinated sense of the self which figures at the heart of modern liberalism.

Charles Taylor, *Hegel* (Cambridge 1975). A richly expansive discussion of Hegel's philosophy around his conception of the self-realization of Spirit, at once free and self-legislating, but equally in rational accord and sympathetic harmony with both mankind and nature, and including a communitarian treatment of the concrete fulfilment of abstract rights in the State.

John Edward Toews, *Hegelianism: The Path Toward Dialectical Humanism, 1805–1841* (Cambridge 1980). An impressive study of the early history of Hegelianism and of the disintegration of religious and metaphysical faith in a world stripped of the last illusions of the sacred.

CHAPTERS 3–4   MARX AND ENGELS

Isaiah Berlin, *Karl Marx,* 4th ed. corrected (first published 1939, Oxford 1983). A still vigorous intellectual biography, especially illuminating with regard to Marx's personal impressions of his radical contemporaries, including Heine, Bakunin, Weitling, Proudhon and Lasalle.

Allen E. Buchanan, *Marx and Justice: The Radical Critique of Liberalism* (London 1982). An analytically incisive attempt to reconstruct the sense of Marx's juridical ideas, in part by way of Marxian objections to the pre-eminent theory of justice in contemporary political philosophy, that of John Rawls.

Jean-Yves Calvez, *La pensée de Karl Marx* (Paris 1956). An expansive study of Marx's critical philosophy and theory of religion from an essentially sympathetic Christian perspective, with special emphasis on the variety of forms assumed by mankind's alienation and dehumanization.

E. H. Carr, *Michael Bakunin* (first published 1937, London 1975). A delightfully engaging and exemplary biography of a romantic fugitive and intoxicated anarchist, as much at home on revolutionary barricades as Marx was in the library of the British Museum, whose constant appeal for a spontaneous uprising of all the people contrasted sharply with the doctrine of the dictatorship of the proletariat.

Terrell Carver, *Marx and Engels: The Intellectual Relationship* (Brighton 1983). An incisive treatment of the character of the intellectual collaboration of the founders of Marxism, which explores Marx's debt to Engels' historical study of the English working class and Engels' wayward fascination with a crude scientific methodology.

G. A. Cohen, *History, Labour and Freedom* (Oxford 1988). A fine collection of essays around themes in historical materialism, the labour theory of value, and the challenge to freedom posed by capitalism, which suggest that analytical philosophy, when pursued as a means to illuminate Marxism, may also dim its attraction.

G. A. Cohen, *Karl Marx's Theory of History: A Defence* (Princeton 1978). The most sharply honed analysis ever produced of the philosophy of history espoused by Marx, placing emphasis upon the primacy of productive forces and in its reconstruction and refinement of Marx's meaning making a striking contribution of its own to current social theory.

Marshall Cohen, Thomas Nagel and **Thomas Scanlon,** (eds.), *Marx, Justice, and History* (Princeton 1980). An important collection of essays, all previously published in the 1970s in *Philosophy and Public Affairs*, around the place of moral principles, and especially justice, in Marx's philosophy, and with regard to the coherence and significance of historical materialism.

Jon Elster, *Making Sense of Marx* (Cambridge 1985). A large-scale critical examination of Marx's philosophy from a methodologically individualist viewpoint only fitfully if at all adopted by Marx himself, embracing certain features of his doctrine but holding much of it, including the labour theory of value and the idea of history as class struggle, to be incoherent.

Michael Evans, *Karl Marx* (London 1975). A comprehensive albeit brief introduction to Marx's life and work, particularly useful with regard to his association with the Communist League, embracing discussions of his theory of history and his conceptions of the State and revolution.

Helmut Fleischer, *Marxism and History*, trans. Eric Mosbacher (first published in German in 1969, London 1973). A scholarly yet concise commentary on the diverse conceptions of history articulated by Marx, or implied in his writings, at different stages of his career.

Alan Gilbert, *Marx's Politics: Communists and Citizens* (Oxford 1981). An engaging account of Marx's political ideas, career and strategies, from his assessment of the French Revolution and English Chartism, to his attempt, in the course of the German Revolution of 1848–9, to form a communist movement, to his subsequent reassessment of his own doctrines in the light of largely disappointing experience.

Sidney Hook, *From Hegel to Marx: Studies in the Intellectual Development of Karl Marx* (first published 1950, Ann Arbor 1962). A notable account of Marx's intellectual debt to Hegelian dialectical method, and of his critique of the Hegelian philosophical system, in the context of an extended commentary on the Young Hegelians, principally Bauer, Ruge, Stirner, Hess and Feuerbach.

Bob Jessop and **Charlie Malcolm-Brown,** (eds.), *Karl Marx's Social and Political Thought: Critical Assessments*, 4 vols. (London and New York 1990). A useful collection of 134 articles and essays originally published between 1911 and 1987, principally in scholarly journals, around the themes of Marx's life and theoretical development; social class and class conflict; the State, politics and revolution; and civil society, ideology, morals and ethics.

Leszek Kolakowski, *Main Currents of Marxism*, trans. from the Polish by P. S. Falla, 3 vols. (Oxford 1978). A remarkably comprehensive history of the ideological career of Marxism, from its origins in German philosophy and the Left Hegelian tradition, through Marx's own writings on the transcendence of alienation by way of communism, and then its development in European social movements and its collapse under the totalitarian State established embryonically by Lenin and completed by Stalin.

George Lichtheim, *Marxism: An Historical and Critical Study* (first published 1961, London 1971). A compelling history both of Marxist historical, political, economic and revolutionary doctrines in their common affirmation of a humanist programme, and of their career as elements of the theory and practice of the socialist labour movement, until the petrifaction of that movement in the mid-twentieth century.

David McLellan, *Karl Marx: His Life and Thought* (first published 1973, London and New York 1983). The best biography of Marx in English, rich in its detail of the peripatetic life of the principal founder of international communism, who died intestate and stateless.

David McLellan, *The Thought of Karl Marx: An Introduction*, 2nd ed. (first published 1971, London 1980). A usefully comprehensive guide to Marx's social thought, in the form of commentaries on his writings, grouped chronologically, followed by thematic discussions, with textual illustrations, on alienation, historical materialism, class, revolution and other themes.

Ralph Miliband, *Marxism and Politics* (Oxford 1977). A general introductory treatment of Marxist politics, around the idea of the State as an essential means of class domination, whose subtle manifestations sometimes ensure that it acts only on behalf of the ruling class and not at its behest.

Ellen Frankel Paul *et al,* (eds.), *Marxism and Liberalism* (Oxford 1986). Notable essays by leading contemporary political philosophers and interpreters of Marx around the themes of Marxism and democracy, self-ownership and self-realization, totalitarianism and violence.

John Plamenatz, *German Marxism and Russian Communism* (London 1954). A study of the links between revolutionary Marxism and Bolshevism, with particular emphasis on the ways that Lenin refashioned Marx's conceptions of the class struggle, to suit peculiar Russian circumstances.

John Plamenatz, *Karl Marx's Philosophy of Man* (Oxford 1975). A detailed treatment of Marx's conception of human nature and alienation, including discussions on ideology, religion, morality, the State, and the proletariat as a revolutionary class, partly by way of comparisons with the moral philosophies of Rousseau and Hegel.

Nicos Poulantzas, *Political Power and Social Classes,* trans. Timothy O'Hagan (first published 1972, London 1973). A notable, if densely argued, account of the relative ideological and institutional autonomy of the State with respect to class conflict, whose limits, concrete forms and manifestations, particularly in capitalist society, remain politically circumscribed.

S. S. Prawer, *Karl Marx and World Literature* (Oxford 1976). A well-documented study of Marx's career as a writer, in the light of his assessments of novels, plays and poetry, as well as the use he made of literature in his social philosophy, drawn from the whole corpus of his writings and correspondence.

S. H. Rigby, *Engels and the formation of Marxism: History, dialectics and revolution* (Manchester and New York 1992). An illuminating study of the Marxist theory of historical materialism, showing how its principles, as espoused by both Marx and Engels in *The German Ideology,* were prefigured in Engels' *Condition of the Working Class in England,* and how the weaknesses of its later formulations by Engels had to do with its lack of correspondence to reality rather than to any striking divergencies from Marx.

Paul Thomas, *Karl Marx and the Anarchists* (London 1980). Contends that, in criticizing Hegel's theory of the State, Marx retained a Hegelian perspective on the need for an ordered community to resolve the atomistic tendencies of civil society, thereby distinguishing a State's oppressive power from a community's benign authority, along lines which anarchists, who drew no such distinction, bitterly opposed.

Allen W. Wood, *Karl Marx* (first published 1981, London 1984). A solid and sensitive, comprehensively illuminating, interpretation of Marx's social philosophy, organized around the themes of alienation, the materialist conception of history, morality, philosophical materialism and the dialectical method.

CHAPTER 5   THE IDEA OF PROGRESS

Bronisław Baczko, *Utopian Lights: The Evolution of the Idea of Social Progress* (first published in French in 1978, New York 1989). A superb study of utopian representations around images of progress and the promise of history, of revolutionary festivals and games, of new cities and their architecture, and generally of the world of political reverie and dreams, mainly with reference to French eighteenth-century thinkers and planners.

Keith Michael Baker, *Condorcet: From Natural Philosophy to Social Mathematics* (Chicago 1975). Much the finest intellectual biography of the pre-eminent social philosopher devoted to the scientific transformation of the social world in accordance with the public good.

J. B. Bury, *The Idea of Progress: An Inquiry into its Origin and Growth* (first published 1920, New York 1955). Essentially a history of ideas of worldly happiness, as distinct from doctrines of felicity in a celestial paradise, focusing predominantly on French thinkers in the period 1650–1850.

D. G. Charlton, *Positivist Thought in France during the Second Empire 1852–1870* (Oxford 1959). A study of the use and abuse of certain philosophical principles in French intellectual history, including a treatment of Comte's attempt to establish sociology as a science capable of predicting future social developments, and an attendant social ethics designed to promote morally desirable change.

Barbara Goodwin, *Social Science and Utopia: Nineteenth-Century Models of Social Harmony* (Hassocks 1978). A study of nineteenth-century naturalist utopias which largely mirrored the intellectual preoccupations and aspirations of the eighteenth-century *philosophes* and their materialist, perfectionist, neo-Newtonian followers, including a treatment of the shift of emphasis from an anthropocentric to a socially oriented utopian social science.

Ghiţa Ionescu, *Politics and the Pursuit of Happiness* (London 1984). A spirited defence of non-ideological political thought for an industrial age.

Frank E. Manuel, *The Prophets of Paris* (Cambridge, Mass. 1962). A masterly study in intellectual history devoted to a collection of prophetic visionaries – Turgot, Condorcet, Saint-Simon, the Saint-Simonians, Fourier and Comte – whose gospels for a civilization in crisis were all preached from Paris to the chosen people, the French.

Alasdair MacIntyre, *After Virtue: A study in moral theory* (London 1981). A wide-ranging, impassioned study of the moral barbarism of contemporary political culture, traced in part to an emotivist ethic of arbitrarily determined principles inspired by the Enlightenment, which has deprived citizens of their sense of shared values and virtues such as once obtained in communities shaped by tradition.

Robert A. Nisbet, *History of the Idea of Progress* (London 1980). A freely expansive account of the diverse manifestations of an idea whose unfurling is perceived as central to the development of Western civilization.

John Passmore, *The Perfectibility of Man*, 2nd ed. (first published 1970, London 1971). A judicious history of classical, Christian and modern doctrines of man's moral capacity to improve his nature and transcend the condition he has attained.

Index

Emile (Rousseau), 303
Encyclopaedia of the Philosophical Sciences (Hegel), 50
Engels, Friedrich, 114
  Anti-Dühring, 204n, 221n
    and the State, 239, 244n, 245, 262n, 273n
  'On Authority', 204n
  and class, 176–208
    conflict, 185–9
    consciousness, 191–5, 224, 237
    divisions, 171, 176–8, 181–91
    and exploitation, 181, 204–8
    inequality, 178–81, 245, 248–9, 266–7
    interests of, 188–208, 216–19, 241–2, 248
      irreconcilable and reconciling, 195–200, 204, 241–8, 250, 254–5, 262
      objective, 200–3
    and the State, 238–62
    structure, 183–5, 258
    types of, 181–3
  on contract, 241
  economics of, 153–4, 219, 268–9
  on government, 185, 239–40, 244, 257–60, 262, 271–2, 291–2
  on ideology, 172–3, 208–37, 247–50
    and class interests, 216–19
    as false consciousness, 211–19
    and religion, 219–31, 251
    theory of, 231–4
    use of word, 208–13
  on inequality, 178–81, 245, 253, 267
  Origin of the Family, Private Property and the State, The, 239, 244n, 245, 254, 255
  on property, 160, 162–4, 170, 176–8, 187–8, 190, 205, 240, 243, 253–4, 266
  and revolution, 185–6, 189–95, 203, 211, 236, 278, 283–4, 299
    Marxian model of, 189–91
  and the State
    and class domination, 251–5
    and conflict in classless society, 276–8
    disappearance of, 252, 262–78, 294
    functions of, 238–76
    and hierarchy, 268–71
    and irreconcilable classes, 244–51
    not controlled by any class, 255–62
    origins of, 238–44

  and organized force, 262–5
  and social classes, 238–62
    three views on, 238–44
  and tribal societies, 238–42
  see also Marx
England, 85, 195, 266, 275, 278–81, 283–5, 291
  Civil War
    and class conflict, 187
Enlightenment, 42, 309
Equality *see* Inequality
Error and vice, 326–30, 339, 343–5
Esquisse d'un tableau historique des progrès de l'esprit humain, see *Sketch for an Historical Picture of the Progress of the Human Mind* (Condorcet)
Essence of Christianity (Feuerbach), 219, 220n
Estates: Hegel on, 137–41
Ethical life: Hegel on, 111, 115–23
Études hégéliennes (Grégoire), 123
Europe: Hegel's bias towards, 81–2
Executive power of government: Hegel on, 135–7, 138
Experience and knowledge: Hegel on, 23–5
Exploitation, 68
  and class, 170, 178, 181, 189, 196, 199, 204–8, 242–5, 252–8, 260, 284
  and the State, 204, 244–5, 251–2

False consciousness
  as ideology: Engels on, 211–19
  religion as, 221–2
Family, 167–8
  and civil society: Hegel on, 111–14, 121–30
  Engels on, 239–41, 243
Fascism, 260–1
Feminism, 236–7
Feudalism, 234
  and capitalism, 165, 183–90, 193
  Marx and Engels on, 157n, 165, 183–6, 241, 270
Feuerbach, Ludwig, 219–23, 228, 231
  Essence of Christianity, 219
Fleming, Sir Alexander, 174
Fontenelle, Bernard de, 310
Force, organized: Marx and Engels on, 262–5, 270, 272
Fragment on Government, A (Bentham), xx
France, 70, 85–6, 278–9, 283–5, 291, 310
  First and Second Empires, 256–7
  French monarchy, 187, 255, 284

Man and Society · Volume Three

see also French Revolution; Paris
Commune
Freedom and liberty, 235–6
of conscience, 86–7
and democracy, 89–90
and happiness, 303–4, 350–2
Hegel on, 28, 31–3, 42–7, 59, 66–73,
77, 89–90, 94–106, 109–10,
119–20, 122, 134–5, 143–6, 148–9
individual, and social change, 317–21
and law, 77, 98, 100–1, 104, 120,
123, 144
Marx on, 177, 283, 298
and morality, 96–7, 99–101, 106–11,
114–15, 119–21, 144–5
and progress, 303–4, 317–21, 332,
350–1
of speech: Hegel on, 140–1
French Revolution, 40, 43–4, 144, 146,
187, 190, 194, 257, 284
Freud, Sigmund, 62

Galileo, 308, 320, 331, 334
*Genèse et Structure de la Phénoménologie de
l'Esprit de Hegel* (Hyppolite), 28, 41n,
43n, 44n
German Ideology, The (Marx and Engels)
and society, 157n, 212, 216n, 237n,
248n
and the State, 255
German Marxism and Russian Communism
(Plamenatz), 154n, 161n, 162n, 278n,
286n
Germans and the German world, 283–7,
348
Hegel on, 72, 80, 85–6, 91
Germany, 260, 271
Marx on, 271, 278, 283–5
God, 8, 33–5, 41–3, 46, 52–3, 61, 76–7,
87–8, 123–4, 175, 213, 216, 218, 220,
223, 251, 301, 305, 325–6
Goethe, Johann Wolfgang von, 73, 143
Government, 67, 171, 214
Engels, on, 185, 239–40, 244, 257–60,
262, 271–2, 291–2
Hegel on, 129, 135–40
Marx on, 156, 160, 185, 257–60, 262,
291–2
bourgeois, 256, 288–9
proletarian, 271–3
of the Paris Commune, 271–6
representative assemblies, 137–40
Greece, 22, 303
Greeks, 174, 304–7, 333
Hegel on, 31, 35–6, 49, 52, 56, 67,
80–1, 86, 88, 91–3, 118

Grégoire, Franz: *Études hégéliennes*, 123
Grotius, Hugo, xv

Happiness
and depth psychology, 339–45
and expansion of knowledge, 301–4,
307–8, 314–15, 326–52
Comte on, 327, 329–30, 336–9,
344–52
Condorcet on, 333–9, 349–52
and science, 308–9
Comte on, 309–13, 345–8
Condorcet on, 336–9
in scientific age, 308–9
and vice, 326–30
and virtue, 302–4, 330–2, 345
Hegel, Georg Wilhelm Friedrich, xvii,
xix, xxii–xxv, xxviii, 1–149
on abstract right and morality,
106–21
on being and becoming, 6–7, 12–13
and Bentham 98, 131–3, 147
compared 125–6
on civil society, 121–31
on communal life *see* ethical life
on community, 67, 102–4
of selves, 16, 19, 24, 47, 53–4, 94,
101, 147–8
and concrete universal, 1–4, 16–17,
19, 53
Spirit as, 9, 15
on conscience, claims of, 118–21
consciousness
ignoble and noble, 40–1
Unhappy, 33–5, 59, 61–2, 81
on contract, 115–16
on corporations, 129–30
on crime and punishment, 116–18,
124
culture, world of, 37
deduction of categories, 12–19, 107
and democracy, 89–90, 145–6
and dialectic, 6–10, 14–15, 28–9, 106,
110, 116–17, 130, 136
and contradiction, 6–7, 60–2,
107–8, 114–15
*Encyclopaedia of the Philosophical
Sciences*, 50–1
on ethical life, 106–7, 111–24
experience and knowledge, 23–5
on family, 118–21, 124–5
and civil society, 106, 111–14,
121–30, 146–8
on finite and infinite, 13–15
self, 19, 24, 47, 53–4, 94

Vice
  and error, 326–30, 339, 345
  and happiness, 326–30
Vico, Giovanni Battista, xv
Virtue
  and expansion of knowledge, 302–4,
    330–2, 345
  and happiness, 302–4, 330–2, 345
Voltaire, 143

Wallace, William, 50n
  Philosophy of Hegel, The, 13
War: Hegel on, 142–3
Weil, Eric: *Hegel et l'État*, 144
Whigs, 140, 146
Whitehead, Alfred North, xxvi
Will, Hegel on, 103, 114
  arbitrary, 98–101
  general, 42–3, 89

  Rousseau on, 43, 139
  holy, Kant on, 45
  moral, 44–6, 100–1, 118–19
  objective, 94
  rational, 97–102, 117
  universal, 43–4, 100–1, 116–17, 126,
    131, 139, 145, 148
World-Historical Individuals: Hegel on,
  82–5, 149, 320
World history: Hegel on, 79–93, 101
World and language: Hegel on, 74
World revolution, 288–9
World-state: Hegel on, 148

Yorktown, 195

Zeno (the Stoic), 22